ENCOUNTER WITH KATYN

Tadeusz Wolsza

ENCOUNTER WITH KATYN

The wartime and postwar story of Poles
who saw the Katyn site in 1943

2018

Originally published as

"To co widziałem przekracza swą grozą najśmielsze fantazje." *Wojenne i powojenne losy Polaków wizytujących Katyń w 1943 roku,* Warszawa: Instytut Historii PAN, Polskie Towarzystwo Historyczne, Wydawnictwo Neriton, 2015.

© Tadeusz Wolsza, Polskie Towarzystwo Historyczne, Wydawnictwo Neriton, Instytut Historii Polskiej Akademii Nauk
ISBN 978-83-7543-388-3

The second Polish edition was published as

Dotyk Katynia. Wojenne i powojenne losy Polaków wizytujących Katyń w 1943 roku,
Poznań: Zysk i S-ka Wydawnictwo, 2018.

© Tadeusz Wolsza, Zysk i S-ka Wydawnictwo
ISBN 978-83-8116-361-3

The Janusz Kurtyka Foundation
al. Waszyngtona 39/25 04-015 Warszawa, Poland
www.fundacjakurtyki.pl, e-mail: nauka@fundacjakurtyki.pl

TRANSLATED FROM THE POLISH BY
Teresa Bałuk-Ulewiczowa, Marta Kapera, Piotr Pieńkowski

PROOF-READING
Teresa Bałuk-Ulewiczowa

DTP
Piotr Perzyna

COVER DESIGN
Piotr Perzyna

Printed in the United States of America

ISBN 978-1-5310-1537-4
Library of Congress Control Number: 2018965044

© Copyright The Janusz Kurtyka Foundation, Warszawa, 2018
© Copyright for the English translation Teresa Bałuk-Ulewiczowa, Marta Kapera,
  and Piotr Pieńkowski

Published by
Janusz Kurtyka Foundation, Poland
for Carolina Academic Press, Durham, North Carolina

Strategic Sponsor of the project is Polish
Security Printing Works S.A.

Co-financed by
the Polish History Museum in Warsaw
as part of the Patriotism of Tomorrow program

Table of Contents

FOREWORD

There are points in history which shape the identity of nations. They are significant vantage points, collections of the most important events, works, and ideas. One such event in Polish history is the Katyń Massacre. The aim of its perpetrators was the genocidal extermination of the Polish national elite. The Polish officers who were taken prisoner without trial or sentence were murdered with a bullet in the back of the head, and buried in a mass grave in a forest, unbeknownst to their families. They were doomed to oblivion because they were Polish, their thoughts were Polish, they looked at the world through the lens of Polish values and the Polish national interest. They were considered incapable of adapting to the Soviet system based on the communist ideology. They were members of the Polish intelligentsia, the elite of the prewar state, therefore they were to perish so as not to lead the nation in defiance against the imminent conquest of its territories by the Soviets.

The story we present in this book is interwoven with the drama of the lives of people who testified to that crime. The Katyń affair is the story of a great lie that spread around the world and was designed to be perpetuated and established forever. The truth about the crimes of the Red Army and the nature of the Communist system was not to be told. For this reason, there were two realities: one that strove for the truth, and the other, the official line. Those who thought or spoke differently were oppressed, not only in Poland by the Communist secret police, but also throughout the world by intelligence agencies and fellow travelers, such as Communist parties in Western Europe. The title of the book, *Encounter with Katyń*, reflects that reality, because those who came into contact with this issue, even by random chance or unintentionally, faced far-reaching repressive measures for the rest of their lives.

The Katyń Massacre challenged the fundamental values recognized by the Euro-Atlantic community – freedom of speech, religious freedom, and human rights. The Polish people professed values which were an obstacle to the totalitarian regimes of Hitler's Germany and the Soviet Union. There was no place for such values in the Communist State. Therefore, the disclosure of the Katyń Massacre was deemed unwelcome by the British, Soviet, and American alliance, and the world could not learn the truth until the Cold War.

Today, the Katyń Massacre is still a relevant issue, not only because the Russian Federation has still not made all the documents accessible to Polish academics for research, the perpetrators have not been brought to justice even symbolically, and the families of the murdered officers have not received compensation. It is important to put these issues, which have been distorted and denied for years, on an international agenda, and to bring them to an honest closure. It is not merely a matter of restoring elementary justice, but also a philosophical and ethical question. Raising this issue is a duty for the civilized world, which holds that the passage of time does not allow the crime of genocide to be swept under the carpet. At a time when the rulers of the Russian Federation invoke the heritage of the USSR, it is indeed worth recalling the nature of that system and issuing a geopolitical warning to the entire free world that the dream of an end to history is about to end.

Paweł Kurtyka
President of the Board,
The Janusz Kurtyka Foundation

INTRODUCTION

The Katyn atrocity has an impressive bibliography; the list scrupulously compiled only for the period up to 2010 contains 5,916 published items of various kinds (monographs, biographies, source editions, studies and articles, interviews, diaries, memoirs, and relations, covering works of scholarship and those for the general reader as well as journalism).[1] It would be impossible to establish the number of all the works written on the subject up to now, but it is certain that every year hundreds of new publications appear on the Katyn atrocity committed on Polish people by NKVD officers in the spring of 1940, and on its Polish and international consequences. Here I am going to focus primarily on the monographs, studies, and articles on various aspects connected with the backdrop to the problem, and to publications of source materials of diverse provenance. In view of the interesting work by the historian Stanisław Jaczyński, which covers the time up to 2007,[2] I shall consider fairly recent publications.

Nonetheless, I shall start from the milestones, the works which created the foundation for this impressive bibliography. Here it will be enough to observe that in recent times for Polish readers the classics in the field which have dominated

---

[1] *Zbrodnia katyńska. Bibliografia 1940–2010*, I. Kowalska and E. Pawińska (eds.), (Warszawa: Niezależny Komitet Historyczny Badania Zbrodni Katyńskiej, 2010), 53–637.

[2] Useful overviews of the research on the Katyn atrocity are in P. Łysakowski, 'W kraju o tragedii w Kozich Górach,' *Dzieje Najnowsze* 1990: 4, 81–95; and for publications to 2007 in S. Jaczyński, 'Stan badań i postulaty badawcze w zakresie problematyki katyńskiej,' *Łambinowicki Rocznik Muzealny* 30 (2007), 9–32. Recently the online publications on Katyn have been addressed by J. Żelazko, 'O Katyniu w Internecie,' in *Wokół spraw trudnych, bolesnych i zapomnianych*, E. Kowalczyk et al. (eds.), (Łódź: Instytut Pamięci Narodowej and Wydawnictwo Uniwersytetu Łódzkiego, 2014), 265–288.

the scholarship on Katyn[3] have been supplemented by dozens of important new publications adding to what we know on the subject. It will be necessary, I think, to mention the monographs wholly or partly on the Katyn atrocity, by authors like Stanisław Jaczyński,[4] Józef Mackiewicz,[5] Wojciech Materski,[6] Eugenia Maresch,[7] Krystyna Piórkowska,[8] Andrzej Przewoźnik and Jolanta Adamska,[9] Witold Wasilewski,[10] Jacek Tebinka,[11] Paweł Jaworski,[12] and Tadeusz Wolsza,[13]

---

[3] The Polish bibliography starts with Czesław Madajczyk, *Dramat katyński*, (Warszawa: Książka i Wiedza, 1989). In the early 1980s another useful publication, by Jerzy Łojek, the son of a Katyn victim, appeared in the samizdat press under a nom de plume: Leopold Jerzewski, *Dzieje sprawy Katynia*, (Białystok: Versus, 1989). Another classic is the book by Janusz Zawodny, *Katyń*, (Lublin and Paris: Editions Spotkania,1989), which first appeared in its English version: *Death in the Forest: The Story of the Katyn Forest Massacre*, (Indiana: University of Notre Dame Press, 1962). Other books in English include J. Mackiewicz, *The Katyn Wood Murders*, (first edition London: World Affairs Book Club, 1951); L. FitzGibbon, *Katyn: A Crime Without Parallel*, (London: Tom Stacey, 1971, and New York: Charles Scribner's Sons); and O. O'Malley, *Katyn: Dispatches of Sir Owen O'Malley to the British Government*, (Chicago: Katyn Memorial Fund Commission 1973).

[4] S. Jaczyński, *Ocaleni z zagłady. Losy oficerów polskich ocalonych z masakry katyńskiej*, (Warszawa: Bellona, 2012).

[5] J. Mackiewicz, *Sprawa mordu katyńskiego*, (London: Wydawnictwo Kontra, 2009).

[6] See the work of Wojciech Materski, *Mord katyński. Siedemdziesiąt lat drogi do prawdy*, (Warszawa: Naczelna Dyrekcja Archiwów Państwowych, 2010); *Od kłamstwa ku prawdzie*, (Warszawa: Oficyna Wydawnicza Rytm, 2012); and 'Z początków wojny propagandowej wokół zbrodni katyńskiej. Sowiecka Komisja Specjalna (tzw. Komisja Burdenki),' in *Represje sowieckie wobec narodów Europy 1944-1956*, A. Adamczyk and D. Rogut (eds.), (Zelów, 2005), 19–28.

[7] E. Maresch, *Katyń 1940*, (Warszawa: Świat Książki, 2014); English edition: *Katyn 1940: The Documentary Evidence of the West's Betrayal*, Stroud: The History Press, 2010).

[8] K. Piórkowska, *Anglojęzyczni świadkowie Katynia. Najnowsze badania*, (Warszawa: Muzeum Wojska Polskiego, 2012).

[9] A. Przewoźnik and J. Adamska, *Katyń. Zbrodnia. Prawda. Pamięć*, (Warszawa: Świat Książki, 2010).

[10] W. Wasilewski, *Ludobójstwo. Kłamstwo i walka o prawdę. Sprawa Katynia 1940-2014*, (Warszawa: Wydawnictwo LTW, 2014).

[11] J. Tebinka, *„Wielka Brytania dotrzyma lojalnie swojego słowa". Winston Churchill a Polska*, (Warszawa: Neriton, 2013), 134–148 (the chapter entitled 'Katyń').

[12] P. Jaworski, *Marzyciele i oportuniści. Stosunki polsko-szwedzkie w latach 1939-1945*, (Warszawa: Instytut Pamięci Narodowej, 2009), 167–177 (the chapter entitled 'Szwedzka dyskusja o Katyniu').

[13] T. Wolsza, *„Katyń to już na zawsze katy i katowani". W „polskim Londynie" o sowieckiej zbrodni w Katyniu (1940-1956)*, (Warszawa: Instytut Historii PAN, 2008).

Ewa Cytowska-Siegrist,[14] and translations of three books originally published outside Poland, by Allen Paul[15] and Franz Kadell.[16] Alongside these monographs we should also mention a few other publications on the comments on the Katyn atrocity in occupied Poland.[17]

I would attribute a signal role in this respect to the publishing activities of Poland's Institute of National Remembrance, amounting to over a dozen items including the collective volume *Zbrodnia katyńska: w kręgu prawdy i kłamstwa*[18] and several items published in different regions of Poland.[19] I should also mention two publications inspired by the Institute of National Remembrance, with contributions from young people in search of unknown facts on the victims of Katyn.[20] Niezależny Komitet Historyczny Badania Zbrodni Katyńskiej (The Independent Historical Committee for Research on the Katyn Atrocity), the publisher of the *Zeszyty Katyńskie* series, is continuing its salient activities.[21] I can hardly overlook the fact that several schol-

---

[14] E. Cytowska-Siegrist, *Stany Zjednoczone i Polska 1939–1945*, (Warszawa: Neriton, 2013), 209–222.

[15] A. Paul, *Katyń. Stalinowska masakra i tryumf prawdy*, (Warszawa: Świat Książki, 2007). Several English editions, recently as *Katyń: Stalin's Massacre and the Triumph of Truth*, (DeKalb, IL: Northern Illinois University Press, 2010).

[16] Two books by Franz Kadell: *Kłamstwo katyńskie. Historia pewnej manipulacji*, (Wrocław: Wydawnictwo Dolnośląskie, 2008); and *Katyn w oczach zachodu*, (Warszawa: PWN 2012), translated from the German original versions, respectively *Die Katyn Lüge. Geschichte einer Manipulation. Fakten, Dokumente und Zeugen*, (München: F. A. Herbig Verlagsbuchhandlung, 1991); and *Katyn – Das zweifache Trauma der Polen*, (München: Herbig Verlag, 2011).

[17] T. Szarota, *Okupowanej Warszawy dzień powszedni. Studium historyczne*, (Warszawa: Czytelnik, 2010), 414–419; K. Sacewicz, 'Katyń w prasie Polskiego Państwa Podziemnego,' *Biuletyn Informacyjny Światowego Związku Żołnierzy AK* 2015: 4, 31–39; P. Gontarczyk, 'Katyń. PPR-owska szkoła kłamstwa,' *Pamięć.pl* 2013: 4, 24–27; *idem, Polska Partia Robotnicza. Droga do władzy 1941–1944*, (Warszawa: Fronda, no date of publication), 222–233.

[18] *Zbrodnia katyńska: w kręgu prawdy i kłamstwa*, ed. S. Kalbarczyk, (Warszawa: Instytut Pamięci Narodowej, 2010).

[19] *Jeńcy wojenni z Łódzkiego – ofiary Zbrodni Katyńskiej*, J. Żelazko and P. Zawilski (eds.), (Łódź: Biblioteka Instytutu Pamięci Narodowej w Łodzi, 2011); P. Szopa, *Zbrodnia katyńska 1940. Pamięci mieszkańców powiatu strzyżowskiego zamordowanych przez Sowietów w Katyniu, Charkowie i Twerze (Kalininie)*, (Rzeszów: Instytut Pamięci Narodowej, 2010).

[20] *Sprzączki i guziki z orzełkiem ze rdzy… Obraz ofiar Zbrodni Katyńskiej w pracach plastycznych młodego pokolenia*, ed. K. Cegieła et al., vol. 1, (Warszawa: Instytut Pamięci Narodowej, 2012); vol. 2, (Warszawa: Instytut Pamięci Narodowej, 2015).

[21] 25 volumes of *Zeszyty Katyńskie* have been published since 1990.

arly and general interest periodicals are disseminating information on the Katyn atrocity in its broad context. While this is absolutely understandable for institutions like Urząd do Spraw Kombatantów i Osób Represjonowanych (the Office for War Veterans and Victims of Oppression), which publishes a bulletin titled *Kombatant*;[22] the Polish Ministry of National Defense unit Wojskowe Centrum Edukacji Obywatelskiej (the Military Center for Civic Education), publisher of the magazine *Przegląd Historyczno-Wojskowy*;[23] and Centralne Muzeum Jeńców Wojennych w Łambinowicach-Opolu (the Polish Central Prisoner-of-War Museum at Łambinowice), which publishes an annual entitled *Łambinowicki Rocznik Muzealny*;[24] the fact that other publishers are presenting the issue merits special commendation and their efforts are an undeniably important contribution. The Katyn atrocity is a regularly addressed subject in the history magazine *Mówią Wieki*,[25] the quarterly *Dzieje Najnowsze* issued by the Institute of History of the Polish Academy of Sciences,[26] the Wrocław annual on oral history *Wrocławski Rocznik Historii Mówionej*,[27] and *Biuletyn Instytutu Pamięci Narodowej* (the bulletin published by the Institute of National Remembrance, now continued in a successor periodical for the general reader, *Pamięć pl*).[28]

I would like to finish this necessarily abbreviated review of the research with a word on the source editions. It is self-evident that the major contributions

---

[22] See, for instance, *Kombatant* 2010: 3.

[23] K. Jasiewicz, 'Rola teorii, hipotez i spekulacji w wyjaśnieniu zbrodni katyńskiej. Rzecz o metodologii i metodyce badań,' *Przegląd Historyczno-Wojskowy* 2012: 4.

[24] See *Łambinowicki Rocznik Muzealny* 30 (2007).

[25] See *Mówią Wieki* 2010: 4; and *Mówią Wieki* 2013: 4.

[26] Only in 2013–2014 *Dzieje Najnowsze* published 4 articles and 1 book review on Katyn (W. Wasilewski, 'Decyzja Politbiura WKP(b) z 29 II 1952 r. ZSSR wobec komisji katyńskiej Izby Reprezentantów USA,' *Dzieje Najnowsze* 2013:1; K. Jasiewicz, 'Mechanizm podejmowania decyzji katyńskiej,' *Dzieje Najnowsze* 2013: 2; E. Cytowska, 'W rocznicę ujawnienia zbrodni katyńskiej. Na marginesie publikacji amerykańskich dokumentów dotyczących sprawy Katynia,' *Dzieje Najnowsze* 2013: 3; S. Maćkun, 'Niechciana prawda. Kanada wobec ujawnienia zbrodni katyńskiej (1943–1945),' *Dzieje Najnowsze* 2014: 1; and T. Wolsza, 'Polska emigracja o zbrodni katyńskiej,' *Dzieje Najnowsze* 2014: 2.

[27] See the work of Krzysztof Łogojda, a young historian who is recording the postwar history of the families of Katyn victims: K. Łogojda, 'Pamięć o ojcu. Refleksje z rozmów z rodzinami katyńskimi. Rekonesans badawczy,' *Wrocławski Rocznik Historii Mówionej* 2014, 89–127.

[28] See, for instance, *Biuletyn Instytutu Pamięci Narodowej* 2005: 5/6; *Biuletyn Instytutu Pamięci Narodowej* 2007: 1–2; or *Biuletyn Instytutu Pamięci Narodowej* 2010: 4.

in this respect were made by books published many years ago, including the invaluable volume accomplished by researchers with a background in the Polish Second Corps and the wartime community of Polish exiles in London.[29] This publication, which has come out in several languages, is well-known world-wide. No less valuable are the other émigré publications containing first-hand documents, such as *Pamiętniki znalezione w Katyniu*,[30] and the émigré journalism on the Katyn atrocity.[31] Of the official publications which have appeared in Poland since 1989, the issue of the book by Jerzy Tucholski was certainly a ground-breaking event.[32] The next milestone was marked out by the initiative launched by two archive institutions, the Polish Naczelna Dyrekcja Archiwów Państwowych (the Head Office of State Archives), and Rosarhiv (the Federal Archival Agency of Russia). Its effect was the edition of a set of documents of first-rate significance, published jointly as *Katyń*.[33] Of the newly published items I would single out two for special mention: *Katyn: A Crime Without Punishment*, compiled by an international team from Poland, Russia, and the USA;[34] and a three-volume publication entitled *Zbrodnia katyńska 1940*, which was the outcome of yet another search in the Polish émigré archives in London.[35]

---

[29] *Zbrodnia katyńska w świetle dokumentów*, with a foreword by W. Anders, (London: Figaro Press, 1948).

[30] J.K. Zawodny, *Pamiętniki znalezione w Katyniu*, (Paris: Editions Spotkania,1989); B. Młynarski, *W niewoli sowieckiej* (London: Gryf, 1974); J. Orlicki, *Poprzez Starobielsk do Piątej Dywizji Kresowej. Pamiętnik wojenny lekarza – rezerwisty*, (London and Warszawa: Hanna Orlicka Kielim,1992); J. Czapski, *Wspomnienia starobielskie* (Roma: Oddział Kultury i Prasy 2. Korpusu, 1944); Z. Peszkowski, *Wspomnienia jeńca z Kozielska*, (Wrocław: Fundacja Centrum Ignacego J. Paderewskiego, 1992); S. Swianiewicz, *W cieniu Katynia*, (Warszawa: Czytelnik, 1990).

[31] *Katyń. Wybór publicystyki 1943–1988*, (London: Polonia, 1988).

[32] J. Tucholski, *Mord w Katyniu. Kozielsk, Ostaszków, Starobielsk. Lista ofiar*, (Warszawa: Instytut Wydawniczy PAX, 1991).

[33] *Katyń*, vol. 1: *Jeńcy wojenni nie wypowiedzianej wojny. Dokumenty zbrodni*, W. Materski et al. (eds.), (Warszawa: Trio, 1995); vol. 2: *Zagłada*, (Warszawa:Trio,1998); vol. 3: *Losy ocalałych*, (Warszawa: Trio, 2001); vol. 4: *Echa Katynia*, (Warszawa: Trio, 2006).

[34] *Katyn: A Crime Without Punishment*, A.M. Cienciala, N.S. Lebedeva, and W. Materski (eds.), (New Haven and London: Yale University Press, 2007).

[35] *Zbrodnia katyńska 1940. Poszukiwanie prawdy 1941–1946*, B. Polak and M. Polak (eds.), (Koszalin: Wydawnictwo Uczelniane Politechniki Koszalińskiej, 2010); *Zbrodnia katyńska 1940. Dr Bronisław Kuśnierz o Katyniu*, B. Polak and M. Polak (eds.), (Koszalin: Wydawnict-

All of these publications provide detailed data and information, thanks to which historians now have far fewer problems with establishing the circumstances and date of the Katyn atrocity, its scale, the personal data of the murderers and their victims, the reasons behind the operation, and the mechanisms applied to misrepresent and conceal the truth about this singularly horrific crime – genocide.

* * *

The book I am giving readers is not a monograph on the circumstances, development, and consequences of the Katyn massacre; neither is it on its international contexts. These unquestionably key issues have been clarified beyond all doubt, and there are many invaluable books on the subject. Suffice it to refer back to the excellent monographs and studies I have already enumerated. Instead, this book is an attempt to establish and describe what happened during and after the War to the individuals (writers, scientists, photographers, journalists, medical doctors, Polish Red Cross associates, factory workers, Polish officers who were prisoners-of-war held by the Germans, representatives of the families of victims of Soviet atrocities etc.), who in 1943 traveled to Smolensk and Katyn, encouraged to do so by the Germans and with their consent, and on their own initiative, to see the scale of the atrocity for themselves and view the incontrovertible evidence as to who did it. Some of the points in this book have been addressed before, but this aspect of the Katyn issue has received the least attention so far and calls for a search for new, hitherto unknown sources.[36]

---

wo Uczelniane Politechniki Koszalińskiej, 2012); *Zbrodnia katyńska 1940. Polacy w Wielkiej Brytanii wobec ludobójstwa katyńskiego 1943–1989*, B. Polak and M. Polak (eds.), (Koszalin: Wydawnictwo Uczelniane Politechniki Koszalińskiej, 2013).

[36] See for instance S.M. Jankowski and R. Kotarba, *Literaci a sprawa katyńska 1945*, (Kraków: Wydawnictwo Towarzystwa Naukowego „Societas Vistulana", 2003); J. Bratko, *Dlaczego zginąłeś prokuratorze?* (Kraków: Stowarzyszenie Twórcze Krakowski Klub Artystyczno-Literacki, 1998); 'Dzieje sprawy katyńskiej na przestrzeni siedemdziesięciu lat historii,' in *Jeńcy wojenni z Łódzkiego: ofiary zbrodni katyńskiej*, J. Żelazko and P. Zawilski (eds.), (Łódź: Instytut Pamięci Narodowej – Komisja Ścigania Zbrodni przeciwko Narodowi Polskiemu; Archiwum Państwowe w Łodzi, 2011), 35–62; M. Golon, 'Kary za prawdę o zbrodni Stalina. Represje polskich organów bezpieczeństwa w okresie stalinowskim (1944–1956) wobec osób ujawniających władze ZSRR jako sprawców zbrodni katyńskiej w świetle inwentarza doku-

In this book I present the extraordinary stories of scores of Polish people who again faced oppressive measures from the Germans after having accomplished their Katyn mission, and after the War were put on the list of particularly dangerous individuals for Polish and Soviet Communists. This point is connected with the evidence court prosecutors and secret agents collected to stage a Katyn trial in Poland which was to lead to a verdict saying that the Germans were culpable for the mass murder of the Polish officers. The Poles who were in danger of arrest in this connection tried to save their skin either by leaving the country illegally, or by taking refuge in a hideout, or else they retracted the statements on the Katyn atrocity they had made earlier, in the spring and summer of 1943. Some of them were wanted by the Communist secret services not only because they had been to Katyn in 1943 or because they had become involved in the Katyn issue, but also because they had engaged in far-reaching co-operation with the Germans, in matters such as editing or publishing the so-called *prasa gadzinowa* (the "reptile press" – newspapers published in Polish to disseminate German propaganda).

Up to 1946, for as long as a group of prosecutors consisting of Dr. Roman Martini, Karol Szwarc, and Dr. Jerzy Sawicki, were working on a Katyn trial in Poland, the problem of co-operation with the reptile press was relegated to a position of minor importance and not given much attention by Communist propaganda. It was only when Prosecutor Martini died in mysterious circumstances and the Soviet idea to put the blame for the Katyn mass murder on the Germans during the Nuremberg Trial ended in fiasco that working for the reptile press (which the Communist newspapers and propaganda called collaboration) came to the fore as the key issue. It was certainly a smart propaganda trick. The Katyn trial the Communists had insisted on and publicly plugged was now defused and abandoned, and what they offered the public as a surrogate was a series of trials against journalists who had been involved with co-operation with the Germans in the reptile press. But whereas the prosecutors had shown an interest in the Katyn affair in the course of their work to collect

---

mentacji przechowywanej w zasobie archiwalnym Instytutu Pamięci Narodowej,' in *Charków–Katyń–Twer–Bykownia. Zbiór studiów w 70. Rocznicę Zbrodni Katyńskiej*, A. Kola and J. Sziling (eds.), (Toruń: Wydawnictwo UMK, 2011), 225–240; P. Gasztold-Seń, 'Siła przeciw prawdzie. Represje aparatu bezpieczeństwa PRL wobec osób kwestionujących oficjalną wersję Zbrodni Katyńskiej,' in *Zbrodnia katyńska. W kręgu prawdy i kłamstwa*, ed. S. Kalbarczyk, 132–153.

evidence, when it came to the court proceedings against particular journalists and other associates of *Nowy Kurier Warszawski*, *Goniec Krakowski*, and other reptilian papers, they no longer mentioned Katyn at all.[37]

In 1952 the Katyn question returned to the official discourse in the People's Republic of Poland, in outcome of the activities, findings, and statements issued by the Madden Committee (the United States House Select Committee to Conduct an Investigation and Study of the Facts, Evidence, and Circumstances of the Katyn Forest Massacre), which conducted an official investigation into the circumstances of the Soviet atrocity committed in 1940. The American findings and their dissemination in the media worldwide forced the Communists in Poland and the Soviet Union to take up the Katyn problem again. Naturally, the special services of the People's Republic again became interested in persons who had had any involvement at all since 1943 in the investigation of the Katyn massacre. Repressive measures were again in store for those who had taken part in the German expeditions to Katyn and Smolensk, and had been invigilated since 1945. This is also how I would explain the high level of interest the Polish Ministry of Public Security showed in about a dozen Polish citizens who fled the country illegally toward the end of the War or after it was over, and joined either General Anders' Second Corps or the Polish exiles in London. Subsequently, as émigrés, they gave witness to the truth about Katyn, in declarations that the Soviets were irrefutably culpable for the deaths of thousands of Polish officers.

The lead characters of this book are several dozen of the nearly sixty Poles whom I managed to identify as participants of the 1943 Katyn expeditions. They are, first and foremost, seven medical practitioners: Dr. Hieronim Bartoszewski, Dr. Edward Grodzki, Dr. Konrad Orzechowski, Dr. Stanisław Plappert, Dr. Tadeusz Pragłowski, Dr. Adam Szebesta, and Dr. Marian Wodziński. Of the Polish Red Cross Technical Commission numbering over a dozen persons under the surveillance of the special services of Communist Poland I tracked down Gracjan Jaworowski, Jan Mikołajczyk, Kazimierz Skarżyński, and Jerzy Wodzinowski. Next come the wanted or invigilated writers, journalists, and press photographers: Kazimierz Didur, Ferdynand Goetel, Władysław Kawecki, Zdzisław Koss, Zygmunt Ipohorski-Lenkiewicz, Józef Mackiewicz,

---

[37] T. Wolsza, 'Gadzinówki przed sądem Polski Ludowej (1946–1949),' in *Polska 1944/45–1989. Studia i Materiały* 14 (Warszawa: Instytut Historii PAN, 2014), 359–360.

Marian Maak, Jan Emil Skiwski, and Bruno Widera. The working class is represented in my shortlist mostly by industrial workers from the General-gouvernement [the GG – the part of German-occupied Poland administered as a purportedly "independent" entity'] and Wartheland [the part of Poland directly incorporated in the Third Reich]: Włodzimierz Ambroż, Dr. Zygmunt Giżycki, Władysław Herz, Edmund Killer, Stanisław Kłosowicz, Leon Kowalewicz, Mikołaj Marczyk, Leon Nowicki, Franciszek Prochownik, Bolesław Smektała, and Jan Symon, though I have not been able to give the full particulars for each of them. Two of the six Polish officers who were held as prisoners-of-war by the Germans and attended a Katyn expedition compiled a statement (and that is why they were invigilated by the Ministry of Public Security). They were 2nd Lieut. Stanisław Gostkowski and Col. Stefan Mossor. My list of lead characters is rounded off with the politicians, churchmen, and associates of charity institutions: Father Stanisław Jasiński, Professor Leon Kozłowski, Father Tomasz Rusek, and Edmund Seyfried. These are the principal characters in this book.

The motto at the beginning of this book is a reference to the headline of Władysław Kawecki's interview with Jan Emil Skiwski, which was published in the reptile paper *Nowy Kurier Warszawski* in April 1943.[38]

I would like to thank Dr. Mirosław Grodzki, Dr. Anna M. Jackowska, Dr. Piotr Kardela, Dr. Krzysztof Langowski, Andrzej Skalimowski, and Zofia Pragłowska-Gorczyńskia, as well as the staff of the Institute of National Remembrance for helping me access records which I found invaluable.

---

[38] 'To co widziałem przekracza swą grozą najśmielsze fantazje,' *Nowy Kurier Warszawski* 1943: 92 (Apr. 18, 1943).

THE WARTIME AND POSTWAR FATE OF THE POLES WHO SAW THE KATYN SITE IN 1943

In April, May, and June of 1943, on the initiative of the German authorities, dozens of Poles visited Katyn, the site of the Soviet atrocity committed on Polish prisoners-of-war. The Polish observers included employees of the Polish Red Cross and the RGO (the Central Welfare Council – a Polish social and charity organization tolerated by the German occupying authorities), journalists, officers held in oflags, and laborers delegated from the GG and Wartheland. Some who went to Katyn, such as the journalists, writers, and Red Cross and RGO representatives, had obtained permission from the authorities of the Polish Underground State to inspect the site of the atrocity, and were obliged to submit a report on their findings. However, it is difficult to verify these claims because there are no sources to confirm them. In many cases all we have to go by is information from the observer in question that he had obtained permission from the Polish Underground State.

There were also Polish observers who did not apply to the authorities of the Underground State or failed to get in touch with them. Some of those from factories in the GG and the part of Poland directly incorporated into the Third Reich, from Kraków, Warsaw, Stalowa Wola, Poznań, Łódź, Radom, and Sieradz, were elected by their workmates to represent them.

THE FIRST FOREIGN DELEGATIONS IN KATYN

The Germans started the Katyn Forest exhumations at the turn of March and April 1943. The team of excavators worked under the leadership of Professor

Gerhard Buhtz of Breslau University. After the work on the site (including the exposure of the graves) and the establishment of the facts relating to the scale and time of the killings, they decided to make the Katyn atrocity public and spread news of it internationally using all the resources and media available at the time, such as the press, radio, newsreels, gramophone records, expeditions to the site, memorial ceremonies, interviews, public addresses and lectures, exhibitions, meetings with local inhabitants and employees etc. To achieve their purpose and make the German version of the events trustworthy, they had to bring in observers to see the scale of the crime for themselves. To help them with the broadcasts they were provided with the indispensable propaganda materials, such as victims' letters and photos, and keepsakes from the site such as buttons and pieces of the uniforms.

The first parties of observers the Germans brought to Katyn were not made up of Poles from the GG or the Polish territories directly incorporated in the Third Reich. They tried to get a group of about 10–20 Polish exiles staying in Hungary or Switzerland to come, but were unsuccessful.[39] Before the arrival of the first inhabitants from the GG, who were on the site on April 11 and 15, 1943, there was a delegation of journalists from several neutral or German–occupied countries. The Poles arrived and saw this group just as it was leaving the hotel in Smolensk.[40] A film and radio crew accompanied this delegation. The press reports and German records show that these journalists worked for papers in countries like Sweden, Switzerland, and Spain. The reason why the Germans invited a group of journalists from neutral countries was to create a situation where they could not be accused of a biased account

---

[39] Zawodny, *Katyń 1940*, 37.

[40] F. Goetel, *Czasy wojny*, Introduction by W. Bartoszewski, footnotes and postscript by M. Gałęzowski, (Kraków: Arcana, 2005), 157. "Chance would have it that at the entrance [to the officers' mess – T.W.] we encounter a group of journalists from various countries who have been brought here as well and who have just finished their Katyn visit. But the Germans attending us and them maneuver us about to prevent a direct meeting and exchange of opinions." (B. Kroll, 'Pierwsze sprawozdanie z Katynia. Raport Edmunda Seyfrieda,' *Życie Warszawy* 1989: 4 (Feb. 24), in a supplement entitled *Życie i Historia*, which also notes the following: "Just as our plane arrived in Smolensk we came across a group of foreign journalists making ready to depart." Already on April 7, 1943, Dr. Karl Grundmann, a German official from the Warsaw office of the German Ministry of Propaganda, notified Goetel of the discovery of the graves and the arrangements for a visit by the Polish delegation. A.K. Kunert, 'Kiedy ujawniono prawdę o Katyniu?' *Niepodległość* 28 (1996), 168.

of the events. At that point the presence of witnesses from Sweden, Switzerland, or Spain meant more for them than the opinion of Poles, who were the most interested. For the Germans the opinion of independent journalists was absolutely invaluable at the launch of the propaganda campaign they wanted to conduct on a mass scale. They were well aware of this, and that is why they only brought in Polish observers later. The third party brought in to Smolensk and Katyn was an international team of medical practitioners. The Germans were particularly concerned to have the doctors' opinion, because they were certain it would confirm Soviet culpability for the crime. The arrival of the medical team was slightly delayed, because the Germans and subsequently the Poles (viz. the Polish government-in-exile under General Władysław Sikorski) were waiting for the International Red Cross to reach a decision on an on-site investigation. When the Soviet Union refused to issue permission to the International Red Cross to send in its commission, the prioritized scheme was to have a team of specialists from several European countries conduct an on-site medical examination. The last groups brought to the site were made up of more delegations consisting of writers and scientists from countries under German occupation, locals, and prisoners-of-war. It would be difficult to give an accurate estimate of the number of people the Germans brought to the site in dozens of delegations, but it was certainly an expensive operation. They used air transport, with several stopovers. The observers were put up in Smolensk, and the organizers saw to it that they were served better than average meals, sometimes with alcohol. A bus service ran between Smolensk and Katyn Forest. Another thing that generated costs was the expenditure on propaganda operations.

Of paramount importance from the propaganda point of view, the world of writers, scholars, journalists and press photographers was represented by individuals from many countries: Belgium, Bulgaria, Denmark, Finland, France, Holland, Italy, Norway, Portugal, the Protectorate of Bohemia and Moravia, Romania, Slovakia, Spain, and Turkey. Out of the scores of journalists who visited the site, several made a special commitment to spreading news of the Katyn atrocity in their respective countries. They included the Swedish newspaperman Christer Jaderlund and the Spaniard Jiménez Cabarello, who wrote for *Ya* and *Arriba*. Max Schnetzer reported on the story in the Swiss paper *Der Bund*. Jiménez Cabarello, who arrived somewhat later, delivered an address in

Katyn condemning the Bolshevik atrocity. Filip De Pillecyn, another popular journalist, came to Katyn from Belgium. On the whole the opinions these journalists presented in their respective papers were like Jan Emil Skiwski's headline, "The horror of what I saw surpasses my wildest phantasmagorias." One of the French delegates, the Vichy minister Fernand de Brinon, said that what he had seen "exceeded the capacity of the human imagination." The Spanish journalist wrote that "the reality surpassed the preliminary information," while the Belgian stressed that "we in the West did not believe that such a thing was possible."[41]

The Germans also put great store on the reports from the site published in the reptile press appearing in the GG, as well as in the German-language press like *Die Deutsche Ukrainier Zeitung* and *Die Minsker Zeitung*, issued in the eastern territories the Wehrmacht still held. And of course I cannot fail to mention *Die Warschaeur Zeitung* and *Die Krakauer Zeitung*.[42]

The first reports on the Katyn massacre published in the Swedish press appeared on April 16, 1943.[43] Swedish papers also referred to items published in neighboring countries, such as Finland. The Finnish writer, poet and journalist Ornulf Tigerstedt visited the Katyn site and wrote that the Soviets were culpable for the atrocity.[44] Paweł Jaworski, a Polish historian working on Polish–Swedish relations during the War, has found that some Swedish newspapers were very cautious about the Katyn issue and did not trust the information the Germans disseminated on the subject. One Swedish journalist

---

[41] T. Głowiński, 'Sprawa katyńska w oficjalnej polskojęzycznej prasie codziennej w Generalnym Gubernatorstwie: lipiec–sierpień 1943,' *Niepodległość* 28 (1996), 155.

[42] The first news to appear in the *Krakauer Zeitung* on Katyn was an article published on April 15, 1943, headlined 'Grausiger sowjetischer Massenmord an Kriegsgefangenen polnischen Offizieren. Aufdeckung von Massengraben bei Smolensk. Die Ermordeten in mehreren Schichten übereinander. 50 Leichen bisher identifiziert darunter bekannte Generale. Eine polnische Kommission am Tatort.' Mieczysław Motas has compiled a list of 42 press articles and news items published on Katyn from April to August 1943. On April 18, 9 photographs of the site of the atrocity were published in the press. M. Motas, 'Materiały dotyczące zbrodni katyńskiej w zasobie archiwum Głównej Komisji Badania Zbrodni przeciwko Narodowi Polskiemu. Instytutu Pamięci Narodowej,' *Biuletyn Głównej Komisji Badania Zbrodni przeciwko Narodowi Polskiemu. Instytutu Pamięci Narodowej* 33 (1991), 233. For the German point of view, see L. Jockheck, *Propaganda im Generalgouvernement* (Osnabrück: fibre Verlag, 2006), 183–185.

[43] Jaworski, *Marzyciele,* 169.

[44] *Ibid.,* 170.

1. A 1943 poster from France (courtesy of Musée de l'histoire vivante, Montreuil)

went as far as to warn the Poles for their own good not to find themselves on the losing side of the War.[45] His remark was, of course, directed at the tactics adopted by the Polish government-in-exile, without taking the circumstances of the atrocity itself into consideration. The Spanish press consistently

---

[45] *Ibid.*, 175.

2. Page One of *La Semaine*, May 13, 1943 (courtesy of Musée de l'histoire vivante, Montreuil)

wrote of Soviet culpability for the Katyn massacre. The best-known of the Frenchmen who saw Katyn was the writer and journalist Robert Brasillach; after the War he was prosecuted, convicted of collaboration with the Germans, and executed.[46] Katyn was given wide coverage in the French press,

---

[46] A.M. Jackowska, 'Kłopotliwy temat. Francuzi wobec Katynia,' *Mówią Wieki* (2013: 4), 64; also P. d'Hugues, *Brasillach. Ofiara „kłamstwa katyńskiego"*, (Warszawa: ARTE, 2013).

with accounts from individual members of the various delegations, and the results of the medical investigation by the German and international doctors. Professor Leon Kozłowski, one of Poland's prewar prime ministers, addressed the people of France in a radio broadcast in French, in which he attributed the blame for the Katyn murders to the Soviets.[47] The Polish writer Andrzej Bobkowski, who was living in Paris at the time, summed up the Katyn question as seen from France: "Katyn is 'the story of the season' this spring, if one may speak of it in this manner. But one could hardly put it in any other way. The photographs, the interviews, the reports. The entire German propaganda stands united on this issue, focused on Katyn. Forensic scientists have gone to the site, but only those from countries which have friendly relations with Germany. The matter has been clear from the very start – at least for me. There is only one point which makes it grotesque, sinisterly grotesque – the fact that the wholesaler is denouncing the retailer, while they both come from the same branch of business in butchery. What the Russians have done – it is uncanny to kill one at a time, bringing the victims one at a time, shooting them in the back of the head and stacking the corpses like sardines in a can – the Germans are doing wholesale, on a factory conveyor-belt. What's intriguing about it is that in this case the ideology of collectivism has applied a radically individualistic form of killing."[48]

The Czech journalists were represented by František Kožík, at the time a highly popular Prague radio broadcaster. The historian Mečislav Borák examined his behavior on his return from Katyn and found that in his articles and radio broadcasts he had "tried to avoid making judgments on the atrocity, nonetheless the facts he presented were against the real perpetrators. For instance, the remark that the dates on the latest documents found on the exhumed bodies were for early April 1940, and likewise what the local people he had talked to said was evidence of who was the guilty party."[49]

---

[47] Archiwum Instytutu Pamięci Narodowej [Archive of the Institute of National Remembrance, hereafter AIPN] Kraków, sign. no. 303/1, Protokół przesłuchania świadka Godzika Adama z 7 VII 1945 r.[Minutes of the hearing of witness Adam Godzik, Jul. 7, 1945], sheet 67.

[48] A. Bobkowski, *Szkice piórkiem*, (Warszawa: Wydawnictwo CiS, 2010), 405.

[49] M. Borák, *Ofiary zbrodni katyńskiej z obszaru byłej Czechosłowacji*, (Opava: Slezské zemské museum, 2011), 9.

In late April 1943 an international medical commission arrived at Katyn. It consisted of 14 doctors from occupied Europe and Switzerland, which was neutral. From April 28 to April 30, 1943 the most distinguished forensic scientists established on the basis of their examination that the atrocity had been committed by the Soviets in the spring of 1940. The document, which the Germans subsequently disseminated far and wide, publishing it in several language versions, including Polish, French, Russian, and English, was signed by Reimond Speleers (Ghent, Belgium), Marko Markov (Sofia, Bulgaria), Helge Tramsen (Copenhagen, Denmark), Arno Saxen (Helsinki, Finland), Vincenzo Palmieri (Naples, Italy), Eduard Miloslavić (Zagreb, The Independent State of Croatia), Herman de Burlet (Groningen, Holland), František Hájek (Prague, The Protectorate of Bohemia and Moravia), Alexandru Birkle (Bucharest, Romania), François Naville (Geneva, Switzerland), František Šubík (Bratislava, Slovakia), Ferenc Orsós (Budapest, Hungary), and André Costedoat (Vichy, France). The team was joined by Gerhard Buhtz, a German medical doctor and professor of Breslau University. According to Mecislav Borák, originally Dr. Herman Krsek of the Institute of Forensic Medicine of the University of Slovakia was due to come from Bratislava, but the Slovaks recommended another specialist, Dr. František Šubík, because Krsek had a Czech background.[50] Professor Piga, the Spanish doctor who had been invited, did not reach Katyn; he was very ill on the flight, and returned to Madrid. When the Katyn mission was over the commission was wound up. For some of its members there were consequences due to their attendance even before the War was over. This happened to those who found themselves on territories taken over by the Red Army. I shall return to this point in greater detail later.

In May of 1943 the Germans brought a group of British and American officers held as prisoners-of-war to Katyn. It consisted of Lt.-Col. John Van Vliet, Capt. Stanley Gilder, and Capt. Donald Steward. They were accompanied by two NCO's from Canada and New Zealand, and Frank Stroobant, a civilian from Guernsey in the Channel Islands, which were under German occupation at the time.[51] Their arrival coincided with the work done by the Polish Red Cross Technical Commission. Dr. Marian Wodziński recalled their visit and in his statement made

---

[50] *Ibid.*, 12.

[51] More on this in Piórkowska, *Anglojęzyczni świadkowie Katynia*; Maresch, *Katyń 1940*.

the following record: "When I came to work around eight o'clock in the morning I noticed the Germans were wearing their gala uniforms and that there was a larger group of them than usual at the entrance road into Katyn Forest. (...) That day the Germans did not allow us to work, saying that we would not be able to continue with our normal work until the British and American delegation left. On the path through the forest for the Dnieper River, about 30 meters from the grave, I noticed an automobile hidden in the forest, with sound recording and phonographic equipment. (...) The newly arrived prisoners-of-war were welcomed by a distinctly excited Lieut. Slovenczyk, who showed them the topography of the graves and gave them a general account of the atrocity. An interpreter translated the whole of his address into English."[52] After the War some of the members of this group testified before the Madden Committee.

THE LIST OF POLES WHO SAW THE SITE OF THE ATROCITY IN 1943

There are difficulties with determining a full list of those who were at Katyn in the spring of 1943. We don't have precise data on all the delegations, especially those consisting of workers representing factories and other workplaces. On the other hand there is no problem with the names of those in the Polish Red Cross and RGO delegations, and the same is true of the journalists, writers, and photojournalists. The group of Polish prisoners-of-war held in German oflags seems to have been established precisely enough. And we also know the names of those Polish people who were in Katyn in 1943 and subsequently, in the latter part of the War, were killed in atrocities committed by the Germans.

How many Poles were in Katyn from April 11, 1943 to June 1943? In light of extant records – I have in mind the reports drawn up by the observers themselves, newspaper articles and interviews including those in the reptile press, as well as the postwar Ministry of Public Security materials – it seems it could not have been less than fifty-odd persons.[53] Taking into account the different institutions which sent representatives, we get the following names:

---

[52] Z.S., 'Raport amerykański o Katyniu,' *Orzeł Biały* 1950: 40 (Oct.7), 4.

[53] I used the following documents to draw up the list of those who were in Katyn in the spring of 1943: AIPN, Warsaw, sign. no. 00231/124, vol. 1, Oświadczenie Bolesława Smektały z 10 IV 1952 r. [Statement by Bolesław Smektała, Apr. 10, 1952], sheet 1; *Ibid.*, vol. 2, Notatka

- The Polish Red Cross delegations from Kraków and Warsaw: Roman Banach, Dr. Hieronim Bartoszewski, Władysław Buczak, Stefan Cupryjak, Adam Godzik, Antoni Godzisz, Gracjan Jaworowski, Hugon Kassur, Stefan Kołodziejski, Franciszek Król, Jan Mikołajczyk, Dr. Stanisław Plappert, Ferdynand Płonka, Zygmunt Pohorski, Dr. Tadeusz Pragłowski, Ludwik Rojkiewicz, Kazimierz Skarżyński, Dr. Adam Szebesta, Jerzy Wodzinowski, and Dr. Marian Wodziński;
- The RGO: Edmund Seyfried;
- Polski Komitet Opiekuńczy (the Polish Welfare Committee): Dr. Edward Grodzki and Dr. Konrad Orzechowski;
- Journalists and writers: Kazimierz Didur (*Krakauer Zeitung*), Ferdynand Goetel (The Polish Academy of Literature, the RGO), Władysław Kawecki (*Goniec Krakowski*, Telpress), Zdzisław Koss (*Dziennik Radomski*), Zygmunt Ipohorski-Lenkiewicz, Marian Maak (writer from Kraków), Józef Mackiewicz (*Goniec Codzienny*), Jan Emil Skiwski (writer), and Bruno Widera (*Nowy Głos Lubelski*).

There is yet another name – that of the journalist Marian Martens – in the Institute of National Remembrance records and the reptile press; and an anonymous associate of *Kurier Częstochowski*.

- Employees of factories and other workplaces: Włodzimierz Ambroż (representing an optical instruments factory from Warsaw), Dr. Zygmunt Giżycki (a dentist working for the Poznań municipal streetcar company), Władysław Herz (for the Centra battery factory, Poznań), Edmund Killer aka Kiler

informacyjna chor. H. Kowalskiego z 8 X 1952 r. [Note drawn up by Ensign H. Kowalski, Oct. 8, 1952]; *Ibid.*, sign. no. 4058/IV, Teczka Zygmunta Lenkiewicza-Ipohorskiego [Dossier on Zygmunt Lenkiewicz-Ipohorski]; C. Madajczyk, *Dramat katyński, passim*; Kroll, 'Pierwsze sprawozdanie z Katynia,' 1; A. Toczewski, 'Raport ppłk. dypl. Stefana Mossora o wizycie polskich oficerów z niemieckich oflagów w Katyniu,' *Niepodległość* 45 [25 in new series] (1992), 77; *Zbrodnia katyńska w świetle dokumentów*, 1980, passim; Jankowski and Kotarba, *Literaci a sprawa katyńska 1945, passim*; F. Goetel, 'Katyń. Rok 1943 i pierwsze wieści,' *Wiadomości* 1949: 43 (Oct. 23), 1; and K. Skarżyński, 'Katyń i Polski Czerwony Krzyż,' *Kultura* 1955: 5, 128–129. I also used a few newspaper articles published in *Nowy Kurier Warszawski* in April, May, and June 1943 ('Bolszewicy zamordowali tysiące polskich oficerów. Delegacja Polaków z Ferdynandem Goetlem na czele oglądała wstrząsające cmentarzysko,' *Nowy Kurier Warszawski* 1943: 89 (Apr. 14), 1; 'Delegacja polskiego świata pracy w Katyniu,' *Nowy Kurier Warszawski* 1943: 126 (May 28), 1; 'Ofiarna praca ekipy PCK,' *Nowy Kurier Warszawski* 1943: 131 (Jun. 3), 2; 'Gehenna oficerów pod „opieką" NKWD w Kozielsku. Opowiadanie byłego jeńca, który wydostał się z obozu,' *Nowy Kurier Warszawski* 1943: 132 (Jun. 4), 1).

(for the Warsaw Steyer-Daimler-Puch works), Stanisław Kłosowicz (for the Radom Steyer-Daimler-Puch Works, competitor in the 1928 Amsterdam Olympics), Leon Kowalewicz (for the Avia mechanical works, Warsaw), Hieronim Majewski (for the Sieradz railroad works), Mikołaj Marczyk (for the Stalowa Wola steelworks), Leon Nowicki (for the Cegielski heavy engineering works, Poznań), Franciszek Prochownik (for the Zieleniewski heavy engineering works, Kraków), Bolesław Smektała (for the Focke-Wulf aircraft works, Poznań), Jan Symon aka Szymon (for the F.S.W. automobile factory, Warsaw), and probably two more unidentified employees from factories in Łódź;

- Prisoners-of-war from the Woldenberg, Neubrandenburg, and Gross Born Oflags: Capt. Konstanty Adamski, Capt. Stanisław Cylkowski, 2nd Lt. Stanisław Gostkowski, Capt. Eugeniusz Kleban, Col. Stefan Mossor, and 2nd Lt. Zbigniew Rowiński;[54]
- Others: Maj. Arthur Glaeser (aka Jan Artur Glezer of Sosnowiec);[55] Father Stanisław Jasiński (representing Archbishop Adam Sapieha); Professor Leon Kozłowski (prewar prime minister of Poland); General Mieczysław Smorawiński's brother; Edward Leśniak, an engineer from Warsaw,[56] and Capt. Stanisław Sitko (a medical practitioner from Grodno).

The delegation from Grodno (now Grodna, Belarus) was joined by a small group of doctors from Białystok. Unfortunately we have no information on the names and number of people in this group. In addition we should also consider the forced laborers the Germans employed for the digging. Members of some of the delegations said in their recollections that these laborers were Poles from Lwów (now L'viv, Ukraine), and that they wore German uniforms with no rank badges.[57] Postwar Ministry of Public Security records mention a few forced laborers from Łódź and Poznań, but I am not at all sure that these men, Stanisław Pawłowski, Stefan Okupski, Kazimierz Stułkowski, and Józef

---

[54] More on this in Toczewski, 'Raport ppłk. dypl. Stefana Mossora,' 77, 79.

[55] 'Gehenna oficerów,' 1.

[56] According to information from Halina Czekalska, Leśniak's wife, he was arrested by the Gestapo and never heard of again. Most probably he was a victim of one of the German crimes. AIPN Warsaw, sign. no. 00231/124, vol. 1, Informacja nr 1 dotycząca dowodów prowokacji niemieckiej w sprawie Katynia [Information no. 1 concerning evidence for the German provocation regarding Katyn], sheet 24.

[57] G. Jaworowski, 'Nieznana relacja o grobach katyńskich,' *Zeszyty Historyczne* 45 (1978), 4.

Zbikowski (all from Łódź), and Mieczysław Lisiecki (from Poznań), whom the Germans sent east, were in Katyn in the spring of 1943; though when interrogated by Ministry of Public Security officers they all insisted that they arrived on the site of the atrocity on May 2, 1943. But their statements were so similar to one another, down to the minor details, that they cast doubt on the truthfulness of these witnesses.[58] We cannot rule out that their testimonials were orchestrated by the secret service.

No doubt this is not the full list, especially as the delegations from workplaces and provincial cities tended to be mentioned only in passing in press articles on Katyn. It would be no use trying to search for the names of these delegates in the reptile press or in the papers that came out in the Polish territories incorporated directly into the Third Reich. The example of the forced laborers from Łódź shows just how futile that would be. The documents the Ministry of Public Security compiled in 1952 say that there were also some residents of Lida (now in Belarus) and several other persons from hitherto unidentified places who saw the Katyn site in 1943.[59]

This is where I should add the persons who had German permission to travel to Katyn to collect the bodies of their relatives. We do not know the scale of this practice, nor of the corruption that presumably attended it. What we know for certain is that situations of this kind did occur. The PSL (Polish Peasants' Party) activist Andrzej Witos recalled one of them: "After the War I met such people. People whom the Germans allowed to travel to Katyn for the body of a friend or relative (e.g. B.S. went there with the wife of Stefan Podhajniuk for the body of her husband, a teacher and captain of the reserve forces who was arrested by the NKVD and was discovered in the pit among the officers and ensigns murdered in Katyn. A Russian living in the locality, at whose house they had a drink of water, apparently told them Stalin and Beria were to blame for it, and that they [the NKVD] shot people every night)."[60] Though

---

[58] AIPN Warsaw, sign. no. 00231/124, vol. 1, Informacja nr 1 dotycząca dowodów prowokacji niemieckiej w sprawie Katynia z 3 IV 1952 r. [Information no. 1 concerning evidence for the German provocation regarding Katyn, Apr. 3, 1952], sheets 112–115.

[59] *Ibid.*, vol. 2, Notatka informacyjna chor. H. Kowalskiego z 8 X 1952 r. [Note drawn up by Ensign H. Kowalski, Oct. 8, 1952], sheets 2–3.

[60] A. Witos, *Wszystko, co niosło życie. Wspomnienia*, ed. C. Brzoza (Wojnicz: Towarzystwo Przyjaciół Ziemi Wojnickiej, 1998), 155. Andrzej Witos also wrote that there was a memorial plaque on Capt. Podhajniuk's grave in Smotrycze cemetery, which said that he was murdered

you can hardly overlook the fact that you won't find a Capt. Stefan Podhajniuk on the list of victims from Kozelsk. But you can't rule out the possibility that the Germans decided not to put his name on the list once they had handed his body over to the family. That is why the Polish Red Cross Technical Commission did not record the name; neither did Władysław Kawecki, who compiled the first, provisional list of victims identified. And you can't rule out the possibility of Andrzej Witos' memory failing him about the name of the Polish officer whose wife set out in search of him.

THEY COULD HAVE GONE, BUT FOR VARIOUS REASONS DIDN'T...

We can also draw up another list – of about a dozen people from the GG and Distrikt-Lemberg who could have traveled to Smolensk and Katyn but for various reasons withdrew. The names of several of them appeared in various documents still during the War as well as after it was over. The individuals concerned from Kraków and Warsaw were associates of the Polish Red Cross, the RGO, the Supreme Court, or chapter members of the respective cathedral; those from Lwów were medical practitioners, journalists, or RGO associates.

In the memoirs of Ferdynand Goetel we read that from Warsaw "Father [Zygmunt] Kozubski is indeed ready to travel to Koziy Gory, but for the love of God he would never venture to do so in an airplane. [Janusz] Machnicki cannot take a flight because of a liver disorder. [Stanisław] Wachowiak had some extremely important conferences with representatives of the authorities to attend to, and the delegate for the courts [Kazimierz Rudnicki] did not know at all what to say when asked if he would go, proffering the excuse that the chairman of the judiciary was down with an illness."[61] None of them eventually decided to travel, and the representative of the courts not only did not turn up at the airport, but did not say anything at all whether he would go on the journey or not. Other prospective observers from Warsaw did not show much of an interest, either. They included the political journalist and

---

in Katyn. The Russians removed the plaque as soon as they entered the area.

[61] Goetel, *Czasy wojny*, 155.

Sovietologist Tadeusz Teslar, and
Stella Olgierd, who had been a secretary with the PEN Club before
the War, and in the war years published minor articles in the reptile
press.[62] Stefan Korboński wrote that
Father Stanisław Trzeciak had been
a member of a delegation, but his
information was wrong.[63] The Board
of the Polish Red Cross wanted the
zootechnician Jan Rostafiński,
a professor of the SGGW [modern
English name: Warsaw University of
Life Sciences], who was organizing
secret education in Warsaw at the
time, to engage in the identification
of the Katyn victims. In May Professor Rostafiński received a letter
signed by Wacław Lachert and Dr.
Władysław Gorczycki inviting him

3. Jan Rostafiński

to a meeting of the Board of the Polish Red Cross "for the reading of the
report drawn up by the Information Office of the Polish Red Cross on the
exhumation, identification, and reburial of the bodies of Polish military discovered at Katyn near Smolensk."[64] I realize that there were far more people
invited, but unfortunately the full details have not been researched yet. Professor Rostafiński turned down the invitation, as in his opinion attending
the meeting could be seen as collaboration.[65] In 1943 the Germans arrested
him and held him in the Pawiak prison, and later sent him to Stutthof concentration camp.

---

[62] Jankowski and Kotarba, *Literaci a sprawa katyńska 1945*, 213–214.

[63] S. Korboński, *W imieniu Rzeczypospolitej...*, (Warszawa: Instytut Pamięci Narodowej,
2009), 159.

[64] P. Kardela, *Wojciech Rostafiński (1921–2002). Powstaniec Warszawy, naukowiec z NASA*,
(Lublin: Norbertinum, 2008), 82–83.

[65] *Ibid.*, 83.

The final decision on the members of the delegation from Kraków was in the hands of Adam Ronikier and Archbishop Sapieha. Apart from the candidacy of Edmund Seyfried, the names of the others being considered were not divulged almost to the last moment. The Archbishop took the duty upon himself to select "a clergyman to conduct the appropriate memorial services on the site."[66] In fact it is hard to say whether all of those from Kraków who had declared they were willing to participate in the delegation actually traveled to Katyn.

When the Poles had already arrived on the site of the massacre the idea was put forward to have Dr. Jan Olbrycht, a distinguished Cracovian physician, join the Polish Red Cross Technical Commission. Lt.-Col. Stanisław Plappert from the Kraków branch of the Polish Red Cross, and Dr. Marian Wodziński spoke on the matter with Dr. Gerhard Buhtz, head of the German medical commission. Their efforts were unsuccessful: "During that conversation I tried to intervene (...) on behalf of Dr. Jan Olbrycht. Prof. Buhtz told me that although he knew Olbrycht very well, nonetheless he would not be able to intervene on his behalf at the time."[67] What made it impossible was the fact that Olbrycht had been sent to Auschwitz-Birkenau. From Dr. Wodziński's information it appears the matter was being considered by the German Ministry of Propaganda.[68] Evidently, not even the Katyn question, which was a key issue for the Germans, could guarantee a release from a concentration camp. For various reasons Dr. Stanisław Manczarski of Warsaw and Dr. Leon Wachholz from Kraków, other candidates suggested somewhat later, were turned down as well. Eventually the man who came nearest to actually joining the Technical Commission of the Polish Red Cross was Dr. Tadeusz Starostka from Tarnobrzeg. But he didn't go, either, because the Germans issued an order for the exhumation project on the site to finish. Another who eventually decided not to travel to Katyn was Dr. Jan Zygmunt Robel, who supported his decision with the argument that a scientific examination could not be conducted on the site of an atrocity.

---

[66] A. Ronikier, *Pamiętniki 1939–1945*, (Kraków: Wydawnictwo Literackie, 2001), 233.

[67] AIPN Kraków, sign. no. 303/1, Protokół przesłuchania świadka Stanisława Plapperta [Minutes of the hearing of witness Stanisław Plappert], sheet 18.

[68] Maresch, *Katyń 1940*, 148.

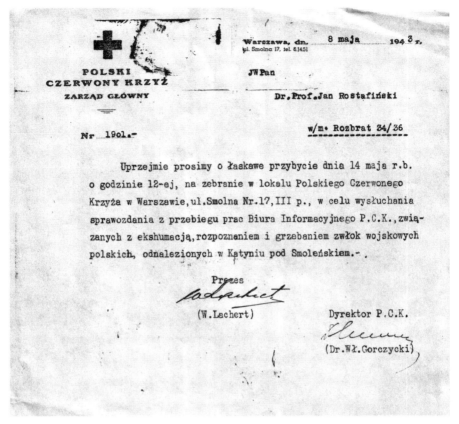

4. Letter from the authorities of the Polish Red Cross inviting Professor Jan Rostafiński to attend the meeting on Katyn, May 1943

Others who boycotted the expedition were a group from Lwów appointed by various institutions and consisting of Stanisław Wasylewski, editor of *Gazeta Lwowska*; Adam Gruca, professor of medicine at Lwów University; and Dr. Leopold Tesznar, RGO plenipotentiary for Distrikt Galizien.[69] Later there was talk in the Red Cross milieu of another prospective member of the team, Dr. Bolesław Popielski from Lwów, but this idea was not put into practice, either. Lwów was one of the few large Polish cities without a representative who decided to travel to Katyn.

---

[69] G. Hryciuk, „*Kumityt". Polski Komitet Opiekuńczy Lwów Miasto w latach 1941–1944*, (Toruń: Wydawnictwo Adam Marszałek, 2000), 68.

33

The extant records of the Ministry of Public Security show that three of the persons the Germans had selected for the Wartheland laborers' delegation did not join the group. They were Konrad Kabuz, Władysław Smętek, and Jan Wojciechowski, all laborers from Karsznice, and all of them used a poor state of health as an excuse. One of them suggested Hieronim Majewski, a trustworthy person who had been an officer in the Polish Army before the War, as a prospective member of the group.[70]

Finally two officers, Gen. Jan Chmurowicz and Maj. Aleksander Nowosielski, both from Oflag II C at Woldenberg, left the prisoners'-of-war delegation. They were already on their way for Katyn, via Stettin (now Szczecin, Poland), Berlin, and Warsaw, when they withdrew because of serious health problems, and got medical certificates from German doctors to confirm their condition.[71]

WHAT HAPPENED DURING THE WAR (1943–1945) TO POLISH OBSERVERS WHO SAW THE SITE OF THE KATYN ATROCITY AND THE ACTIVITIES THEY UNDERTOOK

What all the Poles who saw the Katyn site in 1943 did and how they behaved during the rest of the War had a profound influence on what happened to them after the War. This applied especially to the Polish Red Cross and RGO associates and the journalists, and their professional activities. It was on this basis that a feverish search for witnesses who had seen the site of the Katyn atrocity in 1943 started as soon as the Red Army set foot on Polish territory. Communist security officers assessed witnesses' behavior on the basis of what they had published, the press interviews they had given, and the reports they had compiled. The Ministry of Public Security had the Home Army's counter-intelligence records in their hands.[72] The fullest information they had was on Ferdynand Goetel for 1940–1942. In 1940 agents had reported that

---

[70] AIPN Łódź, Akta śledcze przeciwko Majewskiemu Hieronimowi [Records of investigation against Hieronim Majewski], sign. no. 5657, Sentencja wyroku z 1 VIII 1950 r. [Sentence of verdict of Aug. 1, 1950], sheet 2.

[71] Toczewski, 'Raport ppłk. dypl. Stefana Mossora,' 77, 79.

[72] Currently these records are in the Archive of the Institute of National Remembrance, Warsaw.

Goetel had registered as a writer on the instigation of the German authorities. In July 1942 the authorities of the Polish underground resistance learned that he had made deprecatory remarks about the Polish government-in-exile, calling it a "rabble." A few months later allegations of the most serious kind were made against him in a report submitted by a secret agent known as Hanna, who wrote that he was "an outright supporter of Hitler. For the entire War he has been in favor of cultural co-operation with the Germans, just like that other writer Cybichowski. His latest book is on Fascism. Two years ago, when Goetel was arrested [from his apartment] on ulica Kaniowska due to the discovery of his radio, he was severely beaten up by the Gestapo and spent three days in Pawiak jail. Everyone was surprised when he was unexpectedly released. During the first year of the war he had been a frequent guest of the Pod Pegazem Bar (now the Warta) on ulica Moniuszki. This bar was used as a permanent base for communication with Paris, before the fall of France. The journalist Stanisław Piasecki and others were regulars, too. None of them are still alive, except for Goetel. Why?" Both the Soviet and the Polish secret services had collected enough documentation to be quite well briefed on the Poles' wartime involvement in an attempt to clarify the circumstances of the Katyn atrocity.

Several of the Red Cross and RGO representatives drew up reports on their 1943 visit to Katyn. Ferdynand Goetel was the very first to do so, already by April 13, 1943. He did not keep it for institutional use only by the Red Cross, but also sent copies to several persons in the authorities of OPW [Obóz Polski Walczącej, "the Fighting Poland Movement," a resistance group]. In his recollections he wrote, "On arrival [in Warsaw] I wrote a report for the Polish Red Cross, and sent a copy with a commentary and a list of the first identified victims through the services of Marian Ruth Buczkowski to "Hubert" [Aleksander Kamieński, at the time head of propaganda for the Home Army's Warsaw branch], and to "Koral" [?] Julian Piasecki. Having delivered my letter to the Red Cross I asked for a copy to be sent to Dr. Karl Grundmann of the [German] Propagandaamt. My reason for doing this had nothing to do with 'co-operation' of whatever kind with the Propagandaamt on the Katyn issue. By sending a copy to Grundmann I wanted on the one hand to force the German authorities to entrust the Katyn inquiry to the Polish Red Cross, and on the other hand to break down the reluctance which the Red Cross and other institutions had shown to handle the Katyn issue."[73]

In his report Ferdynand Goetel presented the circumstances of the expedition, the members of the delegation (Dr. Konrad Orzechowski, Dr. Edward Grodzki, Jan Emil Skiwski, Edmund Seyfried, two journalists and two photojournalists), and the conduct of the Germans during the expedition. He wrote of the work done by the International Medical Commission and the documents the Germans collected on the site of the crime. He added a list of the first 36 identified victims, including Generals Bronisław Bohaterewicz and Mieczysław Smorawiński. Finally he ventured on some personal impressions: "the excavation is authentic beyond all doubt; even if the number of bodies, estimated by German experts at ten thousand, is perhaps overrated, one may certainly assume on the basis of the investigation conducted hitherto that all the prisoners-of-war from Kozelsk, of whom nothing has been heard since the spring of 1940, are in the graves at Koziy Gory. The procedure used for execution may be reconstructed as follows: prisoners were removed from Kozelsk in small groups and systematically, about two or three railcars per day. At Smolensk station they were put on a train for Koziy Gory, where their belongings and valuables were taken from them. On arrival they were immediately killed with a shot in the back of the head. Any who resisted were bound with a rope, and those who shouted or screamed had a hood put over their heads or had their mouths stuffed with oakum. The executions went on for the months of March and April. When they finished young pines were planted on the burial ground."[74]

Just a few days later other persons in the OPW resistance movement received the document. This is what Goetel said about his initiative: "I wanted

---

[73] F. Goetel, 'Lot do Katynia,' sent to the press by P. Żaroń, *Przegląd Tygodniowy* 1989:21 (Apr. 22), 10. Goetel wrote of his first meeting after his return from Katyn with members of the Polish Red Cross at their Warsaw headquarters, in a newspaper article entitled 'Katyń. Po powrocie,' *Wiadomości* 1949: 47 (Nov. 20), 2: "I went to the presidium of the Polish Red Cross and handed in my report. I don't know whether the gentlemen assembled there had had a detailed report on what had happened there from one of the doctors, or whether they regarded the information from the radio broadcasts and news in the press as sufficient. Nonetheless, my letter must have shocked them."

[74] F. Goetel, 'Raport z Katynia do Polskiego Czerwonego Krzyża,' sent to the press by M. Kledzik, *Przekrój* 1989: 2297 (Jun. 18), 9.

5. Ferdynand Goetel in 1936

to put it even more drastically, so I made a few copies and gave them to trustworthy persons."[75] He wrote that the persons who had access to his report were Jerzy Zagórski, Marian Buczkowski, Wilam Horzyca, Józef Targowski, and Alfred Wysocki at home, and Wiesław Wohnout and Wiktor Trościanko outside of Poland. Subsequently the document reached Stefan "Grot" Rowecki, Commander-in-Chief of the Home Army. On reading it General Rowecki said that Goetel had "served his country well by what he had done on the Katyn question," (as Goetel later wrote).[76]

Another person who had a very good opinion of Goetel's report was Kazimierz Skarżyński, secretary general of the Polish Red Cross, who observed that it was "the first authentic Polish report, written by an intelligent man who drew his own conclusions from the horrific sight he had before his eyes (...)."[77]

While on the subject of Ferdynand Goetel, there is another problem that cannot be passed over. It concerns his alleged co-operation with the reptile press following his return from Katyn. A scrutiny of the 1943 reptiles, including *Nowy Kurier Warszawski*, leads to the discovery of an article signed "G", supposedly "Goetel."[78] Yet the maneuver brought about a strong protest from the writer, who insisted he had nothing to do with that publication: "So on my return, when I hear that I took part in the delegation as a German

---

[75] Goetel, 'Lot do Katynia,' 10.

[76] *Ibid*. Jankowski and Kotarba (*Literaci a sprawa katyńska 1945*, 60–61, 76–77) present a lot of details on the circumstances of Goetel's travel to Katyn and his recommendation issued from the Polish Underground State. See also K. Polechoński, 'Ferdynand Goetel w Katyniu,' *Arcana* 2009: 1, 85; M. Klecel, 'Pisarze ścigani za Katyń,' *Biuletyn Instytutu Pamięci Narodowej* 2010: 4, 65–75.

[77] Skarżyński, 'Katyń i Polski Czerwony Krzyż,' 129.

[78] (G.), 'Największa zbrodnia dziejów ludzkości,' *Nowy Kurier Warszawski* 1943:90 (Apr. 15), 1–2.

agent and was remunerated with a bottle of vodka, I don't bother to counteract. When I get a mean trick played against me, when *Nowy Kurier Warszawski* feels snubbed and publishes an editorial signed with the initials F.G., which were never there before, all I can do is just shrug my shoulders."[79] He wondered why the paper's editors had done that, and reached a conclusion that it must have been a deliberate move by the Germans, who wanted to draw him into their propaganda machine.[80] Goetel gave a brief radio broadcast, in which he said, "Having been badgered many times to speak out and give my impressions, I shall say one sentence to the microphone: In all likelihood the men lying in the graves of Koziy Gory are the Polish officers from Kozelsk and Starobielsk of whom there has been no sign since April 1940."[81] So we cannot rule out that this incident, too, contributed in one way or another to Goetel's name being put on the blacklist of those who co-operated with the German media. On leaving the site of the atrocity, Goetel and the other members of the delegation took keepsakes of remembrance with them, in his case the ribbon of General Bohaterewicz's Virtuti Militari cross, a few buttons from victims' uniforms, and a handful of soil, which he intended to deposit in a museum.[82]

On the same day Edmund Seyfried handed in his "report on the flight to Smolensk" to the RGO management. Initially he had been quite skeptical about the RGO delegation's immediate departure for Katyn, he went as far as to have doubts about the expediency of their journey. As a result he traveled to the site of the Soviet atrocity in a private capacity.[83] Seyfried, who was the general director of RGO, argued that "the RGO as such had nothing to do with matters relating to cemeteries, which is the business of the Polish Red Cross, which was statutorily appointed to handle such operations (...)." In his report he wrote of two aspects of the Katyn atrocity. He discussed "the state of the matter from the German point of view" and "the state of the matter as established by us on the site." Regarding the former issue, he enumerated all the arguments the Germans had used to persuade the Poles that the Soviets were culpable for the Katyn massacre – witnesses' testimonials, documents found

---

[79] Goetel, 'Katyń. Po powrocie,' 2.

[80] Jankowski and Kotarba, *Literaci a sprawa katyńska 1945*, 241.

[81] Goetel, *Czasy wojny*, 163.

[82] *Ibid.*, 162.

[83] Kroll, 'Pierwsze sprawozdanie z Katynia,' 1.

on the bodies such as letters, daily newspapers etc., which stopped abruptly in the spring of 1940, the three-year pines planted on the site, and the state of the corpses' decay indicating a time of interment of not less than three years. Next he presented his own and other delegates' impressions, mentioning the appearance and layout of the graves, the surviving documents, and the victims who had been identified (he appended a list of names). He ended his report with his "personal conclusions." Here he stressed that the victims were Polish officers from Kozelsk. Then he made an appeal for the setting up of a Polish honorary committee to investigate the matter. He also saw the need to send a Polish Red Cross delegation to the site.[84]

A week later Col. Trapszo, who held the most senior rank among the Polish officers in Oflag IIE/K at Neubrandenburg, received the report compiled by Col. Stefan Mossor, who wrote on behalf of all the Polish POWs in Katyn on April 17, 1943. In August 1943 the Polish government-in-exile and Supreme Commander read Mossor's report. AK units in clandestine contact with the prisoners-of-war in Oflag IIE/K served as go-betweens for the document's delivery.[85] In his report Col. Mossor drew attention to several important points which he and other officers observed on the Katyn site. A large passage of his report was on the appearance of the victims. He wrote of their uniforms and shoes, and of the documents and insignia the Germans found on the bodies – the paper documents, military distinctions and orders, buttons, regimental badges, epaulettes, postcards, photographs, cigarette boxes, money etc. He considered the length of time the bodies had been interred in Katyn Forest, and observed that this question would be resolved by specialists using scientific methods. He also mentioned the German estimate of 10–12 thousand victims.[86]

But the passage which should be regarded as the most important part of Col. Mossor's report is the part on who perpetrated the massacre. On the basis of what he had heard, he wrote that "Witnesses (local people) give fairly consistent estimates of the number of transports arriving at the place. They say that in March and April of 1940, when the executions took place, about three to four prison railcars a day arrived at Gnezdovo station from the

---

[84] *Ibid.*

[85] Toczewski, 'Raport ppłk. dypl. Stefana Mossora,' 76.

[86] *Ibid.*, 81.

Smolensk direction. They were packed with Polish officers, who were driven away from the station on three GPU *chorniye raby* [*chorniye woroni*] ("black crow" trucks), each of which took sixteen men."[87] He went on to write that the documents retrieved which had a precise date, such as letters, postcards, and newspapers, came to a stop in March of 1940. He attached a sketch of the site and the first list of victims, identical with the one appended to Goetel's and Seyfried's reports.

Another person who submitted a detailed report was Kazimierz Skarżyński, who traveled to Katyn as a Red Cross delegate as well as the secret representative of the Polish Underground State. Just before he left for Katyn he read Goetel's observations.[88] Skarżyński was a sharp-eyed and exceptionally attentive observer, and put a lot of details into his report. He noted the behavior of the Germans and the medical commission. He devoted a lot of attention to the appearance of the bodies: "They (...) were all wearing Polish uniforms, most were in the heavy winter coats. The condition [of the uniforms] was extraordinary – the distinctions and buttons looked brand new. The bodies had been through a complex process of decomposition and mummification – no doubt due to the sandy soil. There was no skin on the faces anymore, and you could see the oral cavities and eye sockets through the desiccated muscle and membrane tissue. The skulls had hair which had lost its color. I noticed that only red hair had kept its color (...). But the hands were in an excellent state of preservation, the skin on them was untouched and they had fingernails, you could see the palm lines."[89] Skarżyński was another observer who wondered how the executions had been done. It was no secret to him the murders had been perpetrated by "a team of experts, at a very close range."[90] He challenged the German estimate for the number of victims, and reached a conclusion that the Katyn graves must have held 4–6 thousand victims. He also talked to the German medical commission, including Dr. Gerhard Buhtz, and said afterwards that he could confirm that the German army had treated the Polish team decently.

---

[87] *Ibid.*, 82.

[88] Skarżyński, 'Katyń i Polski Czerwony Krzyż,' 129.

[89] *Ibid.*, 133.

[90] *Ibid.*, 134.

On his return to Warsaw Skarżyński submitted an extensive report to the management of the Polish Red Cross, which he signed with his first name and surname. His report consisted of eight points, and was later published in all the reptile newspapers in the GG and in the German press on the Polish territories directly incorporated in the Reich. Point four on his list made it plain that the atrocity had been done by the Soviets: "on the basis of the papers, documents, and notes found on the corpses the time of the massacre can be determined as March–April 1940."[91]

Despite pressure and insistent appeals, he firmly refused to give an interview for the German press (including the reptiles, of course). He did not agree to write a letter to the editor for them on the details of his visit to Katyn. While he steered clear of all co-operation whatsoever with the German authorities, he arranged for a meeting as soon as possible with Stefan Korboński, who was head of Civilian Resistance. They met in April 1943 and on the basis of Skarżyński's account Korboński reached a conclusion that it was the Soviets who did the crime. That was the opinion he subsequently sent to Jan Stanisław Jankowski, who was Polish Government Delegate for Poland. [92] Later he dispatched numerous telegrams to the Polish government-in-exile.[93] Korboński's telegrams were also used by the Polish radio station Świt, which broadcast to Poland from Britain. Skarżynski's report perished during the 1944 Warsaw

---

[91] 'PCK uczestniczy w ekshumacji,' *Nowy Kurier Warszawski* 1943: 93 (Apr. 19), 1.

[92] Korboński, *W imieniu Rzeczypospolitej...*, 278. This is Korboński's account of the meeting: "During my talk with the Delegate [viz. J.S. Jankowski, the domestic representative of the government-in-exile] it was decided that I should get in touch with one of those who went to Katyn, and we decided to choose a person we were sure would be trustworthy, impartial, and fully reliable as regards security. We ruled out Józef Mackiewicz and Ferdynand Goetel, whose German sympathies were well known. We decided on Kazimierz Skarżyński, Secretary-General of the Polish Red Cross (...). I'll say this: his extensive, unemotional, and objective information based on the facts he had observed left us in no doubt: the Russians were the murderers. (...) After my talk with Skarżyński I rushed first to the Delegate. (...) When I had finished, he asked me to keep the information to be transmitted to London within the bounds of radio security. From the Delegate I rushed to the radio station. Zosia, the telegraphist and monitoring staff were already waiting there, they had been alerted there might be alarm messages to be sent that day" (278–279).

[93] P. Stanek, *Stefan Korboński (1901–1989). Działalność polityczna i społeczna* (Warszawa: Instytut Pamięci Narodowej – Komisja Ścigania Zbrodni przeciwko Narodowi Polskiemu, 2014), 73.

Uprising.[94] Luckily his rough copy with the notes he made while still in Katyn has survived. He used it to draw up a second version of the report and subsequently disseminated it internationally.

Józef Mackiewicz, the delegate from Wilno (now Vilnius, Lithuania), left for Katyn on obtaining the consent of the authorities of the Polish Underground State. Years later he said, "at a secret meeting in Wilno (...) a decision was taken that not only was I to go there, but also that I was to write an article in the pro-German paper *Goniec Codzienny* (this was a demand made by the Germans, as was only to be expected), because after all that paper was widely read."[95] He returned to his home city via Warsaw, where he submitted his first Katyn report. Once he was home he drew up a second report for the local AK. He was interviewed by Feliks Lubierzyński for *Goniec Codzienny*. If we compare his statement on Katyn for the reptile press with other reports, we can say that Mackiewicz's was a full and well-thought-out testimonial which gave a good idea of the atmosphere of the Katyn burial field. He wrote of the graves and the victims, wondering what their last moments might have been like. He quoted a few passages from letters he had retrieved from Katyn. In his description of the graves and their contents he observed that what the staff conducting the exhumation were finding and extricating from them were the bodies of the men who had been murdered, bills of various kinds and currencies, wooden cigarette boxes, cigarettes, scraps of Soviet newspapers, army buttons with the Polish Eagle on them, gloves, scraps of uniforms, handkerchiefs, and leather wallets. "This was so because thousands of murdered men were cast into these horrific pits together with all the personal ballast of their everyday lives."[96] He was in no doubt that the atrocity had been committed by the Soviets – and he stressed this, citing evidence to prove it, such as the results of the medical examination and the documents found on the bodies. He quoted a few passages from the letters. In one a child wrote, "Dear Daddy, We're worried, because we've not had any news or letters from you. We've sent 100 rubles and a parcel (...). We're well and staying at the same address. Please

---

[94] Jankowski and Kotarba, *Literaci a sprawa katyńska 1945,* 105.

[95] J. Malewski (W. Bolecki), *Wyrok na Józefa Mackiewicza,* (London: Puls, 1991), 45.

[96] 'Widziałem na własne oczy. (Józef Mackiewicz o swoim pobycie na miejscu zbrodni w Katyniu),' *Goniec Codzienny* 1943: 577 (Jun. 3).

don't worry about us (...)."[97] He collected a set of souvenirs from Katyn and took it home, just as other delegates had done. In it there were scraps of papers, a small wooden cigarette case containing three cigarettes, Polish army buttons, a Soviet paper dated December 1939, a two-złoty bill, a bullet extricated from a skull, a pair of epaulettes belonging to a major in the Polish Army, and another pair from a captain's uniform.[98]

Another person who compiled a report on his visit to Katyn was Dr. Edward Grodzki, who delivered his statement to Janusz Machnicki, deputy chairman of the RGO and chairman of its Warsaw branch.[99] When interrogated in the Ministry of Public Security nearly a decade later, he said that he had refused to give an interview for the reptile press (probably meaning *Nowy Kurier Warszawski*) on his sojourn at Katyn.[100]

I should also draw attention to the part played in Katyn by Jan Mikołajczyk, who was the AK Headquarters delegate and served as its "secret trustee." Years later Jan Lerski recalled that "our emissary" had said he had talked to the local inhabitants, who had informed him that well before the massacre there had been regular mass executions on the site of Russian "fascists" and "spies."[101]

On the basis of all that had occurred in connection with the Polish visits to Katyn and the way the German propaganda machine had handled the matter, the authorities of the Polish Underground State tried to determine the German aims in their approach to the Katyn question. They drew up the following list of putative German aims: to exploit the Poles' fear of communism in order to persuade them that Germany was defending the West, including Poland; to curtail and block communist undertakings on the Polish territories; to put the Polish government-in-exile in a difficult position and throw the anti-Hitler coalition off-balance; to discredit the London-based government-in-exile in the eyes of Polish society at home, thereby helping potential collaborators take over Polish public opinion; to create favorable conditions for the recruitment

---

[97] *Ibid.*

[98] *Ibid.*

[99] AIPN, Warsaw, sign. no. 00231/124, vol. 2, Dr Grodzki Edward, Oświadczenie w sprawie Katynia z dnia 18 III 1952 r. [Statement by Dr. Edward Grodzki concerning Katyn, Mar. 18, 1952], sheet 2.

[100] *Ibid.*, sheet 3.

[101] J. Lerski, *Emisariusz „Jur"* (London: Polska Fundacja Kulturalna, 1988), 111.

of labor from the GG for work in the Reich; and to justify the Holocaust then being perpetrated on the Jewish population by presenting the Katyn atrocity as the work of Soviet Jews.[102]

Alongside the individual reports by Polish observers on their visit to Katyn, there were also a few articles in the reptile press. I have published a full list of these articles in another book.[103] A regular feature characteristic of most of these articles and interviews was their anonymity. The exceptions to the general rule were the interviews given by Jan Emil Skiwski, Franciszek Prochownik, Włodzimierz Ambroż, and Władysław Kawecki, and the articles by Józef Mackiewicz and Bruno Widera. There is also the question of Zygmunt Ipohorski-Lenkiewicz, whose activities still call for clarification. Ipohorski-Lenkiewicz was an inmate of Auschwitz-Birkenau, but after just a month he was released and started to co-operate with the Germans. It cannot be ruled out that he was the person who collected data on the Katyn site and compiled the articles which subsequently appeared anonymously in the reptile press. It has been established that he spent an unknown period of time in Katyn, as of April 17, 1943. He was also associated with the theaters operating in Warsaw under German control. Krzysztof Woźniakowski has named Zygmunt Ipohorski-Lenkiewicz as one of a small group of actors who appeared in humorous skits, stand-up comic acts, adaptations of comedies and vaudeville shows performed in the legal theaters.[104] He was later sentenced to death by the Home Army's Special Military Court for collaboration with the Germans,[105] and the sentence was carried out on May 25, 1944.[106]

The pictorial records made on the site of the atrocity were done chiefly by Kazimierz Didur, who was Hans Frank's personal photographer and – as has only recently transpired– a Home Army agent who passed on the data in his possession to the authorities of the Polish Underground State. His secret

---

[102] Quoted after Głowiński, 'Sprawa katyńska w oficjalnej polskojęzycznej prasie,' 136–137.

[103] Wolsza, „*Katyń to już na zawsze katy i katowani*", 28–30.

[104] K. Woźniakowski, *W kręgu jawnego piśmiennictwa literackiego Generalnego Gubernatorstwa (1939–1945)*, (Kraków: Wydawnictwo Naukowe WSP, 1997), 73.

[105] AIPN Warsaw, sign. no. 4059/IV, Teczka Zygmunta Lenkiewicza-Ipohorskiego [Dossier on Zygmunt Lenkiewicz-Ipohorski], sheet 1.

[106] L. Gondek, *Polska karząca 1939–1945. Polski podziemny wymiar sprawiedliwości w okresie okupacji niemieckiej* (Warszawa: Instytut Wydawniczy Pax, 1988), 118.

operations did not stop at the Katyn issue. A second person who had a camera on the site was Dr. Edward Grodzki.[107] Other members of the delegation referred to his photographic work, but without giving away his name.

A characteristic feature of the reptile press was its repetitiveness and the anonymity of its authors – a general rule reptile editors used with very few exceptions. Articles published in *Nowy Kurier Warszawski* or *Goniec Krakowski* would subsequently reappear in an identical version, sometimes with a different headline, in *Nowy Głos Lubelski*, *Dziennik Radomski*, *Kurier Kielecki*, *Kurier Częstochowski*, *Gazeta Lwowska* and *Goniec Codzienny*.

I have already said that Ferdynand Goetel refused to work with the reptile press. Such an assertion was put forward by Goetel himself and a few other people who were acquainted with his wartime biography. The exception was the statement made by Stella Olgierd, the secretary of the PEN Club, when she was questioned by Prosecutor Roman Martini in 1945. Olgierd claimed that on their return from Katyn Goetel and Skiwski gave an interview to *Nowy Kurier Warszawski*. She said she had a copy of the paper with the interview in her hands, but didn't read it right through, because – she said – "there were too many suspicious remarks in that article on murders, and I couldn't stand it."[108] Olgierd also claimed that the interview gave a figure of 12 thousand for the number of victims at Katyn. What Olgierd said in her statement to the prosecutor, especially what she said about Goetel, was not true, but it reflected the critical attitude some PEN Club members had of Goetel, who had published a controversial book entitled *Pod znakiem faszyzmu* (Under the Sign of Fascism) just before the outbreak of the War. No joint interview of Goetel and Skiwski ever appeared in the reptile papers, although Skiwski had several interviews on his own with *Nowy Kurier Warszawski* and *Goniec Codzienny*, and he did so of his own free will.[109] According to Maciej Urbanowski, Skiwski had two reasons for going to Katyn. First, he thought it would make it easier

---

[107] Information from Dr. Mirosław Grodzki.

[108] Jankowski and Kotarba, *Literaci a sprawa katyńska 1945*, 214.

[109] J.E. Skiwski, *Na przełaj oraz inne szkice o literaturze i kulturze*, M. Urbanowski (ed.), (Kraków: Wydawnictwo Literackie, 1999), 11. Tomasz Głowiński writes that Skiwski's interviews were dispassionate, and essentially examined the Soviet threat to the region, albeit the title of one of them, 'Czerwony bies atakuje kulturę' (The Red Devil Is Attacking Culture), was most certainly uncouth. Głowiński, 'Sprawa katyńska w oficjalnej polskojęzycznej prasie,' 140.

for him to establish and build up relations with the Germans, which he saw as a chance for the future of Poland with the prospect of a Soviet threat looming ahead. And secondly, he wanted to disclose the Soviet atrocities and get news of them out to the West, which trusted the Soviets absolutely. For some time already the Polish underground authorities had been keeping an eye on Skiwski owing to his views, and in 1941 their underground bulletin *Biuletyn Informacyjny* published a warning addressed to him, for trying to publish his novel *Czad* (Carbon Monoxide) with a German publisher.[110] Moreover, in the spring of 1943, at the instigation of the Germans Skiwski did a tour of several oflags, giving lectures and talks on the Katyn atrocity.

As regards the authenticity of other interviews and articles, those by Władysław Kawecki were published on his own initiative. Reptile journalism provided his source of income. Ferdynand Goetel, Józef Mackiewicz, and Dr. Marian Wodziński all later issued a very bad opinion of him. Wodziński wrote in his report, "we were very distrustful of him, because of his co-operation with the Germans. (...) Yet Mr. Kawecki kept telling us he had a hostile attitude to the Germans. In point of fact he was not very interested in our work at Katyn, though he would go into the forest and talk to Lieut. Slowenczyk. Kawecki was collecting data for his paper, diligently noting down all that we said in connection with the Katyn operation, which irritated us a lot (...)."[111] Later on in the War Kawecki continued to collaborate with the Germans, working for Wanda, a German radio station.[112] When the War was over he tried to rehabilitate himself with the military authorities of the Polish Second Corps, but his attempt failed. He was arrested and sent to prison by the Twelfth Military Court of the Second Corps. Subsequently he was transferred to the civilian camp at Barletta, and later to the camp at Afragola. He was released in 1947 and left for Germany. In the 1950s he collaborated with the Ministry of Public Security, the Ministry of Internal Affairs, and the Internal Military

---

[110] On September 5, 1941 Agent "A. Pras" reported that Skiwski had submitted his latest novel for publication in a German publishing company called Wydawnictwo Polskie, and had also accepted an appointment as the company's literary manager (Home Army counterintelligence card file).

[111] 'Zbrodnia katyńska w świetle dokumentów,' 175.

[112] S. Lewandowska, *Prasa polskiej emigracji wojennej 1939–1945* (Warszawa: Instytut Historii Polskiej Akademii Nauk, 1993), 232–233; R. Habielski, 'Radiostacja „Wanda". Relacja Władysława Kaweckiego,' *Dzieje Najnowsze* 1989: 1.

Service (military police force) of Communist Poland, using the pseudonym Hill.[113] There is no doubt, either, as to the authorship of the texts by Bruno Widera and Józef Mackiewicz, or the opinions of Professor Leon Kozłowski, who came to Katyn directly from Berlin. A former prime minister of Poland, Kozłowski published his statement indicating that the Soviets were culpable for the Katyn massacre in a brochure widely circulated in the GG.[114] He reiterated his opinion in *Gazeta Lwowska*.[115] His decision to speak out in an article in a Lwów newspaper was no coincidence, since he was a distinguished professor of archeology of that city's university. Professor Kozłowski's Katyn visit met with disapproval from members of the Polish Red Cross delegation. Years later Gracjan Jaworski made the following remark, "By that time he was an out-and-out alcoholic. Later he broadcast on German radio, but did not make it plain that the Bolsheviks had done it."[116]

Dr. Marian Wodziński[117] and Franciszek Prochownik[118] denied the authenticity of the interviews in the reptile press attributed to them. In Dr. Wodziński's case the man responsible for the alleged interview was Władysław Kawecki, who listened in on Wodziński's conversations with other members of the Polish Red Cross and RGO delegation and later concocted a fake interview for *Goniec Krakowski*. Wodziński and Kawecki met each other again later on during the War. When Wodziński voiced his well-founded grievance, the reptilian editor "tried to exonerate himself by saying that the Germans forced him to do it, and that it was under pressure from them that he wrote the fake interview on the

---

[113] AIPN Biuro Udostępniania [Data Releasing Office, hereafter BU], sign. no. 01168/243, Kawecki Władysław Ryszard; *Ibid.*, sign. no. 00518/22, Teczka personalna „Hill" – agent [Personal file of Agent "Hill"].

[114] *Masowe morderstwo w lesie katyńskim. Sprawozdanie na podstawie urzędowych danych i dokumentów*, [no place or date of publication] 1943, unpaginated.

[115] 'B. premier prof. dr. Kozłowski w Katyniu,' *Gazeta Lwowska* 1943: 126 (May 30/31).

[116] Jaworowski, 'Nieznana relacja o grobach katyńskich,' 6. Prof. Kozłowski's statement offers no confirmation for Gracjan Jaworowski's remark. On at least two occasions Kozłowski declared that the Soviets were responsible for the Katyn atrocity. L. Kozłowski, *Moje przeżycia w więzieniu sowieckim i na wolności w czasie wojny w Rosji sowieckiej*, B. Gogol and J. Tebinka, (eds.), (Warszawa: LTW, 2001), 11.

[117] 'Potworne szczegóły masowej egzekucji na Koziej Górze. Sensacyjne wyniki badań zwłok w lasku katyńskim,' *Nowy Kurier Warszawski* 1943: 128 (May 31), 1.

[118] 'Wrażenia krakowskiego robotnika w lesie katyńskim. Specjalny wywiad „Telpressu" z członkiem polskiej delegacji Franciszkiem Prochownikiem,' *Goniec Krakowski* 1943: 90 (Apr. 17), 1.

basis of notes he had taken during his sojourn at Katyn (...)."[119] Dr. Wodziński was also remembered for his contribution to the statement published by the Polish Red Cross Commission which had conducted the on-site investigation. The statement appeared in a brochure entitled *Katyń* and printed in the GG. Its author used the nom-de-plume "Andrzej Ciesielski."[120]

Franciszek Prochownik was a blue-collar worker from the Zieleniewski engineering works in Kraków. Two years after his Katyn visit he was accused of collaboration, on the grounds of an interview published in *Goniec Krakowski* on April 17, 1943, and later reprinted in other reptile papers. Prochownik said he had nothing to do with the interview and that it had been forged by a reptile journalist. He claimed that the journalist had spoken to him only about his work in the factory and flying in an airplane. Yet unexpectedly, on the next day the paper published his impressions of the Katyn visit. On the basis of what we already know about the background to Dr. Wodziński's purported interview, in reality forged by Kawecki, we can safely say that Prochownik's argument is highly plausible. Moreover, Prochownik said that he had refused to take part in a documentary film on Katyn that the Germans were making, which had its Kraków premiere on April 22, 1943. He had been asked to deliver an intro-ductory address to the documentary.[121] Thereafter, fearing further German propositions, he pretended to have gone down with a disease and went into hiding. Finally he left Kraków for a time.[122] Stanisław Jankowski and Ryszard Kotarba found that he risked a death sentence from the PPR for visiting Katyn, or being killed by the Gestapo should he have changed his mind about who did the massacre.[123]

Yet another interview given by a member of the workers' delegation from the GG appeared in the reptile press. This group was in Katyn around May 20,

---

[119] 'Zbrodnia katyńska w świetle dokumentów,' 175.

[120] A. Ciesielski, *Katyń* (Warszawa: Gebethner i Wolff [Regierung d. G.G. Hauptabt. Propa-ganda, Abt. Aktivpropaganda], 1943), 23. The Polish prewar publishers Gebethner i Wolff had been taken over by the German propaganda office in the GG, and the brochure's real place of publication was Kraków.

[121] AIPN Warsaw, sign. no.00231/124, vol. 2, Oświadczenie Franciszka Prochownika z 22 III 1952 r. [Statement by Franciszek Prochownik, Mar. 22, 1952], sheet 2.

[122] Jankowski and Kotarba, *Literaci a sprawa katyńska 1945*, 96.

[123] *Ibid.*

1943.[124] Włodzimierz Ambroż, who was named in the interview, never denied having made this statement. It seems that he never experienced any reprisals after the War.

I cannot pass over another man of letters in silence. I mean Marian Maak from Kraków. I have not managed to trace any Katyn publication by him in the reptiles, nevertheless Maak was a writer who co-operated with the Germans during the War and published two novels, *Powrót Krzysztofa Szaroty* (The Return of Krzysztof Szarota, 1941) and *Trzy kwadranse na mężczyznę* (Three-Quarters of an Hour for a Man, 1944). He worked for *Goniec Krakowski* and *Ilustrowany Kurier Polski*, and edited articles from rural areas for the Telpress news agency. In Krzysztof Woźniakowski's opinion the image of the War and occupation conjured up in Maak's books was truly unique. He conjured up "an absolutely fictional, well-nigh fairy-tale world." There was no reign of terror in the GG, no street round-ups, no concentration camps, there were no Germans in it at all."[125]

Another who commented on his 1943 visit to Katyn was Maj. Artur Glezer (that's how his name was spelled in *Nowy Kurier Warszawski*). Maj. Glezer had been a prisoner-of-war held in Kozelsk, but the Soviets released him at the request of the German authorities.[126] No hard evidence is currently available

---

[124] 'Sosnowe krzyże na bratnich mogiłach w Katyniu. Wywiad z uczestnikiem delegacji polskiego świata pracy,' *Nowy Kurier Warszawski* 1943: 127 (May 29–30), 2.

[125] Woźniakowski, *W kręgu jawnego piśmiennictwa*, 327.

[126] In 1943 Maj. Artur Glezer told the readers of *Nowy Kurier Warszawski* that he owed his release to his family, who had petitioned the German authorities to intervene on his behalf with the Soviets for his discharge from Kozelsk. 'Gehenna oficerów,' 1. Arthur Glaeser was indeed released thanks to the efforts of his family, albeit the decisive factor was the support lent by the German authorities. Glezer aka Glaeser had been born in 1892 at Józefów near Wągrowiec. During the First World War he had served in the Prussian army (Lublin was one of the places where he was stationed). After the Great War he lived in Warsaw and served in the Polish army as a sanitation officer. When combat operations started in 1939 he was in eastern Poland, in the military hospital at Białowieża, where on September 19 he was taken prisoner by the Soviets. He was held in Kozelsk from October 1939 to May 1940. Later he was sent to Pavlishchev Bor and Griazovets camps. In December 1940 he was released and handed over to the Germans. He then lived in Poznań, and following the outbreak of the German–Soviet war joined the German army and stayed at Sosnowiec. In 1943 he was presumably a member of the Katowice delegation to Katyn. AIPN Warsaw, sign. no. 0546/126, Glaeser Arthur (Abschrift) [copy], sheets 4–7; Tucholski, *Mord w Katyniu*, 528.

to confirm beyond all doubt that he visited Katyn in 1943, but it is certain that he gave the Germans an account of his spell in Soviet captivity.[127]

I have deliberately gone into such detail on the reports, accounts, and other items published in the press on the Katyn atrocity. Right from the spring of 1945 the persons who had been involved during the War in attempts to clarify the Katyn issue, worked for the Polish Red Cross or RGO, and knew anything about the background to the atrocity caught the interest of the Soviet secret service (viz. the NKVD) and the Ministry of Public Security and judiciary of People's Poland. The persons involved in the Katyn issue were identified on the grounds of the records I have described, although the Communists did not manage to get satisfactory answers to all the problems. Those who were crossed off the list of suspects were those who did not survive the War.

A few of the people who saw Katyn Forest in 1943 or were involved in Warsaw and Kraków in disseminating information on the Soviet crime did not survive the War. In 1944 the Germans shot Capt. Ludwik Rojkiewicz on a Warsaw street. After the 1939 defense campaign he took up employment with the Polish Red Cross. Hugo Kassur and Count Władysław Zamoyski, who was a top-rank Red Cross activist, were killed during the Warsaw Uprising. Ferdynand Płonka died of natural causes in the fall of 1944.[128] Dr. Władysław Gorczycki, a member of the Board of the Polish Red Cross, died in 1945. He had coordinated the work done in 1943–1945 on the Katyn question.[129] Another who did not live to see the end of the War was Zdzisław Koss, chief editor of *Dziennik Radomski*. In 1943 the Germans sent him to Auschwitz-Birkenau, from where he never returned.[130]

Władysław Herz, a parliamentary deputy before the War for the NPR (National Workers' Party) was yet another victim of the War. At the beginning of wartime occupation he was sent to Dachau concentration camp. In 1943 he returned home to Poznań, and on April 23 joined Leon Nowicki, Dr. Zygmunt

---

[127] 'Zbrodnia katyńska w świetle dokumentów,' 98. See also Glezer's article in *Nowy Kurier Warszawski*.

[128] 'Zbrodnia katyńska w świetle dokumentów,' 185.

[129] Władysław Gorczycki had also liaised between the management of the Polish Red Cross and the authorities of the Polish Underground State. In his remarks on Dr. Gorczycki, Kazimierz Skarżyński said that he had truly been "the soul of the organization" [viz. of the Polish Red Cross]. Skarżyński, *Katyń i Polski Czerwony Krzyż*, 128.

[130] Jankowski and Kotarba, *Literaci a sprawa katyńska 1945*, 225.

Giżycki, Bolesław Smektała, and three workers from Łódź in the delegation the Germans sent to Katyn.[131] According to the statements Smektała made a few years later before Ministry of Public Security officers, "The Germans took us to Katyn to see some graves. They showed us some dug up graves. There I saw the bodies of soldiers in Polish uniforms, later we were shown some documents (...). Then we had to say how many there were of those who had been murdered (...). According to the Germans there were about 7,000 bodies in those graves. (...) The Germans did not ask us to say who had murdered those Polish soldiers (...)."[132]

There was extensive press coverage of this visit in the German press in Wartheland and in the Reich itself. Photos of Władysław Herz standing over a Katyn grave appeared in the popular paper *Das Reich* and in *Ostdeutscher Beobachter*.[133] On their return to Poznań Dr. Zygmunt Giżycki and Władysław Herz attended a couple of meetings with the employees of local companies. They also visited Gniezno. They spoke in Polish – a language hitherto prohibited in this region – on what they saw in Katyn. According to Herz's family, he was very careful about what he said at these big meetings: "I was there and I saw it, but I don't know who did it, because I wasn't there at the time it was done."[134] His comments for the German-language press were just as vague. Or at least that's how one of the readers remembered them: "I saw soldiers in Polish uniforms there, you could see they had been shot."[135] Leon Nowicki, another member of this delegation, neither co-operated nor attended talks and meetings with local inhabitants. The Germans sent out search parties to bring him in.

At the end of one of these meetings Herz was arrested by the Gestapo for circulating Polish underground publications. Initially he was held in Fort

---

[131] AIPN Warsaw, sign. no. 00231/124, vol. 1, Oświadczenie Bolesława Smektały z 10 IV 1952 r. [Statement by Bolesław Smektała, Apr. 10, 1952], sheet 1. Hieronim Majewski was one of the delegates from Sieradz.

[132] *Ibid.*, sheet 2

[133] *Ibid.*, Kasper Kuliński. Ważna informacja w sprawie Katynia z 8 III 1952 r. [Kasper Kuliński. Important information re. Katyn, Mar. 8, 1952], sheet 2.

[134] P. Bojarski, 'Gdy prawda jest zdradą,' *Gazeta Wyborcza*, Nov. 14, 2007.

[135] AIPN Warsaw, sign. no. 00231/124, vol. 1, Kasper Kuliński. Ważna informacja w sprawie Katynia z 8 III 1952 r. [Kasper Kuliński. Important information re. Katyn, Mar. 8, 1952], sheet 2.

VII in the Jeżyce district of Poznań (this was the so-called Stronghold of the Unyielding).[136] Dr. Tadeusz Piechocki remembered Herz from this time, and said that he was reduced to the mere shadow of a man, though not much earlier he had weighed about 130 kg (290 lb.). "At the time when I arrived in the Fort," Dr. Piechocki recalled, "Citizen Herz had lost so much weight that he could wrap the skin of his belly over his head."[137] Władysław Herz talked to other prisoners in the Fort about Katyn, but he was not convinced the Soviets had done it. He did not believe the German arguments, and that is why he thought he was in prison. Later, when he was already in the advanced stages of tuberculosis, he was transferred from Fort VII to Gross-Rosen concentration camp, where he died on July 17, 1944, in the presence of Stanisław Pawłowski.[138]

We also have information, albeit modest information, on Dr. Zygmunt Giżycki, a dentist working for the Poznań streetcar company. It is certain that on his return he completed the task the Germans had set him before he left for Katyn. During special meetings at work he spoke extensively on his visit to Katyn, telling his listeners who had done the crime. Home Army Headquarters sent a report on this to the Polish authorities in exile in London: "Excursions from the whole of Poland are being sent out to Katyn. A public address was given in the hall of the Poznań municipal streetcar depot. It was delivered in Polish, in a place where three years ago a notice was put up saying that not a word of Polish would ever be spoken there again." [139] One of the witnesses of this event was the mother of Mieczysław Rakowski, who would later be First Secretary of the PZPR [Polish United Workers' Party, viz. the Communists] and Prime Minister of the People's Republic of Poland, which means that Mieczysław Rakowski must have learned the truth about Katyn in 1943, when he was 20. Years later he wrote the following about his Mom and the Katyn atrocity: "Thanks to her brother-in-law, Maria Rakowska got a job in the kitchen of the streetcar depot. This led to what

---

[136] *Ibid.*, Oświadczenie więźnia Piechockiego Tadeusza odnośnie sprawy zbrodni katyńskiej z 5 III 1952 r. [Statement by prisoner Tadeusz Piechocki re. the Katyn atrocity, Mar. 5, 1952], sheet 1.

[137] *Ibid.*, sheet 2.

[138] *Ibid.*, Oświadczenie Stanisława Pawłowskiego. [Statement by Stanisław Pawłowski]. Bojarski ('Gdy prawda jest zdradą,') gives a different date, July 20, 1944, for Herz's death.

[139] *Armia Krajowa w dokumentach 1939–1945. Studium Polski Podziemnej*, vol. 3: *Kwiecień 1943 – lipiec 1944*, (London: Gryf, 1976), 22.

seems to be a fairly important consequence. It wasn't the fact that sometimes she brought some extra bread or even a piece of meat home, thanks to which she and her son did not go hungry. The point was that when the Germans discovered the Katyn graves and set up an international medical commission to examine them, a Polish doctor employed in the Poznań streetcar company was appointed to the commission. On his return he started telling people what he had seen, and my Mom was one of those who heard his story. We had no doubts at all that it was the work of the Russkies."[140] After the War another Poznań streetcar employee voiced his opinion on Dr. Giżycki and his activities on his return from Katyn: "Dr. Giżycki gave an account of his Katyn experience. Strangely enough, whereas people caught speaking Polish were fined or even flogged, for the first time we heard Polish used [officially] when Dr. Giżycki gave his talk on Katyn. Of course none of us present there believed his story, which was evidently forced upon him."[141] In this person's opinion, Dr. Giżycki fled Poland in 1945, fearing reprisals and imprisonment by the Soviets for his Katyn visit. The Germans who had organized his visit to Katyn informed him of the opportunity to leave for Germany, where he stayed for a short spell, and later went to Australia. Bolesław Smektała, the third of the Poznań delegates, took the risk of staying at home. He was arrested by the Communists and imprisoned in one of the NKVD detention camps in Poznań.

WHAT HAPPENED AFTER 1945 TO THE POLES WHO SAW THE SITE OF THE KATYN ATROCITY AND THEIR POSTWAR ACTIVITIES

The operations undertaken by the Soviet and Polish Communist special services against the persons who saw the site of the Katyn massacre in 1943 may be divided into four stages. In the first few months of 1945 the NKVD conducted an in-depth investigation. In the next stage, which started in June 1945, Henryk Świątkowski, Minister of Justice of the Polish People's Republic, set up

---

[140] Quoted after J. Eisler, *Siedmiu wspaniałych. Poczet pierwszych sekretarzy KC PZPR*, (Warszawa: Wydawnictwo Czerwone i Czarne 2014), 465.

[141] AIPN Warsaw, sign. no. 00231/124, vol. 1, List J. Strzelczyka z 4 III 1952 r. [Letter from J. Strzelczyk, Mar. 4, 1952], sheet 13.

a team headed by prosecutor Dr. Roman Martini to prepare a Katyn show trial to be held in Warsaw with extensive media coverage. The team accomplished its task, collecting a vast amount of documentation to serve as evidence. But the trial was not held, following an outright Soviet prohibition. Thereafter the Katyn question was hushed up. Presumably the Soviets were afraid of being discredited. The third stage was connected with the second, and with the Nuremberg Trial. The Kremlin's tactics look clear enough. They gave up pressing for a trial in Poland, which would have been difficult and likely to end in disaster, and opted for an easier procedure before the Nuremberg Tribunal, where they could select their witnesses and arguments as they liked. The problem surfaced for the fourth time in the early 1950s when the American committee led by Ray Madden started its work.

The list of implicated persons, Poles and people outside Poland, was vast. Virtually all of those who did not manage to leave Poland when combat operations came to an end or shortly thereafter came under the scrutiny of the Polish Communist and Soviet special services. As soon as the Red Army entered Polish soil the Soviets located and detained Dr. Jan Zygmunt Robel, an expert in clinical chemistry. Dr. Robel had a lot to say on the matter, although he had not been to Katyn himself. As of 1943 he had headed a team of scientists in the Chemistry Department of the National Institute of Forensic Medicine and Criminalistics in Kraków, conducting research on the materials brought from Katyn by the Polish Red Cross associates. According to Kazimierz Skarżyński's report the team was examining these samples, and – unofficially, illicitly – investigating the circumstances of the atrocity. "Their official work was to draw up a full list of those who had died in Katyn" and conduct research on the samples, while their unofficial work was to study the victims' notes and diaries. On the basis of this research Dr. Robel established that the records stopped in April of 1940.[142] Hence for the Soviets Dr. Robel was an extremely important witness. And for the purposes of the prospective Katyn trial he would be the key witness, if under duress he could be brought to repudiate the results his research team had established but not published, thereby undermining one of the points in the German evidence compiled by the International Medical Commission in 1943.

---

[142] Maresch, *Katyń 1940*, 272.

The NKVD imprisoned Dr. Robel in a private residential house on aleja Krasińskiego in Kraków. He was interrogated for seven weeks.[143] The Soviets scrutinized his knowledge of the Katyn atrocity and his contacts with the Home Army very thoroughly. Both of these matters turned out to be related when some Home Army documents including Dr. Robel's receipt for the delivery of 22 diaries from Katyn happened to fall into the hands of the NKVD.[144] In mid-1945 the NKVD called off its Katyn interrogations, and Dr. Robel was set free. But almost at once he was obliged to attend Prosecutor Martini's inquiry, which was held in the headquarters of the Kraków Special Criminal Court on June 21, 1945. The only matter Dr. Martini was interested in was Katyn. Dr. Robel, now head of the Institute of Forensic Research, said that in 1943 the Germans offered him the opportunity of traveling to Katyn with the Polish Red Cross delegation. He told Martini he had turned down the offer because the conditions on the site were not good enough for scientific research of any kind whatsoever. But he did agree to collect records from Katyn in the Institute and conduct research on them. His idea received the approval of the management of the Polish Red Cross and Dr. Werner Beck, the Institute's German director.[145] His task was to decipher the documents found on the corpses and identify the names of their owners. In a nutshell, his job was to supplement the Katyn findings of the Polish Red Cross Technical Commission. Dr. Robel gave the prosecutor a detailed account of his working technique.[146] He also told him that the Germans had never interfered with the identification work, but they did observe it closely and asked how it was going. Finally he told Martini the story of how the Germans hid the records to prevent them from falling into the hands of the Home Army, which wanted to intercept the "Katyn packets."

---

[143] Bratko, *Dlaczego zginąłeś prokuratorze?*, 222.

[144] K. Skarżyński, *Katyń. Raport Polskiego Czerwonego Krzyża*, (Warszawa: Oficyna Wydawnicza Pokolenie, 1989), 81 [samizdat publication].

[145] AIPN Kraków, sign. no. 303/1, Protokół przesłuchania świadka Robla Jana Zygmunta z 21 VI 1945 r. [Minutes of the hearing of witness Jan Zygmunt Robel. Jun. 21, 1945], sheet 24.

[146] "The envelopes of items discovered on the bodies and numbered accordingly on the whole contained a compacted lump of materials stuck together with adipocere and soiled with earth. We had to disassemble these lumps extremely carefully in an appropriate bath, remove the adipocere, and clean the objects; this treatment, which took up several hours, was only the start of the decipherment and recording of the texts themselves, virtually all of which had been severely damaged by damp and the processes of decomposition," (*Ibid.*).

At first the Katyn materials were transferred from the Institute's Chemistry Department on ulica Kopernika to the Institute of Forensic Medicine on ulica Grzegórzecka. On August 4, 1944, a convoy carrying the records set off for Beuthen (now Bytom, Poland).[147] The materials collected by the Board of the Polish Red Cross were destroyed during the Warsaw Uprising. According to Dr. Robel, copies of these materials, and those held by the Kraków branch of the Polish Red Cross, fell into the hands of the Soviets.[148]

The NKVD arrested Dr. Hieronim Bartoszewski, a Polish Red Cross delegate who had been to Katyn, and held him for two months in Wieliczka. He is believed to have been released only thanks to an attestation by his fellow medical practitioners that under German occupation he had never spoken out on the Katyn massacre, nor blamed the Soviets for it. That is what Dr. Bartoszewski said years later in a press interview.[149] Also, in mid-1945 the NKVD stopped its Katyn inquiry in Poland, which was another factor speeding up the release of some of the members of the Katyn commissions. Perhaps this is why later Dr. Bartoszewski was very cautious in his comments on the background to the Katyn murders. At one point he even went as far as to speak of "fraudulent German propaganda."[150] He informed the prosecutor that "all the graves were opened up. When we visited the graves there were Germans next to each one of us, so we could neither do anything at all without their knowledge nor engage in any kind of independent examination."[151] Bartoszewski also challenged the medical determination of the date of the atrocity.

---

[147] We now know for certain that the records were subsequently sent to Breslau (now Wrocław) and later, following an abortive attempt to transfer them to the Prague branch of the International Red Cross, dispatched to Dresden. Years later Dr. Werner Beck wrote that due to there being no possibility of hiding the Katyn materials or handing them over to the Americans before the Red Army entered Dresden, an authorized person burned 14 crates of Katyn materials. On occupying the city, the Soviets conducted several searches in Dr. Beck's family house to retrieve the Katyn materials. – B. Popielski and W. Nasiłowski, 'Cienie Katynia w dokumentach i historii medycyny sądowej,' *Archiwum Medycyny Sądowej i Kryminologii* 47 (1997), 189.

[148] *Ibid.*, 25.

[149] 'Byłem w Katyniu. Rozmowa z dr Hieronimem Bartoszewskim, lekarzem, członkiem Komisji Technicznej PCK w 1943 r.,' *Przegląd Tygodniowy* 1989: 18, 15.

[150] Bratko, *Dlaczego zginąłeś prokuratorze?* 250.

[151] *Ibid.*, 247. In a 1989 interview he said the exact opposite: "We could walk anywhere we liked in the area, and nobody stopped us or interfered. Without doubt all of us experienced a shock on seeing the enormity of this crime." ('Byłem w Katyniu,' 15).

In his opinion the condition of the bodies was no evidence that it had been committed in 1940. He said the same about the state of preservation of the uniforms and the new afforestation on the site. And he also said that German ammunition had been used for the executions.[152] He concluded his statement with the following remark: "We traveled to Katyn anticipating that the whole Katyn affair might be biased German propaganda, so once we were there we tried to spot points confirming it was fraudulent German propaganda. As soon as we arrived on the site it was clear to us that the Germans wanted to exploit the murders they had perpetrated for propaganda purposes and skillfully shift the blame onto someone else – and when we were there we (and I myself in particular) became even more convinced of this. Once we were back in Warsaw we tried to present the fraudulence of the Katyn propaganda as best as we could to trustworthy persons."[153] Following this declaration Dr. Bartoszewski left for Wrocław and in 1945 set up the city's first Polish Red Cross hospital. In 1947–1955 and 1956–1959 he was a Ministry of Public Security informer operating under the aliases "Doktor" and "Adam."

In the early 1950s during the Communist propaganda campaign against the Madden Committee, the Ministry of Public Security pressurized Dr. Bartoszewski into making yet another declaration on Katyn. During his interrogation he finally declared that as an eye-witness at Katyn in 1943, he had become convinced "of the reprehensible lies propagated by Hitler's fascists, who were trying to attribute their own atrocity – one of the many mass murders they had committed – to the Soviet Union."[154] In 1989 he changed his mind again about the circumstances of the Katyn atrocity. In Helena Wojtas' interview with him for *Przegląd Tygodniowy* he said that "All the evidence indicates that the officers were murdered in the spring of 1940. There is a scientific proof (...). In one of the skulls [Dr. Ferenc Orsós] observed a multiple layer of calcium salts which had already become integrated with the osteonecrosis on the surface of the brain, which had turned into a clayey lump. This phenomenon could not have occurred if the body had been interred for less than three years. I learned

---

[152] Bratko, *Dlaczego zginąłeś prokuratorze?* 247.

[153] *Ibid.*, 250.

[154] AIPN Warsaw, sign. no. 00231/124, Oświadczenie dr Bartoszewskiego Hieronima, [Statement by Dr. Hieronim Bartoszewski], sheet 5.

PREZES
SĄDU APELACYJNEGO
W KRAKOWIE

DNIA 5 sierpnia ...9 ..

Nr PREZ. 9853/39

Do

Pana Dra Tadeusza Pragłowskiego

Lekarza

w Krakowie

ul.Łazarza Boczna 7.

Na zasadzie § rozporządzenia Ministra Sprawiedliwości z dnia 7 grudnia 1928 r.Nr 104 poz.
945 Dz.U.R.P. ustanowiłem Pana biegłym sądowym
w zakresie m e d y c y n y s ą d o w e j
dla okręgu Sądu Okręgowego w Krakowie.

Załączniki prośby zwracam.

Prezes Sądu Apelacyjnego:

w z. *[signature]*

A. GŁOWACZ
Wiceprezes Sądu Apelacyjnego

Przysięgę odebrano.-
Kraków,dnia 28 sierpnia 1939.
Sędzia spraw.kier.Sądu Gr.
WKZ.

6. Letter issued by the prewar Polish court appointing Tadeusz Pragłowski to serve as a forensic expert, August 5, 1939

of this opinion after the War. But our on-site observations in the spring of 1943 had led us to the same conclusions."[155]

Dr. Tadeusz Pragłowski of the Kraków Institute of Forensic Medicine was in Katyn in the same period, April 14–15, 1943.[156] He had been recommended by the management of the Polish Red Cross to make the journey. This delegation's visit to Katyn was reported in the reptile press and filmed for the German newsreel. The film material was subsequently put into a German documentary. Dr. Pragłowski was in the film and named on its sound-track while he was carrying out a forensic examination of one of the victims. So the film made him widely known. As Kazimierz Skarzyński said, Pragłowski went to Katyn "under orders" to act as a criminologist, but with no specific instructions. On visiting the graves he said that he did not "see a need for his services there and soon left."[157] On his return to Kraków he spoke to Dr. Marian Wodziński about what he had seen. He told him that in view of the age of the pines that had been planted there, the graves must have been made more than two years before. He also confirmed that the bodies buried there were of Polish officers. "He told me that among the bodies exhumed during his stay he found and identified a captain who had been his fellow student at university, so there was no doubt at all that these were the bodies of Polish officers," Wodziński recalled.[158] Pragłowski also told other persons who worked in the Institute what he had seen. Maria Byrdy, who was an Institute employee at the time, recalled that "on his return after three days in Katyn he said that he had seen open graves there and bodies in

---

[155] 'Byłem w Katyniu,' 15.

[156] Tadeusz Pragłowski was born in Lwów on September 21, 1903. He graduated from Strzyżów high school and in 1922 enrolled at the Jagiellonian University Medical Faculty. In 1929 he was appointed assistant in the Department of Pathological Anatomy. He received the doctor's degree in 1937 and took up an appointment in the Department of Forensic Medicine. His academic career was associated with this Department, the head of which was Professor Jan Olbrycht. During the War for a short time following Professor Olbrycht's arrest Pragłowski was Head of the Department. After the War he left Kraków for Silesia and for many years worked in the Medical Academy of Silesia. He received several medals and distinctions, the Knights' Cross, the Officers' Cross of the Order of Polonia Restituta (1973), and the Medal to mark the Thirtieth Anniversary of the foundation of the People's Republic of Poland. He died on January 24, 1983.

[157] Quoted after Maresch, *Katyń 1940*, 122.

[158] *Ibid.*, 132.

Polish uniforms; some of them had been identified, and all the evidence indicated that the Soviets had committed the crime."[159] For a time it looked as if Dr. Pragłowski would travel again to Katyn as leader of the Polish Red Cross' Technical Commission. However, this plan was abandoned due to Dr. Pragłowski's family problems (his wife's illness).[160] Shortly before the end of combat operations Dr. Pragłowski moved to Mielec, and subsequently to Silesia, bypassing Kraków.[161] Most probably a search was conducted for a short time after the War, for him as well as for the other medical doctors in the Polish Red Cross delegation – Dr. Marian Wodziński, Dr. Adam Szebesta, Dr. Hieronim Bartoszewski, and Dr. Stanisław Plappert.[162] However, I have not come across a record of him being questioned by the prosecutor investigating the Katyn massacre. Later Pragłowski settled in Szarlociniec, one of the districts of Chorzów. In May of 1945 he was appointed head of the forensic pathology department for the Katowice region, and in June of the same year he was appointed to the post of forensic expert in the regional court.[163] He was one of the few specialists in the field in the entire region. One of his professional duties was to examine the mass graves of Red Army soldiers at Łambinowice (German name Lamsdorf), where he worked with Dr. Bolesław Popielski. He also conducted examinations on other wartime burial sites, such as those at Jaśkowice Śląskie and Panewniki. In 1952–1974 he was head of the Forensic Medicine Department at the Medical Academy of Silesia. Dr. Pragłowski's visit to Katyn does not seem to have brought him any major problems, but there is one point in his biography which might have been a consequence of his participation in a Katyn delegation. In 1968 the Scientific Council of the Medical Academy of Silesia applied to the Central Commission for Academic Degrees for the award of a professorship to

---

[159] M. Byrdy, 'Prof. dr hab. Tadeusz Pragłowski w moich wspomnieniach' [Unpublished personal recollections of Prof. Pragłowski], 16. I would like to express my thanks to Professor Pragłowski's daughter, Ms. Zofia Pragłowska-Gorczyńska, for making these and other materials available to me.

[160] *Ibid.*

[161] *Ibid.*, 17.

[162] Jankowski and Kotarba, *Literaci a sprawa katyńska 1945,* 99.

[163] I received photocopies of both of these letters of appointment from Ms. Zofia Pragłowska-Gorczyńska.

7. Tadeusz Pragłowski

Dr. Tadeusz Pragłowski, but for reasons unknown the application never reached the decision makers.[164]

Dr. Stanisław Plappert (born 1888) was also a Katyn delegate. Dr. Plappert was a professional officer (a second lieutenant) in the Polish Army, and during the War he served as plenipotentiary of the Board of the Polish Red Cross for the Kraków region. Dr. Adam Szebesta was a colleague working in close co-operation with him. Just before their departure for Katyn Plappert and Szebesta decided they would "be as cautious as possible and refrain from making any kind of statements or declarations" while on the site.[165] They definitely kept to the tactics they had planned. Plappert said that all the time the Germans tried to get them to give an interview or make comments, and "kept filming, to the point of annoyance."[166] But they did not manage to persuade the two doctors to engage in any sort of co-operation. On his return Dr. Plappert submitted a report to the management of the

---

[164] Władysław Nasiłowski, *Życiorys Pragłowski Tadeusz (1903–1983)* [unpublished biography of Tadeusz Pragłowski]. Professor Bolesław Popielski made the following note on this question: "The title of professor was never conferred on Tadeusz Pragłowski, even though he fully deserved it for having organized the Katowice Department of Forensic Medicine, for his educational work in the training of medical academic staff, his contribution to numerous fields of scholarship, and his work as a highly qualified court forensic expert, which he carried out conscientiously and with the utmost sense of professional duty. Time and again the Medical Academy of Silesia issued recommendations full of praise for his achievements and recurrently submitted applications for his professorship, but every time the endeavor failed to bring about the required effect. Today we can say that the cause of all this was his one-day visit to Katyn with the Polish Red Cross delegation." – 'Wspomnienia o pracach sądowo-lekarskich w Katyniu i Łambinowicach,' [unpublished recollections of forensic medicine work at Katyn and Lamsdorf], 18). Materials from Ms. Zofia Pragłowska-Gorczyńska.

[165] AIPN Kraków, sign. no. 303/1, Protokół przesłuchania świadka z 14 VI 1945 r. [Minutes of witness' hearing, Jun. 14, 1945], sheets 1–2.

[166] *Ibid.*, sheet 2.

8. Letter issued by the postwar Polish court appointing Tadeusz Pragłowski to serve as a forensic expert, June 2, 1945

Polish Red Cross and spoke on the matter with Archbishop Sapieha. On June 14, 1945 Prosecutor Martini questioned him and took his statement on his visit to Katyn. Dr. Plappert focused especially on the points Martini wanted to hear. He decided to speak on the intentions of the German organizers. "What struck me throughout my visit to Katyn was that the Germans were engaging too much in propaganda and there were too many stage managers around. In my opinion the matter was clear enough and needed neither propaganda nor special stage arrangements. It was obvious that the Germans had a special purpose with all this propaganda," Plappert declared.[167] He also wondered how it was possible for the bodies of the two generals to be exhumed right at the start, and suggested that the Germans must have had prior information on the matter. He concluded with the following observation: "Personally, my general impression was that the Germans must have had a hand in the entire business."[168] Dr. Plappert looked

---

[167] *Ibid.*

[168] *Ibid.*

promising from the point of view of future expediency, so his name was put on the list of about a dozen other delegates on whom the Communists could count during a trial or to advance a propaganda campaign on Katyn. In 1952 he was listed alongside Dr. Adam Szebesta, Dr. Edward Grodzki, Franciszek Prochownik, and Tadeusz Piechocki, as a prospective witness who would definitely testify that the Germans had arranged all that had happened in Katyn. In a nutshell, he was a safe bet, certain to endorse the Soviet version of the events.

Others who fell into the hands of the NKVD were Dr. Konrad Orzechowski, Stanisław Kłosowicz, and Bolesław Smektała. Orzechowski was deported to the Soviet Union following an in-depth investigation. I have written elsewhere on what happened to him in the Soviet gulags and later.

Stanisław Kłosowicz (born March 4, 1906 at Krasnoyarsk, Russia) was a well-known figure in prewar Poland. He was a competitor in the cycling events at the 1928 Amsterdam Olympics. So we may infer that his election to a Katyn commission was by no means a random choice but based on his popularity as a sportsman. This was precisely the remark made by Mikołaj Marczyk of Stalowa Wola, another delegate, when he and Kłosowicz were on their way from Radom to Warsaw for the flight to Smolensk.[169] After their return the reptile *Dziennik Radomski* published a photo showing Józef Mackiewicz and members of the blue-collar delegation, including Stanisław Kłosowicz.[170] This seems to be the only record in the press of his Katyn visit, of course apart from the article in *Nowy Kurier Warszawski*, which put a list of all the members of this delegation in its report.

Like all the other members of this delegation, Kłosowicz took home souvenirs collected from the Katyn graves, such as gorgets, scraps of uniforms, and buttons. He was to use these materials to prepare a talk and exhibition for his workmates. It is hard to tell whether he did this, though the Germans tried

---

[169] M. Rusek, 'Lot do Smoleńska, 1943,' *Gazeta Wyborcza,* Apr. 6, 2011, 11.

[170] *Ibid.* Neither is there a mention of this delegate from Radom in Sebastian Piątkowski's book, *Okupacja i propaganda. Dystrykt Radomski Generalnego Gubernatorstwa w publicystyce polskojęzycznej prasy niemieckiej (1939-1945),* (Lublin and Radom: Instytut Pamięci Narodowej. Komisja Ścigania Zbrodni przeciwko Narodowi Polskiemu, Oddział Lublin, 2013). On the other hand, on p. 292 Piątkowski pays a considerable amount of attention to an article headlined 'Katyń – Fakty, które stały się symbolem w umysłach sercach i na ustach Radomia' on the reactions of Radom's inhabitants to news of Katyn. In my opinion most of the items originally published in *Dziennik Radomski* were by Zdzisław Koss, while reprints came from Telpress.

to see to it that what they had planned earlier was carried out. So it cannot be ruled out that Kłosowicz had a part in the propaganda campaign of May and June 1943.

When the Red Army entered Polish soil Stanisław Kłosowicz was arrested by the NKVD in Radom on February 8, 1945, sent to the NKVD detention camp at Rembertów, and thereafter deported to the Soviet Union. He was in a gulag at Rezh in the Ural region until November 2, 1947.[171] When he returned home he was debilitated and in a bad state of health in outcome of the slave labor he had done as a lumberjack.[172] Not surprisingly, his name was put on the Communist blacklist, especially as regards chances of employment. It was only after some time and thanks to help from a friend that he got a job with a state transport enterprise. In 1955, as he was on his way home from a day of enforced community work harvesting potatoes, he was killed when a tractor trailer ran over him. The accident came to be associated with a series of issues which have not been cleared up.[173]

Bolesław Smektała was arrested by the Soviets in February 1945.[174] During the search conducted at his house all his documents were confiscated, not only those connected with his visit to Katyn but also things relating to his private life.[175] He was held in one of the NKVD camps in Poznań (perhaps the detention camp on ulica Słoneczna). All the indications are that he was deported to the Soviet Union and held there for several years.[176] On his return home he was constantly under surveillance by Ministry of Public Security agents. In April 1952 he made a statement on his Katyn visit. He declared that on his return from Katyn he had never participated in any propaganda campaigns,

---

[171] Rusek, 'Lot do Smoleńska, 1943,' *passim.*

[172] *Ibid.*

[173] *Ibid.*

[174] Bolesław Smektała was born in 1907 in Dortmund. His father was a miner. In 1919 he left for Poland and settled in Poznań. He worked for a railroad company and later for a law court. Finally he and his wife ran a food store. In 1939 he served in the Polish forces (Armia Poznań). In German-occupied Poznań his store was confiscated and he got a job in the Focke-Wulf aircraft works. He spoke fluent German and was popular with his workmates, and that is why he was chosen to be a member of the 1943 Katyn delegation.

[175] S. Kmiecik, 'Niewygodny świadek mordu na polskich oficerach,' *Głos Wielkopolski,* Apr. 17, 2010.

[176] AIPN Warsaw, sign. no. 00231/124, Oświadczenie Bolesława Smektały z 19 IV 1952 r. [Statement by Bolesław Smektała, Apr. 19, 1952], sheet 76.

as the matter had died down by May of 1943. He also said that the German arguments regarding the atrocity had aroused his suspicions. He claimed that the bodies were in a good condition, and in his opinion they could not have been in such a good state if they had been buried for such a long time.[177] This argument was frequently resorted to by witnesses making statements in 1952.

Canon Stanisław Jasiński, the personal emissary of Archbishop Adam Stefan Sapieha, the Metropolitan of Kraków, was another witness questioned in June 1945. Canon Jasiński insisted that he had traveled to Katyn to administer the last rites to victims and conduct a memorial service.[178] In his account of his stay in Katyn, he said that when he was there a German officer delivered a fairly long address attributing the blame to the Russians. Commenting on this in 1945, Canon Jasiński said, "During his speech I could not help feeling disgusted, since the speaker's sentimentality coupled with the fact that I knew of the enormity of the atrocities committed by the Germans on a mass scale conjured up an image of German hypocrisy and guile."[179] Next the archbishop's emissary gave an account of the Mass he had said near the graves. He also confirmed that the Germans had encouraged members of the delegation to make radio broadcasts. He refused to take part in them, and with that his part in the delegation came to an end, because his health failed him. He repeatedly stressed during the questioning that he distanced himself off and was very critical of the German version of the events. On his return home he firmly refused to be interviewed for *Goniec Krakowski* and to appear in the documentary film. In exchange the Germans offered to release any prisoners he cared to name from the Montelupich prison or from the Plaszow camp, but he firmly declined these offers.[180]

In July 1945 Edmund Seyfried appeared before Prosecutor Jerzy Sawicki. He made a statement declaring that during the War he had been the managing director of the RGO. Then he said that for this reason the Germans made him responsible for selecting the members of a Katyn delegation. To do this he

---

[177] *Ibid.*

[178] AIPN Kraków, sign. no. 303/1, Protokół przesłuchania świadka ks. kanonika Stanisława Jasińskiego z 13 VI 1945 r. [Minutes of the hearing of witness Canon Stanisław Jasiński, Jun. 13, 1945], sheets 1–2.

[179] *Ibid.*

[180] *Ibid.*, sheet 3.

IPN Kr 303/9
(Ds Spec 314/45 L9, IPN Kr 2/2/1A)

126

Prokurator
Specjalnego Sądu Karnego
w Krakowie
dnia 10 lipca 1945,
Nr. II Ds Spec. 314/45.

W odpowiedzi na to pismo
należy powołać datę tego pisma
i numer akt.

List Gończy

Nazwisko: Wodziński

Imiona: Marian, Jan, Julian,

Dzień, miesiąc i rok urodzenia: 8/5.1911.

Miejsce urodzenia: Tarnów pow. Tarnów

Ostatnie miejsce zamieszkania: Kraków, Krowoderska 11, I.piętro

Wyznanie: rzym.kat. - zawód - lekarz, w okresie okupacji starszy
asystent Państwowego Instytutu Medycyny Sądowej i Kry-
minalistyki w Krakowie.

Rysopis: wzrost wzwyż średni, szczupły, szatyn, twarz owalna, czoło
wysokie, nos prosty, bez zarostu.

Według posiadanych informacji znajdować się może w jednej z polskich
miejscowości uzdrowiskowych.

Zarzucane przestępstwo: w okresie okupacji niemieckiej idąc na rękę
niemieckiej władzy okupacyjnej, dopuścił się
działania na szkodę Państwa Polskiego tj. przest.
z art.1.§ 2 dekr.P.K.W.N. z 31/8.1944, w brzmie-
niu dekr.P.K.W.N. z 16/2.1945.

Zarządzenie o aresztowaniu - wydano dnia 7 lipca 1945.

Prokurator Specjalnego Sądu Karnego w Krakowie wzywa każdą osobę zna-
jącą miejsce pobytu oskar. Mariana Wodzińskiego do zawiadomienia o nim
najbliższej władzy sądowej lub najbliższego organu Bezpieczeństwa
Publicznego wzgl. Milicji Obywatelskiej a w miarę możności do zatrzymania go.

9. Warrant for the arrest of Marian Wodziński, July 10, 1945

endeavored to obtain the consent of the authorities of the Polish Underground State and make the arrangements with their knowledge. He also spoke about what he saw on the site of the atrocity, and said that he steadfastly refused to make an official statement for the German media, despite persistent pressure.[181]

For Dr. Edward Grodzki the matter closed with no serious consequences. Initially he went into hiding, but later left for Włocławek. In 1952 he again came under the special kind of concern the Ministry of Public Security tended to exercise.

Other members of the 1943 excursions to Katyn got no peace, either. This applied especially to those regarded as the principal experts – Dr. Marian Wodziński, Kazimierz Skarżyński, Dr. Adam Szebesta, and Dr. Stanisław Plappert. Black clouds hung over the heads of Ferdynand Goetel, Jan Emil Skiwski, and Józef Mackiewicz as well. Some of them went into hiding in Poland, others managed to flee the country before the arrival of the Red Army. For a time Dr. Wodziński, Ferdynand Goetel, and Dr. Szebesta stayed in their hideouts.

Initially Wodziński hid away in a refuge in Jędrzejów, and subsequently in Katowice and Poznań.[182] He was an important, or even the key witness both for the Soviets and for the Ministry of Public Security – this is shown by the vast amount of effort and resources put into attempts to arrest or even eliminate him.[183] Thanks to help from his colleagues in Kraków, close members of Wodziński's family passed information on to him, which let him keep his freedom. As of January 1945 Ferdynand Goetel was in hiding in the Discalced Carmelite Monastery in Kraków.[184] Prosecutor Martini issued warrants for the arrest of both of them. Goetel made the following remark on the danger the warrant meant for him: "That arrest warrant did not scare me off at all, the reason for its issue being my visit to Katyn and my position on the matter. A search on grounds which were so precarious from the prosecutor's point of view should not have given cause for concern. And it didn't. I had no news of any immediate search for me in Kraków or Warsaw."[185] Skiwski, who had left

[181] AIPN BU, sign. no. 01251/151, Edmund Seyfried i in. Protokół przesłuchania świadka [Edmund Seyfried and others. Minutes of the hearing of a witness], sheet 3.

[182] Bratko, *Dlaczego zginąłeś prokuratorze?* 231.

[183] Jankowski and Kotarba, *Literaci a sprawa katyńska 1945*, 99.

[184] Bratko, *Dlaczego zginąłeś prokuratorze?* 230.

[185] Goetel, *Czasy wojny*, 220.

Poland with his family in February 1945, was in a much worse situation.[186] Yet Dr. Martini issued a warrant for his arrest, too. Effectively it was the second document of its kind – the death sentence passed on Skiwski by the judiciary of the Polish Underground State in 1944 may certainly be recognized as the first. Szebesta remained in hiding for several months and only came out after special provisions for an amnesty had been published.[187]

Kazimierz Skarżyński took the risk of staying at home. In consequence of his decision he was questioned by Dr. Roman Martini, one of the team of prosecutors. Skarżyński undertook a responsible task. He drew up a report for the Communist authorities on the 1943 Katyn visit. "I was officially instructed to write up a report on my mission (...), and I was advised 'in my own interest' to highlight every detail that could indicate that the Germans had committed the atrocity. I agreed to submit a statement, but said right at the start that I would not make any references at all to anything that could indicate that Katyn was a German crime," Skarżyński wrote.[188] Apparently the prosecutors were pleased with his first draft and wanted him to provide better documentary evidence from their point of view. For him their response was a sign that things had taken a turn for the worse. He was in serious trouble.

The Soviets ended their Katyn investigation just as unexpectedly as they had started it. As of the summer of 1945 a group of Polish prosecutors led by Dr. Roman Martini was working on the problem in co-operation with the Ministry of Public Security. They questioned dozens of suspects and witnesses. They interrogated Kazimierz Skarżyński at Józefów near Warsaw in December of 1945, and they also interrogated Dr. Hieronim Bartoszewski, Dr. Stanisław Plappert, Jerzy Wodzinowski, Canon Stanisław Jasiński, Franciszek Prochownik, Jan Zygmunt Robel, Adam Godzik, Władysław Buczak, Franciszek Król, Zygmunt Szargut the *Gazeta Lwowska* journalist, General Smorawiński's wife Helena, Marek Arczyński, and a couple of writers, Maria Dąbrowska, Jan Kott, Jerzy Turowicz, Stefan Kisielewski, and Tadeusz Hołuj. They also issued a few arrest warrants. Finally they wound up their investigation. Faced with these developments, some individuals like Dr. Marian

---

[186] Skiwski, *Na przełaj*, 12.

[187] Skarżyński, *Katyń. Raport*, 80–81.

[188] *Idem*, 'Katyń i Polski Czerwony Krzyż,' 141.

Wodziński, Ferdynand Goetel, and Kazimierz Skarżyński decided to leave the country. As I have already written, Jan Emil Skiwski and Józef Mackiewicz had done this earlier.[189] Wodziński got to London illegally, and once there pretty soon produced a report entitled *Relacja dr med. Mariana Wodzińskiego lekarza sądowego Komisji Technicznej PCK w Katyniu* on what he had seen at Katyn. This document was compiled in September 1947 and was put into the first edition of the monumental publication on the Katyn atrocity in light of the documents, *Zbrodnia katyńska w świetle dokumentów* (London, 1948). Ferdynand Goetel traveled to Italy via Czechoslovakia and Germany, using a forged passport for a Dutch diplomat named John P. Menten.[190] In Italy he was cleared by the commanding officers of the Polish Second Corps and resumed his work on the Katyn atrocity.[191] Skarżyński left Poland on May 20, 1946, and traveled via Germany, where he served as a military guard. Eventually he got to London, where he joined the community of Polish émigrés. He was invited to attend sessions of the Polish government-in-exile. Jan Emil Skiwski and Feliks Burdecki got to Neuhaus near Munich, where Hans Frank's headquarters were located at the time. From there Skiwski went to Kufstein, Austria, and finally settled in Wildflecken. In mid-1946 he decided to come out into the open and try to join General Anders' Second Corps. His plan misfired, as the Second Corps intelligence men handed him over to the British, who put him in a detention camp in Rimini, where he stayed until mid-1947. After his release he worked for a short spell as a librarian in the Polish Library in Paris. Disgruntled with life in Europe, in January 1948 he changed his name to Rogalski and emigrated to Venezuela. For a short period he had worked with *Kultura*, the Polish émigré journal that came out in Paris, using the *noms- de-plume* Karol Hołobocki and Karol Rogaliński to publish his articles.[192]

Albeit nonplussed by many of those who had been to Katyn in 1943 evading capture by hiding away or fleeing the country, the prosecutors nonetheless managed to round up some of the Polish people who had been involved. Dr. Adam Szebesta, Edmund Seyfried, and Franciszek Prochownik were in

---

[189] Malewski (W. Bolecki), *Wyrok na Józefa Mackiewicza*, 64–65.

[190] In *Czasy wojny*, 220–227, Goetel describes the background to the visit.

[191] Wolsza, „*Katyń to już na zawsze katy i katowani*", 37–40.

[192] Skiwski, *Na przełaj*, 12; M. Urbanowski, *Człowiek z głębszego podziemia. Życie i twórczość Jana Emila Skiwskiego*, (Kraków: Arcana, 2003).

10. Father Stanisław Jasiński conducting the funeral rites (obsequies) over the graves of Katyn

a difficult situation. Another person who was put on trial was Marian Maak, although in his case involvement in the Katyn affair was of lesser importance. Ferdynand Goetel and Jan Emil Skiwski were tried in absentia.

In 1953 Edmund Seyfried, the RGO delegate, was sentenced to 10 years in prison.[193] The circumstances of the case and verdict against him were not directly connected with his visit to Katyn in 1943. During the War Seyfried had also been involved in the underground activities of PPS–WRN the clandestine Polish Socialist Party, and had operated in close contact with Franciszek Białas, a trade unionist and PPS activist. After the War he was a joint proprietor of a metal foundry in Poznań. When interrogated by Ministry of Public Security agents he could not give a satisfactory explanation of how he had come by the funds for the business. He had obtained this money from Franciszek Białas. For several years secret agents had been collecting evidence against him, for his alleged anti-Polish activities and involvement in the secret independence movement.

---

[193] AIPN BU, sign. no. 01251/151, Teczka Edmunda Seyfrieda [Dossier of Edmund Seyfried].

Adam Szebesta was detained as soon as he came out of hiding and was interrogated by Ministry of Public Security officers. Thereafter he was subject to intensive invigilation. In 1950 the Ministry decided to arrest him. Fearing for his life, he succumbed to pressure from the Ministry and changed his declaration on Katyn. He also changed the spelling of his name – from "Schebesta" (a German spelling) to "Szebesta," a Polonized form. Hieronim Bartoszewski recalled that Szebesta, with whom he was in touch for a time after the War, systematically avoided the subject of Katyn and eventually told him that "he did not want to talk about it."[194]

Franciszek Prochownik was arrested in June 1945. He enjoyed the confidence of his workmates and had an excellent work record. He was in the PPS, which he had joined before the War and continued to be a member during the War and afterwards when the party went underground. The events that followed his visit to Katyn were evidence in his favor: not only did he not co-operate with the Germans, but he actually went into hiding. Eventually he was released in October 1946.

The in absentia trial of Jan Emil Skiwski and a few other reptilian journalists earned notoriety throughout Poland. Ferdynand Goetel's name was bandied about on a well-nigh daily basis in reports on the case in court, but he was never officially charged. Thanks to Jankowski and Kotarba's invaluable book and my own work we know what went on behind the scenes. While none of the writers who gave evidence in court testified in Skiwski's or Feliks Burdecki's favor, they all spoke up for Goetel. The chief defendants were given life sentences.

Jan Mikołajczyk, who had worked in the Polish Red Cross' Technical Commission at Katyn, was arrested in in the early 1950s.[195] One of his duties on the site had been to keep a record of the items and documents retrieved from the pits. Some of these objects – handmade wooden artifacts, badges and distinctions, a pocket calendar in which a victim had made notes, and a large

---

[194] 'Byłem w Katyniu,' 15.

[195] Jan Mikołajczyk was born in Szczuczyn on Aug. 17, 1916. He trained as an electrical engineer, and worked for the Polish Red Cross from November 1939 to 1949. In 1942 he joined the underground resistance movement ZWZ [Union of Armed Struggle] and took "Wiesław" as his nom-de-guerre. In 1946 he made a public declaration on his activities in the resistance movement. He died in Warsaw on Mar. 19, 1973.

collection of photos of the bodies and the burial ground – he took back to Warsaw. On many occasions during the War he had spoken in public on the Soviet culpability for the crime. As a result, when combat was over Mikołajczyk, who had been a second lieutenant in the Home Army, was put under close surveillance by Ministry agents on account of his operations in the underground resistance movement (he had served in the Syrena (Mermaid) unit, which handled Allied airdrops) and his "slander campaign against the Soviet Union." During his interrogation he handed in eight of his Katyn photographs and the original of his letter of appointment to the Polish Red Cross delegation.[196] Under constant duress and intimidation, he decided to work for the Ministry of Public Security.[197] Operating as its agent under the pseudonym Kot ("Cat"), he participated in a secret investigation code-named Siatka ("Net") against the Home Army's Syrena unit. After the political thaw of 1956 he withdrew from all activities connected with the Ministry.[198]

The Katyn question hit the national and international headlines again in 1952, when Congressman Ray Madden's Committee started its operations.[199] The authorities of the Polish People's Republic were alarmed at the scale of the Committee's activities, and embarked on undertakings of various kinds, including attempts to blackmail individuals who had taken part in the 1943 visits to Katyn. The search resumed for witnesses – those who had been to Katyn, and others who could present new evidence. It was no coincidence that people like Franciszek Prochowniak, Dr. Adam Szebesta, and Dr. Edward Grodzki were again being approached by Ministry of Public Security officers.

The Ministry's agents went as far as to draw up a list of those who visited Katyn in 1943 – amazingly also containing the names of victims of Soviet murders and individuals not connected in any way with Katyn, mixed in with the roll-call of persons who had indeed taken part in one or other of the excursions the Germans had organized. The administrative officer employed in the Ministry's Department VII responsible for compiling it put Seyfried,

---

[196] AIPN BU, sign. no. 0718/40, Notatka opracowana na podstawie materiałów archiwalnych z 15 III 1977 r. [Note drawn up on the basis of archival materials, Mar. 15, 1977].

[197] AIPN Warsaw, sign. no. 01355/120/806/4, Wydarzenia katyńskie. [Katyn incidents].

[198] AIPN BU, sign. no. 0718/40, Notatka opracowana na podstawie materiałów archiwalnych z 15 III 1977 r. [Note drawn up on the basis of archival materials, Mar. 15, 1977].

[199] Wolsza, *„Katyń to już na zawsze katy i katowani"*, 109–125.

Orzechowski, Grodzki, Prochownik, Father Jasiński, Szebesta, Pragłowski, Bartoszewski, Plappert, Skarżyński, Wodzinowski, Kołodziejski, Banach, Wodziński, Rojkiewicz, Kassur, Płonka, Jaworowski, Godzik, Cupryjak, Mikołajczyk, and Kawecki on the list.[200] If we discard those who had died in the interim (e.g. Kassur, Płonka, and Rojkiewicz), there were no misgivings about the rest of these persons, although some of them were no longer in Poland and therefore beyond the Ministry's reach. In a subsequent part of the document the compiler, one of the Ministry's warrant officers, put down the names of people like Zygmunt Berling and Leon Bukojemski, who had visited the site with the Soviets in 1944. Lieut. Bronisław Młynarski, an inmate of Kozelsk who survived by sheer chance, was on the list as well, along with the names of people who were not so lucky and perished in the massacre – Maj. Adam Solski and Lieut. Janina Lewandowska, Gen. Dowbór-Musnicki's daughter. Kazimierz Gumowski, also on the list, died in another Soviet atrocity completely unconnected with Kozelsk and Katyn. The Soviets shot him in 1941. Witold Daszkiewicz, another person on the list, was killed by the NKVD in 1944. The body of Maj. Adam Sołtan, an inmate of Starobielsk, has not been recovered, yet on the list his name was entered under a sub-heading "other delegation members," along with Lieut. Wacław Kruk and Lieut. Piotr Krahelski, who were murdered in Katyn.

We may wonder why this list drawn up by a low-rank officer in the Ministry of Public Security has such a large number of names on it of people who had absolutely nothing to do with the delegations which visited Katyn in 1943. There is a simple answer. All these names appear in the volume of documentary sources, *Zbrodnia katyńska w świetle dokumentów*, first published in London in 1948. Most probably the warrant officer did not do his job properly and failed to read through the book. To be on the safe side he expanded his list with a couple of names of people generally associated with Katyn.

Another name which appeared on the Ministry's list in the early '50s was of one Bochenek, who had apparently escaped execution by fluke and managed to flee from the site of the Katyn atrocity.[201] Officers working in the Min-

---

[200] AIPN Warsaw, sign. no. 00231/124, vol. 2, Notatka informacyjna chor. H. Kowalskiego z 8 X 1952 r. [Note drawn up by Warrant Officer H. Kowalski, Oct. 8, 1952].

[201] *Ibid.*, sign. no. 01419/78, Amerykański Komitet dla Zbadania Zbrodni Katyńskiej [US Select Committee To Investigate the Katyn Forest Massacre].

istry notified their superiors that the British were keeping the said Bochenek in a hideout, and that he would be of service to the Madden Committee. Actually there was a Bochenek on the list of Katyn victims. However, Mieczysław Roman Bochenek, a captain in the artillery, of Szkoła Podchorążych Rezerwy Artylerii (the junior officers' college of the reserve artillery), did not survive Katyn, or at least that is what Jerzy Tucholski writes.[202] On the other hand, the compilers of the Ministry's list failed to put Tadeusz Ślaski on it. This person was in Poland, writing articles on Katyn which were published in the Polish émigré press under the pen-name Tadeusz Nieczuja.[203]

At about the same time in the early '50s another list of names was drawn up – of "Members of the 'commissions' sent out by the Germans, who have submitted declarations to the effect that at Katyn they saw evidence that the Germans had rigged up that provocation." The Ministry pressurized five persons, Dr. Adam Szebesta, Dr. Edward Grodzki, Franciszek Prochownik, Dr. Stanisław Plappert, and Dr. Tadeusz Piechocki, into making such declarations. The first four had been to Katyn, while Tadeusz Piechocki was a witness of a statement made by Władysław Herz. The Communist authorities put Dr. Szebesta's statement in the limelight, lavishing a great deal of publicity on it. It was originally published in the daily *Dziennik Zachodni*, where he said, "when I left Katyn I had no illusions at all who had perpetrated the crime. There is absolutely no doubt that it was done by Hitler's henchmen – the very same people who have a lot of Polish blood on their hands."[204]

Following on from the discussion in the press, the unrelenting criticism of the Madden Committee and distorted representations of its members, the time came for the first book on Katyn published in People's Poland. It was issued in a print-run of ten thousand copies with a highly telling title, *Prawda o Katyniu* (The Truth about Katyn). It was envisaged to refute the findings of the Madden Committee and counteract the re-issue of *Zbrodnia katyńska w świetle dokumentów*, the volume of Katyn documents published by Polish

---

[202] Tucholski, *Mord w Katyniu*, 77.

[203] T. Nieczuja, 'Zbrodnia katyńska,' *Przegląd Polski* 1948: 7. I was able to establish that the nom-de-plume "Nieczuja" was used by Jerzy Ślaski and his father Tadeusz thanks to assistance from Dr. Kamila Churska, who accessed documents kept in the Archive of the Bydgoszcz branch of the Institute of National Remembrance which identified them.

[204] Quoted after B. Wójcicki, *Prawda o Katyniu* (Warszawa: Czytelnik, 1952), 188–189.

émigrés in London. The book relating the Communist version was written by Bolesław Wójcicki, a journalist working for *Życie Warszawy*, who had an eventful prewar and wartime CV.[205]

The events of 1952 led in outcome to further developments in 1953 – the engagement of the pathologist Jan Olbrycht in the Katyn project. I have already mentioned Professor Olbrycht in connection with the activities of the Polish Red Cross' Technical Commission on the site of the atrocity. Putting it briefly – his opinion corroborated the new statements issued by two of the international medical experts, Professors František Hájek and Marko Markov. Under duress they now changed the opinion they had given in 1943. There was no other option for them: their new opinion saved their lives. As regards Professor Olbrycht's opinion, we do not know what was going on behind the scenes. Olbrycht was a distinguished expert in his field and a close friend of Dr. Marian Wodziński and Dr. Jan Zygmunt Robel, like them associated professionally with the Kraków Institute of Forensic Medicine. His expert opinion was based on an assessment of the German materials published in a book of fundamental importance, *Amtliches Material zum Massenmord von Katyn* (Official Materials on the Katyn Mass Murder), which also appeared in the GG in a Polish synopsis.

It should be pointed out that Professor Olbrycht's expert opinion was certainly not written in 1952. He had been working on it for a long time, having received a request from Prosecutor Michał Trembałowicz in a letter dated December 12, 1945.[206] We may assume that the Ministry intended to use Olbrycht's opinion in a prospective Katyn trial. The trial failed to materialize, but the document was preserved.

---

[205] Bolesław Wójcicki was born in Łódź in 1908. He graduated in Romance Philology and Education from the University of Warsaw. In the 1920s and '30s he worked in the Institut Français in Warsaw. When the War broke out he evacuated to Lwów, where he taught Russian. In 1941 he returned to Warsaw after the outbreak of the German-Soviet war. He was wounded during the Warsaw Uprising. In February 1945 he started a job with the *Życie Warszawy* newspaper. He joined the PZPR in 1948, but had not been a member of its predecessor, the PPR. In 1951 he was appointed editor-in-chief of *Życie Warszawy*. Later he joined the editorial staff of *Trybuna Ludu* [the daily regarded as the mouthpiece of the government of the People's Republic]. He died in Warsaw in 1991. P. Libera, 'Za kulisami prawdy o Katyniu,' *Mówią Wieki* 2013: 4, 55.

[206] AIPN Kraków, sign. no. 303/8, Do prokuratora Specjalnego Sądu Karnego w Krakowie. Opinia sądowo-lekarska z 12 XII 1945 r. [For the attention of the Prosecutor of the Kraków Special Criminal Court. Forensic Opinion, December 12, 1945].

Jan Olbrycht started his extensive opinion with an observation that the German book *Amtliches Material zum Massenmord von Katyn* published in Berlin in 1943 contains "a collection of materials to prove that the mass murder of Polish officers at Katyn was committed by the Soviets in the spring of 1940. The main part of these materials consists of the report drawn up by Dr. Gerhard Buhtz, a German forensic scientist and professor of pathology from Breslau, and the report compiled by the International Medical Commission (...). The claim that the Katyn mass murder was committed by the Soviets in the spring of 1940 is based first on the statements made by witnesses, second on the documents, letters, newspapers, notes etc. discovered on the bodies of the victims, and third on the results of the examination of the corpses."[207] Regarding the first point, he observed that "in general one cannot attribute very much importance to the witnesses' statements, and certainly one should not treat them as the decisive evidence."[208] His remark on the second point went as follows: "As regards the second grounds, that is the documents, letters, notes, diaries etc. discovered on the bodies, and their use to identify the victims of Katyn and to establish when they died – these documents should be tested chemically and technically to determine the quality of the paper, the handwriting and print, and to determine the changes which could have ensued in them in outcome of the decomposition of the bodies and the fairly long period of interment in the ground – and moreover these documents should be examined by expert graphologists with the use of a sufficient amount of material for comparative purposes. One should be very cautious about jumping to conclusions on the identity of the Katyn victims and the time of their death until such tests are carried out."[209] He then passed on to a medical critique, with a separate review of the two reports, by the German and the international commission. He alleged the former had conducted their medical examinations very hastily, arguing that three German doctors and one doctor from Poland could not have examined over 4,100 corpses with the required precision, and identified 2,815 of them, in the time available. He made the following remark: "Anyone who has had anything to do with such examinations will admit that they call for far more time

---

[207] *Ibid.*, sheets 1–2.

[208] *Ibid.*, sheet 2.

[209] *Ibid.*, sheet 3.

than an ordinary postmortem carried out in a scientific institute (...)." He went on to observe that there were other problems as well, for instance groundwater in the graves. The doctors emptied the victims' pockets, which caused additional delay with the autopsies. In his opinion the German commission could not possibly have conducted 4,134 flawless postmortems.[210] He devoted most of his attention to the foreign medical experts and referred to them by name – Ferenc Orsós, Helge Tramsen, Vincenzo Palmieri, Marko Markov, František Hájek, Eduard Miloslavić, and Alexandru Birkle. He assessed the work of each of them: "Pathologist Markov only gave an account of the external and internal examinations he carried out but did not give an opinion. Of the particulars in his autopsy report which are of interest to us, he observed a bullet hole in each of the skulls, from the back of the head to the forehead with no evidence for a shot at close range, and well-preserved, partly coriaceous outer skin, with adipocere forming in the fatty tissue on the mesentery of the small intestine. Pathologist Hájek observed a bullet wound running over a path from the back of the head to the forehead in both of the bodies he examined, but without the features typical of a shot at close range. For the autopsy of corpse no. 831 he writes that the brain was completely soft and he did not manage to observe the bullet channel, yet in his report on this case he writes that the brain was crushed. In neither case does he say that he observed adipoceratous changes. Pathologist Birkle observed a similar bullet wound as the cause of death, with no features characteristic of a shot at close range, and mentioned the occurrence of adipoceratous changes on the surface of the corpse and in the muscles of the limbs and heart. Pathologist Tramsen observes that death had been caused by a similar bullet wound, with no evidence for a shot at close range, and he also writes of the occurrence of corpse wax on the chest. Pathologist Orsós observes that death was due to a similar bullet wound running from the back of the skull to the left side of the nose cavity, with no features of a shot at close range, and with internal and external adipoceratous changes. Yet whereas on this corpse (no. 835) he could distinctly observe not only the diverse components of the brain and its cerebral ganglia, but even a pink color on the cortex and an almost white color on the cerebral core, on the skull of corpse no. 526 he observed a hard, layered incrustation on the surface of its

---

[210] *Ibid.*, sheet 6.

brain turned into a clayey, mushy substance, and on the grounds of this change he concluded that the body must have lain in the ground for at least three years. Pathologist Palmieri observed three wounds in the back of the head where bullets had entered, with no features characteristic of shots at close range, two exit wounds in the forehead, and a caliber 7.65 mm bullet lodged in the brain. On the grounds of the observed changes he determined that the victim must have died more than a year before. Pathologist Miloslavić observed a similar bullet wound in the skull, with the entrance wound giving rise to a blackish stain on the inner part of the skin and on the occipital bone. In addition he held that the post mortem changes (adipocere) observed on the corpse corresponded to the dates on the documents found on the body, viz. that death occurred in the spring of 1940."[211] In his conclusion Professor Olbrycht wrote, "Summing up, I shall observe that the foreign pathologists concurred that the cause of death of the victims they autopsied were shots in the back of the head, but with the exception of pathologist Miloslavić, none of them observed features characteristic of shots at close range; that some of the pathologists did not mention adipoceratous changes at all, others said that adipocere had started to set in, while still others described it as having reached an advanced stage; that most of the pathologists did not establish the time of death, or the time for which the body had been in the ground at all, while only pathologist Palmieri said it was more than a year, and pathologists Orsós and Miloslavić determined this time as 3 years."[212] Professor Olbrycht also said that in neither the German nor the international expert opinions was there any information on the provenance of the ammunition used for the executions. "It must seem at least strange that neither the international commission's report nor Prof. Buhtz's summary says that the ammunition used was of German origin (...)."[213] He also commented on the observation made in both reports on "the experienced hand of the executioner," writing that "examinations of the victims from numerous mass graves, murdered by the Germans on the territory of Poland give incontrovertible proof that they, too, had a deft hand for this kind of murder."[214] Finally he

---

[211] *Ibid.*, sheets 7–9.

[212] *Ibid.*, sheet 9.

[213] *Ibid.*, sheet 10.

[214] *Ibid.*, sheet 12.

expressed his doubts as to the date of the executions, which both commissions had determined as the spring of 1940.

The highly detailed analysis Professor Olbrycht conducted in 1945 was still significant and trenchant after a few years. It was published in a Belgian scientific journal, as part of the international propaganda campaign against the Madden Committee.[215] Professor Olbrycht's critique was circulated internationally, and it may well have attenuated the persuasive power of the American argument. One person who expressed his satisfaction with this was Jakub Berman, the man who supervised the Stalinist system of repression in People's Poland, in his reply to a question from an American journalist.

WHAT HAPPENED AFTER THE WAR TO THE INTERNATIONAL COMMISSION DOCTORS AND THEIR POSTWAR OPINIONS

Several of the doctors who were members of the International Medical Commission, out of the total of fourteen including Dr. Gerhard Buhtz and Dr. André Costedoat of Vichy France, were in danger of Soviet reprisals already in 1944. The most at risk were of course those from countries which fell under the direct control of the Red Army – Dr. František Hájek, Dr. František Šubík, Dr. Marko Markov, and Dr. Alexandru Birkle. Theoretically two others, the Hungarian pathologist Dr. Ferenc Orsós and Dr. Arno Saxén from Finland, could have been in jeopardy as well, if they had let the NKVD outwit them. But they were not the first to be severely punished for co-operating with the Germans. In 1947 Dr. André Costedoat, head of the French Medical Inspectorate, who had been the delegate of the Vichy government, died in "unexplained" circumstances.

František Hájek was arrested when combat operations came to an end and charged with collaboration. One of the grounds for his arrest was that in 1943 he had published an article on the Katyn atrocity with the claim that the Czech intelligentsia would have suffered the same fate if the Bolsheviks had reached the West sooner. In detention he was subjected to a thorough program of "Katyn re-education," the intention being to utilize his opinion for

---

[215] Libera, 'Za kulisami prawdy o Katyniu,' 54.

the disavowal of the German arguments. The program did not last very long: in fear for his life, Dr. Hájek soon acquiesced to all the suggestions put forward by Czech and Soviet Communists. He published a book entitled *Důkazy katynské* with the Czech Medical Association (Spolek českých lékařů). "In this book he ostentatiously upheld the Soviet version of the crime, attributing the blatant discrepancy between what he had said on Katyn during the War and what he was now saying to the unreliability of journalists under the Protectorate."[216] For a time the Soviets were planning to make use of Dr. Hájek when the subject of Katyn came up at the Nuremberg trial. Eventually they abandoned this idea and instead forced Dr. Marko Markov to participate in their lies about Katyn. In their opinion this medical practitioner from Sofia, Bulgaria, was better suited for the job. He was arrested in 1945 and sentenced to death by the Supreme Chamber of the Bulgarian People's Court.[217] In its closing remarks the court said that by working with the German Commission Dr. Markov had "committed a crime against the Bulgarian Nation and its liberator, Russia, as well as against civilized mankind."[218] Dr. Markov was so terrified by the severity of the sentence that he immediately declared his readiness to co-operate with the Communists. On his release from prison he resumed his professional practice under the permanent surveillance of the Bulgarian special services. He died in 1967 following a third heart attack.

As of 1946 František Hájek was ready to help the Czechoslovak security services at any time in the event of a special situation. A special situation did indeed arise in 1952, and Dr. Hájek was given a key part in the anti-American campaign in connection with the Madden Committee. His statements were translated into the languages of the countries within the Soviet sphere of influence and utilized in the propaganda campaign. In Poland an interview he gave was published in March 1952. In it he said, "The aim Hitler's war criminals had in mind, and the purpose of their deceitful campaign on the so-called 'Katyn question' was clear already at the time. They wanted to turn the world's attention away from the dreadful atrocities they had committed in Poland and the Soviet Union, crimes which they were later proved guilty of

---

[216] Borák, *Ofiary zbrodni katyńskiej,* 11.

[217] Zawodny, *Katyń,* 63.

[218] A. Basak, *Historia pewnej mistyfikacji. Zbrodnia katyńska przed Trybunałem Norymberskim,* (Wrocław: Wydawnictwo Uniwersytetu Wrocławskiego, 1993), 68–69.

and sentenced by the International Military Tribunal in Nuremberg." He went on to claim that "On the grounds of my observations and autopsies of a few cadavers I confirmed that they definitely could not have lain there for 3 years, as the Nazi Germans claimed, but only for a very short time, at most just over a year." In addition he said that "the bodies were in a very good state of preservation, only in a few cases was there a loss of soft tissue on the crown of the head, but the joints were not separated, and the noses, lips, fingers, and even skin were preserved." [219] In short, his objective was to conclude that the Germans had committed the atrocity in the fall of 1941. Finally he appealed to "all the world's scholars and scientists to join in the protest against the American campaign on the so-called 'Katyn issue,' and the attempt to yet again make shameful use of it against the Soviet Union."[220] This was Hájek's best-known postwar statement on the Katyn atrocity, and it was countered with a resolute protest from Drs. Vincenzo Palmieri, Helge Tramsen, and François Naville, the medical experts who did not revoke the opinions they had issued earlier. Palmieri said that Hájek's conduct was due to the presence of the Red Army and the NKVD in Prague. "If the Red Army had liberated Naples, perhaps I would have gone back on my earlier opinion as well," he said.[221] František Hájek died in Prague on March 15, 1962.

Drs. Ferenc Orsós, František Šubík, and Alexandru Birkle were in serious trouble, too. Dr. Orsós fled to Germany. Dr. Šubík fled as well, and got as far as Bavaria, where he gave himself up to the Americans, hoping they would help him with the further part of his journey. But unexpectedly, in the summer of 1945 they handed him over to the Czechoslovak authorities, and he was put on trial on charges in connection with the anti-Jewish laws in force during the War. He categorically refused to revoke his signature on the report drawn up at the end of the Katyn visit in 1943. He was held in prison until the end of 1947.[222] After he had served his sentence he worked in a hospital at Trnava, under permanent surveillance by security agents. When the anti-American

---

[219] Quoted after Wójcicki, *Prawda o Katyniu,* 183–184.

[220] *Ibid.,* 185.

[221] G. Herling-Grudziński, 'Dziennik pisany nocą,' *Kultura* (Paris), 1978: 4, 17.

[222] M. Lacko, *Dwuramienny krzyż w cieniu swastyki. Republika Słowacka 1939–1945,* (Lublin: Oficyna Wydawnicza El-Press S.C., 2012), 234. Mečislav Borák (*Ofiary zbrodni katyńskiej,* 12) claims that during his hearing he said he had signed the Katyn report under duress.

propaganda campaign escalated in 1952 he and his wife fled to Austria, making an illegal crossing over the Morava River. In 1953 he emigrated to the USA, where he spent the rest of his life. He died in 1982.[223]

Dr. Ferenc Orsós, who had served as a doctor on the eastern front during World War I, posed a double threat to the Soviets, because he had seen both Katyn and Vinnytsia (where in 1943 the Germans discovered another set of mass graves of victims killed by the Soviets). He knew very well how dangerous he could be, and fled Budapest in December 1944. "He anticipated that no-one who had been to an atrocity site could expect any mercy if they got into the hands of the Soviet political police (...)."[224] He got to Halle with a medical team, and from there moved to Bavaria, and finally to West Berlin. At this time the Soviets were trying to get the Americans to hand him over. A Hungarian special commission with a readymade list of persons due to get an instant sentence from a people's court applied for his extradition as well. So he gave up medical practice, presumably to make them lose track of him, and started a job in Mainz lecturing in fine arts.[225] One of his paintings shows what happened in Katyn Forest.[226] In 1952 Drs. Ferenc Orsós, Vincenzo Palmieri, Helge Tramsen, and Alexandru Birkle testified as witnesses before the Madden Committee. Ferenc Orsós died in Mainz, Germany, in 1962.

Dr. Alexandru Birkle of Romania went into hiding in 1944, as soon as the Red Army set foot in his country. According to the Romanian security service, he was liable for visiting Katyn and Vinnytsia. He remained in hiding until 1946, when a Romanian court sentenced him in absentia to 20 years in a labor camp. He left Romania illegally, using forged documents. Later his wife and daughter, who stayed in Romania, paid the consequences for his Katyn visit and testimony before the Madden Committee. Their property was confiscated and they spent several years in prison. More repressive measures were applied against them in 1952. Dr. Birkle died in New York in 1986.

Dr. Eduard Miloslavić left Zagreb for the USA while the War was still in progress. In postwar Yugoslavia a death sentence was handed down on him

---

[223] Borák, *Ofiary zbrodni katyńskiej*, 12. Lacko (*Dwuramienny krzyż w cieniu swastyki*, 234) gives 1983 as the year of his death.

[224] S. Orsós, 'Mój stryj Ferenc tam był,' *Biuletyn Katyński* 33, (1991: 1), 41.

[225] *Ibid.*, 43.

[226] Maresch, *Katyń 1940*, 255.

in absentia. In 1952 he testified before the Madden Committee. He died in the USA in 1952. Dr. Arne Saxen of Helsinki was also in serious danger, because the NKVD was very active in Finland. Dr. Saxen was a member of the Finnish Red Cross and an associate of the Helsinki Institute of Forensic Medicine. On his return from Katyn he made only one public statement on the subject, in an interview for *Turun Sanomat* (April 28, 1943),[227] thereafter steadfastly refusing to take part in any propaganda operations or talks the Germans suggested. Fearing for his life, when hostilities were over he emigrated to Sweden and stayed there for a few years. On his return home he was questioned on his Katyn visit and it was suggested he withdraw his signature on the International Medical Commission's report. This was done without doubt under Soviet pressure. He refused categorically, thereby definitely putting himself in a worse position.[228] He died suddenly on November 19, 1952, although he was in good health, during a conference in Zurich, Switzerland.

The stories of the medical experts from countries beyond the Soviet sphere of influence show that straight after the War the Kremlin decided to deal with the remaining members of the delegation. The Soviets employed various methods of blackmail and repressive measures, which they either applied themselves or through the services of local communists.

Dr. Helge Tramsen traveled to Katyn on instructions from his superiors at the Copenhagen Institute of Forensic Medicine and with the knowledge and consent of the Danish resistance movement, as recorded in his diary, which is shown in the Danish documentary film *Kraniet fra Katyn* (The Skull from Katyn; 2006). Dr. Tramsen took the skull of one of the victims, a Polish office from Kraków, from the site of the massacre and smuggled it back to Denmark in his baggage. In 1945 he was arrested by the Gestapo for his involvement in the anti-German resistance movement and put in the Froslev labor camp. In 1945 he lost his job in the Institute of Forensic Medicine and was continually harassed. Nonetheless he continued to assert that it was the Soviets who had committed the Katyn atrocity in the spring of 1940, and repeated his statement on many occasions.[229] He said it on Radio Free Europe in the 1960s. In 1970 his

---

[227] *Kontakt. Pismo Zjednoczenia Polskiego w Helsingforsie, dodatek* [Supplement] 2008: 2.

[228] A.E. Jessen, *Kraniet fra Katyn. Beretning om massakren i 1940*, (København: Høst & Søn, 2008), 233.

[229] H. Kuberski, 'Świadkowie ludobójstwa,' *Mówią Wieki* 2013: 4, 44.

daughter died in Warsaw in unexplained circumstances. Dr. Tramsen believed it was an act of revenge on the part of the Communists, maybe even Soviet Communists, for his position on Katyn. He compiled a detailed report on his Katyn visit, which was published in a Polish version entitled *Wrażenia z podróży do Katynia w 1943 roku* (My Katyn visit in 1943).[230] Helge Tramsen died in 1979.

Drs. Reimond Speleers, Herman Maximilien de Burlet, Vincenzo Palmieri, and François Naville also suffered reprisals for their presence in Katyn in 1943. Dr. Reimond Speleers of Ghent University paid the greatest price. In September 1944 he was arrested by members of the Belgian resistance movement, in which communists had a lot to say. The grounds for Dr. Speleers' arrest were his involvement in the Flemish nationalist movement and his Katyn visit.[231] The communists saw to it that his personal documents and the notes he made on the site of the atrocity were confiscated and destroyed. He was put on trial and sentenced to 25 years in prison, a longer sentence than the verdicts passed against German war criminals. He died in the prison hospital at Aalst on April 29, 1951. After the War Dr. Herman Maximilien de Burlet, the Dutch member of the Commission, was removed from the office of president of the University of Groningen, but that was the only consequence that befell him in Holland for his travel to Katyn. However, he had also been a wartime member of the pro-German National Socialist Movement, and to avoid trouble he decided to emigrate to the USA. He died in Königswinter, West Germany, in 1957.[232]

The story of the Swiss doctor François Naville has been examined in several research papers.[233] Like several other members of the International Medical Commission not in Iron Curtain countries, he was on the Soviet schedule for reprisals, not only theoretically. The first to attack this professor from Geneva was the Communist parliamentary deputy Jean Vincent. In his allegations made in court against Naville, Jean Vincent claimed outright that it was the

---

[230] H. Tramsen, 'Wrażenia z podróży do Katynia w 1943 roku,' *Zeszyty Historyczne* 1989:87, 155–157.

[231] Kuberski, '*Świadkowie ludobójstwa*,' 44.

[232] *Ibid.*

[233] Wolsza, „*Katyń to już na zawsze katy i katowani*", 42–44; M. Komaniecka, 'Orędownik sprawy katyńskiej. Profesor François Naville,' *Biuletyn Instytutu Pamięci Narodowej* 2010: 4, 82–85; *Zbrodnia katyńska 1940. Dr Bronisław Kuśnierz o Katyniu*, 40–41; Kuberski, '*Świadkowie ludobójstwa*,' 46.

Germans who had committed the Katyn atrocity, and accused Naville of collaboration.[234] Dr. Naville answered the charge by saying that his aim was certainly not to collaborate with the Germans, but to discover the truth and help the Poles as much as he could. He gave a detailed account of his work at Katyn and, countering the opinion circulated by Dr. Markov, denied that the members of the commission had succumbed to German pressure of any kind.[235] Acting chiefly under Soviet inspiration, Swiss communists tried to discredit Dr. Naville, and the proceedings dragged on. The decisive meeting of the Grand Conseil of the Canton of Geneva was held in January 1947. Naville explained why he had traveled to Katyn, saying that he did so for the benefit of Poland and the Polish people. If he had refused to go there, he argued, his conduct would have been immoral: "If a country which has been cut up by the armies of two powerful neighbors learns of the murder of nearly ten thousand of its officers who did not commit any crime but were only defending their country, and tries to determine the circumstances in which the massacre could have occurred (...)."[236] On hearing the arguments put forward by Dr. Naville, the members of the Grand Conseil including Albert Picot, its president, concluded unanimously that his conduct had been honorable and in compliance with professional ethics.[237] The *Parti Suisse du Travail* (Swiss Labor Party), which had communist leanings, could not be reconciled to such a verdict, and hence Picot and others continued to hold that the Germans were culpable for the atrocity. This did not make any difference to Dr. Naville's situation: in 1948–1950 he was dean of the Medical School at the University of Geneva. He collected books and documents on the Katyn atrocity and corresponded on the issue with the International Red Cross. And most importantly, he testified before the Madden Committee, having inquired whether the Swiss Ministry of Foreign Affairs considered there was anything against the law about his decision to testify and received an answer that it was his private business. Dr. Naville died in Geneva on April 3, 1968.[238]

---

[234] Komaniecka, 'Orędownik sprawy katyńskiej. Profesor François Naville,' 84.

[235] *Ibid.*

[236] A. Korczyński, 'Sprawa Katynia przed genewskim „Grand Conseil". List ze Szwajcarii,' *Dziennik Polski i Dziennik Żołnierza* 1947: 20 (Jan. 23), 2.

[237] Wolsza, „*Katyń to już na zawsze katy i katowani*", 43.

[238] Komaniecka, 'Orędownik sprawy katyńskiej. Profesor François Naville,' 82.

Professor Vincenzo Palmieri was one of the most distinguished Italian experts in forensic medicine. He was appointed to a university chair already at the age of 35. In his recollections of his Katyn visit he wrote, "There were no doubts, no-one out of the twelve of us had any doubt at all, no reservations were put forward. An autopsy of one of the skulls performed by Professor Orsós from Budapest decided the issue; a new substance which only starts to form three years after death was observed on the skull's inner wall. Also a birchwood planted three years earlier was on the grave."[239] The first propaganda attacks against Palmieri started in May of 1944. The Communist paper *l'Unità* described his Katyn expedition as unworthy of a conscientious scholar: "Someone who has offered his services to Nazi propaganda, someone who has failed to respect his dignity as a scientist by applying scientific method to endorse a lie and acknowledge utterly ridiculous Nazi fabrications as absolute truth, may certainly not continue to teach young people. Such is the case of Professor V.M. Palmieri, who traveled to Katyn at the request and expense of the German Chief-of-Staff, who has declared that he has identified bodies from the graves of Katyn, and has organized a series of conferences in Naples, Venice, and Milan to uphold a dirty Nazi claim, on the basis of his alleged scientific authority."[240] In July of 1944 Professor Palmieri published an article in his defense in *Il Popolo*, a newspaper associated with the Christian Democrats. After the War he was put under surveillance. Under pressure from the Communists, the president of his university advised Palmieri to resign his chair. Palmieri refused and later said, "I did not let myself be intimidated, somehow I stood my ground…"[241] Italian Communists kept the Soviet ambassador to Rome informed on Palmieri and his attitude, calling him "a collaborator and flunky of Goebbels' propaganda." The Soviets recommended Palmieri's elimination from the discourse on Katyn, but their measure proved abortive. In the early 1950s Palmieri appeared before the Madden Committee as a witness. He also compiled a report on his sojourn on the site of the Soviet atrocity.[242] Vincenzo Palmieri died on December 23, 1994. "No-one from the Italian Left

---

[239] M. Patricelli, 'Osaczony świadek Katynia,' *Do Rzeczy* 2013: IV, 48.

[240] *Ibid.*

[241] Herling-Grudziński, 'Dziennik pisany nocą,' 17.

[242] V.M. Palmieri, 'Rezultaty dochodzenia w Lesie Katyńskim,' *Tygodnik Demokratyczny* 1989: 22 (May 28), 18–19, 29.

ever apologized to him for the smear campaign that was conducted against him for years on ideological grounds."[243]

Another point concerning the postwar attitudes of individual members of the medical commission which should be noted here is the questionnaire compiled by the American journalist Julius Epstein, who devoted a considerable part of his life to investigating the Katyn atrocity and earned a vast amount of merit in this field.[244] In 1948 he launched a questionnaire addressed to the twelve doctors on their visit to Katyn. The questions were as follows: 1. Did the German government exert any pressure on you before, during, and after the Commission's investigation? 2. Do you still hold the opinion now that the murdered Polish officers discovered in Katyn Forest were killed by the Soviets? 3. Would you be ready to come to the United States to testify as a witness in the case before a private or Congress investigating committee? Understandably, not all the interested parties got a copy of the questionnaire. One of them, Dr. André Costedoat, had died by that time. Epstein did not send the questionnaire to him. Some were in prison or had recently been released from a penitentiary. A few were under constant surveillance or were being harassed. So it is no wonder that only four replied. František Hájek wrote back that "while no pressure had been put on him, in the meantime he had changed his mind and was no longer of the opinion that the Soviets had committed the crime." The other three, Vincenzo Palmieri, Helge Tramsen, and François Naville, confirmed the opinion they gave in 1943, denied the Germans had put any pressure on them, and declared they were willing to come to the United States, even at their own expense.[245] Shortly afterward all three, along with a few other witnesses, delivered their testimony before the Madden Committee in the USA or in Europe.

After some time Stefan Korboński gave an assessment of the importance of the Madden Committee's work and the role and significance of the diverse witnesses. Quite naturally, he gave special consideration to the experts of the International Medical Commission and named five of them, "Dr. Eduard Miloslavić from Croatia, Dr. Helge Tramsen from Denmark, Dr. Ferenc Orsós from

---

[243] Patricelli, 'Osaczony świadek Katynia,' 49.

[244] Wolsza, „*Katyń to już na zawsze katy i katowani*", 76–77.

[245] S. Korboński, *W imieniu Polski walczącej*, (London: B. Świderski, 1963), 170.

Hungary, Dr. François Naville from Switzerland, and Dr. Vincenzo Palmieri from Italy, whom the Germans invited to come to Katyn, and who assisted in the exhumations, carried out autopsies, and examined letters, documents, and other items of evidence which they found there. Two of them, Tramsen and Naville, submitted material evidence retrieved from the Katyn site, such as samples of paper, army buttons and officers' badges, to the Committee. All five confirmed on the basis of the changes they had observed in the bodies and in accordance with the report they and seven others had signed on April 30, 1943, that the massacre had been done in the spring of 1940, when the area of Smolensk where the Katyn site is located was part of Soviet Russia and under Soviet control. The crime was committed a year before the outbreak of the Soviet–German war (June 21, 1941)."[246]

---

[246] *Ibid.*, 176–177.

THE POLISH ÉMIGRÉ COMMUNITY IN LONDON ON THE KATYN ATROCITY. THE POLISH GOVERNMENT'S LONELY BATTLE FOR THE TRUTH, FROM 1940 TO THE MID-1950s

BEFORE THE DISCOVERY OF THE KATYN GRAVES IN THE SPRING OF 1943

Before the War was over the London-based Polish émigré community had already become engaged in the question of the atrocity the Soviets committed on Polish officers in 1940. Initially the government-in-exile, the diverse political parties, groups, and institutions, as well as private individuals focused on finding out what had happened to the officers who had gone missing in mysterious circumstances in the Soviet Union. Nobody dared to speculate that they could have been murdered. Everybody thought the right thing to do was to look for them in the labor camps scattered over the vast expanses of the Soviet Union. Hence in 1941, when diplomatic relations were established between the Polish government-in-exile and the Soviet Union, Józef Czapski, one of the very few to have survived Starobielsk, was appointed head of Biuro Opieki (the Welfare Office), his principal duty being to search for his missing fellow-officers. He immediately set down to work on this challenging task, conducting talks on the matter with top Soviet politicians, carefully listening to their answers, and analyzing the information he obtained.

Czapski's mission was not the only effort being made. It was part of a broad sweep of operations undertaken by the Polish émigré authorities on the one hand, and by General Władysław Anders in the Soviet Union. The most senior officers of the Polish Army in the Soviet Union and Ambassador Stanisław Kot focused their attention on negotiations with Joseph Stalin, Vyacheslav Molotov, and Andrei Vyshinsky – these were the individuals with reliable information on what had happened to the Polish prisoners-of-war. Unfortunately, things were going far worse than what the Poles had expected. The Soviet dignitaries rambled, beat about the bush, and told them things which seemed preposterously unlikely. They alleged that the Polish prisoners-of-war had escaped to Romania. They insisted that all the detainees had been released and no-one was being held against their will. Stalin went as far as to assert that "there were no exceptions to a Soviet amnesty," which was meant to suggest that even those who were the most hostile to the Soviets had definitely been released. With his back against the wall when it was suggested to him that the amnesty was not all that it should have been, he delivered a thoroughly discrediting utterance which has gone down as a classic of deceitfulness. He actually said that the Poles held in Soviet POW camps had escaped to Manchuria. "They escaped," he announced to the astonished Generals Władysław Sikorski and Władysław Anders. When Anders asked, "Where on earth could they have escaped to?" Stalin said, "Well, to Manchuria, of course." General Anders observed that they could not have all fled to Manchuria – there were thousands of them. Whereupon Stalin again insisted that they had all been released, but had not yet reached the assembly points."[247]

The key document Czapski compiled in the fall of 1941 was a concise factsheet on the missing prisoners-of-war. He wrote that POWs from three camps, Starobielsk, Ostashkov, and Kozelsk, had still not turned up, with the exception of a few (2-3%), who had gotten to the camp at Griazovets.[248] He went on to observe that in April of 1940 the Soviets had started to wind up camps, and he understood this to mean transferring POWs to other "distribution centers." But there was something that made him suspicious. He recalled that officers and NCOs had returned from Vorkuta and Kolyma, but not from

---

[247] *Zbrodnia katyńska w świetle dokumentów*, 73.

[248] M. Polak and B. Polak, *Zbrodnia katyńska 1940. Poszukiwanie prawdy 1941–1946*, 9.

Starobielsk, Ostashkov, and Kozelsk, and the Soviets could not offer a rational explanation for their absence.[249] Toward the end of 1941 another important witness turned up: Lieut. Bronisław Młynarski, who had been held in Staro-bielsk from September 1939 to May 1940. His report was of the same caliber as Czapski's account – an eyewitness' story. We should also bear in mind that this Polish officer passed this information on to the British and Americans, asking them to help with the search for the POWs from Starobielsk and secure their release. Młynarski estimated the number of Polish officers in Starobielsk at about 3,920 in April 1940, and then wrote that every day from April 5 to April 26 a group of them were taken from the camp and driven away in an unknown direction. The same happened in May. He mentioned the camps at Pavlishchev Bor and Griazovets, where he was sent from Starobielsk. He concluded with a demand the Soviets inform the Polish authorities where they were holding thousands of Polish officers.[250] It is evident that he had not seriously consid-ered the possibility that his fellow-officers from Starobielsk and other camps might no longer be alive.

The want of specific information on what had happened to thousands of Polish officers gave rise to a variety of speculations. Apart from searching for the missing officers and conducting talks with the Soviet authorities, Poles in the Soviet Union and in Britain continued to collect any data they could on the fate of their compatriots in the Soviet Union. They collected even information that looked unbelievable.

In June 1942 one of the Polish officers who had left a Soviet labor camp just two months earlier submitted an anonymous written report that on April 30, 1940 he had witnessed Polish officers being transported from Kozelsk to a rail-road station near Smolensk, from where his colleagues were taken in buses with blackout windows in the direction of an area of woodland.[251] The note reached Gen. Romuald Wolikowski, the Polish military attaché in Kuybyshev.[252] A few years later it turned out that the anonymous officer was Lieut. Stanisław Swi-aniewicz, who for several reasons used the alias Jerzy Lebiedziewski, and who

---

[249] *Ibid.*, 11.

[250] Maresch, *Katyń 1940*, 24.

[251] *Zbrodnia katyńska w świetle dokumentów*, 47.

[252] Maresch, *Katyń 1940*, 21.

was saved from the Soviet bloodbath by a quirk of fate, to become an extremely important witness and the author of a book which exposed the Soviet lies about Katyn.[253] A lot of interesting information was collected by Franciszek Bała, an employee of the Missing Persons Unit. A report he drew up for the Polish government in June 1942 at a place called Yangiyul says that he had established a group of locations where Polish officers unaware of the amnesty might still be staying. On the basis of information from dozens of witnesses he listed Novaya Zemlya, Franz Josef Land, Kolyma, Komi, and the taiga between the Ob and the Yenisei as likely places. He supplemented this with information on places like Norilsk, Chelyabinsk, Yakutsk, Omsk, Krasnoyarsk, Dnepropetrovsk, and Samarkand.[254] He concluded with a somewhat self-confident assertion: "In 1940, after Kozelsk, Starobielsk, and Ostashkov were closed down, only a small group of those from Kozelsk were sent to Novaya Zemlya and Franz Josef Land, via Arkhangelsk. 1) A larger group of POWs, probably from Starobielsk, was dispatched to Kolyma. 2) The remainder (Kozelsk and Ostaszkov) were scattered throughout the taiga of Komi (in camps along the Vym, Ukhta, Izhma, and Pechora). 3-4) In the spring and summer of 1941 the POWs were moved on. Some of those in Komi or its environs were sent further north to Novaya Zemlya or Franz Josef Land. 5) Some of those from Kozelsk in Novaya Zemlya were transferred to Kolyma. 6) Conversely, some of those from Starobielsk were moved to Novaya Zemlya. 7) Another group of them were put in the taiga along the Ob and Yenisei. 8) It cannot be ruled out that following the amnesty some of the Polish POWs were transferred from the islands in the Far North to the continent in the region of Norilsk and Dudinka, and 9) they could not be transported any further because of climatic conditions. Therefore now they should be sought in three centers: a) the islands of the Far North and the areas around the mouths of the Ob and Yenisei, b) Kolyma, and c) Narimski Krai; d) a small number might still be in Komi."[255] Franciszek Bała added that the Polish ex-POWs from Kozelsk, Starobielsk, and Ostashkov were being treated as a separate group hitherto not covered by the amnesty. Finally he suggested a procedure – a continuous series of notes sent

---

[253] Swianiewicz, *W cieniu Katynia.*

[254] M. Polak and B. Polak, *Zbrodnia katyńska 1940. Poszukiwanie prawdy,* 12–13.

[255] *Ibid.,* 18.

to the Soviet authorities and an intensification in the operations undertaken by the Polish institutions attached to the embassy and army.[256]

Interesting information relating to this issue also came in the recollections of ex-prisoner Tadeusz Kiersnowski. As soon as he was liberated Kiersnowski made his information available to the Polish authorities in exile. In October 1942 he submitted an invaluable document, *Moje spostrzeżenia o Rosji Sowieckiej (1940–1942)*, on his observations in Soviet Russia, 1940–1942, important not only from the point of view of the Katyn atrocity. This Vilnian lawyer did not believe that the Soviets could not locate the whereabouts of the missing officers. Like Swianiewicz, he was a trustworthy witness, albeit not an eyewitness. Somewhat earlier he had experienced confinement in Soviet labor camps himself. He knew all the details of the procedure for imprisonment and the transfer of prisoners to new places. He said explicitly that every prisoner in the Soviet Union, not just a Pole sent to a Soviet gulag, had a dossier with his photo and all the particulars relating to his place of confinement. "So it is absolutely impossible for the authorities to be unaware of where twelve thousand persons had gone," he stated.[257] He recalled the stories and rumors he had heard about Poles who had been drowned in the Barents Sea, or imprisoned in Franz Josef Land or Komi. Gen. Zygmunt Szyszko-Bohusz added Kamchatka to this list.[258] Everyone who expressed an opinion on the subject referred to remote places somewhere in the Far North, far away from human settlement – places which were hard of access and from which it seemed virtually inconceivable to return. Perhaps this kind of reasoning was applied to keep hope alive and hold off the moment of truth – the bitter truth for all the people of Poland. Though Tadeusz Kiersnowski had no illusions: "yet one thing is clear about it all (...) that alas these people are no longer alive, and maybe one day history will clear up the mystery and explain where and how they gave their lives."[259]

The Poles saw to it that the effects of their searches were passed on to their closest allies. In February 1942, acting on instructions from Gen. Anders, Józef Czapski paid a visit to the British military mission in Moscow. Following the

---

[256] *Ibid.*, 21.

[257] T. Kiersnowski, *Moje spostrzeżenia o Rosji Sowieckiej (1940–1942)*, Introduction by P. Łossowski, (Warszawa: Wydawnictwo DiG, 1997), 33.

[258] Z. Szyszko-Bohusz, *Czerwony sfinks*, (Roma: Polski Dom Wydawniczy, 1945), 102.

[259] Kiersnowski, *Moje spostrzeżenia o Rosji Sowieckiej (1940–1942)*, 33.

meeting, during which Czapski was explicit that his endeavors had foundered chiefly in his talks with the NKVD, the British must certainly have had enough to go by to build up an opinion of the nature of the problem. A member of the mission's staff dispatched a note to London, putting it quite plainly: "There is not the slightest doubt that the N.K.V.D. must (?know) what has happened to these Poles as the most detailed nominal rolls and information are kept up at every concentration camp and prison."[260] Over the next few months Stanisław Kot, the Polish ambassador to the Soviet Union, would bring up the subject of the missing POWs on several occasions in his talks with the British. He sought their diplomatic assistance. In May of 1942 Archibald Clark Kerr, the British ambassador in Moscow, notified Whitehall that the Poles had asked for help with finding out what had happened to over eight thousand officers who had still not been traced. However, Foreign Secretary Anthony Eden did not issue consent for the British Embassy in the Soviet Union to support the search. As Jacek Tebinka has observed, in the opinion of Whitehall the solution to the problem lay entirely with the Poles and the Russians.[261] Yet the intention was to return to the matter as soon as possible. An opportunity arose when Molotov visited Britain and the USA. The British decided to examine the matter in the Soviet Union, and appointed Col. Leslie Hulls of the War Office to handle it. In June, October, and December of 1942 Hulls drafted three memoranda on the condition of the Polish army in the Soviet Union. He traveled to Yangiyul to conduct a thorough examination. He recorded the number of soldiers in the Polish army, their weapons and equipment, and the conditions in which the men were living, with temperatures going down to $-45°C$ ($-47°F$). Naturally, he presented his position on the question of the missing officers. Those confined in Kozelsk, Starobielsk, and Ostashkov, a total of 8,300, had disappeared

---

[260] J. Tebinka, 'Dyplomacja brytyjska wobec sprawy katyńskiej w latach 1943–1945,' in *Z dziejów Polski i emigracji (1939–1989). Księga dedykowana byłemu Prezydentowi Rzeczypospolitej Polskiej Ryszardowi Kaczorowskiemu*, M. Szczerbiński and T. Wolsza, eds. (Gorzów Wielkopolski: IKF, 2003), 453. See also J. Tebinka, „*Wielka Brytania dotrzyma lojalnie swojego słowa". Winston Churchill a Polska*, (Warszawa: Wydawnictwo Neriton, 2013), chapter entitled 'Katyń,' 134–148. Transcript of British cipher telegram, 5 Feb. 1942, from 30 Military Mission Moscow to The War Office. MIL 2706 cipher 2/2. Public Record Office Kew, FO 371/31078, C1370/19/55. Cited after Tebinka, 'Dyplomacja brytyjska,' 453. The translator is grateful to Professor Tebinka for providing a photograph of the original document.

[261] Tebinka, 'Dyplomacja brytyjska,' 453. British diplomatic correspondence cited after Tebinka.

without trace. No-one had heard of them since 1940, and despite the promise Stalin made personally to General Sikorski and General Anders what had happened to these officer was still a complete mystery.[262] Hulls' reports gave the British an insight into the matter, but brought no changes to their behavior. The British and Americans trod very cautiously in this respect – until the events of April 1943 triggered an international discussion on the fate of the Polish officers missing since 1940, a discussion badly needed in 1941.

APRIL 1943

The Germans started the first exhumations at Koziy Gory already on February 18, 1943. They seem to have been unaware as yet of the scale of the occurrence, and perhaps they were not sure what they were dealing with. To be on the safe side, they were careful not to spread too much news of the matter. They only launched their largescale operation on March 28, 1943. At this time no-one in the Polish émigré community in London was still pursuing the matter of the Polish officers missing in the Soviet Union. It was the German radio broadcast on April 11, followed by another broadcast on the night of the twelfth and thirteenth, that set off the avalanche. In President Władysław Raczkiewicz's office a note dated April 13 said: "News – morning: the Germans find grave of 11,000 Poles murdered by the Bolsheviks near Smolensk. Evening: details from Germany." On the next day the following note was entered in the President's diary: "Further details on the discovery of the grave of Poles near Smolensk. The auxiliary bishop of Kraków has set off for the site. The Germans have summoned (...) a Spanish commission."[263]

On April 15 *Dziennik Polski* published the first article on the subject. It was front-page news and the headline was 'Sprawa zaginionych oficerów polskich. Huraganowy ogień propagandy niemieckiej – nakaz ujawnienia prawdy Kozielska i Starobielska' (The Missing Polish Officers: A Barrage of German Propaganda. A Call for the Truth about Kozelsk and Starobielsk). In the morning British Prime Minister Winston Churchill received Gen. Sikorski and Edward Raczyński, Polish Ambassador to Great Britain. The news broadcast by

[262] Maresch, *Katyń 1940*, 34.

[263] *Dziennik czynności Prezydenta RP Władysława Raczkiewicza 1939–1947*, vol. 2, ed. J. Piotrowski, (Wrocław: Wydawnictwo Uniwersytetu Wrocławskiego, 2004), 54–55.

Radio Berlin was one of the items on a busy agenda for discussion.[264] During the meeting Raczyński gave Churchill a memorandum with information on the disappearance of 7–9 thousand officers and 8 thousand policemen, gendarmes, prosecutors, judges, doctors etc. in the Soviet Union. An annex was attached to the document, with a list of the names of 4,664 missing officers, including 12 generals (Mieczysław Smorawiński and others), and 94 colonels. The detailed nature of the document left Churchill impressed, since on receiving it he responded that the German disclosure could well be true, unfortunately. He knew what the Bolsheviks were capable of and how cruel they could be, he was perfectly aware of that and appreciated the numerous difficulties the Poles had been having. He shared many of their opinions, yet no other policy was possible. It was his government's duty to save the fundamental aims the British had set themselves and to serve them as efficiently as they could.[265] The position of the British authorities was clear. They knew who had committed the crime. But because of their wartime priorities and international alliances they did not intend to press the matter in order to keep the coalition against Hitler united.

On the same day the Polish government decided to refer the matter to the International Red Cross through the services of its diplomatic outpost in Berne (Switzerland). The note was delivered by Stanisław Albrecht Radziwiłł on behalf of the Polish government. Thereby the Polish Red Cross was faster than the German Red Cross, which handed in its note later. A few days later Adam Ronikier, head of the RGO in occupied Poland, sent a telegram to Geneva requesting the International Red Cross to initiate an investigation on the site of the atrocity.[266]

On April 16 the Polish Ministry of National Defense issued a statement. The Minister, Gen. Marian Kukiel, demanded an investigation on the site of the atrocity, presenting the following arguments on behalf of Poland: "We are used to the lies disseminated by German propaganda and we realize what

---

[264] W. Materski, 'Zerwanie stosunków polsko-sowieckich,' in *Historia dyplomacji polskiej*, vol. 5: *1939–1945*, ed. W. Michowicz, (Warszawa: Instytut Historii PAN, 1999), 374.

[265] *Na najwyższym szczeblu. Spotkania premierów Rzeczypospolitej Polskiej i Wielkiej Brytanii podczas II wojny światowej*, M.K. Kamiński and J. Tebinka, eds., Polish translation of English documents by Iwona Sakowicz, (Warszawa: Wydawnictwo LTW, 1999), 84.

[266] Ronikier, *Pamiętniki 1939–1945*, 235.

the aim of its recent revelations is. Nevertheless, in view of the detailed information broadcast by the Germans concerning the discovery of the bodies of thousands of Polish officers in the neighborhood of Smolensk, and in light of their categorical declaration that these men were murdered by the Soviets in the spring of 1940 – it is necessary to examine the mass graves which have been discovered, and for the appropriate international institutions such as the International Red Cross to establish the facts (...)."[267] Gen. Kukiel's official statement shows that he must have considered the German radio broadcast trustworthy. The Polish government was aware of the significance of the statement and of the consequences it could bring about. Years later Edward Raczyński said, "At any rate, when I got the communiqué, I made a few alterations, not to mitigate the sense, but the form, as I realized the Soviets would use it as a pretext for moves against us."[268]

On April 17, 1943, Gen. Władysław Sikorski, Chairman of the Council of Ministers (viz. the Polish Prime Minister), called an extraordinary cabinet meeting, which was attended by Ministers Stanisław Mikołajczyk, Gen. Józef Haller, Henryk Strasburger, Karol Popiel, Marian Seyda, Stanisław Kot, Jan Kwapiński, Edward Raczyński, and Gen. Marian Kukiel. The Prime Minister gave an account of his meeting with Winston Churchill. Next he asked the members of the cabinet to adopt a four-point resolution on the Katyn atrocity. His postulates were as follows: to issue a communiqué on the murder of the officers, to dispatch a diplomatic note to the Soviet government, to send a request to Pope Pius XII to take up the matter, and to issue a directive to the Government's Delegate in Poland to establish a united policy and procedure. The Prime Minister invited Minister Wacław Komarnicki, one of the very few POWs to have survived Kozelsk, to attend the meeting and deliver

---

[267] *Zbrodnia katyńska w świetle dokumentów*, 88. Somewhat earlier Gen. Marian Kukiel telegraphed Gen. Władysław Anders, asking him to collect information on the search for the Polish officers in the Soviet Union. Anders replied on April 15, saying that the Soviet authorities had been hedging over giving an answer to the Poles' questions. He added that the suggestions concerning Kolyma, Novaya Zemlya, and Franz Josef Land had not been confirmed; furthermore, the volunteers sent out there to verify this version had not returned. He finished by saying, "In fact not one of the 8,300 officers from Kozelsk and Starobielsk, or of the 4,000 gendarmerie and police NCOs from the Ostashkov camp has joined the army." *Zbrodnia katyńska 1940. Polacy w Wielkiej Brytanii wobec ludobójstwa katyńskiego 1943–1989*, 17.

[268] E. Raczyński and T. Żenczykowski, *Od Genewy do Jałty. Rozmowy radiowe*, (London: Puls, 1988), 70.

an account of what he knew about the circumstances in which officers had been removed from Kozelsk.[269] This was, of course, not the only information available to the cabinet on the POWs at Kozelsk and the site, time and circumstances of the atrocity. Reports compiled by a handful of Poles who had seen the site of the atrocity on the German invitation on April 10–11 and 14–15, 1943 had been successively reaching the Polish émigré community in London.[270] Some of these witnesses had been granted permission to travel to the site by the Polish Underground State or by institutions such as the Polish Red Cross and the RGO which the Germans recognized as legal. Katyn reports of this kind were submitted by Ferdynand Goetel, Edmund Seyfried, Kazimierz Skarżyński, and Father Stanisław Jasiński on their return home to Warsaw or Kraków. Col. Stefan Mossor, one of the members of the POW delegation the Germans brought to the site on April 17, 1943, also delivered a report.[271] Secret units of the Polish Underground State were sending clandestine radio reports to London as best they could.[272] Presumably prior to April 17, the day of the extraordinary cabinet meeting, the information available to its ministers which had come in from Poland and foreign statements was very fragmentary. It was only after a few days, in late April 1943, that Lt.-Col. Michał Protasewicz managed to draw up a fairly detailed bulletin for Gen. Sikorski, the Commander-in-Chief, with information on the delegations from the GG which had been to Katyn.[273] He listed the names of the members of the delegations, gave an account of their stay on the site, described the technique used for the executions (a shot in the back of the head), and quoted the conclusion of

---

[269] *Protokoły posiedzeń Rady Ministrów Rzeczypospolitej Polskiej*, vol. 5: *Wrzesień 1942–lipiec 1943*, M. Zgórniak, W. Rojek, and A. Suchcitz, (eds.), (Kraków: Secesja, 2001), 384.

[270] Madajczyk, *Dramat katyński*, 36–40; Wolsza, „*Katyń to już na zawsze katy i katowani*", 32–34.

[271] Toczewski, 'Raport ppłk. dypl. Stefana Mossora,' 77–85.

[272] S. Korboński, *Polskie Państwo Podziemne. Przewodnik po Podziemiu z lat 1939–1945*, (Paris: Instytut Literacki, 1975), 150.

[273] The telegram of April 18, 1943 sent to London from occupied Poland contained a brief note on the first delegation's Katyn visit. On April 19, 1943 Gen. Stefan Grot-Rowecki dispatched news of the visit by Goetel and the Polish Red Cross, with information that there were Polish officers' graves there, and that the Germans had identified scores of bodies. *Zbrodnia katyńska 1940. Polacy w Wielkiej Brytanii*, 21. According to Janusz Zawodny, the first radiogram reached London on April 22, 1943, and the next ones on May 7 and 13. He also writes of Gen. Anders' ciphertext of April 15, 1943, Zawodny, *Katyń 1940*, 37, 48.

Kazimierz Skarżyński's report, that the documents found on the bodies show that the murders were done in March and April of 1940.[274] A few days later Protasewicz compiled another document, this time on the basis of information from the reports which had come in from Poland. We may assume that by this time the data which reached London were the first-hand documents drawn up by delegates who had traveled from the GG to Smolensk. Interestingly, Protasewicz juxtaposed the Katyn atrocity with extermination operations the Germans were carrying out on the Polish population: "The German propaganda is making very efficient use of the Katyn atrocity in the press and broadcasting news of it on loudspeakers, trying to turn Polish public opinion against the Soviets, against the Allies and the Polish Government. The reaction of the people of Poland has been anger against the Bolsheviks, but at the same time the recollection that the Germans have perpetrated similar murders."[275]

Another source of invaluable information for the Polish government was the press – not only the German papers, where the atrocity was obviously front-page news and the coverage very extensive.[276] On April 9 and 10 the Germans hosted a group of journalists from Spain, Switzerland, Sweden, and a few of the occupied countries, in Smolensk and on the site.[277] The group included political commentators and photojournalists, some of them from France, which in view of the proximity of Britain may have been important from the aspect of information transfer, particularly of the photographic images. A few days later journalists working for the reptile press in the GG (*Nowy Kurier Warszawski*, *Goniec Krakowski*, *Nowy Głos Lubelski*, and the Telpress agency) arrived in Smolensk and saw the site. Prior to April 17, 1943 neither the underground resistance organizations in occupied Poland nor the government-in-exile could have had access to photographs of the site made by Polish observers (apart from the images published in the reptiles). Yet on the other hand the émigrés in London would have had information on Katyn obtained from France, Spain, Switzerland, and Sweden.

---

[274] *Ibid.*, 51.

[275] *Ibid.*, 40.

[276] P. Łysakowski, 'Prasa niemiecka o Katyniu. Jak niemiecka propaganda przedstawiała w 1943 r. sprawę mordu popełnionego na polskich oficerach,' in *Katyń. Problemy i zagadki*, ed. J. Jackl, (Warszawa: PoMOST, 1990), 88–114.

[277] Madajczyk, *Dramat katyński,* 37.

Once the Polish government had a certain amount of information on what had happened in the spring of 1940, its ministers set up a special commission consisting of Stanisław Kot, Gen. Marian Kukiel, and Edward Raczyński to investigate the Katyn atrocity. The Polish government also announced that May 3, 1943 would be a day of prayer "for our brothers who have been murdered during this war, wherever and at whoever's cruel hands they happened to fall victim."[278] And finally it drafted a press communiqué to calm incensed emotions and call the people of Poland to refrain from passing overhasty judgments. This document says, "There is not a single Polish person who has not been thoroughly appalled at the news disseminated by the German propaganda as loudly as possible, of the discovery near Smolensk of a mass grave with the massacred bodies of Polish officers missing in the Soviet Union, and of the bloodbath of which they were victims. On April 15 this year the Polish Government instructed its representative in Switzerland to request the International Red Cross in Geneva to send a delegation to examine the true state of affairs on the site."[279] In the next part of the communiqué the Polish government declared that the Germans had no right to exploit the atrocity for propaganda purposes: "The absolutely hypocritical anger voiced by German propaganda cannot obscure from the world's view the cruel, recurrently perpetrated and continuing crimes the Germans have committed against the Polish Nation."[280] There followed a list of German atrocities: Majdanek and Treblinka (misspelled in the original document), the deportation of Poles for slave labor, and the forced conscription of Polish men into the Wehrmacht. The government started to keep an eye on public utterances on Katyn, and even Bishop Józef Gawlina was not immune from censure for his "irresponsible statements." It was also decided that *Dziennik Polski*, the paper regarded as the mouthpiece of the Polish government, should remove "anything written in an aggressive vein" from its articles.[281] An example of this way of thinking is presented in the anonymous article signed with the initials St. Sz., which says, "We Poles are endeavoring by sheer willpower not to yield to the inevitable

---

[278] *Protokoły posiedzeń Rady Ministrów*, 385.

[279] *Ibid.*, 386.

[280] *Ibid.*

[281] *Ibid.*, 389.

suspicions, which could evoke an emotional reaction urging us to pass judgment on criminals who have not yet been identified."[282] Gen. Anders did not expressly name the perpetrators, either. At a memorial service in Baghdad, in an address to Polish soldiers who had been held in Soviet labor camps, he spoke of the suffering the people of Poland were going through at home in an occupied country, and on their compatriots who were still in the Soviet Union: "Always remember that we still have hundreds of thousands of our people out there, in the Soviet Union, hundreds of thousands of starving children (...) . Atrocity upon atrocity is being committed, yet I deeply believe, as I see you before me, that justice shall always win in the end, and that our Polish cause, which is so pure, so true, and so right, shall be victorious, despite the losses, despite the blood which has already been shed in each of our families, and that we shall achieve our aim."[283]

But on the other hand the Polish government did not manage to impose its control on the editors of *Wiadomości Polskie*, a London-based weekly which published an obituary by Zygmunt Nowakowski, who blamed the Soviets outright, in defiance of the government's recommendation of restraint. "The situation of our true allies," he wrote, "is not at all easy. On the contrary, it will be extremely troublesome, but that cannot force us to keep silent, neither does it permit us to conceal the dreadful truth, or even to pretend that we are not clear about the matter. Because it is clear to us already, while our allies will have their misgivings for a while. Because they, people who live in a civilized world, yet far removed from Russia, cannot comprehend the sense and the aim of the atrocity. For this atrocity lies beyond the scope of the normal person's imagination. And it is even harder to bring to light [the logic behind it]."[284] As Rafał Habielski, a historian of Polish émigré journalism, has observed, Zygmunt Nowakowski's article in *Wiadomości Polskie* – to my mind clear enough in its intent – still showed tell-tale signs of the British censor's interference.[285] Unsurprisingly, it was well received by the GG reptiles.

---

[282] St. Sz., 'Nad grobami polskich żołnierzy,' *Dziennik Polski* 1943: 854 (Apr. 22), 3.

[283] Quoted after *Zbrodnia katyńska 1940. Polacy w Wielkiej Brytanii*, 24.

[284] Z. Nowakowski, 'Castrum Doloris,' *Wiadomości Polskie* 1943: 18 (May 2), 1.

[285] R. Habielski, *Niezłomni, nieprzejednani. Emigracyjne „Wiadomości" i ich krąg 1940–1981* (Warszawa: Państwowy Instytut Wydawniczy, 1991), 52.

11. 'The Wedge,' a David Low cartoon (1943). Ribbentrop drives a wedge held up by Gen. Sikorski into British–Russian–American unity. Originally published in *Punch*.

Notwithstanding the clear and logical tactics the government adopted, it also made a serious mistake. Its diplomatic note on the German disclosure to the Soviet government, which was ready on April 17, only reached Ambassador Aleksandr Bogomolov three days later. After a few days the Soviets turned this fact to their advantage. On April 21 Stalin sent a letter to Churchill accusing Gen. Sikorski's government of collaborating with the Third Reich. It was a clear allusion to the two separate requests addressed to the International Red Cross, one by Poland and the other by Germany. Stalin simply put them together. Moreover, he notified Churchill that he had decided to break off diplomatic relations with Poland.[286] Churchill

---

[286] Tebinka, 'Dyplomacja brytyjska,' 455.

was informed of the Soviet position two days later. His reaction was firm: at this point in time he took the Polish side.[287]

The émigré community passed the following days waiting for the decision of the International Red Cross. It came fairly soon, already on April 22, though Germany got its decision earlier. *Dziennik Polski* published a series of recollections by people who had been through Soviet camps. Władysław Jan Furtek published his memories, entitled *Byłem jeńcem w Kozielsku* (I was a prisoner-of-war in Kozelsk).[288] However, we should note that there was a distinct tendency in the Polish press and in the official statements at the time to inhibit anti-Soviet attacks. The Polish government was counting on Britain to support its position and expecting an International Red Cross commission to travel to Katyn. Briefly speaking, it did not want to provoke the Soviets.

On April 24 there was a "last chance" meeting, as I think it could be called, between Anthony Eden and Władysław Sikorski. Eden informed Sikorski about Stalin's letter to Churchill and put forward a way to deflate the crisis, proposing two matters on Churchill's behalf. First, he suggested Poland withdraw its request to the International Red Cross. And second, he urged Sikorski's government to say the Germans were culpable for the Katyn massacre. Sikorski categorically refused, arguing that "Russia had power on its side, while justice was on Poland's side."[289] A day later the Soviet Union broke off diplomatic relations with the Polish government. Molotov wrote in a diplomatic note that Poland's conduct should be recognized as execrable: "The German Fascists have propagated a campaign of slander against the Soviet Union in connection with the mass murder of Polish officers, which they themselves committed in the neighborhood of Smolensk on territories occupied by German forces. The Polish Government immediately joined in this campaign, which has been

---

[287] *Ibid.*

[288] I have discussed this aspect in greater detail elsewhere. T. Wolsza, 'GUŁag z polskiej perspektywy emigracyjnej 1939–1956,' in *Sowiecki system obozów i więzień. Przykłady wybranych państw*, ed. J. Bednarek, (Łódź: Instytut Pamięci Narodowej – Komisja Ścigania Zbrodni przeciwko Narodowi Polskiemu. 2013), 111–131.

[289] M. Hułas, 'Rząd Władysława Sikorskiego czerwiec 1940 – lipiec 1943,' in *Władze RP na obczyźnie podczas II wojny światowej*, ed. Z. Błażyński, (London: Polskie Towarzystwo Naukowe na Obczyźnie, 1994), 228. See also M. Dymarski, *Stosunki wewnętrzne wśród polskiego wychodźstwa politycznego i wojskowego we Francji i w Wielkiej Brytanii 1939–1945*, (Wrocław: Wydawnictwo Uniwersytetu Wrocławskiego, 1999), 273–279.

conducted in the official Polish press. Far from repudiating the mean Fascist libel against the Soviet Union, the Polish Government did not even deem it necessary to put a request or a demand to the Soviet Union to examine and explain the matter."[290] Naturally enough, Tadeusz Romer, Poland's ambassador to the Soviet Union, declared this completely untruthful note inadmissible. As he wound up his diplomatic mission, he "firmly denied these groundless accusations against our honor as an ally and refused to accept a diplomatic note proffered in that spirit." He tried to "keep calm and make a public declaration that we were still on the same side, fighting to the end against Germany, and to safeguard the future of the Polish deportees who were still in Russia."[291] A few days later the Polish government issued another statement denouncing the Third Reich for exploiting the Katyn atrocity for its propaganda purposes, and countered the Soviet allegations against Poland's trustworthiness. Sikorski's government denied the Soviet insinuations that Poland had made no attempt to ask the Soviet authorities to investigate and elucidate the Katyn affair. The Poles said that they had sent a diplomatic note to Ambassador Bogomolov. They also had several other cogent facts in their favor – the negotiations which had been conducted in the Kremlin between Sikorski, Anders, and Kot with Stalin and Molotov. So Ambassador Romer's reaction turned out to be fully warranted. The British response was just as clear: henceforth His Majesty's government sided with the Soviets.

The following entry was made on the matter in President Raczkiewicz's official diary for April 26, 1943: "British radio broadcast on the Soviets breaking off relations with Poland. The government's nine o'clock evening news said that the Soviet Government had broken off relations with Poland because the Poles had alleged the Soviets had murdered the Polish officers. The news bulletin said that that the officers were murdered by the Germans."[292] A couple of days later Churchill apologized to Stalin for the Polish publications on Katyn which had come out in Britain and assured him that the press would be "called to order." He also stated his position on the Polish application to the International Red Cross, explaining that the Poles had not informed the British government that they

---

[290] *Zbrodnia katyńska w świetle dokumentów*, 91.

[291] T. Romer, 'Moja misja jako ambasadora RP w Związku Sowieckim,' *Zeszyty Historyczne* 30 (Paris, 1974), 163.

[292] *Dziennik czynności Prezydenta RP*, 58.

intended to do this, hence the British could not have warned them of the risk the decision to take such a course would involve.[293] Churchill's dispatch of May 10, 1943 left the Poles with no illusions. They had been definitively left on their own regarding an investigation to elucidate the circumstances of the Katyn atrocity, albeit there were a few in the British' political sphere who were still engaged in the matter, with a considerable amount of commitment. Sir Owen O'Malley, British ambassador to the Polish government, wrote a memorandum endorsing the Polish point of view on Soviet guilt for the Katyn murder. The document was sent to Churchill, Eden, and Sir Alexander Cadogan. It is self-evident that O'Malley's report was classified information. No-one identified in public with his position on the matter. On August 13, 1943 Churchill ordered a copy sent to the President of the USA.[294] But it did not bring about any change in the American view of the matter, either, all the more so, as the Roosevelt administration had already formed its opinion on Polish–Soviet relations.[295] The mission of the American diplomat Joseph Davies to Moscow in May shows unequivocally that the United States wanted to have friendly relations with the Kremlin, and Katyn could simply have wrecked them.

In the first days of May 1943 the Polish government-in-exile continued to focus a lot of attention on the Katyn issue. The whole of one of its special sessions concerned the atrocity and the Soviet severance of diplomatic relations. Alongside all the members of the government, the meeting was attended by Professor Stanisław Grabski, chairman of the National Council (Rada Narodowa). The Prime Minister gave an account of the British position on the developments, saying that they had recommended a crackdown on the press, and in particular stiffer censorship on articles which touched on Polish–Soviet relations. The Polish government had issued a strong protest against this. On the other hand it saw a need to have a representative working with the British censorship office.[296] During this and its next meeting three days later the Polish

---

[293] Maresch, *Katyń 1940*, 42.

[294] *Ibid.*, 45.

[295] Cytowska-Siegrist, *Stany Zjednoczone i Polska 1939–1945*, 212–218. Also E. Cytowska-Siegrist, 'W rocznicę ujawnienia zbrodni katyńskiej. Na marginesie publikacji amerykańskich dokumentów dotyczących sprawy Katynia,' *Dzieje Najnowsze* 2013: 3,147–169; *Katyn: A Crime Without Punishment*, 220–221.

[296] *Protokoły posiedzeń Rady Ministrów*, 418–419.

government compiled a set of rules defining tactics to handle Polish–Soviet relations in political negotiations with foreign entities (*Instrukcja wewnętrzna w sprawie zasad naszej taktyki w sprawach polsko-sowieckich w rozmowach politycznych na zewnątrz*). This document addressed territorial disputes, the army, Poles deported to the Soviet Union, and Katyn. The government recapitulated all the main developments in the search for the Polish soldiers missing in the Soviet Union: "From the very outset, following the restoration of Polish–Soviet relations, the Polish government had been making a continuous effort to find and save the nearly 15,000 missing (...) prisoners-of-war, including 8,300 officers."[297] *Instrukcja* went on to state that the Soviet authorities had never given the Poles a clear-cut answer on this point. The Polish government queried the International Red Cross' decision not to send a mission to the site of the Katyn atrocity, following the Soviet refusal to admit such a mission. Finally *Instrukcja* concluded with a paragraph on German intentions: "We must not conceal the fact that Germany has been exploiting the Katyn question and the circumstances attending it not only to weaken the Polish resolve to fight, and to discredit the Soviet Union, but also to undermine the faith the nations have put in Britain and the sincerity of the principles it proclaims."[298]

The Polish émigré community closely followed the work of the International Medical Commission headed by Professor Gerhard Buhtz from Breslau. Polish exiles in London knew not only the partial results of the medical examination, but also the conclusions arrived at by the medical experts, which indicated that the Soviets were to blame for the Katyn atrocity. A full list was drawn up of the internationally renowned specialists who had served as members of the Commission and whose professional authority offered a guarantee of the reliability of their work. And it was no coincidence that when the War was over the Polish government-in-exile kept track of what happened to the Czech František Hájek, Marko Markov from Bulgaria, Ferenc Orsós from Hungary, the Slovak František Šubík, and the Swiss expert François Naville – those of the doctors in the Commission from countries which found themselves in the Soviet sphere of influence, or who were in jeopardy for various other reasons.

---

[297] *Ibid.*, 432.

[298] *Ibid.*, 433.

THE POLISH REACTION TO THE RESULTS
OF THE BURDENKO COMMISSION

In outcome of the Red Army's offensive launched in mid-1943 the Germans left the environs of Smolensk, and Katyn Village and Wood came under Soviet control. With the memory of Goebbels' propaganda campaign still fresh in their minds, the Soviets decided to set up a commission of their own to examine the circumstances of the atrocity, which as a result of Germany's doings had been attributed up to that time to the NKVD. Moreover, the Soviets were encumbered with their refusal to allow access to Katyn to the International Red Cross, which had intended to send in a special commission to the site.

Quite obviously, then, a Soviet commission could not expect help from foreign experts. The supreme authorities of the Soviet Union knew very well who was guilty of the crime, hence they decided to entrust the duties incumbent on a commission to medical practitioners and propagandists from the Soviet Union with a small contribution from a few Polish Communists ready to endorse any version Stalin and his associates cared to propose. Wanda Wasilewska and Jerzy Borejsza, generally regarded in émigré circles as agents of the NKVD, renegades and traitors to Poland, took part in the Soviet farce, bringing utter ignominy upon themselves.[299]

The results reached by the Burdenko Commission were by no means unplanned. One by one it refuted the arguments put forward by Professor Buhtz's group, applying a diversity of scientifically questionable methods. The Soviets emulated the Germans by giving a bogus number of victims – 11 thousand. They conjured up new camps, in which they said the Poles were detained after April 1940, right up to June 1941, again not coincidentally, because of course that was when Germany invaded the Soviet Union, and hence the invaders murdered the Polish POWs. It all fitted in neatly – according to Burdenko's men – giving a logical story. Naturally enough, they discovered new witnesses of the events, having dismissed the statements of those who testified in the spring of 1943, calling them untrustworthy and traitors to the Soviet

---

[299] T. Wolsza, *Rząd RP na obczyźnie wobec wydarzeń w kraju 1945–1950*, (Warszawa: Wydawnictwo DiG, 1998), 130. See also J.K. Kwiatkowski, *Komuniści w Polsce. Rodowód – Taktyka – Ludzie*, (Brussels: Polski Instytut Wydawniczy, 1946).

Union. Despite the broad scope of Burdenko's activities, few gave credence to his revelations. In an overall assessment of the work of Nikolai Burdenko's Commission, Wojciech Materski made the apt observation that it played "the role of a façade, formulating what had been cooked up earlier by Kruglov and Merkulov's *opertivniki*. A comparison of the 'preliminary investigation' drawn up by the NKVD and NKGB (the People's Commissariat for State Security) with the text of the communiqué closing the Special Commission's work shows a far-reaching congruence in the structure of the documents as well as in their conclusions."[300] As soon as the Commission had compiled its final communiqué its text was published in the leading Soviet newspapers, especially *Pravda* and *Izvestia*, which were in the vanguard of the official Soviet storyline and the anti-Polish theme of its propaganda campaign. The British leader in this respect was *The Daily Worker*, which claimed that the results obtained by the Burdenko Commission would restore the Soviet government's reputation and discredit the Polish government.[301]

As soon as the Burdenko Commission had completed its task, the Soviets followed the German example and sent in some Polish delegations to the Katyn site. In January of 1944 there was a visit by General Zygmunt Berling and soldiers of his First Infantry Division. A military parade was held. As Joanna Żelazko has aptly observed, "it was a gesture intended to lend credence, especially in the eyes of world opinion, to the Soviet claim that it was the Germans who were guilty of the murder of the Polish officers."[302] The Communists followed up these events with a propaganda publication entitled *Prawda o Katyniu* (The Truth about Katyn), which came out in Moscow in 1944.

The Polish émigrés in London assiduously recorded everything that appeared on Katyn and commented on it, albeit very frugally. The Polish government had made an appeal for Poles to follow the example of the British press and refrain from making public statements on the matter.[303] But in a remark not intended for the media Minister Tadeusz Romer said, "The new Soviet

---

[300] Materski, 'Z początków wojny propagandowej wokół zbrodni katyńskiej,' 27.

[301] Maresch, *Katyń 1940*, 218.

[302] J. Żelazko, 'Pamięć i propaganda. Sprawa Katynia po 1945 r.,' in *Represje sowieckie wobec narodów Europy*, 399.

[303] *Protokoły posiedzeń Rady Ministrów*, 390.

arguments are not convincing."[304] The Polish papers in the British Isles, which hitherto had not avoided making assessments of the documents relating to the Katyn atrocity, this time maintained a meaningful silence. *Dziennik Polski i Dziennik Żołnierza* only published a summary of the Burdenko report. At the end of the article it added that the authors of the Soviet document had put the Katyn massacre into the context of several atrocities committed by the Germans at Orlo, Voronezh, Krasnodar, and in the Polesie region.[305] As Habielski writes, this editorial policy was due to concern for the paper's future. The recalcitrant *Wiadomości Polskie*, which had defied the British authorities, had been suspended because of its articles on the Soviet Union.[306] A laconic note found its way into President Raczkiewicz's official diary of events, "Soviet radio has broadcast news that a commission has been set up to investigate the Polish officers' murder by the Germans at Katyn."[307] Raczkiewicz never returned to the subject again, since the perpetrators of the crime were overtly and unambiguously named at the very outset of the investigation. Moreover, he acquiesced to pressure from the British not to evoke any further inflammatory matters of contention among the Allies, and was extremely circumspect and reticent about pointing a finger at the Soviets. Tebinka has given an elegant explication of the issue: "whereas British diplomacy wanted to hush up the matter as much as possible, the Kremlin did its best to exonerate itself." And he adds, "One of the items on the Soviet agenda was to invite a group of Moscow-based Western diplomats and journalists to come to Katyn round about January 21, 1944. Britain's diplomats did not participate in the project, unlike Kathleen Harriman, the daughter of the American ambassador, and John F. Melby, third secretary of the US embassy, both of whom came away convinced that the Germans had done it. But most of the British and American journalists had reservations, not to say they were skeptical about the Soviet claim.[308] This was because they felt

---

[304] *Ibid.*, 389.

[305] 'Raport komisji sowieckiej o Polakach zamordowanych w Katyniu,' *Dziennik Polski i Dziennik Żołnierza* 1944: 22 (Jan. 27), 1, 4.

[306] Habielski, *Niezłomni, nieprzejednani,* 58.

[307] *Dziennik czynności Prezydenta RP,* 212.

[308] This attitude is evident in Minister John Balfour's report from Moscow, in which he wrote that some of the correspondents considered insufficient evidence had been produced to prove that the victims had been murdered after 1941. Maresch, *Katyń 1940,* 222.

that the excursion was an attempt to bribe them. Never before during the War had an excursion been organized for journalists in the Soviet Union with such splendor – luxury railcars, good cuisine and drinks (...)."[309] The most concise way of summing up British policy on the Katyn affair and the Polish government would be to say it was an attempt to get the Poles to accept the conclusions of the Soviet commission and try once more to embark on talks with Stalin. "The old grievances are festering. We hope that the publication of this report on what happened at Katyn will help the Polish government to put aside those grievances and find grounds for a reconciliation with Moscow, because – as the London-based *Dziennik Polski* recently observed – our enemy may benefit from the present crisis in Russian–Polish relations."[310] In late January 1944 General Kukiel, Minister for Military Affairs, sent a circular to Polish diplomatic outposts with instructions on how (not) to make public statements on Katyn. The circular reached the hands of Polish soldiers, including internees in Switzerland. Kukiel wrote that the Polish government had not been able to conduct an on-site investigation. The International Red Cross had not undertaken this task, either. The Polish government had never officially named the Soviet Union as the perpetrator culpable for the atrocity, he continued, but on the other hand it had insisted that "over ten thousand Polish POWs had died in Soviet captivity." As regards the Soviet allegations against the Germans, his recommendation was to hedge the question.[311]

Nonetheless, contrary to the wishes of Britain and the United States, the Polish authorities continued steadfastly in their endeavors to get an explanation for what had happened at Katyn. The next installment of their struggle to get the Soviet Union recognized internationally as the party guilty of the Katyn massacre started after a short lull once hostilities were over.

After the War Boris Olshanskiy, a fugitive from the Red Army, passed on an important piece of information to the Poles, namely that Stalin had personally appointed General Nikolai Burdenko, surgeon-general of the Red Army, to head the commission and had laid down what its results would be even before the commission started its work. Burdenko is reputed to have said that Stalin

---

[309] Tebinka, *Dyplomacja brytyjska*, 459.

[310] *Ibid.*; 'Przegląd prasy,' *Dziennik Polski i Dziennik Żołnierza* 1944: 24 (Jan. 29), 2.

[311] *Zbrodnia katyńska 1940. Polacy w Wielkiej Brytanii*, 53–54.

himself had told him to go to Katyn. "All the corpses were four years old. To me as a medical professional the case was absolutely clear. Our friends from the NKVD had made a mistake."[312]

AFTER THE WAR (1945–1948)

Now the chief task for the Polish government-in-exile and the commanding officers of the Second Corps, who were working on this issue in close co-operation with Tomasz Arciszewski's cabinet, was to assemble as much documentation on Poles in the Soviet Union as they could. The Katyn atrocity was evidently part of this task. As regards the Second Corps, its principal agency working in this field was Office K (Kostar, where the initial K stood for Katyn, and other letters of the acronym for Kozelsk, Ostashkov, and Starobielsk).[313] Eugenia Maresch has written that Kostar's basic aim was to highlight the moral and human aspect of Katyn, without prioritizing the political dimension of the crime. She has also observed that those who participated in this project wanted to collect the records which would one day enable Britain and America conduct an in-depth investigation of the matter. There were two phases in the team's work. In phase one they collected documentary evidence for the Nuremberg Trial. Phase two involved the publication of the records they had assembled.[314] The most active contributors to the project were Marian Heitzman, Alfred Hergesell, Zdzisław Stahl, and Wiktor Sukiennicki.

A side-effect Project Kostar achieved was to accumulate a vast number of records, thousands of statements and questionnaires which made up the Anders Collection. These documents contained a brief account of respondents' arrest by the Soviet authorities, and the timeline of their deportation East, living conditions and slave labor in exile and in the gulags, the circumstances of their release and what happened to them later, once freed. Thanks to this project an invaluable repository of records was created, and later it was used by journalists, scholars, and politicians. It also provided evidence for court proceedings, such as David Rousset's case against the Communist paper *Les*

---

[312] Korboński, *W imieniu Polski walczącej*, 177.

[313] For the Second Corps secret offices, see K. Zamorski, *Dwa tajne biura 2. Korpusu*, (London: Poets and Painters Press, 1990).

[314] Maresch, *Katyń 1940*, 294, 316.

Lettres françaises concerning the Soviet labor camps, which French Communists said did not exist or minimized their criminal nature. Except for the trial of Viktor Kravchenko, it was perhaps the best known court case concerning the Soviet Union and the genocide it had committed on its own citizens as well as people from well-nigh the whole of Europe.[315]

Thanks to the efforts of the Polish government-in-exile and particularly the military commission headed by Dr. Wiktor Sukiennicki, the first publications on the fate of Polish POWs in the Soviet Union in 1939–1941, including documentary records, were in print already by the end of 1945. The principal item was the 450-page volume *Facts and Documents Concerning Polish Prisoners of War Captured by the USSR During the 1939 Campaign*, which also appeared in a Polish-language version.

The Poles also collected statements made by witnesses. After 1945 Ferdynand Goetel, Władysław Kawecki, Kazimierz Skarżyński, Józef Mackiewicz, and Dr. Marian Wodziński, who had all seen the site of the atrocity in 1943 as delegates of the RGO or as journalists, made such statements once they had reached the émigré community in Italy, Germany, or Britain. Some, like Goetel, Jan Emil Skiwski, Władysław Kawecki, and Józef Mackiewicz, reported as soon as they could to the commanding officers of the Second Corps, to clear their names; others such as Kazimierz Skarżyński got to the Polish Guard Company in Germany; while Dr. Marian Wodziński made it straight to the British Isles. Józef Mackiewicz was in deep waters. When he got to Italy he was accused of collaboration and had to stand before a peer tribunal consisting of fellow journalists.[316] He was cleared of the charges. Sergiusz Piasecki, Władysław Studnicki, Zygmunt Jundziłł, Adam Ronikier, and Kazimierz Okulicz all testified in his favor, while a few other witnesses were against him.[317]

---

[315] A.M. Jackowska, 'Polska emigracja polityczna wobec procesów sądowych Wiktora Krawczenki i Davida Rousseta (1949–1951). Przyczynek do historii zimnej wojny,' *Polska 1944/45–1989. Studia i Materiały* 10 (Warszawa, 2011), 61–122.

[316] Malewski (W. Bolecki), *Wyrok na Józefa Mackiewicza*, 80. See also 'List Zygmunta Jundziłła do prezydenta Raczkiewicza,' *Zeszyty Historyczne* 19 (1971), 76–79; K. Jeleński, 'List do Redakcji,' *Kultura* 1957: 10, 151; and Stanek, *Stefan Korboński (1901–1989). Działalność polityczna i społeczna*, 311–320.

[317] Naturally, the court decided to examine Mackiewicz's Katyn visit as well. Bolesław Rutkowski, a witness for the prosecution, testified that on the one hand Mackiewicz's visit to Katyn was suspect, to say the least. Apparently in the Warsaw office of the Government's Home Delegate he had been told to be wary in Mackiewicz's presence. But on the other hand

President Raczkiewicz received Goetel, Skiwski, and Skarżyński, writers and journalists involved in the Katyn affair. Wodziński and Skarżyński delivered their statements at a session of the Polish government-in-exile. The Second Corps archives unit (or actually Goetel) managed to procure an invaluable testimonial from Ivan Krivoziertsev, who had been an eyewitness to the Soviet executions carried out by the NKVD on Polish officers at Katyn in 1940, and after the War got out to Western Europe and found a safe haven with the Second Corps. By this time he was using the alias Michał Łoboda. His later life took a complicated course. He left Italy for Britain and went into hiding. Unfortunately, in November 1947 he died in unexplained circumstances. The British police said it was suicide by hanging, but the Poles did not believe that story.[318]

In 1946, thanks to the endeavors of the Polish government-in-exile and its Ministry of Information and Records, a brochure of several dozen pages entitled *Masowe morderstwo polskich jeńców wojennych w Katyniu* was published,[319] with an English-language version, *The Mass Murder of Polish Prisoners of War in Katyn*, which came out in a fairly large print-run (900 copies).[320] In their conclusion its authors put a series of questions which they believed could help to establish the truth about the Katyn atrocity. Question

---

Mackiewicz had consent from the Home Army's deputy commander for the Wilno region for his visit Katyn and interview for *Goniec Codzienny*. Rutkowski added that in principle the underground authorities did not issue consent for collaboration with the reptile press. He had been told this by one Jerzy Wyszomirski, but later it turned out that after the War Wyszomirski got a job with *Polska Zbrojna*, a paper that came out in Communist Poland. Wiktor Trościanko, the second witness for the prosecution, testified that "everyone in Wilno knew that the Soviets were capable of committing the atrocity, so there was no need to persuade anyone." Next he said that therefore Mackiewicz must have traveled to Katyn on his own initiative. When cross-examined by the accused, Trościanko said that he had heard of the death sentence issued by the PPR against Ferdynand Goetel, but he had never heard of an analogous death sentence on Józef Mackiewicz. Eventually Mackiewicz testified that it was the Germans who had suggested he should travel to Katyn. Instytut Polski i Muzeum Sikorskiego [The Polish Institute and Sikorski Museum [hereafter IPMS], sign. no. Kol. 401/12.

[318] J. Mackiewicz, 'Tajemnicza śmierć Iwana Kriwozercowa, głównego świadka zbrodni katyńskiej,' *Wiadomości* 1952: 15/16 (Apr. 20), 1.

[319] 'Raport Rządu Rzeczypospolitej Polskiej na Uchodźstwie. Masowe morderstwo polskich jeńców wojennych w Katyniu. Londyn 1946 r.,' in *Zbrodnia katyńska 1940. Poszukiwanie prawdy*, 39–96

[320] Zamorski, *Dwa tajne biura*, 257.

no. 2 was "Why were the results of the German Katyn investigation dismissed as untrustworthy, even though it was conducted with the participation of outside persons who had no interest in the outcome, while the results of the Soviet investigation, in which no third parties participated, were deemed reliable?" Question no. 3 was "Why did the Germans not murder the Polish officers they held as prisoners-of-war in large numbers, most of them front line officers including dozens of generals, the majority of whom survived six years in captivity and were freed by the victorious Allied forces? Why would they have made such a dreadful exception for the POWs in Kozelsk, Starobielsk, and Ostashkov, if indeed these POWs were murdered by the Germans?" Question no. 13 was "Why did no-one either in the Soviet Union, in occupied Poland, or abroad, ever hear after April 1940 from or of the Polish officers whose bodies were discovered at Katyn in 1943?"[321]

But the most important development in postwar Europe in connection with the Katyn atrocity was undoubtedly the Nuremberg Trial. As of November 1945 German war criminals were being tried by the Nuremberg Tribunal. In June 1946 news reached the Polish émigrés in London that the Katyn issue would come up in the proceedings, but its scope would be very limited. This was what the Soviets wanted, in order to shift the blame onto the Germans at a cost of as small an effort as possible. General Anders tried to get the tribunal to hear Polish witnesses, primarily Józef Czapski. Members of the Polish government-in-exile tried to get evidence across to Germany. [322] Unfortunately not all of their plan was accomplished. But they did manage to get some of their materials and publications, mostly in English versions, into Germany. Col. Henry Szymanski, an American officer with Polish roots, acted as the Polish émigrés' go-between with the British and American prosecutors at Nuremberg. Col. Szymanski had served since 1943 as the American liaison officer with the Polish army in the Soviet Union, and had been working on the Katyn problem for some time, amassing a considerable collection of documentary records. He even wrote a special report on the issue. After the Nuremberg Trial he continued to perform the duties of an American officer for special tasks,

---

[321] 'Raport Rządu Rzeczypospolitej Polskiej na Uchodźstwie,' 94–95. 'The Mass Murder of Polish Prisoners of War in Katyn,' Questions translated into English from the Polish version.

[322] Wolsza, „*Katyń to już na zawsze katy i katowani*", 50.

particularly ones involving Polish affairs, such as those that occurred during the "discharge" of the Murnau displaced persons' camp.[323]

During this part of the proceedings the British and Americans reached a conclusion that the Soviet prosecutors were the ones who had to prove that German war criminals were guilty of the Katyn atrocity. The German attorneys, who used documents collected by Polish émigrés in their defense, managed to undermine the Soviet allegations and discredit their witnesses for the prosecution (the parties were permitted to call three witnesses each).[324] In conclusion the court acquitted the Germans of the Katyn atrocity, but it did not name any specific guilty party. Yet for the Polish émigrés the outcome was plain – it marked the first step on the road to international recognition of Soviet guilt for the Katyn murders. Janusz Laskowski, a journalist working for the (prewar) Polish Telegraphic Agency, reported on the proceedings directly from Nuremberg, and articles commenting on the trial appeared in *Dziennik Polski i Dziennik Żołnierza*, *Orzeł Biały*, and the London-based *Wiadomości*. Zygmunt Nowakowski wrote, "Katyn is not a tall tale. One criminal grassed on another criminal. He drew up precise maps of the scene of the crime, collected the statistical data and material evidence, brought in experts, wrote up a report, and denounced his ex-ally. The German criminal did all this with true German accuracy and the application of scientific method. For the six years of the War the German criminal never hid his crimes, on the contrary, he stressed their scope, saying that as a German he had the right to kill. Having caught out the other criminal, his business colleague, he said, 'Katyn is *your* doing. By way of exception, I didn't put my fingers in *this* pie.'"[325]

In 1946–1948 there were two major initiatives launched in émigré circles. The first was the dynamic journalistic commitment of Józef Mackiewicz, who had seen the site of the Soviet atrocity in 1943. The second was the work done under the leadership of Zdzisław Stahl and General Anders' watchful eye in connection with the publication of the book *Zbrodnia katyńska w świetle*

---

[323] *Generał broni Władysław Anders. Wybór pism i rozkazów*, ed. B. Polak, (Warszawa: Wydawnictwa Uniwersytetu Warszawskiego, 2009), 111, 187.

[324] For more on the Nuremberg Trial and Katyn see Basak, *Historia pewnej mistyfikacji*, 68–69.

[325] Z. Nowakowski, 'Towary norymberskie,' *Wiadomości* 1946: 29 (Oct. 20), 1.

dokumentów. The edition of all the publications on Katyn marked the completion of phase two of the Kostar agenda.

Józef Mackiewicz was planning to publish his own monograph on the Katyn atrocity. Moreover, he was encouraged to do so by Capt. Zdzisław Stahl, who in June 1945 commissioned him to write a book on the subject.[326] Mackiewicz had taken the first steps for this project still during the War, when he published the account of what he had seen at Katyn in the reptile paper *Goniec Codzienny*. In exile after the War he reiterated his 1943 observations. He wrote the book in 1945–1946 – Part One from July to October of 1945, and Part Two from January to November 1946 – on the basis of a large amount of knowledge on the subject.[327] He notified General Anders he was writing the book, but surprisingly, the Second Corps did not show much interest in it, so he sent the 370-page typescript to the Piłsudski Institute in New York, for publication in the United States.[328] A translation was made of a few chapters and an excerpt appeared in

---

[326] Maresch, *Katyń 1940*, 316.

[327] Zamorski, *Dwa tajne biura*, 259.

[328] Eugenia Maresch asked why the Second Corps publishers rejected Mackiewicz's book, and reached a conclusion that it was because a decision had been made to publish all the Katyn documents within the framework of Operation Kostar, and to withdraw from the publication of Mackiewicz's book. Maresch, *Katyń 1940*, 316. Mackiewicz left his own account of the episode: "The quarrel went on for a long time (...). In outcome there was a breach [of contract]. Stahl started to pass himself off as the author of my book, because he was head of that project management office at the time. For political reasons, I didn't want to stand up against Gen. Anders. (...) Straight after the breach I wrote a more florid version of the book and had it translated into English. (...) It came out in several languages (English, German, Spanish, Italian, Portuguese, and French). I couldn't issue it in Polish, because it would have been a too-muchness. True enough, Stahl put some materials I didn't have into subsequent editions, e.g. Wodziński's testimony. Nonetheless, the book as a whole is mine, both as regards the writing and the composition." – J. Mackiewicz, *Fakty, przyroda i ludzie*, foreword by B. Topolska, (London: Kontra, 1993), 274. In 1949 he published the German version of his book, *Katyn – ungesühntes Verbrechen* (Zürich: Thomas-Verlag, 1949), and somewhat later the English version, *The Katyn Wood Murders,* (London: Hollis & Carter, 1951). The headline of Wacław Zbyszewski's review of Mackiewicz's book alluded to the Nobel Prize ('Nagroda Nobla,' *Kultura* 1955: 10, 148–158). Another review was penned by Kazimierz Zamorski ('Katyń,' *Kultura* 1951: 10, 144–148). Mackiewicz thanked Jerzy Giedroyc, editor of *Kultura*, for these reviews. Their relations cooled in 1954, with the publication of Stefan Korboński's book *W imieniu Rzeczypospolitej*, which mentions Mackiewicz's wartime collaboration. M. Ptasińska, 'Korespondencja Jerzego Giedroycia z Józefem Mackiewiczem 1951–1982. Zarys problematyki,' in *Zmagania z historią. Życie i twórczość Józefa Mackiewicza i Barbary Toporskiej*, N. Kozłowska and M. Ptasińska (eds.), (Warszawa: Instytut Pamięci Narodowej. Komisja Ścigania Zbrodni przeciwko Narodowi Polskiemu, 2011), 58.

```
Wyciąg z listu                          Warszawa dnia 23.2.1952r.
ks. A.Kwiatkowskiego.                                            23.

      / Odpis /                              Ściśle tajne.


            W miedzyczasie pan Zarębski spowodował, że zostałem
      zmuezony do napisania ilustrowanej broezury p.t."Katyn", której
      tekst wraz z 49 ilustracjami wysłałem już panu Zarębskiemu. W tej
      broezurze największy nacisk położyłem naideologiczny charakter
      zbrodni ze wekazaniem na bezposrednich sprawców tego mordu.Jedno-
      czesnie wyjasniłem znaczenie Katynia jako emblematu a nie faktu
      dotyczącego tylko Polaków. Podkreśliłem b.mocno,że takie Katynie
      mogą się powtórzyć w USA.


      Odb. w 1 egz KS
```

12. Transcript of a letter from Father Kwiatkowski, dated Feb. 23, 1952; marked "Strictly Confidential". Document from the records of the Ministry of Public Security

the daily *Dziennik Związkowy*, but no publisher was interested in publishing the book. It was not until three years later, in 1949, that Katyn became a hot subject in America. Mackiewicz's project had simply jumped the gun. But it elicited a salient episode. The first attempts by Wacław Jędrzejewicz, one of the Institute's co-founders in 1943, to have the book translated, attracted the attention of the Polish Communist secret service, and Wacław Komar, head of intelligence, ordered the invigilation of Jędrzejewicz and the historian Professor Oskar Halecki, who was working on the Katyn issue.[329] All that Mackiewicz could do was to publish excerpts in *Lwów i Wilno* and *Wiadomości*, Polish-language periodicals in Britain. A series of articles – 'Klucz do parku kultury i odpoczynku' (The Key to the Cultural and Recreation Park), 'Tajemnica szwedzkiego dossier' (The Mystery of the Swedish Dossier), 'Dymy nad Katyniem' (Smoke over Katyn), 'Tajemnica archiwum mińskiej NKWD' (The Secret of the Archives of the Minsk NKVD), 'Ostrożnie z wiadomościami o Katyniu' (Careful with News

---

[329] S. Cenckiewicz, *Długie ramię Moskwy. Wywiad wojskowy Polski Ludowej 1943–1991*, (Poznań: Zysk i Spółka Wydawnictwo, 2011), 113–114.

about Katyn) and 'Mikołajczyk o Katyniu' (Mikołajczyk on Katyn) – showed what a vast amount of knowledge he had on the subject. *Lwów i Wilno* also published an article by Col. Jerzy Grobicki on the Kozelsk camp.[330]

Capt. Stahl occasionally voiced his opinion on Katyn, but on the other hand he took an active part in the organizing work. In 1947 he left for England with Mackiewicz's almost complete typescript and there put in the finishing touches and a foreword by General Anders. The first edition of *Zbrodnia katyńska w świetle dokumentów* contained Mackiewicz's text along with an equally important special report drawn up for the book in 1947 by Dr. Wodziński, who had led the on-site work of the Polish Red Cross Commission in 1943.[331]

The book generated a great deal of interest. Reviews, notes and comments appeared in many of the Polish émigré papers and magazines (*Dziennik Polski i Dziennik Żołnierza, Orzeł Biały, Wiadomości, Polska Walcząca, Przegląd Polski, Myśl Polska,* and *Kultura*).[332] Prof. Stanisław Stroński, Dr. Stefan Mękarski, Stanisław Lubodziecki, Wiktor Trościanko, and Ryszard Wraga (real name Jerzy Niezbrzycki) contributed to the discussion on the book conducted in the émigré community, while Tadeusz Nieczuja (the pen-name of Tadeusz Ślaski), sent in his review from Poland, for publication in *Przegląd Polski*. The book's publishers had it translated and published in several languages, albeit after a certain time lapse. Its French version came out in 1949, followed by the English translation (1965 and 1977), the Italian version (1967), and somewhat later the Spanish version. Unfortunately, none of the leading figures in the Polish émigré community came up with the idea to translate the book into Russian for distribution in the Soviet Union.

The reviewers noted the book's assets and its shortcomings. There was general consensus that it wanted a list of victims. This postulate was promptly addressed. In 1949 Maj. Adam Moszyński, an ex-prisoner of Starobielsk, published a list of POWs missing from Kozelsk, Starobielsk, and Ostashkov (*Lista Katyńska. Jeńcy obozów Kozielsk, Starobielsk, Ostaszków zaginieni w Rosji Sowieckiej*). Kazimierz Zamorski and Jerzy Lebiedziewski published their comments to Moszyński's list. Incidentally, somewhat later

---

[330] J. Grobicki, 'Fakty katyńskie,' *Lwów i Wilno* 1947: 47 (Nov. 3), 2.

[331] *Zbrodnia katyńska w świetle dokumentów*, 157.

[332] I have discussed the review in detail in Wolsza, *„Katyń to już na zawsze katy i katowani"*, 65–73.

it turned out that the latter reviewer was in fact Stanisław Swianiewicz using a nom de plume.[333]

Father Antoni Wincenty Kwiatkowski was another émigré who aspired to the reputation of a Katyn expert. He had spent several years in Russia and the Soviet Union, and had been working on the Katyn question since 1943, when he was in Berlin and came across the records of the Smolensk branch of the Communist Party which the Germans had confiscated when they occupied that city. Father Kwiatkowski never saw the site of the atrocity himself. After the War he spent a short period of time working for Vatican Radio, and later moved to Nottingham, England.[334] He wrote a typescript brochure entitled *Katyń*, with nearly 50 photographs of the site, but presumably never published it.[335] He could not find a publisher or patron to sponsor his work, and complained that when he was researching in the Second Corps archives after the War he had met with distrust on the part of the military archivists. Years later he said, "They observed me, to see if I was not making any public statements, and generally kept an eye on what I was up to."[336] He compiled a document entitled *Memorandum* on the Katyn atrocity. In his opinion a "renewal of the Katyn proceedings" should be made in two stages. Stage One should entail a comprehensive discussion of the Bolshevik ideology, on which he was an expert. Stage Two should be proceedings in court with evidence supplied from the documents collected by Poles, Germans, Americans, and others, to identify those guilty of the crime. In the conclusion of his *Memorandum* Father Kwiatkowski wrote, "The renewal of the Katyn proceedings should serve as one of the ways of combating Bolshevism, and to prove that the Katyn atrocity is neither the first nor the only Bolshevik crime,"[337] and

---

[333] Swianiewicz, *W cieniu Katynia*, 310.

[334] T. Wolsza, 'Kolaborant? Burzliwa biografia ks. Antoniego Wincentego Kwiatkowskiego (1890–1970),' in *Niepiękny wiek XX*, B. Brzostek et al. (eds.), (Warszawa: Instytut Pamięci Narodowej. Komisja Ścigania Zbrodni przeciwko Narodowi Polskiemu, 2010), 307.

[335] My opinion is based on a search in the bibliography compiled by Dr. Zdzisław Jagodziński in *The Katyn Bibliography (Books and Pamphlets)*, (London: The Polish Library, 1976), which does not register such an item.

[336] AIPN Warsaw, sign. no. 01224/511, Antoni Kwiatkowski, 'Czapski. Opracowanie Antoniego Kwiatkowskiego dla Komitetu katyńskiego z 2 II 1950 r.' [unpublished document: Czapski: A Study Compiled by Antoni Kwiatkowski for the Katyn Committee, Feb. 2, 1950], sheet 2

[337] *Ibid.*, sign. no. 01419/78, Amerykański Komitet dla zbadania zbrodni katyńskiej. Notatka informacyjna dotycząca organizacji tzw. Komitetu Katyńskiego, 6 XI 1950 r. [unpub-

he enumerated several other mass murders committed by the Bolsheviks in St. Petersburg, Kharkov, Perekop, Yelsk, Oryol, Voronezh, Tula, Kursk, Minsk, and Gomel, as well as the Vinnytsia massacre, which he considered "twice as big" as Katyn. For the rest of his life (he died in Nottingham on May 6, 1970) Father Kwiatkowski continued to collect records relating to communism and the Soviet Union. After his death his entire collection was sent to the Hoover Institution in the United States.[338]

THE ÉMIGRÉ COMMUNITIES AND THE AMERICAN COMMITTEES FOR THE INVESTIGATION OF THE KATYN ATROCITY (1949–1952)

In August 1949, on the initiative of Arthur Bliss Lane, former US ambassador in Warsaw, the American Committee for the Investigation of the Katyn atrocity was set up within the framework of the National Committee for a Free Europe. The Committee's members included representatives of America's political elite and the Polish American community.[339] Its most prominent activist, alongside Arthur Bliss Lane, was its secretary, the journalist Julius Epstein, who at the turn of the 1940s and '50s dedicated a huge sum of money as well as his personal commitment to the clarification of the atrocity.[340] One of the Committee's successes was the questionnaire Epstein dispatched to the experts on the International Medical Commission who carried out the on-site examination in the last days of April 1943. For various reasons only four of the members of the International Medical Commission, Professor František Hájek, Dr. Helge Tramsen (Denmark), Professor Vincenzo Palmieri (Italy), and Professor François Naville (Switzerland), sent in answers to Epstein's questionnaire. In 1945 Hájek had withdrawn his consensus with the conclusion to the International Medical Commission's report, which indicated Soviet culpability for the crime. The other three professors of medicine who got Epstein's questionnaire upheld their 1943 opinion.

---

lished document: US Select Committee To Investigate the Katyn Forest Massacre. Note on the Organization of the So-Called Katyn Committee, Nov. 6, 1950], sheet 280.

[338] Wolsza, 'Kolaborant?' 311.

[339] Wolsza, „Katyń to już na zawsze katy i katowani", 76.

[340] IPMS, sign. no. Kol. 419/16, Notatka Z. Stahla z rozmowy z J. Epsteinem z 9 IX 1957 r. [unpublished document: Z. Stahl's note on his talk with J. Epstein, Sept. 9, 1957].

Not to be released before
Monday, November 21, 5 P. M.

AMERICAN COMMITTEE FOR THE INVESTIGATION OF THE KATYN MASSACRE, INC.

470 Fourth Avenue

Room 1209

New York 16, N.Y.

MU 6-4488

OFFICERS AND COMMITTEE MEMBERS

Arthur Bliss Lane
        Chairman

Max Eastman
        Vice Chairman

Dorothy Thompson
        Vice Chairman

Montgomery M. Green
        Treasurer

Julius Epstein
        Executive Secretary

Constantine Brown
George Creel
Rev. F. John F. Cronin
William J. Donovan
Allen W. Dulles
James A. Farley
Blair F. Gunther
Sol M. Levitas
Clare Boothe Luce
Charles Rozmarek
George E. Sokolsky
Virginia Starr Freedom
James A. Walsh

13. List of members of Arthur Bliss Lane's committee, the first American committee set up to investigate the Katyn atrocity

Not even a press campaign launched by local Communists against the distinguished Swiss medical specialist Professor Naville, which eventually led to legal proceedings against him in the cantonal court, could make him go back on his earlier opinion. In his presentation of the reasons why he had agreed to participate in the work of the International Medical Commission at Katyn, Naville said in court that it would have been immoral for him to refuse in the situation when "a country that had been cut up by the armies of two powerful neighbors learned of the murder of nearly ten thousand of its officers who had committed no crime except for defending their country, and was trying to establish the circumstances in which it had occurred (...)."[341] On hearing Professor Naville's explanation, the court ruled that his conduct was honorable and in compliance with professional ethics. The court's decision was received with acknowledgement and appreciation by Polish émigrés in Britain, who had been following the case in press reports. Articles on the progress of the trial had appeared in several Polish dailies and periodicals abroad, including *Dziennik Polski i Dziennik Żołnierza*, *Orzeł Biały*, and *Przegląd Polski*. The other two outstanding forensic scientists continued to be invigilated and harassed by Communist secret agents throughout the 1950s and later.

Polish émigré politicians in London and journalists working on Katyn gave the Bliss Lane Committee a high rating for its work. As the Committee operated in the United States, its work was given extensive coverage by Vigil (pen-name of Władysław Besterman), the émigré papers' American correspondent, who appealed to experts and journalists first, and next to politicians, to turn their attention to the Katyn question.[342] Besterman's idea was then taken up by the émigré Sovietologist Aleksander Bregman, who called for a tribunal to be set up to examine the Katyn question. He wrote of a tribunal operating "unofficially," but in his opinion this could launch further initiatives in the legal field which would gain international recognition. Bregman argued that tactics of this kind would be a guarantee that for some time Katyn would not fall into oblivion.[343]

---

[341] A. Korczyński, 'Sprawa Katynia przed genewskim „Grand Conseil". List ze Szwajcarii,' *Dziennik Polski i Dziennik Żołnierza* 1947: 20 (Jan. 23), 2.

[342] Vigil, 'Gdy milczą rządy niech się wypowie opinia. Trybunał dla sprawy Katynia,' *Dziennik Polski i Dziennik Żołnierza* 1949: 25 (Jan. 29), 4

[343] A. Bregman, 'Kto ma wyświetlić zbrodnię katyńską. Wolne narody powinny powołać nieoficjalny trybunał,' *Dziennik Polski i Dziennik Żołnierza* 1949: 28 (Feb. 2), 2.

The Committee's work attracted the interest of American and Western European political journalists. It certainly activated political commentators and experts associated with the Polish émigré community, especially those who were personally committed to the investigation of the Katyn atrocity for one reason or another, such as, for instance, having been to the site in 1943. This meant, of course, Ferdynand Goetel and Józef Mackiewicz, and their work on the issue. A salient contribution was made by the London-based periodical *Wiadomości*, which pressed the matter as much as it could. Goetel published a series of articles in *Wiadomości* on his attendance at Katyn in 1943. In a letter to its chief editor, Mieczysław Grydzewski, he made the following declaration: "I have a big gun on Katyn, and it's rather dangerous and new."[344] He then published three large articles on the background to the Polish delegates' travel to Katyn.[345] Next he gave a detailed account of their attendance on the site.[346] Finally he described the atmosphere in Warsaw on the announcement of the news from Katyn by the delegates themselves and in the reptile press.[347] Mackiewicz voiced his opinion on articles on Katyn published in the foreign press, especially the articles in the Swedish periodical *Dagens Nyheter* (1948); and those appearing in 1949 in *The New York Herald Tribune*, the Swiss weekly *Die Wochenzeitung*, and the German *Die Zeit*. The articles in the three latter periodicals were by Julius Epstein. The *Dagens Nyheter* article featured a passage on Dr. Roman Martini, who was the prosecutor assigned the investigation of the Katyn case by the Communist authorities in Poland in 1945. Dr. Martini did not finish the investigation although he did interview a few of the key witnesses, members of the Polish delegation of 1943. He was murdered by a young couple, Stanisław Wróblewski and Jolanta Słapianka.[348] Julius Epstein's articles convey an apt observation – that there was a conspiracy of silence over Katyn. Mackiewicz went even further in his comments, and wrote that in fact it was a double conspiracy of silence – a kind of "two-way sabotage." There was

---

[344] *Z listów do Mieczysława Grydzewskiego 1946–1966*, R. Habielski (ed.), (London: Polonia, 1990), 174.

[345] F. Goetel, 'Katyń. Rok 1943 i pierwsze wieści,' *Wiadomości* 1949: 43 (Oct. 23), 1.

[346] F. Goetel, 'Katyń. Wizja lokalna,' *Wiadomości* 1949: 45 (Nov. 6), 2.

[347] F. Goetel, 'Katyń. Po powrocie,' *Wiadomości* 1949: 47 (Nov. 20), 2.

[348] Bratko, *Dlaczego zginąłeś prokuratorze*; Zawodny, *Katyń 1940*, 141.

14. A witness (probably Kazimierz Skarżyński) testifying before the Madden Committee

"a conspiracy of the Soviet lie acting against the disclosure of the truth, and it was indeed meeting with silence on the part of the West," he argued, but there was "also another conspiracy at play, by people deliberately muddying the waters and thereby (...) helping the perpetrators, who wanted to stop the truth from coming out."[349]

In 1951 the US Congress set up the Select Committee to Conduct an Investigation and Study of the Facts, Evidence, and Circumstances of the Katyn Forest Massacre.[350] It would be true to say that the establishment of this Committee was associated with the activities of its predecessor under the leadership of Arthur Bliss Lane. Rep. Ray J. Madden was head of the new Committee, which is therefore known as the Madden Committee. Several of the congressmen who were its members had Polish roots.

The Madden Committee seems to have met the expectation of the Poles living in exile. For a long time Polish émigrés in Britain and the USA had been trying to get a foreign institution established to investigate the circumstances of the Katyn massacre and disseminate information on the matter. An American select committee attached to the House of Representatives would have no trouble with accomplishing this aim. In addition, its setting up obliged the Soviet Union and the government of the People's Republic of Poland to declare their position on the subject scrutinized by the American committee,[351] espe-

---

[349] J. Mackiewicz, 'Tajemnica szwedzkiego dossier,' *Wiadomości* 1949; 41 (Oct. 9), 3.

[350] W. Wasilewski, *Ludobójstwo. Kłamstwo i walka o prawdę. Sprawa Katynia 1940–2014*, (Łomianki: Wydawnictwo LTW, 2014), 143–176; Zawodny, *Katyń 1940*, 145–155; Maresch, *Katyń 1940*, 323–341; Wolsza, „*Katyń to już na zawsze katy i katowani*", 109–125.

[351] This point caught the attention of Zdzisław Stahl: Z.S., 'Moskwa zmuszona do zabrania głosu w sprawie Katynia,' *Orzeł Biały* 1952: 10 (Mar. 8), 4. See also 'Kreml przerwał milczenie w sprawie Komisji Kongresu USA. Bierut zaniepokojony rozgłosem śledztwa w sprawie Katynia,' *Dziennik Polski i Dziennik Żołnierza* 1952: 53 (Mar. 3), 1.

cially as the Madden Committee sent official letters to Moscow and Warsaw with a request for access to their Katyn records. The government of People's Poland replied that it did not intend to return to the matter.[352]

The Madden Committee heard witnesses in the USA, Britain, and West Germany, albeit its sessions in London were not officially recognized by the British government. Anthony Eden actually said he didn't like it at all, and that the results could be fatal for British–American relations.[353] Initially the Committee also planned to hold a session in Paris, but the idea was dropped. The Congressmen in the Committee attributed an important role to witnesses recommended by the Polish Association of Former Soviet Political Prisoners in Great Britain, which again did not happen by sheer chance. Kazimierz Skarżyński testified before the Committee in the USA, with a white hood over his face to hide his identity. Prewar premier and former deputy prime minister of the postwar Provisional Government of National Unity Stanisław Mikołajczyk also appeared before the Committee as a witness, and made an important fact public. He said that in 1944 the Soviet ambassador Viktor Lebedev had proposed a deal to the Polish government-in-exile. If they declared the Soviet Union was innocent of the Katyn atrocity, Moscow would cut down its territorial claims on Poland.[354]

In April 1952 more witnesses appeared before American investigators in London. They included Poles who had been through Soviet camps, Lieut. Władysław Furtek, Lieut. Władysław Cichy, and Lieut. Stanisław Swianiewicz, all of whom had been Kozelsk prisoners. Maj. Adam Moszyński spoke of the circumstances in which the Katyn list was compiled. Lt.-Col. Tadeusz Felsztyn, another ex-prisoner of Kozelsk, testified as an expert on German ammunition. Others who delivered statements included the generals (Marian Kukiel, Zygmunt Szyszko-Bohusz, Władysław Anders, and Tadeusz Bór-Komorowski), and the ambassadors (Stanisław Kot and Edward Raczyński). The Committee also heard the evidence given by writers Ferdynand Goetel and Józef Mackiewicz. Equally relevant was the testimony given in Frankfurt-am-Main, by

---

[352] Zawodny, *Katyń 1940*, 142.

[353] Maresch, *Katyń 1940*, 329.

[354] *Polski ruch ludowy na emigracji: dokumenty i materiały*. Part 1 (1944-1954), R. Turkowski (ed.), Introduction by S. J. Pastuszka, (Pińczów: Wyższa Szkoła Umiejętności Zawodowych, 2005.), 234.

Sedno Sprawy

Tajemnica zaginięcia pierwszego raportu pułkownika Van Vliet'a o zbrodni katyńskiej pozostaje po d'à niewyjaśniona. Van Vliet złożył potem drugi raport, już nie tak dokładny, gdyż nie posiadał zapisków. Sprowadzony z Japonji po służbie na froncie w Korei, Van Vliet stanął w zeszłym tygodniu przed komisją kongresową Maddena. Potwierdzi szczegóły obu swych raportów, zgodnych z zeznaniami ppłk. Stewarta, który razem z nim był w niewoli u Niemców podczas wojny i razem z nim został sprowadzony do Kantynia na pierwszą ekshumację zwłok pomordowanych oficerów armji polskiej. Dotychczasowe przesłuchy komisji Maddena nie wyjaśniły jednak okoliczności, w których z archiwów Pentagonu zginął pierwszy raport Van Vliet'a.

Onegdaj kongresman Madden wyjawił, że poza raportem płk. Van Vliet'a zaginął również i raport płk. Henryka Szymańskiego, który podczas wojny był łącznikiem Armji St. Zj. przy 1 Korpusie Armji Polskiej, której dowódcą był gen. Anders. Szymański zbierał przez szereg miesięcy dokumenty dotyczące zbrodni katyńskiej i przesłuchiwał Polaków, którzy przeszli więzienia i różne „lagry" (obozy) w Rosji sowieckiej. Z tego wszystkiego złożył raport swym przełożonym.

Departament obrony potwierdził oświadczenie kongresmana Maddena o zaginięciu raportu Szymańskiego. Jakkolwiek Madden pozyskał już odpisy (kopje) raportu płk. Szymańskiego—fakt zaginięcia oryginału tego raportu jest znamienny.

Społeczeństwo ma prawo DOWIEDZENIA SIĘ, komu tak bardzo zależy na niszczeniu, czy wykradaniu raportów o zbrodni katyńskiej, tj. dokumentów, wskazujących wyraźnie na to, że sprawcami jej są Sowiety. Całe społeczeństwo amerykańskie, a nie tylko jego odłam pochodzenia polskiego, jest zainteresowane w ujawnieniu TAJEMNICY wykradania tych dokumentów z tajnych archiwów Pentagonu. Tu nie chodzi już o sprawę Katynia. Tu chodzi o BEZPIECZEŃSTWO AMERYKI. Kongres MUSI dojść do sedna tej sprawy i to całkiem niezależnie od tego, że mamy rok wyborczy.

15. An article on Katyn, 'Sedno sprawy' (Heart of the matter), which appeared in 1952 in the Polish periodical *Nowy Świat* published in the USA

Examination of the evidence leaves little room for doubt

Condensed
from Commentary

G. F. Hudson

Who Is Guilty
of the Katyn Massacre?

W HAT IS now called the Katyn Forest Massacre was first reported by the Germans in April 1943. On a spruce-covered hill overlooking the Dnieper River near Smolensk, Russia, Nazi soldiers had found, stacked in mass graves, the bodies of several thousand Polish officers.

The Nazis, charging that the Russians had committed the mass murder after their invasion of Poland in 1939, sent teams of non-German doctors to Katyn to corroborate their findings, and brought several Allied prisoners to view the bodies.

The Russians promptly countercharged that the Nazis had done it. The Russian story: When the Red armies retreated from Smolensk in July 1941 they had to leave behind their Polish officer-prisoners. The Nazis had shot the Poles, rigged the Katyn story as a propaganda plant.

During the postwar period of Soviet-Western cordiality, the Russian version became accepted as true. But a number of U. S. Congressmen, urged on by a group headed by former U. S. Ambassador to Poland Arthur Bliss Lane, persistently sought a reinvestigation of Katyn. Last fall a special Congressional investigating committee was appointed to examine all the evidence.

— Condensed from Time (November 26, '51). Copyright 1951 by Time Inc.

T HE Katyn massacre is unique among the famous atrocities of history in that there has long been

ᗏᗏᗏᗏᗏᗏᗏᗏᗏᗏᗏᗏᗏᗏᗏᗐᗐᗐᗐᗐᗐᗐᗐᗐᗐᗐᗐᗐᗐ

G. F. HUDSON, Fellow of All Souls College, Oxford University, England, is a regular contributor to the *London Economist* and other well-known magazines.

doubt by whom it was committed. Evidence now available, however, is sufficient for reaching a conclusion.

For Poland, the Katyn massacre was a national disaster. About a third of the prewar officer corps of the Polish Army, including both regu-

Commentary (March, '52), copyright 1952 by American Jewish Committee,
14 W. 33 St., New York 1, N. Y.

127

16. Page one of the article on Katyn published in 1952 in the American edition of *Reader's Digest*

127

witnesses like Józef Czapski and Władysław Kawecki. Apart from taking statements from Polish witnesses, the Committee also interviewed German and American witnesses, including ex-soldiers of the German 537th Signal Corps Regiment, whom the Soviet prosecutors at Nuremberg wanted to blame for the Katyn atrocity. There were also the doctors who did the on-site examination, François Naville, Ferenc Orsós, and Helge Tramsen for the International Medical Commission, and the German medical doctor Wilhelm Zeit, who worked for Professor Buhtz. Invaluable testimonies were delivered by American witnesses, Robert Kampner, a Nuremberg prosecutor; and Col. John H. Van Vliet Jr., who had written a report on Katyn in 1943. After the War his report was lost, and it was not until the early 1950s that Col. Van Vliet managed to reconstruct his invaluable account, confirming that the Soviets had perpetrated the Katyn atrocity.[355] So it was hardly coincidental that the Poles regarded John Van Vliet's report as key evidence in the proceedings. [356]

According to an estimate by Witold Wasilewski, 81 witnesses testified before the Madden Committee in its American session. The Committee also received about a hundred written statements and accounts. Father Antoni Wincenty Kwiatkowski wanted to offer his large Sovietological archive, but his offer was not accepted. However, the Americans used his knowledge of the history of the Soviet Union and communism for general reference. The Madden Committee heard the testimonies of 54 witnesses in its European sessions in London and Frankfurt-on-Main.[357] In London the Polish Association of Former Soviet Political Prisoners submitted material evidence to the Madden Committee.

In June of 1952 the Madden Committee finished its work. Its members reached a conclusion that the Katyn atrocity had been committed by the Soviets.

---

[355] For more on this, see Piórkowska, *Anglojęzyczni świadkowie Katynia*. Following his Katyn mission, Col. Van Vliet was sent to Oflag 64 (near Szubin in present-day Poland) and detained there until January 1945. In letters to his family in the USA he wrote of his visit to the site of the Soviet atrocity. When the camp was evacuated he and other prisoners-of-war, including Capt. Donald Steward, who had also been in the Katyn delegation, set out on foot and eventually reached Uznam Island. Next the Germans sent Van Vliet to a camp near Berlin. When the Soviets entered the camp he managed to escape, eventually reached American troops, and submitted his first report on his visit to Katyn.

[356] Z.S. [Z. Stahl], 'Raport amerykański o Katyniu, *Orzeł Biały* 1952: 40 (Oct. 7), 4.

[357] Wolsza, *„Katyń to już na zawsze katy i katowani"*, 120.

Unfortunately, the Americans did not manage to put Katyn on the agenda for a debate in the United Nations. The attempt to set up an international court to try the direct culprits proved abortive, too. But the article on Katyn which appeared in the March 1952 edition of *Reader's Digest* was certainly connected with the activities of the Madden Committee. Polish émigrés, including Generals Bór-Komorowski and Anders had been endeavoring since 1946 to disseminate information on Katyn in a large-circulation magazine for general readers.[358]

The operations of the Madden Committee received extensive coverage in the Polish émigré press, *Dziennik Polski i Dziennik Żołnierza* and *Orzeł Biały* in London, *Narodowiec* in France, and *Nowy Świat* in the USA. In People's Poland *Trybuna Ludu* and *Szpilki* tried their best to discredit both the members of the Committee and the witnesses. They were presented as collaborators of Goebbels, traitors to the Polish nation, and foreign intelligence agents. The Ministry of Public Security launched a campaign in and beyond Poland to denigrate the most prominent figures in the Committee and their witnesses.[359] Its secret agents kept its Warsaw headquarters informed who was testifying and what information and data had been submitted. The records kept by the Ministry of Public Security contain instructions dispatched to agents in the USA relating to the Madden Committee's interviews of witnesses. The Ministry of Public Security also compiled propaganda materials for American communists on various individuals who testified, with fake histories of collaboration with the Germans for many of them.

POLISH ÉMIGRÉ MEMORIALS OF THE KATYN ANNIVERSARY TO THE MID-1950s

From 1949 on the chief organizer of Katyn anniversary commemorations was the Polish Association of Former Soviet Political Prisoners in Great Britain. This veterans' organization was supported by the Polish government-in-exile, the Polish Ex-Combatants Association, the leaders of émigré political parties and organizations, and representatives of other émigré organizations such as

---

[358] G.F. Hudson, 'Who Is Guilty of the Katyn Massacre? Examination of the Evidence Leaves Little Room for Doubt,' *Reader's Digest* 1952: 7, 127–130.

[359] AIPN Warsaw, sign. no. 014119/78, Amerykański Komitet dla zbadania zbrodni Katyńskiej [US Select Committee To Investigate the Katyn Forest Massacre].

the Józef Piłsudski Institute, the Polish Institute and Sikorski Museum, the Polish Women's Union, the Supreme Council of the Home Army, the Journalists' Union of the Republic of Poland, and the Polish Scouting and Guiding Association. Gen. Anders was appointed head of the committee coordinating the events.[360]

Commemorations of the Katyn anniversary before the committee was set up usually consisted of special articles in the press, a memorial Mass, and a special commemorative meeting. To mark the tenth anniversary (1950), the organizers issued a special appeal addressed to the entire émigré community, entitled *10. Rocznica Zbrodni Katyńskiej* (The Tenth Anniversary of the Katyn Atrocity). The authors of this text recapitulated the basic facts relating to the fate of the Polish POWs in the Soviet Union, naming the three camps (Kozelsk, Ostashkov, and Starobielsk), and giving a figure of 14,500 for the missing victims. They also called for the punishment of the perpetrators of the Katyn Atrocity, viz. the Union of Soviet Socialist Republics. "The world of the free nations proclaims the ideas of justice and human rights and is proud of the democratic and humanitarian principles of its political systems and way of life, yet it shudders in horror and loathing, and fights shy of the prospect of fighting for these ideals and principles when the brute force of Soviet totalitarianism abuses and violates them without scruple."[361]

The main events were held in April 1950, and were attended by about 1,000 persons. The chief guests of honor were Polish President in exile August Zaleski and Prime Minister in exile Tadeusz Tomaszewski. Gen. Anders chaired the meeting. Addresses were delivered by Gen. Anders; Franciszek Haluch, a PPS activist who had been held captive by the Soviets during the War until 1941; and Zbigniew Stypułkowski, one of the 16 political leaders of the Polish Underground State abducted by the Soviets to Moscow in 1945, put on trial and imprisoned in the USSR. Stypułkowski spoke on how the NKVD obtained "voluntary statements" (*Jak NKWD wydobywa „dobrowolne zeznania"*), on the basis of his personal experience. His speech was later translated and published in Greek, Turkish, Portuguese, Spanish, and Italian magazines. Another study on Katyn was written in this period by Dr. Bronisław

---

[360] Wolsza, *„Katyń to już na zawsze katy i katowani"*, 120.

[361] 'Wobec 10-ej Żałobnej Rocznicy Zbrodni Katyńskiej,' *Biuletyn Informacyjny Stowarzyszenia Byłych Sowieckich Więźniów Politycznych w Wielkiej Brytanii* 1950: 3,1.

Kuśnierz, Minister of Internal Affairs in the government-in-exile. The book was published as *Stalin and the Poles: An Indictment of the Soviet Leaders,* with its Chapter 3 on 'Murder and Ill-Treatment of P.O.W.s; Mass Murder of the Katyn Forest.' Naturally enough, its Polish version was available to émigrés in Britain.[362] In his conclusion Dr. Kuśnierz wrote that the discovery of the Katyn graves provided an explanation for what had happened to about 4,500 POWs "missing" from Kozelsk, who were removed from the camp in April and May of 1940. They were transported to Gnezdovo railroad station and from there to Katyn Forest, where they were murdered. There were reasons to believe that at around the same time another 4,000 officers from Starobielsk and about 6,500 officers and members of the Polish educated classes held in Ostashkov met with the same tragic fate. Their graves were not in Katyn and had not been found hitherto (viz. to 1949).[363] Dr. Kuśnierz toured places with large resident émigré communities of Polish veterans to deliver his Katyn lecture.

In late April 1950 the Polish Association of Former Soviet Political Prisoners in Great Britain organized a press conference for journalists from all over the world. Newspapermen from Britain, the USA, Spain, France, and Italy attended. In his closing remarks Gen. Anders summarized the evidence available to the Polish émigrés in six points: 1) the time of the atrocity, viz. the spring of 1940; 2) the incoherent and circuitous explanations the Soviets offered in 1941–1943 when asked what had happened to the Polish POWs; 3) the unsoundness of the Soviet claim that the POWs were still alive in August 1941; 4) the fact that the Soviets never agreed to an International Red Cross on-site examination; 5) the opinions of specialists like Prof. Naville, which the Poles considered authoritative, and 6) the invalidity of the conclusions reached by the Burdenko Commission, whose final communiqué was full of contradictions, incoherence, and fabrications.[364] A second edition of *Zbrodnia katyńska w świetle dokumentów,* with a foreword by Gen. Anders, was issued to mark the commemorative events.

---

[362] The Polish version of Kuśnierz's book was entitled *Sprawa traktowania jeńców polskich i ich mordu. Masowe mordersto w Lesie Katyńskim.* See *Zbrodnia katyńska 1940. Dr Bronisław Kuśnierz o Katyniu,* 15–41.

[363] *Ibid.,* 41.

[364] 'Katyń wobec opinii świata,' *Orzeł Biały* 1950: 18 (May 6), 1.

17. An April 1952 article on the annual Katyn memorial events, in *Orzeł Biały*, a Polish émigré paper published in London and registered as *White Eagle*.

A documentary film on Katyn was made by Polish émigrés and turned out to be a landmark in the dissemination of news on the atrocity. Work on the film began in the early '50s. It was directed by Stanisław Lipiński and created on the basis both of the 1943 German documentary (which had been shown in the GG in April 1943) and the 1944 Soviet film of the Burdenko Commission on the site.[365] The Polish filmmakers received copies of both films from the Americans. The script to the Polish film was written by Dr. Zdzisław Stahl and Władysław Cichy on the basis of the book *Zbrodnia katyńska w świetle dokumentów*, and both scriptwriters appeared as commentators. A reviewer in *Dziennik Polski i Dziennik Żołnierza* wrote, "The film itself and the commentary have been made objectively. Their appeal lies first and foremost in the persuasive power of the dry facts and documentary records they present."[366] The film received a high rating from Radio Free Europe journalists.

---

[365] *Zbrodnia katyńska 1940. Polacy w Wielkiej Brytanii*, 58.

[366] 'Film o Katyniu,' *Dziennik Polski i Dziennik Żołnierza* 1956: 103 (May 1), 4.

In 1955 the filmmakers made several foreign-language versions, including ones with an English and a Spanish soundtrack. Copies were shipped to the USA, Canada, Japan, and Argentina. There was no demand for a French version at this time, and no-one thought of making a Russian version – perhaps because the Soviet Embassy in London had tried to do all it could to stop the showing of the English version (*The Graves of Katyn*) for an international audience of journalists.[367]

Another important series of commemorative events took place in 1956, and coincided with a visit to Britain by Soviet leaders Nikita Khrushchev and Nikolai Bulganin. Polish émigrés decided to take the opportunity to remind public opinion of the Katyn atrocity. Their April program began with the by now traditional memorial Mass celebrated by Bishop Józef Gawlina. Next the organizing committee led a march through the streets of London to the Tomb of the Unknown Warrior. 20,000 people took part in what I believe was the biggest march in the history of the Polish exile community in London. Gen. Anders walked at the head of the march, with a wreath from the Nation. The journalist Stefania Kossowska wrote that thousands marched in absolute silence, in a procession that seemed endless. "There were generals and soldiers marching with their combatants' distinctions pinned on their civvies, Polish miners from the Welsh coalmines, Polish students from Oxford (...) the Home Army, paratroopers, airmen, grenadiers (...)."[368] The marchers carried flags in the Polish colors, and banners reading "We demand the release of thousands of prisoners held in Soviet labor camps," "We want to go back home to our Country," and "We did not come here as immigrants, but to fight for freedom." 50 thousand copies of a special plaque with the inscription *Freedom for Poland* and a brochure entitled *The Soviet Visit and the Poles* (in a print-run of 50 thousand) were issued to mark the occasion. The Polish government-in-exile delivered a memorandum to the Soviet Embassy calling on Khrushchev to make public the circumstances of the atrocity. 60 thousand Polish people in the British Isles signed this document. *Dziennik Polski i Dziennik Żołnierza* issued an English-language edition with articles by Gen. Anders and Zdzisław Stahl's recollections of being Khrushchev's prisoner in Lwów. A flyer entitled *Deported*

---

[367] Wolsza, „*Katyń to już na zawsze katy i katowani*", 135–136.

[368] S. Kossowska, *Mieszkam w Londynie*, (London: Polska Fundacja Kulturalna, 1994), 263.

Poles in Soviet Captivity 1939–1956, by Professor Władysław Wielhorski, was attached as a supplement to this English edition.[369]

The chief aim of the London demonstration – apart from commemorating the victims of the Soviet atrocity – was to protest against the refusal of the British authorities of a request for the erection of a monument to the Polish officers murdered in Katyn. But in 1956 there was also hope that in the wake of the political thaw in the Soviet Union Khrushchev would break down the wall of silence and admit Soviet culpability for the murders.[370] Some Polish émigrés and journalists from Western Europe and the United States were expecting Władysław Gomułka, the new First Secretary of the Central Committee of the PZPR, would undertake steps to make this a reality. There were even tentative suggestions that a Katyn monument might be erected in Warsaw with facts on the real perpetrators and a White Book published on the background to the atrocity. Alas, all these speculations turned out to be wishful thinking. The proof of the policy People's Poland would be pursuing came during a press conference given by Minister Adam Rapacki in the USA. When Julius Epstein asked him about the Katyn atrocity and the prospect of a White Book, Rapacki said, "Gomułka has never given instructions for the publication of a White Book on Katyn. In any case, there has been no need for it. Because the matter was cleared up a long time ago." The next question put to him was whether in the opinion of the authorities in Warsaw the Germans were to blame for the murders. Rapacki gave an answer in the affirmative and added that on the basis of the results of the Madden Committee he was even more convinced that the Germans were to blame.[371]

The conclusion which may be drawn from all this is that the Polish émigrés were still as isolated as ever in their battle for the truth on Katyn and an international court verdict that the Soviets were culpable for the deaths of the Polish POWs of Kozelsk, Ostashkov, and Starobielsk.

---

[369] Wolsza, „*Katyń to już na zawsze katy i katowani*", 134.

[370] 'Cień katyńskiej zbrodni,' *Życie* 1956: 38 (Sept. 16), 4.

[371] Korboński, *W imieniu Polski walczącej*, 181–182.

THE OPINIONS OF POLISH
AND SOVIET COMMUNISTS
ON THE KATYN MASSACRE FROM
THE 1940s TO THE MID-1950s

The Polish and Soviet Communists voiced their opinions on the Katyn massacre more than ten times. One can distinguish two phases here, although the attitude as such remained inflexible. The Communists were consistent in that they assiduously undermined the German findings after the site had been examined by the German and international forensic commissions in 1943. They challenged that set of data by presenting the results of the Soviet commission headed by Gen. Nikolay Burdenko. The Soviets examined the site in early 1944, following painstakingly careful preparations by the NKVD. Those prearrangements involved two aspects. Firstly, a special unit of the NKVD (including Sergei Kruglov and Vsevolod Merkulov) put documents into the graves indicating that the killings must have taken place not in the spring of 1940, but later. Secondly, the NKVD officers intimidated those witnesses whose previous testimonies had corroborated the findings of the Germans.[372]

In this chapter I am going to describe the position of the leaders of the PPR and the Polish Communists on the Katyn massacre as demonstrated in 1943–1945 and during the propaganda campaigns in the aftermath of the War. The important point is that following 1945 the Polish Ministry of Public Security launched two initiatives which were connected with the Katyn trial that was going to be held in Poland (on the Kremlin's orders) and with concerted attempts to discredit the efforts of the Madden Committee which was

---

[372] Materski, *Mord katyński*, 34. Cf. also Wasilewski, *Ludobójstwo*, 116–118.

working in the United States. The first plan was carried out in 1945–1946, and the second was launched at the turn of the 1940s and continued to 1952. The last significant Communist opinion on who should be held responsible for the Katyn massacre was undoubtedly expressed in 1956, which marks the cut-off point for the discussion in this part of the book.

THE WAR YEARS

The PPR commented on the Katyn massacre for the first time immediately after the Germans had announced their discovery of the mass graves and stated the Soviets were responsible for the murder of the Polish officers. Appropriate texts were printed in Communist papers, *Głos Warszawy, Trybuna Wolności,* and *Gwardzista*. The first paper presented the small group of its readers with the opinions of the Party leadership in articles entitled "Smoleńsk – *łajdacka prowokacja*" (Smolensk: a villainous provocation) and "Piętnujemy hitlerowskich prowokatorów" (We condemn the Nazi provocateurs). *Trybuna Wolności* printed the official statement of the PPR and an article headlined "W sprawie niemieckiego 'odkrycia' zbrodni katyńskiej" (On the German "discovery" of the Katyn crime). In May new articles were released: "Klęska niemieckiej akcji propagandowej" (German propaganda campaign fails) and "Klęska reakcji" (Defeat of the reactionaries). The Communists continued to be quite excited about Katyn, discussing it until the fall of 1943 in connection with two other problems which called for criticism: the Polish Underground State and the Polish government-in-exile.

The first Communist response was to disbelieve the German information on Katyn disseminated in April 1943. The Communists considered it a big hoax. They conceded a mass burial site could have been found near Smolensk, but said the victims were more likely to be Russians murdered by the Germans. One of the tell-tale press headlines was "Smoleńsk – *łajdacka prowokacja*" (Smolensk: a villainous provocation). It was only somewhat later that they modified their tactics. Piotr Gontarczyk says the change occurred once they had received strict guidelines from their Moscow comrades. Presumably the Soviets confirmed it was Polish officers who were buried in Katyn Forest, but at the same time they imposed their own interpretation, claiming that the perpetrators were the Germans, and the events had taken place in the fall of 1941.[373] The reader may rightly guess that the small yet clamorous group of Communist conspirators complied, and adopted this explanation in their next publications. The journalists of *Głos Warszawy*, *Trybuna Wolności*, and *Gwardzista* started assuring their readers that the mass graves at Katyn were the work of German evildoers, which was tantamount to declaring that the Germans were responsible for murdering the victims of Katyn.

In their 1943 May Day proclamation, the PPR wrote on Katyn that "the slaughter of the Polish officers whose bodies were found near Smolensk was perpetrated by Hitler's beasts (…). As criminals tend to do, by crying 'Stop thief!' they want to divert the genuine moral outrage of every Pole from those who actually committed the crime and turn it against the Soviet Union, the country which has allowed a Polish army of one hundred thousand men under General Anders' command to be established on its own territory. The Hitlerite murderers, who have set the whole world on fire, know too well that the Polish nation hopes to regain its freedom and independence before long, thanks to the heroic struggle and victory of the Red Army. (…) It is a vain effort on the part of Hitler's provocateurs to use 'delegations,' reptile newspapers, and loudhailers. It is a vain effort for reactionary rags which support the prewar ruling class and fascists to launch their attacks [on the Soviet Union]."[374] Practically every publication by the Polish Underground State, such as texts printed in *Biuletyn Informacyjny* or leaflets that concerned Katyn, became the butt of Communist criticism.[375] Also some members of the delegations were verbally abused. The writer Ferdynand Goetel was probably the most severely

---

[373] Gontarczyk, 'Katyń. PPR-owska szkoła kłamstwa,' 26.

[374] Quoted after *P. Gontarczyk, Polska Partia Robotnicza. Droga do władzy 1941–1944* (Warszawa: Fronda, 2003), 223.

[375] Cf. e.g. the underground resistance leaflet entitled *Katyń. Zamordowani. Mordercy. Oskarżyciele* ([no place of publication] 1943), compiled by the Government Delegation for Poland. It was printed beyond all doubt in the period when the German propaganda was giving much publicity to the circumstances of the Katyn atrocity, in April 1943. Its author begins by saying: "On April 14, 1943 the German press disclosed a heinous crime, the murder of thousands of Polish officers who had been interned in Russia. This time the German propaganda did not lie. Only the estimated number of victims was too high." Then he comes to the crux of the matter: "In the spring of 1940, the Bolsheviks, who at that time were in close alliance with the Germans, killed the Polish officers who were imprisoned in the Kozelsk camp. The officers were unarmed. They were not even prisoners-of-war, because, formally, Russia had not declared war on Poland. And so those defenseless, captive Polish officers were slaughtered, although according to the law recognized by all the nations they had the right to be protected by the

KATYŃ

ZAMORDOWANI
MORDERCY
OSKARŻYCIELE

18. Title page of the brochure published in 1943 by the Polish Underground State

criticized. Before the War he had authored a book entitled *Pod znakiem faszyzmu* (Under the sign of fascism). The book, his participation in one of the delegations the Germans invited to see Katyn, and a short radio statement on the visit made Goetel an easy target for a vicious attack instigated by leading Communists like Wanda Wasilewska, who stressed, "The Nazis did their best in that matter, indeed. Katyn Forest was inspected by various delegations: 'foreign' journalists from occupied or subjugated countries as well as Polish delegations, 'representatives of the nation.' We had a chance to find out about the fortunes of our old friend, ex-writer Ferdynand Goetel, a home-grown enthusiast of fascism. We never heard of him when news was reaching us of the Polish people's struggle against the invaders. (…) Only now did his name re-emerge when the Germans needed help, when someone had to go to Smolensk and take part in a macabre anti-Soviet affray. (…) He went and saw – the bodies of people murdered by the Germans, and he started touring Poland to poison Polish hearts and souls with his wild story about Bolshevist crimes."[376] Goetel's name, side by side with Skiwski's, was also in a leaflet of the Warsaw Committee of the PPR, where he was represented as a "mercenary rascal and Volksdeutscher."[377]

Naturally, the PPR used the opportunity to vilify the Polish government-in-exile for treating the German findings about the Katyn massacre as

---

state on whose territory they were residing. The facts about the Katyn crime unambiguously point to the responsibility of Moscow" (*ibid.*, 3). See p.147 below.

[376] M. Polak, 'Wanda Wasilewska o Katyniu. Przyczynek do pocztu renegatów polskich II wojny światowej,' *Mars* 2002: 12.

[377] Goetel, *Czasy wojny*, 168.

reliable. A similar attitude to the Polish government-in-exile was adopted by Communists of Polish origin in the Soviet Union. The biographer of Jakub Berman says that they watched the course of events "full of suspense," criticizing the Świt radio broadcasts as well as the "London cesspit full of all kinds of Doboszyńskis and Sosnkowskis."[378] *Trybuna Wolności* wrote, "The Polish nation censures and with utmost indignation condemns all the helpers of Goebbels, both in Poland (…) and in London, who, of their own accord, have rushed to the rescue of the foundering Nazi regime."[379] The offensive against the Polish government in London was accompanied by the censure of the Polish Underground State and anti-German resistance organizations. A relevant comment came from Władysław Gomułka, who authored most of the Communist Party proclamations made at that time. Comrade Wiesław, as he was called, voiced his view not on the crime as such, but on the policies adopted by the leaders of the underground resistance forces. The Katyn crime was just a pretext, while the essence of his statement was that the Home Army was avoiding combat. We may assume he was trying to deflect public attention from what had happened in April 1943. "Let even more Poles die in the grip of the German terror, let them spew a surging river of blood, let the cities and villages burn, let not one stone be left upon another on Polish soil, still the Polish nation may not fight, and in particular it must not win, as that could contribute to a 'premature' victory over the Hitlerite monster."[380] While on the subject of Władysław Gomułka, I cannot pass over his best-known Katyn comment without mention, in which he defined his strategy of dealing with the matter. "Personally, I have never had (…) the slightest doubt that the Polish officers in POW camps in the Soviet Union were murdered by the Germans. I can see no reason why the supreme Soviet authorities, including Stalin, should be interested in the extermination of those people. First and foremost, it is my deepest conviction that Soviet rule, which is Socialist and humanist by nature, is not capable of committing such a deed."[381] Thereafter, shedding his camouflage,

---

[378] 7 A. Sobór-Świderska, *Jakub Berman. Biografia komunisty* (Warszawa: Instytut Pamięci Narodowej – Komisja Ścigania Zbrodni przeciwko Narodowi Polskiemu, 2009), 86.

[379] Gontarczyk, 'Katyń. PPR-owska szkoła kłamstwa,' 26.

[380] P. Gontarczyk, *Polska Partia Robotnicza. Droga do władzy 1941–1944*, 226.

[381] W. Gomułka, *Pamiętniki*, vol. 2 (Warszawa: Polska Oficyna Wydawnicza BGW, 1994), 288–289.

he stressed that even if he had complete knowledge of the circumstances of the 1940 atrocity, he "would never blame the USSR, but instead, following all the leaders of the [Communist] Party, give his full, unstinting support to the statement issued by the Soviet Information Bureau on April 16, 1943."[382] At this point we clearly see that he remained faithful to this conviction until the end of his political career.

The Katyn massacre was also commented upon by another Communist activist, Jerzy Borejsza, who was living in the Soviet Union at that time. In the May 1943 editions of the Polish-language press issued by the Soviets he assessed the efforts of the Polish government-in-exile and used the occasion to mention Katyn and the ways in which the atrocity was being used by the German propaganda. In an article published in *Wolna Polska*, entitled "Czekać, zwlekać, szczekać...?" (To wait, to procrastinate, to snarl?) he said: "Some people in London say that Poland has to be discredited in the eyes of the democratic world by pinning faith on the words of the Berlin-based provocateurs, nay, by joining in their propaganda hoax, as if Berlin were the dwelling place of the defenders of the Poles and their assets."[383] Borejsza's biographer Eryk Krasucki was right to ask why this Communist campaigner called the discovery of the Katyn graves a "propaganda hoax." He suggested two possible answers: either Borejsza believed the Soviet Union had had nothing to do with the murder, or he was being extremely cynical. In his conclusion he wrote that the possibility of Borejsza "not knowing the truth seems rather incongruous."[384]

I would supplement this analysis of the events of the spring of 1943 with one important fact. In April 1943 the Germans brought several Polish delegations to Katyn, mainly from the GG, including the victims' relatives, doctors, journalists, writers, POWs, social workers from the Polish Red Cross and the RGO, and factory workers. The state-of-the-art historical research indicates that the delegations comprised over fifty members. Some of them were representatives of the civilian agencies of the Polish Underground State, *incognito* members of the Home Army, members of the PPS-WRN and a representative of OPW [the Fighting Poland Movement]. I assume it is not a risky proposition to say

---

[382] *Ibid.*, 289.

[383] E. Krasucki, *Międzynarodowy komunista. Jerzy Borejsza – biografia polityczna* (Warszawa: Wydawnictwo Naukowe PWN, 2009), 93.

[384] *Ibid.*

that the Germans realized who was traveling to Katyn and why. The presence of delegates associated with the Polish Underground State or the Home Army was calculated to advance their plans. The reasons were simple. Upon their return to the GG, those people would immediately inform their supervisors and superiors about what they had seen and heard in Katyn. It is no secret, either, that the Germans were willing to guarantee immunity to a delegation of the Polish government-in-exile, which was to be led by Gen. Marian Kukiel.

The only question that remains to be answered is whether the group of over fifty delegates from German-occupied Poland who visited Katyn in 1943 included Communists or their supporters. The extant documents of the postwar Ministry of Public Security show that one of the delegates, Mikołaj Marczyk of Stalowa Wola, was a prewar Communist. On his return to his steelworks he was an active participant in the German propaganda campaign that was to publicize Soviet responsibility for the atrocity. After the War he had to bear the brunt of the crackdown on delegates: he was sentenced to two years' imprisonment.[385] Dr. Edward Grodzki, another Katyn delegate, had to seek the assistance of the PPR because, rightly or not, he feared prosecution and arrest by the Germans when he returned to Warsaw from Katyn, as he did not want to join their propaganda efforts. Grodzki relied on the help of Franciszek "Witold" Jóźwiak, who provided him with forged documents. From then Grodzki as "Stanisław Kamiński" was protected by the Party's security agents. I am going to discuss this episode in more detail later on.

The Communist interpretation of the events associated with the Katyn crime was criticized by the civilian and military leaders of the Polish Underground State in *Biuletyn Informacyjny* and other samizdats. Gen. Stefan Grot-Rowecki was right to indicate that "the Polish–Soviet animosity and the problem of Katyn have shown the general public and the rank and file of the Communists that the PPR is in fact an agency of the Soviet Union. By supporting the Soviet stance, which is antagonistic to Poland, the PPR has lost some of its popularity among the masses and brought about the social isolation of the Communists as well as a better grasp of reality for their followers. (…) The hostile attitude of the Soviet Union and the PPR to the Polish government

---

[385] AIPN Rzeszów, sign. no. 108/6521, Akta dotyczące Mikołaja Marczyka 1950–1951. Wyrok z dnia 14 II 1951 r., [Records on Mikołaj Marczyk 1950–1951. Sentence of Feb. 14, 1951], sheet 2.

and its representatives on Polish territories as well as the issue of Poland's eastern borders and Katyn (…) have produced a radical change in Polish society's perception of the Communist movement and have resulted in its spontaneous self-destruction nationwide, especially in the East."[386] Generally, almost all the Communist statements or opinions on Katyn were responded to by the leaders of the Polish Underground State or commented upon in *Biuletyn Informacyjny*.[387] One of the articles said: "We cannot forget that our future is overshadowed by the policies of Soviet Russia, with its many unambiguous measures. (…) The enmity between Russia and Poland has been clear since the fateful September 1939 (…), when hundreds and thousands of Poles were imprisoned, murdered, or shot. (…) Tell-tale signs of this hatred and brutality against the Polish nation (…) are evident in dreadful atrocities like Katyn. A Pole could never be a Communist, or else he would cease to be Polish. Communism is a contrivance of the Soviet mind."[388]

Historical research shows that it was absolutely justifiable to produce polemical writings. Tomasz Szarota observes that the inhabitants of occupied Warsaw read a range of different papers, those issued by the Underground Polish State, but also ones known as the rags (*szamatławce*) as well as the publications of the PPR. Opinions, including those on the Katyn crime, were shaped by the press.[389]

The second time Katyn emerged as a subject in everyday discussion in Poland and abroad was early 1944, and the impulse was the outcome of the Soviet forensic commission, headed by Gen. Nikolay Burdenko, Surgeon-General of the Red Army. First, following the Soviet offensive in November 1943, an unofficial NKVD commission arrived in Smolensk to prepare the ground for the investigation by the official Burdenko team. The Soviets faced a particularly difficult task, because they had to counter all the German arguments concerning the date and circumstances of the Katyn crime, disseminated internationally since April and May 1943. The Germans established the date at 1940 and the Soviets as the perpetrators. They amassed a body of irrefutable

---

[386] *Armia Krajowa w dokumentach 1939–1945*, vol. 3, 11, 13.

[387] Sacewicz, 'Katyń w prasie Polskiego Państwa Podziemnego,' 31–39.

[388] *Ibid.*

[389] Szarota, *Okupowanej Warszawy dzień powszedni*, 415–419.

evidence,[390] additionally corroborated by arguments advanced by journalists and scientists from several countries (such as Belgium, France, Spain, Switzerland, and Sweden), publications in the reptile press printed in the GG, and expert opinions of doctors from Belgium, Bulgaria, Denmark, Finland, France, Germany, Holland, Hungary, the Independent State of Croatia, Italy, the Protectorate of Bohemia and Moravia, Romania, Slovakia, and Switzerland.

Aware of its guilt, the Soviet Union could not take the risk of letting an international commission investigate the crime. Faced with such an impasse, they could only rely on arguments put forward by their own citizens, trusted comrades, or people who were totally under the sway of the Communist Party. The commission did not include those Poles who expressed their wish to travel to Katyn and in principle would be bound to accept the Soviet version of the events. Stalin himself crossed Wanda Wasilewska and Bolesław Drobner off the list of prospective members of the commission. Reportedly, when it was being compiled, he wondered whether Polish Communists "would be capable at all of maintaining a proper attitude to what had happened if they were allowed to stand over the mass graves, where they would surely take an informed guess."[391] At this point one more fact should be presented which proves that the Soviets made every endeavor to obstruct attempts to throw light on the circumstances of the crime. In May 1941, when the Germans were examining the Katyn site, it was attacked by Soviet bombers. Gracjan Jaworowski, a representative of the Board of the Polish Red Cross, said that "the Soviet air force bombed the area of the mass graves. The attack was unsuccessful, as the bombs fell on a place called Katino, so there was no damage to the site."[392] Dr. Ferenc Orsós, a Hungarian doctor and member of the International Medical Commission, recalled that Soviet pilots strafed them with machine-gun fire, but

---

[390] For more information see *Zbrodnia katyńska w świetle dokumentów*; Zawodny, *Katyń 1940*; Swianiewicz, *W cieniu Katynia*; Jerzewski, *Dzieje sprawy Katynia*; Tucholski, *Mord w Katyniu*; Madajczyk, *Dramat katyński*; Wolsza, „*Katyń to już na zawsze katy i katowani.*"; Wasilewski, *Ludobójstwo, passim*; Maresch, *Katyń 1940*, English edition: *Katyn 1940*; Materski, *Mord katyński, passim*.

[391] Materski, *Mord katyński*, 35. For Wanda Wasilewska's position on the Katyn crime see M. Polak, 'Wanda Wasilewska o Katyniu,' 145–154.

[392] Jaworowski, 'Nieznana relacja o grobach katyńskich,' 6. Józef Mackiewicz did not confirm there had been any bombings and treated Gracjan Jaworowski's report with caution. J. Mackiewicz, 'Do Zeszytu nr 45,' *Zeszyty Historyczne* 1978: 46, 226.

fortunately no one was badly wounded. The intentions of the Soviet fighters were clear: they wanted to destroy the graves, the excavated bodies, and the unearthed evidence, as well as to intimidate the doctors and discourage them from persisting in their work. At the turn of April and May 1943 that was all they could do.

The Soviet explanation of the Katyn atrocity had to be credible and look reliable at least superficially. The hoax was orchestrated both at Katyn and in other places. For instance, the NKVD looked for new "eyewitnesses" to the crime and found some German POWs who, in order to save their lives, were ready to admit even to having participated in the atrocity. The whole campaign was supervised by a special NKVD commission which, as I have said above, arrived in Smolensk a few months ahead of Gen. Burdenko's team. Wojciech Materski, who is an expert on the Polish–Soviet relations during the Second World War and in the later periods, has determined that the NKVD investigators questioned 95 people and obtained 17 new testimonies. They drafted a document on the results of the preliminary investigation of "the so-called Katyn case" (*Справка о результатах предварительного расследования так называемого "Катынского дела"*). The carefully prepared document was to serve as a solid foundation for the further work to be carried out by the official state commission.[393] From the very outset it had nothing to do with honesty nor with concern for the truth. The Soviet press informed readers about the project's contrived timetable and apparent progress. Not surprisingly, the Soviets quickly dismissed all the facts presented by the Germans and accused the Wehrmacht of having committed the crime. On January 22, 1944 they welcomed foreign correspondents in Katyn and Smolensk, whom they had invited to a press conference to discuss the findings of their commission. The Soviets claimed the killings had taken place in August and September 1941, following the German invasion of the Soviet Union. Burdenko's commission said all the POWs were shot by the Germans.

There is an interesting aspect in the background of the visit of foreign journalists in Katyn, as their publications were to lend credence to the conclusions reached by the Soviet investigators. After all, British and American journalists kept their countries informed and shaped the opinions of the general public.

---

[393] Materski, 'Z początków wojny propagandowej wokół zbrodni katyńskiej,' 20–22.

The Soviets were quite sure what the response of the governments on either side of the Atlantic would be: once the Kremlin had broken off diplomatic relations with the Polish government-in-exile, Stalin was positive that in the case of Katyn he would receive the support of the British and the Americans. Jacek Tebinka, an expert on 20th-century Polish–British relations, notes that by January 1944 the Soviets were very well prepared for the arrival of foreign journalists in Katyn and Smolensk. Their guests traveled in luxury carriages and were served the best food and drinks, such as caviar and cognac. It was all too obvious that the Soviets wanted to make a good impression all round. British diplomats boycotted the event, but the Americans did not. They were represented by Ambassador Averell Harriman's daughter and a diplomatic service officer. The British journalists did not trust the Soviet pronouncements on the Katyn atrocity and were suspicious about the glamor surrounding the trip. The Americans, on the other hand, approved the Soviet "forensic evidence" and "readily available witnesses."[394] The only Polish journalist who was allowed to join the delegation, but only after Wanda Wasilewska's intervention, was Jerzy Borejsza.[395] He was a representative of *Wolna Polska* and *Nowe Widnokręgi*. Having returned from Katyn, he published two texts: *Tragiczna karta katyńska* (Katyn: a tragic story) and *Mord w Katyniu. Śladami zbrodni – od naszego specjalnego wysłannika* (Murder in Katyn. Our Special Correspondent investigates the crime). In one of them he said: "Katyn, which the German fomenters intended to use to arouse dissent between our allied armies, is now binding us even more closely together, so that together we can fight and take revenge."[396] For some time Borejsza posed as an expert on the Katyn crime, especially when

19. Józef Sigalin and Jerzy Borejsza

---

[394] Tebinka, 'Dyplomacja brytyjska wobec sprawy katyńskiej w latach 1943–1945,' 459; idem, 'Wielka Brytania dotrzyma lojalnie swojego słowa,' 134–148.

[395] *Katyń. Dokumenty zbrodni*, vol. 4, 325.

[396] Krasucki, *Międzynarodowy komunista*, 94.

it was being widely publicized as the deed of the Germans. From that point of view, his participation in the delegation brought the desired effect.

In January 1944 the Katyn site was also inspected by a delegation of the Polish Tadeusz Kościuszko First Infantry Division, commanded by Gen. Zygmunt Berling. The few previously opened graves had already been refilled, so the delegation could not find out how decayed the bodies were, neither were they shown the artifacts examined by Professor Burdenko's team.[397] However, Berling's soldiers took part in a military parade, which was filmed, and in a memorial service.[398] Before the parade, a short briefing was arranged for those officers who had served longest in the division. They issued a special statement condemning the Germans for the Katyn atrocity. On January 30, 1944 elaborate solemnities were held to commemorate the victims. The event was staged next to a new common grave, covered with snow and with an inscription made up of pinecones arranged to read "Cześć poległym! 1941" [Glory to the fallen of 1941].[399] Mass was celebrated by Father Wilhelm Kubsz, chaplain of the First Corps. Next representatives of particular units and their commanders, Gen. Zygmunt Berling, Gen. Karol Świerczewski, and Maj. Stanisław Zawadzki, laid memorial wreaths. Berling, Commander-in-Chief of Polish units in the Soviet Union, delivered a speech in which he said it was the Germans who had committed the crime: "We're standing next to the graves of our brothers in arms, eleven thousand officers and rank-and-file men of the Polish Army. They were not killed in action against the enemy, it wasn't honorable armed combat. They were shot by the Germans like animals, with their hands tied behind their backs."[400] He took the Soviet interpretation of the Katyn killings, spelled out and propagated by the Burdenko Commission somewhat earlier, as the binding version. Other high-ranking officers present included Col. Leon Bukojemski-Nałęcz, Capt. Tadeusz Pióro, and Capt. Józef Sigalin; all of them

---

[397] Żelazko, *Pamięć i propaganda*, 398.

[398] More on this in S. Jaczyński, *Zygmunt Berling. Między sławą a potępieniem*, (Warszawa: Książka i Wiedza, 1993), 217–227; T.P. Rutkowski, *Adam Bromberg i „encyklopedyści." Kartka z dziejów inteligencji PRL*, (Warszawa: Wydawnictwa Uniwersytetu Warszawskiego, 2010), 26–27; T. Pióro, 'W lesie katyńskim,' *Polityka* 1989:7, 12; *Wspomnienia Józefa Sigalina* (Józef Sigalin's recollections, document in the holdings of Andrzej Skalimowski, courtesy of Andrzej Skalimowski).

[399] Jaczyński, *Zygmunt Berling*, 221–222.

[400] *Ibid.*, 222.

returned to the Katyn case later on, for various reasons and in different political circumstances. Especially Pióro and Sigalin were affected by the atrocity, as their relatives were victims. Lieut. Roman Sigalin, a military engineer, was killed in Kharkiv.[401] Col. Jan Maria Pióro, chief physician for the Headquarters of the Tenth Corps, was imprisoned and murdered in the same camp.[402] Tadeusz Pióro, his son, recollected that shreds of military uniforms were scattered all over the site, as well as fragments of soldiers' and officers' belts, rusted Polish Eagle emblems that had been worn on the caps, as well as buttons and lengths of wire and rope. Moreover, he found

20. Józef Sigalin

he could not explore the site unassisted, as the perimeter was guarded by the NKVD.[403] The same observations were made by Józef Sigalin: "(…) during an interval in the program of events (and it was a very cold day) we broke ranks and wanted to withdraw into the forest to answer the call of nature. Suddenly, several NKVD officers came up from behind the trees, shouting: 'Where are you off to? It's forbidden!' The trees grew right along the road, and as the front had receded scores of kilometers away from Smolensk, we could not figure out why we were 'forbidden' to walk a short distance away, what they were keeping an eye on. We were left clueless and absolutely amazed."[404]

At another time the site was visited by Capt. Adam Bromberg, an erudite encyclopedia editor who later worked for Poland's top academic publishing house, Państwowe Wydawnictwo Naukowe. He remembered the event was

---

[401] Tucholski, *Mord w Katyniu*, 485.

[402] *Ibid.*, 470.

[403] Pióro, 'W lesie katyńskim,' 12.

[404] *Wspomnienia Józefa Sigalina* (unpaginated document).

rigged and described it as follows: "After the Battle of Lenino several officers of the First Army were told to get on a bus. I shall never forget the village leader (…). He was the only Russian witness. Just one look at him was enough. He was scared to death and just paid attention to the KGB officer, not to us. He stammered that he had heard shots when the Germans were there. Not a single officer had any doubts over who had killed those people. We discussed it quite openly in the group (…). Later, talking to our soldiers, we called it a German crime."[405]

This statement is important as evidence of propaganda strategy. We can guess that from January 1944 onward the Soviets organized several such "trips," taking groups of Poles to Katyn, just like the Germans did in 1943. This surmise is corroborated by the statement made by Michał Goldfarb in the Ministry of Public Security in 1952, which he repeated in a letter sent to the editors of the Communist daily *Trybuna Ludu*, and published by them. Goldfarb said: "On January 16, 1944, I was a delegate of the First Division, saw the crime scene at Katyn and read a postcard that had been found there, addressed to a second lieutenant from Warsaw, dated June 18, 1941."[406] So he implied the crime was committed by the Germans soon after that date. Regrettably, we do not know what the scale of this operation was and how many similar trips were arranged in early 1944. We may also wonder if all the participants were Polish.

The memorial ceremonies of late January 1944 did not close the Katyn case. The Soviets continued to explore the opportunities it presented and intensified their propaganda efforts. For instance, they used the film showing the Tadeusz Kościuszko First Infantry Division marching in their parade. It was screened in Polish towns liberated or captured by the Red Army. I perceive that as a deliberate step, premeditated by the Soviet propagandists, given that from April 22, 1943 the inhabitants of the same towns could have watched, sometimes even for six months, the German documentary on Katyn, featuring a statement by Władysław Kawecki, a profile of Dr. Tadeusz Pragłowski, and the materials of the Polish Red Cross which evidenced that the Soviets were culpable for the crime. The propaganda machine was gaining more and more momentum, as by January 1944 the Red Army had already entered the former territory of the Polish state.

---

[405] Rutkowski, *Adam Bromberg i „encyklopedyści,"* 26.

[406] AIPN Warsaw, sign. no. 00231/124, Vol. 1, Informacja nr 1 dotycząca dowodów prowokacji niemieckiej w sprawie Katynia z 3 IV 1952 r., [Information no. 1 concerning evidence for the German provocation regarding Katyn, Apr. 3, 1952], sheet 10.

In 1944 the Union of Polish Patriots [a pro-Communist group] published a book on Katyn, *Prawda o Katyniu*.[407] It came out in Moscow and its launch was accompanied by press articles in *Nowe Widnokręgi* and *Wolna Polska*.[408] Perhaps both the book and the articles were published in response to the newspaper texts and anonymous leaflets released by the Polish Underground State in German-occupied territories. Some of them should be mentioned, e.g. the leaflet written by "Andrzej Ciesielski" and entitled *Katyń* (Warsaw, 1943);[409] and a text which was a few pages long and had the title *Katyń. Zamordowani. Mordercy. Oskarżyciele* (1943); as well as a brochure *Dokumenty mówią…* signed by T. Pietrzak (Warsaw, 1944).

The first part of the leaflet *Katyń. Zamordowani* (…) asserts that the Katyn atrocity is a fact and says that "In the spring of 1940, the Bolsheviks, who at that time were in close alliance with the Germans, killed the Polish officers who were imprisoned in the Kozelsk camp. The officers were unarmed. They were not even prisoners-of-war, because, formally, Russia had not declared war on Poland. And so those defenseless, captive Polish officers were slaughtered, although according to the law recognized by all the nations they had the right to be protected by the state on whose territory they were residing. The facts about the Katyn crime unambiguously point to the responsibility of Moscow."[410] As the title said, the leaflet contained information on the number of victims, their social background and prewar profession. The author went on to describe the murderers and identify their country of origin: "Now we understand Katyn. We know who the killers are. They are natives of the grim Russian

---

[407] In March 1945 the book was re-issued on the initiative of the Communist Office of Information and Propaganda based in Kraków.

[408] Journalists who wrote for the Communist press included Leon Bukojemski-Nałęcz ('Katyń'); Wanda Wasilewska, ('Mord w Katyniu' [Murder in Katyn]); and Jerzy Borejsza ('Śladami zbrodni' [Investigating the crime]). All of them presented the Germans as responsible for the Katyn killings.

[409] It cannot be ruled out that the leaflet was issued by the Germans posing as an agency of the Polish Underground State. I found a German version in the Ministry of Public Security records. We may thus assume the Germans either commissioned a German translation of the Polish text so as to assess the merits of the content, or that their specialists drafted a German version which was then translated into Polish and published, apparently as the work of "Andrzej Ciesielski." Nonetheless, so far the real author has not been identified. AIPN Warsaw, sign. no 0546/126, Abschrift. Andrzej Ciecielski, Katyn, sheets 46–53.

[410] *Katyń. Zamordowani. Mordercy. Oskarżyciele*, 3. See p.136-137, footnote 375.

state, which has been breeding identical generations for several centuries. They are people who are still what their fathers, grandfathers, and great-grandfathers used to be, regardless of all the changes and whether their country is ruled by a tsar or Soviet commisars."[411] Lastly, he dealt with the accusers, stressing that the Poles were well aware that the German motive was strictly political. "Now, when the war has been going on for four years, the Germans are the accusing party. Now, when at any moment they could be up on trial for their crimes, accused by all humanity. Is Katyn indeed an exceptional case when viewed in the context of what the Germans have been guilty of during those three and a half years? Have no other mass killings taken place? Those three and a half years, with the Germans occupying Poland, have been a long, long sequence of atrocity, equally cruel and appalling."[412]

The book published by the ZPP Union of Polish Patriots contained texts by Wanda Wasilewska ('Mord w Katyniu'), Jerzy Borejsza ('Śladami zbrodni'), Marian Klimczak ('Byłem jeńcem w lesie katyńskim,' I was a POW in Katyn Forest), Leon Bukojemski-Nałęcz ('Katyń'), Gustaw Buttlow ('Nad mogiłą w lesie katyńskim,' Over the graves in Katyn Forest), as well as Jerome Davies, Edmund Stevens, and Alexander Werth. The last three contributors were a deliberate choice: in January 1944, they and Jerzy Borejsza had taken the trip for foreign journalists organized by the Soviets and succumbed to the Communist arguments, so later on they could be put on the team of writers. The publishers of *Prawda o Katyniu* treated the German investigation and final conclusions as concocted lies. According to them, the witnesses had given their testimonies under duress.[413] We can only guess at the grounds on which Wanda Wasilewska said that "the Germans (...) had trumpeted their monstrous lies all over the world. They suborned their witnesses by beating and torture or by bribery. They destroyed the documents that spoke against them."[414] Jerzy Borejsza voiced an identical opinion.[415]

---

[411] *Ibid.*, 5.

[412] *Ibid.*, 5–6.

[413] *Prawda o Katyniu* (Moscow, 1944), 8.

[414] Wasilewska, 'Mord w Katyniu,' *Wolna Polska* 1944: 4/45 (Feb. 1).

[415] The issue is discussed in more detail, but still inadequately, in my opinion, in Krasucki, *Międzynarodowy komunista, passim.*

The intentions of the Polish Communists seem clear enough. They made their public statements on Katyn after the Red Army had entered former Polish territory. They claimed the Soviets could not have committed any crimes against the Poles; indeed, Soviet soldiers were liberating them. As supporters of the Red Army, the Polish Communists were making ready to seize power in the country. They could not ground their authority on crime. That was the origin of the lie about Katyn perpetuated in the Communist propaganda and other undertakings. It was the lie lodged in the cornerstone of the People's Republic of Poland.

AND AFTER THE WAR ...

After 1945 there were two basic models of discussing the Katyn atrocity. The first, which I intend to touch upon briefly, was applied by the Polish political émigrés and some people living in postwar Poland. It was based on continuing the work that had been initiated during the War and reached the conclusion that the crime had been committed by the Soviets. The other model also relied on continuing wartime efforts; it involved the steps taken by the Polish Communists, according to whom the guilt lay with the Germans. The two models meant a confrontation between two political forces, the "London-based Poles" and "Soviet Warsaw," in their attempts to analyze the same issue. I think it is necessary to include this aspect in the discussion of the timeline of events in 1945–1956.

In 1945 the Soviets made the decision that the Katyn case should be tried before a court in Communist Poland. The prosecution was represented by Dr. Jerzy Sawicki, head of the Supervisory Board for the Prosecution and Special Courts; Dr. Roman Martini; and Karol Szwarc. They were supported by intelligence agents and the NKVD as well as specially appointed officials from the Ministry of Public Security, the Polish Cheka. The Ministry sent out a special instruction to security police units: "In connection with the Katyn provocation, the Germans made the German and Polish-language press publish the names of the Polish officers allegedly murdered on the orders of the Soviet authorities. The lists included the names of people who, as we know, died in German prisons and concentration camps, or are living either in Poland or abroad. All those in your jurisdiction who may have indirect or direct information on the issue or can make statements should be found and questioned, and the material obtained sent back to us, along with their precise addresses (...)."[416] The instruction was signed by Col. Roman Romkowski, Head of Department 1 (intelligence).

As the Ministry of Public Security had received the Burdenko report, which the Communists considered absolutely binding, the prosecutors started collecting statements from members of the delegations the Germans had shown the Katyn graves in 1943. The findings of the Polish prosecutors were of utmost interest to their Soviet overseers. They must have treated the case as serious, because the NKVD was carrying out a parallel investigation on Polish territory.

The first thing the Ministry of Public Security did was to draft a register of all who had been involved in Katyn inquiries since 1943. The list included the names of the journalists, writers, employees of the Polish Red Cross and the RGO, as well as relatives of victims. However, the compilation was a time-consuming task, as the Communists did not have enough documentation to collect the necessary data. There were even problems with the reptile press (*Nowy Kurier Warszawski, Goniec Krakowski, Nowy Głos Lubelski, Dziennik Radomski, Kurier Kielecki, Goniec Codzienny, Gazeta Lwowska,* and *Kurier Częstochowski*) which had published reports and interviews with members of the delegations. The documents produced by the Ministry say that the libraries did not hold all the issues of the relevant papers. The Polish and Soviet political police looked not only for the delegates who had visited Smolensk and Katyn in 1943, but also for members of the team supervised by Dr. Jan Zygmunt Robel of the National Institute of Forensic Research and Criminalistics in Kraków, because the Institute had examined all the evidence (such as scraps of victims' clothing, and their personal belongings, notes, and diaries) collected in Katyn Forest by the Polish Red Cross associates.[417] The list drawn up by the Ministry also named members of the Polish Red Cross and the RGO staff who had not visited Katyn but had worked on the case in their Kraków and Warsaw offices.

---

[416] Quoted after M. Klecel, 'Pisarze ścigani za Katyń,' 70.

[417] M. Wieliczko, 'Na śladach dokumentacji prawdy o Katyniu,' (in) J. Faryś and M. Szczerbiński, eds., *Historia i bibliologia. Księga dedykowana pamięci doktora Zdzisława Konstantego Jagodzińskiego (1927–2001)*, (Gorzów Wielkopolski: Zamiejscowy Wydział Kultury Fizycznej poznańskiej AWF, 2005), 301–306.

Initially the NKVD conducted its investigation fairly vigorously, and detained Drs. Jan Zygmunt Robel and Konrad Orzechowski. Robel was held in jail in Wieliczka and submitted to intensive interrogation, while Orzechowski was put in the NKVD camp at Rembertów. Edward Grodzki and Marian Wodziński attempted to find a hideout, though with varying degrees of success. Grodzki soon gave up and turned himself in, while Wodziński managed to avoid a confrontation. At first he was at Jędrzejów. Then his friends helped him move to Katowice, and finally he settled in Poznań. In September 1945 the NKVD decided Dr. Wodziński should be pursued relentlessly, but his arrest was to be done "on the quiet, with no unnecessary publicity."[418] He was regarded as an extremely important witness in the Katyn case, who could do a lot of harm to the Soviets, knowing as much as he did about the crime. A Soviet general who talked to Jan Zygmunt Robel was quite right to argue that "this (…) man could ruin our foreign policy even in ten years' time by publishing some stupid article or book on the subject."[419] Eventually, Wodziński managed to leave Poland illegally and arrived in Liverpool, where in the fall of 1947 he prepared a detailed report on his inspection in Katyn, which was subsequently published as *Zbrodnia katyńska w świetle dokumentów*.

In the later phase the Polish prosecutors took the lead. In 1945 one of them, Dr. Jerzy Sawicki, interrogated the first group of witnesses, some of them very important for the investigation. Thanks to the archive search carried out by Józef Bratko, Stanisław M. Jankowski, Ryszard Kotarba, and myself,[420] we now know that the witnesses interrogated included Kazimierz Skarżyński, Dr. Hieronim Bartoszewski, Dr. Stanisław Plappert, Dr. Jan Zygmunt Robel, Jerzy Wodzinowski, Father Stanisław Jasiński, and Franciszek Prochownik, a blue-collar worker from the Zieleniewski factory in Kraków. Sawicki also discussed the Katyn massacre with Stanisław Mikołajczyk, leader of the PSL (Polish Peasants' Party), asking how he would respond to the upcoming Katyn trial in Poland. Mikołajczyk replied, "I will present only the facts and the truth, which I know." He added that in the proceedings one could use the relevant German and foreign documents. Reportedly, the Communist prosecutor was highly

---

[418] Jankowski and Kotarba, *Literaci a sprawa katyńska 1945*, 99.

[419] *Ibid.*

[420] *Ibid., passim*; Bratko, *Dlaczego zginąłeś prokuratorze?*; Wolsza, „*Katyń to już na zawsze katy i katowani*", *passim*.

dissatisfied with this answer.[421] A few years later, two of the witnesses, Kazimierz Skarżyński[422] and Stanisław Mikołajczyk,[423] ex-Deputy Prime Minister
of the Provisional Government of National Unity, managed to leave Poland
and testified before the Madden Committee.

Quite naturally, the investigation conducted by the Polish prosecutors
received no coverage in the media, but there were some official publications
on the Katyn atrocity. This was also the time when three arrest warrants were
issued in connection with Katyn, for Ferdynand Goetel, Jan Emil Skiwski, and
Marian Wodziński. On August 1, 1945 *Polska Zbrojna* and *Robotnik* informed
their readers that Professor František Hájek had withdrawn his support for
the International Red Cross report. On September 1, 1945 *Rzeczpospolita*
published an article entitled "Od Katynia po Niemodlin" on German atrocities in Katyn and Łambinowice (Lamsdorf). On September 17, 1945 *Dziennik
Powszechny* asked if it was not high time to identify the Gestapo officers and
SS men guilty of the Katyn crime. More articles on the subject, in fact scores
of them,[424] appeared over the next months. Only a handful of authors were
brave enough to point out that the case was far from clear. Yet even those few
press texts from late 1945 did not come out into the open on the background
of the crime. For instance, Ksawery Pruszyński, one of the leading journalists
of the period, published an article in *Odrodzenie*, cautiously venturing on the
following: "The fact that about 8 to 12 thousand Polish officers, interned in the
three large camps at Ostashkov, Starobielsk, and Kozelsk, have been missing,
had for a long time loomed like a black cloud over the already overcast sky
of Polish–Russian relations. Indeed, those people had disappeared without
a trace, and the Soviet authorities had been unable to explain what had happened to them, either (…)."[425]

Summing up, during the latter months of 1945 the prosecutors were preparing for the Katyn trial, while a massive propaganda campaign was to mold

---

[421] *Polski Ruch Ludowy na emigracji (1944–1954). Dokumenty i materiały*, part 1; editor's
note and introduction by R. Turkowski (Pińczów: Wyższa Szkoła Umiejętności Zawodowych,
2005), 234.

[422] For the minutes of his interrogation see Korboński, *W imieniu Polski walczącej*, 174–176.

[423] *Polski Ruch Ludowy*, 232–235.

[424] Motas, 'Materiały dotyczące zbrodni katyńskiej,' vol. 33, 246–247.

[425] K. Pruszyński, 'Katyń i Gibraltar,' *Odrodzenie* 1945: 53 (Dec. 2), 4.

public opinion. However, in 1946 the idea of holding such a show trial in Poland was abandoned. The decision was certainly not taken in that country; the Polish Communists had to consult their Moscow comrades. Stefan Korboński is of the opinion that Henryk Świątkowski, a Cabinet member, and Jerzy Sawicki were told they had absolutely no right even to "touch upon that case."[426]

Such instructions from Moscow made the Ministry of Public Security change its policy. For some time the problem was hushed up, but not for long.

In the late 1940s more people were committed for trial in connection with their involvement with the Katyn case. Some of them were blue-collar workers from industrial plants in the GG who had been to Katyn Forest: Hieronim Majewski, the railroad worker from Sieradz; Mikołaj Marczyk, employed in the Stalowa Wola steelworks; as well as journalist Marian Maak; Dr. Adam Szebesta; and Edmund Seyfried of the RGO. Also Jan Mikołajczyk, erstwhile member of the Technical Commission of the Polish Red Cross, was kept under close surveillance.

Realizing how the political situation was going to develop and seeing that the Soviets were deeply engaged in the Katyn issue, several members of the delegations who had traveled to Katyn in 1943 decided to flee before the Red Army entered Polish territory or immediately afterward, or remained in hiding for a while, hoping to be able to leave Poland some time later. The group of émigrés included the writers and journalists Józef Mackiewicz, Jan Emil Skiwski, Ferdynand Goetel, and Władysław Kawecki. Kazimierz Skarżyński was questioned three times by Karol Szwarc, and in all his depositions he denied German responsibility for the crime. Fearing arrest, he decided to leave the country illegally.[427] Helped by the British diplomat Robin Hankey, he went to Paris, where he finished his report on the Katyn inspection of 1943.[428]

Secret police agents implemented radical repressive measures (such as surveillance, interrogation, blackmail, and detention) against the 1943 delegates and carefully watched the activities of those organizations that wanted to learn the truth about the Katyn massacre, usually resorting to clandestine

---

[426] Korboński, *W imieniu Polski walczącej,* 174.

[427] Skarżyński, 'Katyń i Polski Czerwony Krzyż,' 141.

[428] Maresch, *Katyń 1940,* 114.

operations. At the same time, security police officers recorded any statements issued by those Poles who persistently rejected the Communist version of the Katyn crime. Researchers have estimated that by 1956 dozens of people had suffered such reprisals.[429] Przemysław Gasztold-Seń says that in the Stalinist period twenty-five were victimized for spreading information about Katyn. Mirosław Golon adds another forty to the list. The Ministry of Public Security arrested clergymen, students, and relatives of those who had been killed by the Soviets in Katyn or other places. One of the victims of the repressions was Father Tomasz Sapeta of Bardo Śląskie, who died after two years in jail.[430] In 1949 seven young people were arrested in Jarocin on conspiracy charges as members of an illegal organization (a junior offshoot of the Home Army), and for slandering the Soviet Union. Their sentences ranged from five to nine years' imprisonment.[431] In 1947–1950 public security officers suppressed an organization called Katyń which operated in Sieradz. The maximum sentences passed by the military court on its members were ten years' imprisonment.[432] In 1951 Zofia Dwornik, a student of the Łódź Film School, stood trial for saying in public that "the Polish officers in Katyn had been murdered by the Soviets." She was sentenced to one year in jail. Dwornik's family had been bitterly affected by Soviet crimes: Maj. Stefan Dwornik, her father, was killed in Kharkiv, and Capt. Kazimierz Dwornik, her paternal uncle, in Katyn.[433] More cases like these are described in studies by Przemysław Gasztold-Seń and Mirosław Golon.

More reprisals against those who were brave enough to say the truth about the Katyn atrocity began in 1952. That campaign was carried out not only on the national, but also on an international scale.

---

[429] More details in Gasztold-Seń, 'Siła przeciw prawdzie,' 133–141; Golon, 'Kary za prawdę o zbrodni Stalina,' 225–240.

[430] *Ibid.*, 233.

[431] Gasztold-Seń, 'Siła przeciw prawdzie,' 136.

[432] K. Krawczyk, 'Działalność i rozbicie organizacji Katyń w Sieradzu (1947–1950),' in D. Rogut, ed., *"Precz z komuną!" Niepodległościowe organizacje młodzieżowe na Ziemi Łódzkiej w latach 1945–1956* (Zelów: Atena, 2011), 220–222.

[433] Gasztold-Seń, 'Siła przeciw prawdzie,' 138.

A NEW CAMPAIGN IN THE EARLY 1950S AGAINST THE SEEKERS OF THE TRUTH ABOUT KATYN

The second campaign launched by prosecutors' offices and the press started in the early 1950s in response to the work of the Ray Madden Committee in the United States,[434] in particular to Madden's letter to Alexander Panyushkin, Soviet ambassador to the United States. Ray Madden requested the Soviet authorities to state their position on the Katyn atrocity and the circumstances of the crime as well as the witnesses' testimonies. The letter reached the ambassador on February 25, 1952. Witold Wasilewski's invaluable research has shown that the Soviet Union refused to cooperate with the Committee. As a reply would have been a signal that it was possible for the parties to enter into dialog,[435] the Soviets decided to return the letter without comment, unconvincingly explaining that the embassy was not authorized to serve as an intermediary in forwarding such documents. Simultaneously, as the problem was receiving a lot of publicity, especially in the US and West European media, Andrei Gromyko, Soviet Deputy Minister of Foreign Affairs, prepared a statement in which he drew the attention of the press to two aspects. He proved to be an extremely shrewd politician and beat the Americans at their game, employing two arguments connected with the findings of the Burdenko Commission, dated January 26, 1944. As a matter of fact, they had remained unchallenged for eight years, so the Soviets, scrupulously enough, decided to capitalize on the procrastination on the part of the superpowers and to lean on those findings, which had been, in a way, accepted internationally, as it was only the Polish government-in-exile that rejected them, which regrettably went unnoticed. At that time no one was aware of the fact that prior to his death Gen. Nikolay Burdenko informed Boris Olshansky, a Red Army officer, that the Katyn crime "had been committed by the NKVD, on Stalin's orders."[436]

---

[434] On the Committee see also W. Wasilewski, 'Komisja Katyńska Kongresu USA (1951–1952),' *Biuletyn Instytutu Pamięci Narodowej* 2005: 5–6, 71–84; *idem*, 'Decyzja Politbiura WKP(b),' 107–133; and Wolsza, „*Katyń to już na zawsze katy i katowani*", 109–125.

[435] Wasilewski, 'Decyzja Politbiura WKP(b),' 112.

[436] AIPN Warsaw, sign. no. 00231/124, Wyciąg z raportu Ambasady RP w Waszyngtonie z dn. 16.6.1952 r. dot. Katynia [Abstract of report from the Polish Embassy in Washington D.C., dated Jun. 16, 1952, concerning Katyn], sheet 131. For Olshansky's story see Zawodny, *Katyń 1940*, 130–131; and Korboński, *W imieniu Polski walczącej*, 177.

The Kremlin sent out Gromyko's statement for publicity and dissemination to all the Soviet-dominated countries.

The first papers to respond officially were *Pravda* in the Soviet Union and *Trybuna Ludu* in the People's Republic of Poland. They did so on the same day, March 1, 1952, which was not coincidental.[437] The Soviet scenario was clear. The first to speak were the Poles and the Russians, who according to the "insinuations of the Americans" were the victims and the murderers respectively. The Communists in both countries vehemently denied the American accusations that the Soviets had been the perpetrators, and presented the charges as ungrounded. In brief, the statement that was issued by the government of the People's Republic of Poland decried the US "provocation." But that was not the end of it at all. Within the next few days opinions on Katyn were voiced by other Communist newspapers published in Prague, Bratislava, and Sofia (*Rude Pravo, Pravda*, and *Robotnichesko Delo*).[438] The response on the part of Czechoslovakia and Bulgaria met the Soviet scenario too, as it was known since 1945 that Marko Markov and František Hájek, two of the doctors who had worked on the International Medical Commission in 1943, had changed their minds on the Katyn massacre. That fact was immediately utilized by the Communist propaganda.

As the Katyn case was being discussed and contested internationally, the Communists in the Soviet Union and Poland put it on their list of priorities. Their realized its importance and therefore decided to enlist all the available means and resources. On March 12, 1952 Col. Julia Brystygier, Head of Department 5 in the Ministry of Public Security, issued Instruction no. 6/52 on "how to counter the dissemination of information on Katyn

---

[437] The first Polish document on the Madden Committee was drafted by Minister Henryk Świątkowski already in December 1951, as if in anticipation that the topic would soon become a regular feature in the mass media worldwide. This memorandum was prepared for Jakub Berman and entitled *Notatka w sprawie Katynia*. Świątkowski suggested the political background of the German provocation should be described more carefully, e.g. by using the diaries of Goebbels and Frank, Himmler's archival collection, and the documents of the Nuremberg trial, and also that the reliability of the Madden Committee's witnesses should be challenged. On the other hand, he thought the findings of the International Medical Commission would be hard to undermine. In this case his advice was to tap the knowledge of Professor Jan Olbrycht. Libera, 'Za kulisami prawdy o Katyniu,' 54.

[438] Wasilewski, 'Decyzja Politbiura WKP(b),' 121–122.

as a Soviet crime."[439] The document laid down guidelines on several issues. It called the results of the work of the Madden Committee, which was bluntly labeled "Hitlerite American," as the "Katyn affray," which apparently calumniated the Soviet Union and was to start a new war. Julia Brystygier ordered her officers to sniff out all those who were spreading information on Katyn imputing the guilt to the Soviets. Further, she told the security police to seek out people who knew anything on the Katyn massacre, pointing out that even false witnesses should be found, ones who had never been to Katyn Forest. Local administration offices were obliged to respond instantly upon receiving information about any person spreading rumors about Katyn or speaking about it in public, any priest mentioning it in a sermon, illegal leaflets or graffiti, anonymous letters sent to broadcasting stations or other institutions, or circulating pamphlets about Katyn. The punitive measures Brystygier recommended were arrest, detention, and interrogation.[440]

The security police opted for the easiest solution and generally used data collected in 1945–1946. A special section was set up in the Ministry and drafted a list of people who had previously decided, or rather were coerced, to support the Communist story of the Katyn crime. The first person on the list was Dr. Adam Szebesta. The Communist press published texts in which he revoked his earlier statements and said instead that it was the Germans who were guilty of the killings. Dr. Szebesta's change of mind was highly publicized by the Communist authorities, just as they promoted the new assertions of Professor František Hájek of Prague, who withdrew the statement he made about Katyn in 1943. The list compiled by the Polish security police also named Dr. Edward Grodzki, who assured them he intended to confirm the version of the events he had given in 1946, for instance in *Gazeta Kujawska*. Franciszek Prochownik, a factory worker from Zieleniewski's in Kraków, was another man whom the Ministry had recruited, as shown in the list. The relevant annotation states he intended to confirm that the Polish officers at Katyn had been killed after 1940. Moreover, he stressed that the witnesses produced by the Germans were unreliable. The Ministry's list contained more names of people who had not

---

[439] *Księga bezprawia. Akta normatywne kierownictwa resortu bezpieczeństwa publicznego (1944–1956)*, selected and edited by B. Kopka (Warszawa: Instytut Pamięci Narodowej, 2011), 567.

[440] *Ibid,*, 568.

visited Katyn in 1943 but were purported to possess some knowledge about the crime. For instance, Tadeusz Piechocki had been held in a German POW camp during the War and one of his fellows there was Władysław Herz. During interrogation by a security police officer, Piechocki claimed he had heard Herz saying that the Germans were culpable of the Katyn atrocity. None of these witnesses was detained by the security police. Having been suborned earlier, they followed the instructions of the Ministry without demur.

In 1952 many Poles were again imprisoned for taking part in the operations of illegal anti-Soviet organizations or rejecting the Communist version of what had transpired at Katyn. Mirosław Golon has pointed out that an outstanding figure in the latter group was Father Leon Musielak, a survivor of the Kozelsk camp who did not leave Poland and talked openly about the Katyn massacre.[441] He was arrested in Oświęcim, where he was working, put on trial, and sentenced to five years' imprisonment. However, he was discharged in 1955. Also Hieronim Majewski, who had been a member of one of the delegations visiting Katyn, was sentenced to six years' imprisonment for spreading word of the German findings about the massacre. He was the second (alongside Mikołaj Marczyk) of the representatives of "the labor force of the GG" convicted on a Katyn charge. The majority of the Poles who got into trouble over Katyn broke the Communist law by distributing leaflets or relaying information about the atrocity. Consequently, they were tried by and received their sentences from the Special Committee to Fight Embezzlement and Economic Sabotage (*Komisja Specjalna do Walki z Nadużyciami i Szkodnictwem Gospodarczym*, a punitive institution formally established to fight private enterprise).[442]

The Ministry of Public Security operated on a large scale in Poland and additionally embarked on several ventures abroad. It closely surveilled all the work of the Madden Committee in the United States and Europe. The most important item on the agenda was to ruin the reputation of its individual members. Having identified all of them by name, agents sent their personal

---

[441] Golon, 'Kary za prawdę o zbrodni Stalina,' 230.

[442] A few examples of this kind can be found in M. Chłopek, *Szeptane procesy z działalności Komisji Specjalnej 1945–1954* (Warszawa: Baobab, 2005), 111–112, 157, 228. The rumors about Katyn are also described in K. Pogorzelski, 'Sprawa katyńska w oczach mieszkańców Białostocczyzny,' *Biuletyn Instytutu Pamięci Narodowej* 2007: 10–11, 127–128.

data to the Ministry of Public Security, where the first article on the Committee's members was compiled. The text was subsequently forwarded to all the editorial offices to be published in newspapers. All the members of the Committee, especially those of Polish origin, were branded renegades and traitors, supporters of Adolf Hitler, challengers of the incorporation of the [formerly German] territories in the north and west of Poland, enemies of the Soviet Union, and in general of peace between the nations of the world. The article said that George Dondero did business with "gangs of criminals." Thaddeus Machrowicz and Alvin O'Koński were, apparently, "minions of the old Polish ruling coterie in London and pro-Nazi circles in the United States." Henryk Podolski, the article's author, attempted to outline a collective portrait of the leaders of the Madden Committee: "They are all active or former agents of fascists operating in Germany and Poland. Their aim is neither to throw light on the terrifying mass murder that the Germans committed in Katyn, as the truth has already been established on the basis of the documents, nor to disclose the macabre provocation that Goebbels staged over the mass graves, but to generate more and more war hysteria and stronger anti-Polish and anti-Soviet sentiment, and to whitewash Hitler's criminals, whom the US imperialists want to use to unleash another world war."[443]

Reportedly, the Ministry's security police officers even mixed in with the Poles and Americans questioned by the Madden Committee either in Chicago or in Europe (London and Frankfurt-am-Main). Then they systematically sent their reports to headquarters in Warsaw or to a Polish consular office in the United States. Some documents were also received by the press agency which produced the special news releases. The data included details of the testimonies and the persons appearing before the Committee. Even the atmosphere of the sessions was described. One of the commentaries said: "The spectators are mostly Catholic priests and a mob of migrant miscreants. You can get an impression that Jan Wszelaki, once [Józef] Beck's minister, or the infamous Besterman is stage-managing it."[444]

---

[443] H. Podolski, 'Reżyserzy „komisji katyńskiej,'" *Trybuna Ludu* 1952 (Mar. 3).

[444] AIPN Warsaw, sign. no. 00231/124, Waszyngton. Minister Skrzeszewski, 8.02.1952 r. [Washington. Minister Skrzeszewski, Feb. 8, 1952], sheet 29. Władysław Besterman, who is named in the document, was the US correspondent for *Dziennik Polski i Dziennik Żołnierza*. His pen name was Vigil. On his involvement in the problem see T. Wolsza, *„Katyń to już na*

Every witness was assessed individually on the merits of his testimony and the detriment it could potentially bring to the Soviet Union. This is how an officer of the Polish security police described Father Leopold Braun, who had served for a few years as chaplain to Polish diplomatic missions in Moscow: "His was an exceptionally villainous testimony, but also a most clever one, specifying that genocide is a special feature of Soviet rule. (…) Braun, who should be viewed as a supporter of the official stance of the Church, stated he knew Bierut, Gottwald, and Pieck. The questions and answers were formulated so as to establish a connection between these names and responsibility for the Katyn killings, and to demonstrate what dangers the poor American flock may expect from the governments led by those persons."[445]

The Ministry of Public Security records include information on how the general public in particular countries was responding to news on Katyn. The security police agents cited the opinions in the press of the United States, Great Britain, France, Spain, Italy, and West Germany. Their reviews included Polish newspapers published abroad, also those that supported the Communist regime. When the Madden Committee presented its final report, the Ministry of Public Security in Warsaw received important news from all over the world. The French papers (such as *Le Figaro*, *Populaire*, *Aurora*, and *Le Matin*) published information that the Soviets were culpable of the Katyn crime, and suggestions that the case should be examined by an international board of investigators. *The Daily Telegraph* signaled the content of the article with a headline saying that Russia had slaughtered Poles at Katyn, in a conspiracy to annihilate the nation's leaders. Another security officer wrote that the members of the Madden Committee pledged to request a thorough investigation of the case by the United Nations and the International Court of Justice in The Hague. The Communist authorities in Poland perceived the matter as extremely significant, since all the materials were sent out in a circular to several representatives of the political elite, namely Bolesław Bierut, Józef Cyrankiewicz, Jakub Berman, Hilary Minc, Edward Ochab, Stanisław Radkiewicz, Franciszek Mazur, Ostap Dłuski, Mieczysław Mietkowski, Stanisław Skrzeszewski, and Stefan Wierbłowski.

---

zawsze katy i katowani", 77 and 106.

[445] AIPN Warsaw, sign. no. 00231/124, Waszyngton. Minister Skrzeszewski, 9.02.1952 r. [Washington. Minister Skrzeszewski, Feb. 9, 1952], sheet 30.

The political thaw of 1956 gave hope both to the émigrés and the general public in Poland that the Katyn Forest massacre as well as other crimes of the Stalinist period would be ultimately explained in light of historical facts, and punished. That was the belief of American and West European journalists as well as of Polish émigrés, who were particularly affected by the problem. So it was not purely coincidental that correspondence on the matter was sent from the West to Nikita Khrushchev in Moscow and Józef Cyrankiewicz in Warsaw. Regrettably, all those hopes proved groundless. The case was eventually closed by Adam Rapacki, Polish Minister of Foreign Affairs. During his visit to the United States he was asked by the American journalist Julius Epstein if the truth about the Katyn atrocity would be revealed. Without a moment's hesitation, Rapacki replied that following the Madden Committee's inquiry and the way it was conducted, the Communist authorities of Poland had become even more strongly "convinced that the guilt lay with the Germans."[446]

---

[446] Korboński, *W imieniu Polski walczącej,*182.

WŁADYSŁAW KAWECKI AND HIS EFFORTS TO SPREAD NEWS OF THE KATYN MASSACRE. BACKGROUND EVENTS IN GERMAN-OCCUPIED POLAND AND WESTERN EUROPE

THE KATYN MASSACRE AS USED FOR PROPAGANDA PURPOSES

In the spring of 1943 the discovery of the NKVD's mass execution of Polish officers at Katyn drew a great deal of public attention on an international scale. Unsurprisingly, the Germans decided to use the windfall for their own political purposes, particularly to provoke discord within the anti-Nazi alliance, especially a split between the English-speaking powers and the Soviet Union. The German authorities adopted all the available means and methods to generate maximum global publicity. They applied to the International Red Cross to investigate the matter, intending to use the massacre for their propaganda purposes. The Minister of Propaganda of the Third Reich admitted, "My guidelines were to utilize the propaganda material to the fullest. We'll be able to thrive on it for several weeks."[447] The officer who was responsible for promoting the matter was Georg (aka Gregor) Slowenczyk, a Viennese journalist who served in the Wehrmacht in the rank of lieutenant.

---

[447] Quoted after J. Mackiewicz, 'Katyń w *The Daily Telegraph*,' *Lwów i Wilno* 1949: 101 (Jan. 16), 1.

Katyn was promptly visited by two forensic committees, first a German one and an international one about a fortnight later.[448] But these were not the only measures the Germans took once they had discovered the Katyn graves. Slowenczyk, who went to Katyn too, suggested several other delegations from different European countries should be invited to come over and inspect the site to corroborate the findings of the international committee and inform public opinion worldwide about the circumstances of the crime. In one of his letters from Katyn to his closest relatives in Vienna, Slowenczyk stressed, "Katyn,

21. Władysław Kawecki

which is ultimately my discovery, is giving me loads of work. I am responsible for everything that is going on here: the exhumations have to be carried out in such a way as to support the opinions I proclaim, all the delegations have to be given a proper welcome etc. My greatest success is (…) the severance of diplomatic relations between the Soviet Union and Poland. I'm constantly being congratulated on the achievement."[449]

The Germans realized that it was the Poles who were to play the most important role in disseminating the information, and invited representatives of the Polish Red Cross, the RGO, employees of some industrial plants, and

---

[448] More details can be found in *Zbrodnia katyńska w świetle dokumentów*, (pp.144–155 in the 1980 edition).

[449] This letter, dated Apr. 25, 1943, was sent to his mother-in-law, who lived in Vienna. A copy of the letter, made in 1948, as well as other materials on Georg Slowenczyk from his police files, were obtained by Bruno Frei, a journalist with the Communist paper *Der Abend*. He handed the materials over to Edward Jankowski, a representative of PAP, the Polish Press Agency (of People's Poland) in Austria. The Agency's Vienna branch notified the Ministry of Foreign Affairs of the papers, yet the reply, signed by Stefan Wierbłowski, read, "They are of no interest to us." AIPN Warsaw, sign. no. 001168/243, Sprawa „Wanda IV," Kawecki Władysław Ryszard [Wanda IV case; Kawecki, Władysław Ryszard].

```
                                                    Katyń, 25.4.1943 r.


    Moja kochana Vesla!

            Nie piszę już do Ciebie ze Smoleńska, gdyż jestem od ra-
    na do wieczora tutaj - przy moich trupach. Są to nieprzyjemni
    chłopcy, nie bardzo towarzyscy, gdyż wydzielają odór jak świeży
    ser ementalski.
    Mimo to kocham ich, tych biednych chłopaków z wykrzywionymi twarza-
    mi, jeżeli takowe jeszcze znajdują się na kościach. Kocham ich
    gorąco, gdyż przez nich mogłem wreszcie zrobić coś dla Niemiec.
    A to jest piękne!
            Katyń - którego wynalazcą ostatecznie jestem ja - daje mi
    strasznie wiele pracy. Jestem odpowiedzialny za wszystko, co się
    tutaj robi i kierownictwo odgrzebywania w tym sensie, aby mieć sta-
    le odpowiedni materiał propagandowy, przyjmowanie wszystkich dele-
    gacji, które codziennie przybywają tutaj samolotami, wykład z prze-
    roczami, które opracowuję, miejsca i książka "Epilog Katynia"; nad
    którą również pracuję. Każdy, kto mówi przez radio o Katyniu, jest
    kierowany przeze mnie, ja sam również.
            Od 4-ch tygodni śpię 4 godziny na dobę. Ale sprawa jest tak
    piękna i wartościowa, że ona sama daje mi siłę do wytrzymania. Zaś
    najpiękniejsze jest to, że wszyscy koledzy, od komendanta aż do mo-
    jego szofera mówią . Niktby tego sklepu tak nie wymiótł jak ten aus-
    triacki pomocnik z Wiednia.
            Fakt, że przy tym wszystkim znajduję jednak czas, aby dla
    Was, moje kochane dzieci, przesłać jajka samolotem, winien wam po-
    kazać, że cała praca tutaj jest robiona jednak tylko dla naszej
    rodziny. Powinnaś zrozumieć, mała Veslo, że tak mało czasu mam, aby
    do Ciebie napisać. Może po zakończeniu tej roboty propagandowej tu-
    taj otrzymam kilka tygodni urlopu na ukończenie mojej książki. Wte-
    dy poprosiłbym Cię o radę w niektórych sprawach.
            Na dobitek wszystkiego spotkałem wczoraj w kasynie dra.Muttin. Poz-
    drowiłżoń jako sławę europejską. Jest on w moim oddziele w charakte-
    rze oficera specjalnego. Także takie 7-miesięczne dzieci są tutaj.
    W każdym razie mogę mu pomódz.
    Czy mam postarać się dla Ciebie o jakąś służącą rosyjską? Mogłabyś
    ją ... z Berlina.
    Od Haserl otrzymałem dzisiaj dalszych 5 pakunków wielkanocnych.
    Bardzo dziękuję. Może będę mógł Wam posłać tłuszczu. Oliwy tutaj
    niema, ale mogę zaoszczędzić trochę z mojego masła przydziałowego.
    Prawie że nie odkładam pióra z ręki, jeśli nie jestem w Katyniu.
    Mój największy sukces dzisiaj: zerwanie stosunków dyplomatycznych
    między CSRR a Polską. Wszyscy mi gratulują.
            Obok mnie stoi już skrzynka, w której są 3 dni odejdą jajka
    dla Was.  Do Berlina samolotem, potem pocztą.
            Ściskam Was wszystkich serdecznie. Pozdrówcie moją Haserl,
    Twoją wspaniałą córkę.

                                            Wasz Gregor.
```

22. 1948 Polish translation of Lieut. Slowenczyk's letter to his wife on Katyn, 1943

journalists working for the reptile press.[450] In this way they made sure that people representing various professions and circles,[451] both from the GG and the Polish territories that had been incorporated into Germany in October 1939, were invited as members of Polish delegations, whose activities in Katyn

---

[450] Madajczyk, *Dramat katyński*, 37–40; Wolsza, *„Katyń to już na zawsze katy i katowani"*, 32–37.

[451] T. Wolsza, 'Wojenne i powojenne losy Polaków wizytujących miejsce zbrodni katyńskiej w 1943 r.,' in *Polska 1944/45–1989. Studia i Materiały*, vol. 9 (Warszawa, 2009), 7–29.

would form part of the German scheme to use the massacre for propaganda purposes. That much becomes clear when we consider how the Germans arranged the inspections for the visitors. Moreover, they were resolved to obtain official Polish statements on the massacre directly from the crime scene.

Practically all the members of the Polish delegations admitted the Germans had received them politely first in Smolensk and then at Katyn, and were considerate enough to appear friendly and sympathetic. Dr. Marian Wodziński, head of the Polish Red Cross Technical Commission that worked on the site for five weeks, stressed that at the beginning of their mission Georg Slowenczyk announced he was ready to provide the Polish delegation with any assistance needed and declared they could explore the site unhindered.[452] In his conversation with one of the German officers, Kazimierz Skarżyński said he could confirm the German soldiers treated the Polish delegation fairly.[453] Gracjan Jaworowski, who arrived at Katyn on May 7, 1943 as a representative of the Polish Red Cross, wrote, "As to the rapport with the Germans, I have to admit that Slowenczik, commandant of the site, behaved appropriately. The other officer, whose name I can't remember (Lieut. von Arndt – TW), was a martinet whose strictness and rigor often interfered with our work."[454]

However, some of Wodziński's suggestions were not accepted by the Germans. For instance, the number of forensic experts was not increased. No specialists from Lwów or Warsaw arrived, contrary to previous arrangements. The German Ministry of Propaganda rejected Wodziński's proposal to have the site inspected by Professor Jan Olbrycht, a world-recognized expert, who was imprisoned in Auschwitz at the time. Two years later Hieronim Bartoszewski said that the Germans "insisted that those members of the Polish delegation who could speak German well should present their stance to the mass media, they picked especially on Skarżyński to do that."[455] At one point Georg Slowenczyk demanded that Kazimierz Skarżyński should make an official statement over the graves and say that the Soviets were the perpetrators of the crime.[456] Skarżyński gave his steadfast refusal both to Slowenczyk and von

---

[452] *Zbrodnia katyńska w świetle dokumentów*, 160.

[453] K. Skarżyński, 'Katyń i Polski Czerwony Krzyż,' *Kultura* 1955: 5, 136.

[454] Jaworowski, 'Nieznana relacja o grobach katyńskich,' 5.

[455] Bratko, *Dlaczego zginąłeś, prokuratorze?*, 248.

[456] *Ibid.*

Arndt.[457] He concluded that in the event neither his resolute response nor his earlier negative comment on the 1939 German–Soviet alliance against Poland affected the affable attitude of Lieut. Slowenczyk, which Skarżyński ascribed to the latter's service in the Austrian army and acquaintance with Dr. Stanisław Plappert of the Kraków branch of the Polish Red Cross: during the Great War they had been in the same regiment.[458] The Poles who visited Katyn in the spring of 1943 knew it for a fact that the Germans had concealed microphones in the vicinity of the mass graves in order to record what the delegates said.

The Germans wanted to obtain as many comments, impressions, and opinions as they could from the Poles concerning their survey of the site. Again, I would like to quote Dr. Marian Wodziński, whose report said that on numerous occasions Lieut. Slowenczyk had openly and harshly criticized certain members of the Polish delegation, that is officers who were held in German POW camps: they ignored his earnest endeavors and did not intend to voice their views on the Katyn massacre, pointing out that as POWs all they had were duties to perform and no rights.[459] The only Pole who decided to release a public statement for a German broadcasting station was Władysław Kawecki. Ferdynand Goetel observed he gave "an elevated speech, which presumably had been prepared for him in advance."[460] It was later used in a German documentary about the Katyn crime. From April 22, 1943 the film was screened in the GG (Kraków, Warsaw, and other cities), and then on those territories that had been incorporated into Germany. For instance, in Bydgoszcz it was shown from August 1944.[461] Finally, it was viewed by audiences in other German-occupied states, especially the countries of origin of the members of the International Medical Commission.

POLISH JOURNALISTS AT KATYN IN 1943

It seems that in the spring of 1943 Katyn was visited by at least fifty Polish journalists, including ten writers, who worked with the reptile press to

---

[457] Skarżyński, 'Katyń i Polski Czerwony Krzyż,' 135.

[458] *Ibid.*

[459] *Zbrodnia katyńska w świetle dokumentów*, 164.

[460] Goetel, *Czasy wojny*, 163.

[461] W. Stankowski, '*Życie codzienne ludności niemieckiej,*' in M. Biskup, ed., *Historia Bydgoszczy*, vol. 2, Part 1: *1939–1945* (Bydgoszcz: BTN, 2004), 452.

a greater or lesser extent. They were Kazimierz Didur (press photographer for *Krakauer Zeitung*), Zygmunt Ipohorski-Lenkiewicz (*Nowy Kurier Warszawski*), Władysław Kawecki (*Goniec Krakowski* and the Telpress agency), Zdzisław Koss (*Dziennik Radomski*), Ferdynand Goetel (member of the Polish Academy of Literature), Marian Maak (writer and journalist from Kraków, the Telpress agency), Józef Mackiewicz (*Goniec Codzienny*), Jan Emil Skiwski (writer), and Bruno Widera (*Nowy Głos Lubelski*). The group may have included one more journalist from Częstochowa (*Kurier Częstochowski*), but so far he has not been identified by name. Another large group of delegates, besides the Poles, were journalists, poets, and writers from over ten German-occupied European states (such as Belgium, Bulgaria, Denmark, France, Holland, Italy, the Protectorate of Bohemia and Moravia, Romania, and Slovakia) as well as neutral states (Portugal, Spain, Sweden, and Switzerland).

The extant documentation points to one important conclusion. Some of the Polish journalists not only represented the reptile press, but they also acted under the mandate of the Polish Underground State. We know that Kazimierz Didur was in the Polish resistance movement. He worked as Hans Frank's private photographer, but was also an active supporter of the Polish Underground State. There is no doubt that Ferdynand Goetel had been authorized to act in the same capacity.[462] Remarkably, Józef Mackiewicz, who had previously been sentenced to death by an underground court of law, eventually left for Katyn with the permission of the Polish Underground State and was only obliged to present his report after the inspection. The sentence was quashed prior to his departure. Yet Mackiewicz, who lived abroad after the War, had to work hard to win the approval of the Polish émigré circles.[463] Jan Emil Skiwski was not so lucky: after the War he was interned by the Allies in a camp in Rimini, Italy.[464] Zygmunt Ipohorski-Lenkiewicz paid the highest price for his collaboration with the Germans even before the War was over: his death sentence, issued by a special military court, was carried out in 1944.[465] Marian Maak, a writer and journalist from Kraków, was imprisoned after the War. Zdzisław

---

[462] Wolsza, „*Katyń to już na zawsze katy i katowani*", 34–35.

[463] Malewski, *Wyrok na Józefa Mackiewicza*, 81–83.

[464] Skiwski, *Na przełaj*, 12.

[465] Gondek, *Polska karząca 1939–1945,* 118.

Koss probably died in a concentration camp.[466] It is not known what happened to Bruno Widera after the War. He definitely left Lublin before the Red Army entered the city, but his destination has not been identified. The Communists issued an arrest warrant, yet he was never apprehended. Some foreign journalists and writers were also punished, sometimes severely, after the War. Robert Brasillach, a French author, playwright, literary critic, and polemical writer who visited Katyn in 1943, was sentenced to death for his collaboration with the Germans and shot in 1945.

So far I have not discussed Władysław Kawecki, a journalist whose collaboration with the Germans was particularly intense. In 1943 he showed the strongest interest in the Katyn massacre and made the greatest effort to spread news of it both in German-occupied Poland and in other countries. His Katyn mission was the longest. In my opinion, his case requires a look from a wider perspective and the clarification of many ambiguities.

THE CONVOLUTED LIFE OF WŁADYSŁAW KAWECKI

In an assessment of Władysław Kawecki, Stanisława Lewandowska, author of a book on journalism during the Second World War, said that "his life was convoluted: he was a journalist affiliated with the reptile press and a Polish Army reservist in the rank of captain who was taken to Katyn with a Polish delegation from the GG."[467] Rafał Habielski used materials from the Polish Institute and Sikorski Museum in London to reconstruct Kawecki's life until the end of the War. Describing the 1939–1945 period, he said that "from October 1939 Kawecki had written for the Polish-language newspapers that were issued by the Germans in the GG. The ties became stronger after 1942, when he helped the Germans achieve their most important propaganda purposes on the occupied territories of Poland."[468]

---

[466] Zdzisław Koss, according to Tadeusz Hołuj, who met him in Auschwitz I, personally visited Katyn as a member of one of the delegations from the GG. In 1943 Koss was arrested by the Germans on the charge of neglecting his editorial duties: the reptile daily *Dziennik Radomski* had printed a poem where the first letters of the lines formed a Polish patriotic slogan. Jankowski and Kotarba, *Literaci a sprawa katyńska 1945*, 225.

[467] Lewandowska, *Prasa polskiej emigracji wojennej 1939–1945*, 232.

[468] R. Habielski, 'Radiostacja „Wanda." Relacja Władysława Kaweckiego,' *Dzieje Najnowsze* 1989: 1, 167.

We now have two CVs penned by Kawecki. The first was drafted on September 2, 1945 prior to a trial before the court of the Polish Second Corps.[469] The second was written for the Communist secret police in the 1950s.[470] The contents of both documents are in many parts identical. What is also visible is the journalist's tendency to manipulate the facts and interpret the events to show himself in a favorable light.

Kawecki's life before the War was exceptionally exuberant, with many mysterious incidents. Władysław Ryszard Kawecki was born on April 3, 1898 at Łowce near Jarosław.[471] He attended high school in Lwów. In October 1914 he joined the Polish Legions. The years of the First World War were particularly eventful for him, which is not surprising, given the checkered history of Polish military units at that time. Initially he served in the Field Gendarmerie of the Legions. After the military oath crisis of July 1917, when the Polish soldiers, instigated by Józef Piłsudski, did not want to swear allegiance to the German Emperor, Kawecki's unit was joined with the Polish Auxiliary Corps and then with the units under General Józef Haller. He was interned in a POW camp in Khust (then in Hungary, now in Ukraine). Having escaped, Kawecki went to the then Austrian province of Galicia and stayed in Kraków; later he moved to Warsaw. When Poland regained independence, he again joined the ranks. In 1918–1920 he served in the Grodzisk Mazowiecki, Pułtusk, and Grudziądz garrisons. He took part in the Polish–Soviet War of 1919–1920. Afterwards, he was relocated to Poznań, where he ran training courses for gendarmerie NCOs. By the end of his military service he was a captain. Next he embarked on a career in journalism. He had started writing for the press (*Ilustrowany Kurier Codzienny* in Kraków and *Gazeta Poranna* in Lwów) still in wartime. In the 1920s and 30s he worked for several Polish newspapers, but especially for papers coming out in Poznań, Kraków, Katowice, and Warsaw. Having finished his military service, he settled in Poznań and worked for *Kurier Poznański*, a local daily. Then he moved to Katowice, where he wrote for *Polska Zachodnia* until 1927. Roughly at that time he was recruited by the military intelligence service.

---

[469] *Ibid.*

[470] AIPN Warsaw, sign. no. 001168/243, Sprawa „Wanda IV," Kawecki Władysław Ryszard [Wanda IV case; Kawecki, Władysław Ryszard].

[471] Some documents prepared for the Ministry of Public Security erroneously give Łowicz as his birthplace.

In the late 1920s he relocated to Warsaw and lived in Dom Prasy (literally the Press House, a journalists' residence) as a regular contributor to *Express Czerwony* and *Express Poranny*. In the early 1930s he was editor-in-chief for *Nowy Czas*, a version of the morning paper *Dzień Dobry* which was distributed in Silesia and the Dąbrowa Górnicza Basin. When he was living in Upper Silesia, he also sat on the board of and acted as secretary for Klub Sprawozdawców Parlamentarnych (the Parliamentary Commentators' Club) in the Silesian Parliament. His glittering journalistic career included writing for *Targi Wschodnie*, *Postęp*, and *Ilustrowany Kurier Codzienny*. In 1938 Kawecki left for Budapest as a correspondent for the Press House. During his stay in Hungary he completed an intelligence mission. When the Second World War broke out in 1939, the next stage in his journalistic career began: he worked for what was called the reptile press, that is German-censored papers coming out in Polish. Upon his return from Budapest, he settled in Kraków, where he started to write for *Goniec Krakowski*. At this time, in early 1940 he was hired by the Telpress agency, a news provider for the reptile press in the GG.

In the CVs I discussed above, Władysław Kawecki stressed that he joined the Polish resistance movement, or more precisely the ZWZ (Union of Armed Struggle, the predecessor organization of the Home Army). Apparently he was unmasked by the Germans in April 1942, arrested and imprisoned in the Montelupich jail in Kraków, where he spent a few months, as he said before the court of the Polish Second Corps (Kawecki estimated his imprisonment had lasted seven months).[472] After the War Tadeusz Hołuj gave a very different account of the events. He had been detained in the Montelupich jail too and interrogated by the Gestapo about Władysław Kawecki, whom he saw on the premises. According to Hołuj, Kawecki had never taken up his offer to join the underground army and, to make matters worse, he could have been the Gestapo agent who had informed upon several inhabitants of Kraków, including Stanisława Jankowska, Jadwiga Kapturkiewicz, Zbigniew Gonerowicz, and Hołuj himself.[473] Finally, he

---

[472] Jankowski and Kotarba, *Literaci a sprawa katyńska 1945*, 224.

[473] *Ibid.* In 1944, when Kawecki was staying in Italy and managing the Wanda station, he suggested the Germans could hire Tadeusz Hołuj, Zbigniew Gonerowicz, and Włodzimierz Długoszewski, for instance, because he knew they were being held in Auschwitz and wanted to bring about their release. Yet the Germans showed no interest in the idea. Habielski, 'Radiostacja „Wanda",' 188.

said Kawecki had spent only about two months in jail.[474] We cannot rule out the possibility that the Gestapo may have broken Kawecki down and extorted a great deal of important information in exchange for his release. So perhaps Kawecki regained his freedom after having accepted the conditions put forward by the Germans, e.g. having pledged his loyal collaboration. Indeed, Kawecki rejoined the Telpress agency and continued to write a lot for the reptile press. During the War his name was associated with two events: his trips to Katyn and his work for Wanda, a German broadcasting station.

THE KATYN MISSION

In the spring of 1943 the Germans dedicated as much media attention as they could to their discovery of mass graves of Polish officers near Smolensk. They established that the heinous crime had been committed by the Soviets in 1940, and all the efforts of the German propaganda were focused on that fact. The mass media coverage on the site was provided by the Telpress agency, reptile press journalists, a film crew, and press photographers. Kawecki was in Katyn twice, and on the first occasion he used the false surname Wąsowicz.[475] This version of the story was presented by Ferdynand Goetel, who had not made his acquaintance previously. When they met at Warsaw airport before their departure for Smolensk, Kawecki introduced himself using the assumed name. Interestingly, it also appeared in the reptile press, e.g. in *Nowy Kurier Warszawski*. It seems that Kawecki was quick to realize that he had been recognized and therefore he immediately gave up the alias for the real name.

His first visit to Katyn was short, lasting less than a full day (10–11 April). The second one was considerably longer, beginning in early May 1943. Kawecki joined the delegation of Allied POWs. He was the only one the Germans allowed to extend his stay to about two weeks. Therefore he had an opportunity to watch the Polish Red Cross Technical Commission working on the site, he met the delegation of representatives of the working class from the GG (in Smolensk, he was even put up in the same room with Mikołaj Marczyk, one of the workers), and he made the acquaintance of Józef Mackiewicz, a distinguished writer and journalist

---

[474] Jankowski and Kotarba, *Literaci a sprawa katyńska 1945*, 224.

[475] Goetel, *Czasy wojny*, 156.

from Wilno (now Vilnius, Lithuania). At this time Katyn Forest was inspected by journalists from several European countries. Kawecki was a particularly active delegate. He saw the mass graves and was eager to meet the members of other delegations, offering to interview them for the reptile press. Władysław Buczak, one of the experts on the Polish Red Cross Technical Commission, who worked at the Pathological Anatomy Department of the Jagiellonian University, recalled that Kawecki had been inspecting the site every day. "He loitered around, trying to strike up conversations, and approached all the Polish delegates," said Buczak. "One day he accosted me, asking for material for an article or for an interview. (…) He styled himself as an honest Pole, wanted to discuss politics, talked disparagingly about the Germans, and it was clear he was keen to win our trust."[476] Dr. Marian Wodziński had similar memories of Kawecki's behavior on the site of the Soviet crime. He said that the correspondent for *Goniec Krakowski* and the Telpress agency did not find favor with other members of delegations from German-occupied Polish territories, the journalists or the representatives of the Polish Red Cross. The Germans appeared to have deliberately given him lodgings in the building where the other Poles were staying. One of the Polish Red Cross employees said, "We were very unhappy about that, as we viewed him as a man collaborating with the Germans and so we really mistrusted him. The fact that we had to live under one roof with him made it impossible for us to discuss any matter freely. Kawecki, on the other hand, was eloquent about his imprisonment in the Montelupich jail and his hostile attitude to the Germans. The essence of the work that was going on at Katyn was of relatively little interest to him, but he frequently went to the forest and talked to Lieut. Slowenczyk. Kawecki must have been gathering materials to be published in his newspaper, because he diligently put down anything we said about the exhumations, which was terribly upsetting. His attention was attracted by the letters that had been found on the unearthed bodies; when we returned to our barrack after a day's work, we always copied them. Kawecki stayed in Katyn longer than he had intended to because he missed a chance to board an early plane to return to Kraków. As far as I remember, he later managed to join the delegation of foreign journalists or Polish workers from the GG, and flew back."[477] We can infer that the Polish workers' delegation returned home in late May 1943 on the basis of materials

---

[476] AIPN Kraków, sign. no. 303/1, Protokół przesłuchania świadka z dnia 3 VII 1945 r. [Minutes of the witness' hearing dated Jul. 3, 1945], sheet 3.

[477] *Zbrodnia katyńska w świetle dokumentów*, 175.

published by the reptile press. For instance, *Nowy Kurier Warszawski* printed an interview with Włodzimierz Ambroż in the issues dated May 29–30, 1943.

I have already said that Władysław Kawecki published plenty of articles in 1943 and in the next years. In Katyn he represented the Telpress agency and *Goniec Krakowski*. According to Tadeusz Hołuj, a group which included Kawecki as well as Karl Hans Fenske, head of Telpress, and a man called Zenziger, was responsible for mounting the press campaign to publicize the Katyn massacre.[478] We should also accept Hołuj's conclusion that all the reptile press texts signed by a "Telpress special correspondent" were actually authored by Kawecki.[479] In my opinion, this conclusion pertains also to the texts signed with the letters "tp.," which probably stood for Telpress. Finally, Kawecki signed some of the materials with his own initials or full name.

At this point I ought to describe some of Kawecki's other undertakings. The reptile press published more interviews with other members of the Katyn delegations, but based on the statements of some purported interviewees (e.g. Dr. Marian Wodziński and Franciszek Prochownik), it can be inferred that Kawecki fabricated these stories.[480] One more rather important fact is that the reptile newspapers circulating in smaller towns, such as Częstochowa, Kielce, Lublin, Radom, and in the Dąbrowa Górnicza Basin, reprinted slightly modified versions of Kawecki's texts that had previously appeared in *Goniec Krakowski* and *Nowy Kurier Warszawski*. The first article that can be ascribed to Kawecki with absolute certainty was entitled "GPU zlikwidowało cały obóz polskich oficerów" (Soviet political police killed all Polish officers in camp) and was published in *Goniec Krakowski* on April 16, 1943. *Kurier Kielecki* reprinted the text with a new headline: "Bezgraniczne bestialstwo bolszewików. GPU zlikwidowało obóz polskich oficerów" (Infinite Bolshevik cruelty. Soviet political police killed all Polish officers in camp). On the same day *Nowy Kurier Warszawski* published Kawecki's interview with Franciszek Prochownik, which was titled "Wrażenia krakowskiego robotnika w lesie katyńskim. Specjalny wywiad Telpressu z członkiem polskiej delegacji Franciszkiem Prochownikiem" (Kraków worker's impression of Katyn Forest. Telpress special interview with Franciszek Prochownik,

---

[478] Jankowski and Kotarba, *Literaci a sprawa katyńska 1945*, 225.

[479] *Ibid.*

[480] Wolsza, 'Wojenne i powojenne losy,' 17–18.

member of Polish delegation). The same text appeared in the next day's issue of *Goniec Krakowski*, followed by more local papers: *Kurier Kielecki, Kurier Częstochowski, Dziennik Radomski,* and *Nowy Głos Lubelski.* Sometimes the editors changed the headline into, for instance, "Ręce złożyć w pięść" (Clench your fist), "Robotnik polski na miejscu krwawej zbrodni" (Polish worker at crime scene), "Żydzi z GPU mordowali polskich oficerów" (Jews in Soviet political police murdered Polish officers), "Naoczny świadek polski robotnik opowiada" (Report by eyewitness Polish worker). On April 16, 1943 *Nowy Kurier Warszawski* published one more text by Kawecki, "Widok był wstrząsający i potworny" (Shocking and appalling sight). The next day, the same article was reprinted by *Goniec Krakowski* "Wstrząsający i potworny widok. Tajemnica cmentarzyska w lesie na Koziej Górze. Specjalny wywiad Agencji Prasowej Telpress z redaktorem Wł. Kaweckim" (Shocking and appalling sight. Secret graves in Koziy Gory forest. Special Telpress interview with journalist Władysław Kawecki). On April 17 *Dziennik Radomski* printed Kawecki's text "Na krwi polskiej zasiali las. Brzozowy krzyż nad mogiłą bestialstwa sowieckiego. 12 000 zamordowanych Polaków oskarża" (They grew a forest on Polish blood. Birch cross over graves of victims of Soviet ruthlessness. 12 thousand murdered Poles cry out in accusation). *Nowy Głos Lubelski* presented an article "Na miejscu masowej kaźni dotychczas ustalono nazwiska 50 zamordowanych oficerów polskich" (50 Polish officers identified on site of mass killing). On April 18, 1943 an article by Kawecki reached readers in Częstochowa. It was entitled "Zdarta maska zbrodni katyńskiej" (Katyn crime unmasked). In the issues dated April 18–19, 1943, *Nowy Głos Lubelski* reprinted "Na Koziej Górze. Wywiad agencji prasowej Telpress z W. Kaweckim" (In Koziy Gory forest: Telpress agency interviews Władysław Kawecki), which had appeared previously in other towns in the GG. On April 18–19, 1943 *Nowy Kurier Warszawski* published Kawecki's interview with Eugeniusz Kukulski's widow. The conversation with the wife of this Polish officer and doctor was entitled "Tragiczna wieść (Specjalny wywiad Telpressu z wdową po śp. płk. lek. dr K.)" (Tragic news. Telpress special interview with widow of the late Col. Dr. K.). These texts were written after Kawecki's first visit to Katyn. He used his second visit to fabricate the interview with Dr. Marian Wodziński, which was published in *Goniec Krakowski* as "Tragedia katyńska widziana oczami lekarza" (Katyn tragedy in doctor's eyes). It was reprinted in other papers, which was the common reptile press practice.

After his visits to Katyn, Kawecki took even more steps to publicize the fact that the Soviets had murdered Polish officers. He authored a German-language pamphlet discussing the Katyn massacre. It was distributed in Vienna, Berlin, and elsewhere; he may have written its Polish version too. I will venture a suggestion that he published his work under a *nom-de-plume*, as Stanisław Ciesielski. Czesław Madajczyk conjectures that Kawecki also wrote *Wykaz członków b. armii polskiej, zamordowanych przez bolszewików w Katyniu, zidentyfikowanych do dnia 1 czerwca 1943 r.* (List of the members of the Polish army, murdered by the Bolsheviks in Katyn and identified up to June 1, 1943 – no date or place of publication).[481] This claim seems to be plausible, as the Telpress correspondent said Kawecki visited Katyn for the identification and compilation of lists of the victims. Moreover, Kawecki prepared a register of all the documents that had been found in the mass graves.[482] He took all those materials to Kraków. I think this is why he published relatively little on the Katyn massacre in late May 1943. Having returned to the GG, Kawecki gave several talks on his Katyn stay. All his efforts to spread news of the massacre culminated in his participation in an international press conference in Berlin, held by the Ministry of Propaganda of the Third Reich.[483] A similar course of action was taken by Father Antoni Wincenty Kwiatkowski, famous for his anti-Communist views even before the War, when he was one of the co-founders of the Warsaw Institute for Research on Communism. He arrived in Berlin in July 1943. His timing was by no means a random choice, as the excavation works in Katyn were over and the graves had been filled in again. In German cities, including the capital, and in the Polish cities in the GG, the propaganda campaign was still going on and Father Kwiatkowski was involved in it.[484]

The biography that Kawecki wrote when he was tried by the military court of the Polish Second Corps contains the information that there had been a plot to assassinate him. Apparently that was why he had to leave Kraków and seek

---

[481] Madajczyk, *Dramat katyński*, 80.

[482] Habielski, *'Radiostacja „Wanda",'* 168; AIPN Główna Komisja [GK; the Main Board], sign. no. 164/100, Spis współpracowników prohitlerowskiej radiostacji „Wanda" [List of associates of Wanda, the pro-German radio station], sheet 3.

[483] Jankowski and Kotarba, *Literaci a sprawa katyńska 1945*, 226.

[484] T. Wolsza, "Kolaborant? Burzliwa biografia księdza Antoniego Wincentego Kwiatkowskiego (1890–1970)," in B. Brzostek et al., ed., *Niepiękny wiek XX* (Warszawa: Instytut Pamięci Narodowej, 2010), 304.

a hideout in Krynica.[485] In his opinion, the plotters were Communists. Examining that period in Kawecki's biography, Rafał Habielski expressed his doubts as to whether any assassination attempt had ever taken place.[486] His stance seems to be justified, as the second biography, drafted by Kawecki for the Ministry of Internal Affairs, does not mention any assassination attack at all. We cannot rule out that in 1945, about to be tried by the court of the Polish Second Corps, Kawecki wanted to stress his merits and his anti-Communist attitude, therefore he concocted a story about assassination plans hatched by the PPR. In the fall of 1945 Kawecki and Father Alfons Krawczyk from Katowice went to Borysowo (now in north-eastern Poland) to inspect a POW camp for Polish soldiers who had either defected to, or had been taken captive by the Germans during the Battle of Lenino.[487] He included this point in the CV drawn up for the Polish Second Corps, but omitted it in the Ministry of Internal Affairs version. After his visits to Katyn, Kawecki went back to Kraków and prepared for a long time away from the city. The Germans offered him work in Katowice for *Gazeta Ogłoszeń*, a reptile daily for the Poles living in the neighborhood of Żywiec and in the Dąbrowa Górnicza Basin. Eventually, Kawecki did not accept the job. Instead he traveled to Berlin and then to Italy, where the Polish Second Corps, commanded by General Władysław Anders, was engaged in combat against the German Armed Forces.

THE WANDA BROADCASTING STATION

In Italy, from March 1944, Kawecki and other journalists collaborating with the Germans, such as Jan Godziemba-Maleszewski (who wrote for the *As* magazine before the War) and Joanna Czarkowska-Bekierska, were on the staff of the German radio station Wanda. The programs were targeted at soldiers of the Polish Second Corps. The first broadcast was aired on March 3, 1944. Its signature tune was the first bars of the song of the Polish Legions during WWI, "My, Pierwsza Brygada" (We are the First Brigade).[488] The announcer

---

[485] Habielski, 'Radiostacja „Wanda",' 168.

[486] *Ibid.*

[487] Madajczyk, *Dramat katyński*, 74.

[488] Habielski, 'Radiostacja „Wanda",' 180. Scraps of information on the Wanda station and Kawecki's work there can be found in Jankowski and Kotarba, *Literaci a sprawa katyńska 1945*, 227.

was Maria Kałamacka, whose professional names were Marysia and Wanda.[489] The station took the name Wanda.

Kawecki was head of the station until October 1944.[490] It is highly probable that in Italy he authored another pamphlet on the Katyn massacre, this time for the soldiers of the Polish Second Corps.[491] The leaflets were airdropped over the positions taken by the Poles. As Kawecki wrote in his CV for the Polish Second Corps, he was later arrested by the Germans.[492] Initially he was interned in the Bolzano-Gries camp. In late October he was transferred to the Innsbruck jail. The charges were espionage, sabotage, breach of professional confidentiality rules, as well as contempt of his superiors and the Führer.[493] In the spring of 1945 he was in jeopardy of imprisonment in Dachau, and even the date of his transport was set (April 6, 1945). The sentence was deferred on grounds of poor health. According to Kawecki, that saved his life. On May 3, 1945 he was liberated by the Austrian resistance movement. He quickly came into contact with other Poles in Innsbruck. However, he did not reveal the secrets of his "convoluted life" and managed to find favor with Capt. Wacław Skibiński, head of the local branch of the RGO. In May 1945 Kawecki started to work as a secretary for that organization.

Three months later he decided to join the circles of the Polish Second Corps and went back to Italy. In August 1945 he turned himself in to the Gendarmerie of the Polish Armed Forces in Porto Civitanova and was subsequently taken to Ancona and San Giorgio, where he was questioned by the intelligence officers of the Polish Second Corps.[494] He wrote a report on his visits to Katyn, in which he

---

[489] AIPN GK, sign. no. 164/100, Spis współpracowników prohitlerowskiej radiostacji „Wanda" [List of associates of Wanda, the pro-German radio station], sheet 1. During the War Maria Kałamacka's husband was sentenced to death by the Polish Underground State's Special Military Court for collaborating with the Germans and executed.

[490] Kawecki's duties involved preparing political programs and selecting other programs that fitted the profile of the station. *Ibid.*, 'Sprawa prohitlerowskiej radiostacji „Wanda",' [The case of Wanda, the pro-German radio station], sheet 2.

[491] *Armia Krajowa w dokumentach 1939–1945*, vol. 3: *Kwiecień 1943 – lipiec 1944* (London: Studium Polski Podziemnej, 1976), 396.

[492] Habielski, '*Radiostacja „Wanda",*' 170.

[493] *Ibid.*, 223.

[494] AIPN Warsaw, sign. no. 001168/243, Sprawa „Wanda IV", Kawecki Władysław Ryszard [Wanda IV case; Kawecki, Władysław Ryszard] sheet 62.

described the mass graves and exhumations.[495] Kawecki included some other episodes from his flamboyant life. The fact that he had been collaborating with the Germans was known to the Polish government-in-exile as early as 1943, when the Home Army notified its authorities of his involvement, which obviously worked to his disadvantage. One of the Home Army dispatches sent to London labeled Kawecki as a "reptile journalist."[496] His work for the anti-Polish Wanda radio station was even more incriminating. Not surprisingly, Kawecki's attempts to be rehabilitated were doomed to fail. In August 1945 the Gendarmerie of the Polish Second Corps brought him for trial before the Twelfth Court-Martial, which was investigating the case of the Wanda radio station. Stanisław Borkowski and Antoni Żukowski, two soldiers of the Polish Second Corps who had been taken captive by the Germans and participated in a program broadcast by Wanda, were sentenced to fifteen and ten years' imprisonment respectively. Adolf Wysocki, who had served in the Polish First Tadeusz Kościuszko Infantry Division and been taken captive during the Battle of Lenino, was also brought to justice by the Polish Second Corps.

All the Wanda broadcasters were imprisoned. Kawecki was detained until June 1946.[497] In that period he wrote a long text of 239 pages on the Katyn massacre, planning to have it published. Regrettably, we do not know what happened to the typescript. Kawecki was transferred to a civilians' camp in Barletta near Bari, where he was head librarian. In July 1946, following an application from the British and American intelligence service, he and thirty other Poles were sent to a POW camp in Afragola near Naples. I suppose the transfer was an outcome of an investigation pursued by the Polish Second Corps. The British and American intelligence questioned all the Wanda journalists as well. Kawecki was later transferred from Afragola to Riccione near Rimini, which had a similar camp for POWs and internees. Ultimately, he was sent to a camp for displaced persons in Reggio Emilia, where he stayed until November 1947.[498]

---

[495] *Ibid.*

[496] *Armia Krajowa w dokumentach*, vol. 2: *Czerwiec 1941 – kwiecień 1943* (London: Studium Polski Podziemnej, 1973), 501.

[497] AIPN Warsaw, sign. no. 001168/243, Sprawa „Wanda IV", Kawecki Władysław Ryszard [Wanda IV case; Kawecki, Władysław Ryszard] sheet 62.

[498] *Ibid.*

At this time he established contact with Communist intelligence officers. One of the aides-de-camp, an attaché of the Polish People's Republic military mission in Rome, learned Kawecki was at Riccione. At a secretly arranged meeting, he offered Kawecki money in return for the withdrawal of his former statements on the Katyn massacre.[499] At this point we may come to the conclusion that Kawecki had wanted to be rehabilitated and decided to do the same as a few other Poles who had inspected the Katyn site in 1943, namely Ferdynand Goetel, Józef Mackiewicz, and Jan Emil Skiwski. After 1945 Goetel and Mackiewicz were finally admitted into the circles of the Polish Second Corps and some (but not all) émigré groups in the West, but Skiwski and Kawecki were not exonerated.

KAWECKI'S COOPERATION WITH THE COMMUNIST INTELLIGENCE SERVICE IN POLAND

The Reggio Emilia internment was the final stage in Kawecki's stay in Italy. The extant documents imply he could have used the false name Władysław Gromadzki in that period. He left the camp for Germany. In 1948 he commenced talks with the representatives of the intelligence service of People's Poland in West Germany,[500] which initially did not proceed too quickly. Presumably, Kawecki would have been a person of practically no importance for the Polish intelligence and secret police if it had not been for his knowledge on the Katyn massacre. The preserved materials of the secret police evidence that the Katyn crime was never discussed with him anyway, even after the Madden Committee had heard his testimony as a witness in Frankfurt-am-Main in April 1952.[501] Oddly enough, *Dziennik Polski i Dziennik Żołnierza*, which normally provided detailed reports on the hearings that were conducted in that city between April 23 and 28, 1952, did not make the slightest mention of Kawecki's statement. It was only later that his importance and role as a potential agent became apparent. He was able to initiate contact with the US secret service, and he knew several journalists of Radio Free Europe and the organization of its Munich broadcasting center. The fundamental question

---

[499] Zawodny, *Katyń 1940*, 141.

[500] AIPN Warsaw, sign. no. 001168/243, Sprawa „Wanda IV", Kawecki Władysław Ryszard [Wanda IV case; Kawecki, Władysław Ryszard] sheet 24.

[501] Wolsza, „*Katyń to już na zawsze katy i katowani*", 119–120.

23. Władysław Kawecki and his wife

here is why Kawecki wanted to come into contact with the Polish intelligence service, especially as he was the one who made the first move. After all, he was known as a fanatical anti-Communist and a bitter attacker of the Soviet Union. Yet this man, who would have definitely received a death sentence had he entered any of the countries east of the Iron Curtain, began a dialog with Communist intelligence and secret service officers. In order to answer this question, we need to return to German-occupied Poland. On his departure from Kraków in 1944, Kawecki left behind his wife Elżbieta and four-year-old son Andrzej. They did not manage to slip out of Poland in 1944–1945 or later, but only moved to Wrocław, perhaps to be nearer the German border. Kawecki knew the predicament his family was in, and this was his main concern when he started his talks with the secret service. What he wanted was to be given a chance to reunite with his wife and son in exchange for the information he provided. At the turn of the 1940s he supervised several DP camps in West Germany and served the longest in Würzburg. This seems to be the time when he made contact with the US secret service, to become their agent in 1957.[502] As an ex-journalist of the reptile press and the Wanda broadcasting station, Kawecki joined the National Committee for a Free Europe, which operated in West European countries. In West Germany alone, there were five mobile sections headed by Michał Dachan, Czesław Bruner, Alfred Ruebenbauer, Zygmunt Jędrzejewski, and Władysław Kawecki. Kawecki testified that his section was soon closed down and he started cooperating with American intelligence officers in Berg.[503]

Kawecki notified the Polish intelligence officers of the type of work he did for the Committee for a Free Europe and his collaboration with the US intelligence. He prepared relevant documentation for the Ministry of Public Security, listing the names of the Poles living abroad who cooperated with the CIC (Counter Intelligence Corps), such as Stanisław Mikiciuk, Kajetan Gołejewski-Czarkowski, and Kazimierz Zamorski.[504] Kawecki informed that Mikiciuk had previously been employed by the broadcast monitoring section of the Voice of America and added that his work for the CIC went on under the guise of running the Veritas libraries and writing for the Polish émigré paper *Orzeł Biały*. Kawecki also provided the Ministry with the personal data of Gołejewski-Czarkowski and Zamorski, such as their addresses and even their telephone numbers. He described some important events in their private lives, e.g. that Zamorski was divorced, and included a great deal of information about his second marriage.

Kawecki dutifully updated the Ministry on the personnel turnover in Radio Free Europe and gave fairly accurate characteristics of the employees, head of the Polish section, and all the journalists and technical staff. Additionally, he provided the names of many people who wanted to work for Radio Free Europe and had submitted their job applications: Tadeusz Chciuk-Celt, Feliks Chrzanowski, Jan Krok-Paszkowski, Wawrzyniec Czereśniewski, Roman Grzymała, Feliks Broniecki, Włodzimierz Sznarbachowski, Jan Tabaczyński, Wiktor Trościanko, Stanisław Kodź, Zbigniew Stypułkowski, Zbigniew Promirski, Zbigniew Błaszczyk, Bronisław Orłowski, and Bogusław Chabot. Kawecki did not know all

---

[502] AIPN Warsaw, sign. no. 001168/243, Sprawa „Wanda IV", Kawecki Władysław Ryszard [Wanda IV case; Kawecki, Władysław Ryszard] sheet 17.

[503] *Ibid.*, sheet 37.

[504] *Ibid.*, sheet 64.

24. Władysław Kawecki at the time when the Communist intelligence kept him under surveillance

of them personally, so sometimes he could not supply any details. Yet if he did know somebody, he procured all the information the Ministry required. He said that Tadeusz Chciuk-Celt, aged 43–45, "chaired the association of Polish journalists in Germany, headed the economic section in Radio Free Europe, married a Polish woman (aged 30) while in Britain, where his family lived. Apparently some of his relatives also lived in Poland. (…) He seemed to be kind and friendly to his workmates."[505] Jan Tabaczyński was characterized by Kawecki as follows: "A senator's son, he received his master's degree in philosophy. Until 1939 he was the most important news commentator for *Polonia*, a Katowice weekly. He was working as a foreign correspondent in Budapest both for *Polonia* and *Kurier Poznański* when the War broke out. He reached the Near East via Yugoslavia to serve in the Polish army. Before he was hired by Radio Free Europe, which happened ten years ago, he was employed in the press office of the 'London-based government.' At present he has a job in the political section. He is a bachelor, aged 55. His brother Stanisław Tabaczyński, a journalist, lives in Poland, perhaps

---

[505] *Ibid.*, sheet 14.

184

still in Sosnowiec. (…) He is politically active in the Alliance of Democrats."[506] Kawecki also gathered data on those employees of Radio Free Europe who came from other East European countries, e.g. Czechoslovakia and Hungary, and on Ukrainian émigrés. Given the wealth of the information on Radio Free Europe that Kawecki obtained for the Ministry of Public Security, we could say he was one of the best agents the Polish secret service had at that time. However, neither that aspect nor Władysław Kawecki as such are discussed in Paweł Machcewicz's book on Radio Free Europe.[507]

Continuing his collaboration with the Communist secret service in Poland, Kawecki prepared a report on Polish political parties that operated abroad: SN (the National Party), PPS-WRN, and PRW NiD (the Polish Freedom Movement Independence and Democracy). I am of the opinion that he had to describe those parties whose members worked for various departments of Radio Free Europe and served as commanders in the Polish Guard Companies (*Polskie Kompanie Wartownicze*) in Germany. Therefore Kawecki must have known them personally.

In the late 1950s Kawecki's cooperation with the Ministry of Internal Affairs (viz. the old Ministry of Public Security, operating under a new name as of 1956 – translator's note) dwindled down and finally came to an end. It can be surmised, though, that he was viewed as a valuable agent by the Internal Military Service (*Wojskowa Służba Wewnętrzna*) because he was well-informed and could easily approach Polish émigrés living in West Germany. Indeed, he started working for the Internal Military Service in 1962 and stayed on the job until the early 1970s. His alias was Hill.[508] Kawecki proved to be so useful that in the late 1960s the counterintelligence chiefs planned to bring him back to Poland secretly (they even considered kidnapping) and to extort from him all the information that he had not revealed earlier. This operation was code-named Fala (Wave) and could have been carried out quite easily. Kawecki was simply to be blackmailed. The Polish court would have sentenced him for his wartime collaboration with the Germans, and foreign courts for his

---

[506] *Ibid.*, sheet 15.

[507] P. Machcewicz, „*Monachijska menażeria.*" *Walka z Radiem Wolna Europa 1950–1989* (Warszawa: Instytut Pamięci Narodowej, 2007).

[508] AIPN Warsaw, sign. no. 00518/82, Teczka personalna "Hill" – agent [Personal file of agent Hill].

collaboration with the Communist secret service. He would have been cornered. However, the plan was never put into practice, as other events intervened: the operation was going to be conducted in June–July 1968,[509] but then the Warsaw Pact armed forces invaded Czechoslovakia. The attack probably saved Kawecki from imprisonment in Poland or Germany.

We may wonder what made Hill such a prized agent for the Polish military counterintelligence. First and foremost, he knew the personal data of the agents of the CIC and the German intelligence, not just the Poles, but nationals of other countries behind the Iron Curtain. Internal Military Service records say that Kawecki supplied the names of 350 people who worked as agents for the USA and West European states. The next batch of information concerned scores of émigrés who were active in Polish émigré political parties. The Polish counterintelligence statistics show that Kawecki provided personal data on 22 individuals cooperating with Polish Communist intelligence and counterintelligence, 38 persons affiliated with Radio Free Europe, the Polish Veterans' Association (*Stowarzyszenie Polskich Kombatantów*) and the Union of Polish Émigrés (*Zjednoczenie Polskiego Uchodźstwa*), 11 persons cooperating with the CIC, 38 persons whom the CIC kept under surveillance, and 39 émigrés from Bulgaria, Czechoslovakia, Yugoslavia, and the Soviet Union.[510] The decision to bring Hill to Poland was made because the representatives of the Internal Military Service appreciated his expertise, which he always shared with them sparingly, and were pressurized by the secret service officers from other Eastern Bloc countries, who appraised Kawecki's revelations regularly and favorably. We do not know what happened to him later. In the 1970s he may have given up working for the Internal Military Service due to old age, or the Polish secret service dropped him for some reason. The matter requires further investigation in the archives.

---

[509] *Ibid.*, sheet 189.

[510] *Ibid.*

THE SECOND KATYN DELEGATION: THE LIFE OF LT.-COL. ADAM SZEBESTA DURING AND AFTER THE WAR

Adam Szebesta (who spelled his name Schebesta until the end of the War) was born on December 24, 1893 in Stryj (now Stryi, Ukraine). He completed his secondary education in Buczacz (now Buchach, Ukraine) and began medical studies in 1914 at the University of Lwów. When the First World War broke out, Szebesta was drafted into a medical unit in the Austrian army, where he initially served as an ordinary medic. In 1918, on orders from his Austrian superiors, he traveled to Albania, but immediately after the ceasefire returned to his family home in Austrian Galicia. At the end of the war he held the rank of second lieutenant.[511]

He found a job in a Lwów hospital and resumed his medical education. However, it was impossible for him to give all his time to the study and practice of medicine. During the Polish–Ukrainian conflict he took part in the defense of Lwów. Later he served as a military medic in the Polish–Soviet war. Therefore it was not until 1921 that he could focus on his education again, and in 1923 received a doctoral degree in medicine. The next year he moved to Warsaw to continue his studies and specialize in neurology and psychiatry. At that time he worked in the military hospital at Ujazdów and carried out his research in the Medical Aviation Research Institute (Centrum Badań Lotniczo-Lekarskich). He became a military doctor for the Fortieth Infantry

---

[511] AIPN Katowice, sign. no. 02/1340, Streszczenie sprawy nr 164/52 dotyczące dr Szebesty Adama [Summary of case no. 164/52 concerning Dr. Adam Szebesta], sheet 58.

187

Regiment and served in that capacity until 1926. Later he was employed in several military hospitals.

In 1930 he moved to Katowice in the region of Silesia and was chief physician for the local garrison and the Seventy-Third Infantry Regiment, where he was promoted to the rank of lieutenant colonel. While living in Silesia, he was involved in the initiatives of the Airborne and Anti-gas Defense League, the Polish Scouting and Guiding Organization, and the Polish Red Cross. Dr. Szebesta was one of the founders of pediatric neurology in that region.

THE RESISTANCE MOVEMENT AND THE KATYN INSPECTION

When the War broke out in 1939 Szebesta was nominated chief physician of the Śląsk (Silesia) operational group. In the campaign of September 1939 he served in the Twenty-Third Division, which surrendered to the Germans in the vicinity of Zamość. In that area Dr. Adam Szebesta supervised a makeshift field hospital, which operated until December 1939. Subsequently he worked in Kraków in the hospital run by the Brothers of Mercy, and for the Polish Red Cross, as its chief sanitary inspector and deputy plenipotentiary.[512] Additionally, he took up charity work in the RGO. All those activities were legal, viz. conducted in registered organizations recognized by the German occupying forces. However, Szebesta was active in other fields too. He was authorized by the PPS to engage in the work of the Polish Underground State. He was chief physician of the underground ZWZ (Union of Armed Struggle, later renamed the Home Army) for the Kraków region. In April 1941 Dr. Adam Szebesta and Lt.-Col. Jan Cichocki, Chief of Staff for Region IV, were arrested by the Gestapo. Szebesta was released fairly soon.[513] Regrettably, I do not have any further information concerning this intriguing period in his life.

Arguably, the most important event in the wartime years, and perhaps in his entire career, was his Katyn sojourn in April 1943. Szebesta was a member of the second Polish delegation organized by the Germans to disseminate news of the crime and propagandize Soviet culpability. On April 14, 1943 Szebesta

---

[512] *Ibid.*

[513] Bratko, *Dlaczego zginąłeś prokuratorze?*, 238.

25. The second delegation from the GG at Katyn, April 1943

flew to Katyn in a group that included Father Stanisław Jasiński, special representative of Archbishop Adam Sapieha; Marian Maak, a reptile journalist from Kraków also working for the Telpress agency and responsible for the local news coverage; Kazimierz Skarżyński, Secretary General of the Polish Red Cross; as well as Drs. Tadeusz Pragłowski, Stanisław Plappert, and Hieronim Bartoszewski, medical practitioners from Warsaw and Kraków. I have information from the postwar records of the Ministry of Public Security that there was one more reptilian journalist in the group, Zygmunt Ipohorski-Lenkiewicz. Other members were the technical staff of the Polish Red Cross, initially supervised by Capt. Ludwik Rojkiewicz,[514] who was replaced by Dr. Marian Wodziński on April 29. As Dr. Szebesta was a resistance movement activist at that time, we may assume that he was authorized to travel to Katyn by the Polish Underground State. This hypothesis is confirmed by what transpired when the delegation returned to the GG. Adam Szebesta became engaged in a number of important missions connected with his Katyn inspection.

His first task was to write a report on his Katyn inspection. We know for certain that he compiled such a report, because in May 1943 Sir Owen

---

[514] C. Madajczyk, *Dramat katyński*, 40.

O'Malley, British ambassador to the Polish government-in-exile, had a copy at his disposal when preparing documentation pertaining to the Katyn atrocity for the highest British officials, including Winston Churchill, the Prime Minister, and Anthony Eden, the Secretary of State. Szebesta's document was made available to the British authorities by General Stefan Grot-Rowecki, Chief Commander of the Home Army.[515] The report drafted by Dr. Szebesta included key information about the condition of the mass graves in which the Polish officers had been interred, the number of the victims as well as the evidence that had been found at the scene of the crime: shreds of newspapers, letters, and diaries, in which the latest dates were for April 1940. These materials were sent to London by radio communication and had a powerful impact on the British politicians. A copy of O'Malley's memorandum was also expedited to President Roosevelt.[516] This course of events is enough to demonstrate that Szebesta played a significant part in the struggle to reveal the truth about the Katyn atrocity. In 1943–1945 he continued to spread news of Soviet culpability for the massacre.

Upon his return to Kraków, Dr. Adam Szebesta issued a few statements in which he was quite explicit about the Soviet responsibility for the crime. Anonymous letters sent to the Ministry of Public Security after the War say that "when he came back from Katyn, he was telling everybody this awful crime was definitely the deed of the Bolsheviks, that all the evidence linked them to the crime."[517] Additionally, he may have expressed such opinions in the reptile press and official German publications on Katyn. Although I have not found any texts signed by Szebesta in *Goniec Krakowski* or *Nowy Kurier Warszawski*, it is highly probable that he was interviewed at least once by Władysław Kawecki for *Goniec Krakowski*, or that he authored one

---

[515] Maresch, *Katyń 1940*, 44. I am not questioning Eugenia Maresch's findings about how Szebesta's statement concerning his stay in Katyn was used, but in two reports that I am acquainted with, which were prepared by Lt.-Col. Michał Protasewicz for the Polish government-in-exile and later presented to the British, Szebesta is named only as a member of the Katyn delegation. Though the main source for Protasewicz's report was obviously the information from Edmund Seyfried and Kazimierz Skarżyński, it cannot be excluded that Protasewicz, a high-ranking officer of the Polish Armed Forces, had access to other documents. Cf. *Zbrodnia katyńska 1940*. B. Polak and M. Polak (eds.), 40–41, 49–51.

[516] *Ibid.*, 45.

[517] AIPN Katowice, sign. no. 02/1340, Streszczenie sprawy nr 164/52 dotyczące dr Szebesty Adama [Summary of case no. 164/52 concerning Dr. Adam Szebesta], sheet 56.

of the anonymous articles.[518] The Germans also used his name in his formal capacity as a Polish Red Cross delegate in their official publication on the Katyn massacre.[519]

Dr. Szebesta was also involved in the appointment of the head of the Polish Red Cross' Technical Commission working in Katyn at that time. The Germans treated this nomination as one of their priorities and pressured the decision-makers in the Polish Red Cross to name their candidate as soon as possible. To speed up proceedings, on April 22, 1943, they set up a Katyn Committee consisting of Wacław Lachert, Kazimierz Skarżyński, and Dr. Szebesta (representing the Polish Red Cross), Count Adam Ronikier and Edmund Seyfried (representing the RGO). Szebesta was responsible for the nomination of the head of the Polish Red Cross' Technical Commission. Initially he wanted to present three candidates, experienced physicians and researchers with a global reputation, from Kraków, Lwów, and Warsaw. Ultimately he recommended only one candidate, Dr. Marian Wodziński from the Institute of Forensic Medicine in Kraków; the other two candidates, Prof. Bolesław Popielski from Lwów and Dr. Stanisław Manczarski from Warsaw, were never officially considered. At the same time, Szebesta stressed that one of the three, Dr. Wodziński, was available immediately, ready to leave for Katyn at any moment, accompanied by three of his assistants.[520] Perhaps this was the decisive factor determining Wodziński's appointment. A delegation headed by him set off for Katyn in late April 1943.

There was a potential rival candidate, Dr. Jan Stanisław Olbrycht, however, his participation was not very likely, as he had been imprisoned in Auschwitz-Birkenau since 1942. Szebesta thought that because of the importance the Germans attached to the Katyn question, they might be willing to release Olbrycht from the concentration camp, and he would then have a better chance to survive the War if he was engaged to investigate the crime in Kraków's Institute of Forensic Medicine. Unfortunately, the Germans rejected

---

[518] For instance, 'Nad grobami polskich żołnierzy,' *Nowy Kurier Warszawski* 1943:93 (Apr. 19), 1; or 'Grudki polskiej ziemi padły na groby oficerów. Reportaż z pobytu delegacji PCK na miejscu kaźni pod Smoleńskiem,' *Nowy Kurier Warszawski* 1943: 94 (Apr. 20), 1.

[519] I am referring to a Polish-language leaflet about the work of the International Forensic Commission in Katyn, issued by the Germans in April 1943.

[520] Maresch, *Katyń 1940*, 130.

Szebesta's suggestion.[521] The postwar statement made by Kazimierz Skarżyński, head of the Polish Red Cross, shows that there was yet another candidate, Dr. Leon Wachholz from Kraków, an internationally recognized criminologist. Skarżyński implied the Germans did not accept Wachholz because he was imprisoned in Auschwitz-Birkenau at the time,[522] but his information was wrong. Dr. Leon Wachholz had died in Kraków on December 1, 1942. Most probably Skarżyński's memory failed him.

When Dr. Wodziński completed his five-week mission, the supervisory staff of the Polish Red Cross found another doctor to replace him. Dr. Szebesta suggested they should choose Dr. Tadeusz Starostka, a physician from Tarnobrzeg, who wanted to participate in the enterprise as an unpaid volunteer. Yet it turned out that the Germans finished the work in Katyn Forest because of the onset of the hot summer weather which made exhumation unviable, and the new appointee did not visit the site. The other members of the Technical Commission returned to the GG, taking with them the correspondence found on identified victims and some of their personal belongings, along with the forensic reports.

The next task for the Technical Commission under Szebesta's vigorous supervision was to hide the records compiled by the Polish doctors and specialists from the Institute of Forensic Medicine, keeping them out of reach both of the Germans and the Soviets. A great deal of relevant information on this aspect of the work is in the report by Kazimierz Skarżyński. It was Dr. Szebesta who informed the Board of the Polish Red Cross that following the exhumations, the Institute received "nine numbered cases holding envelopes with the Katyn finds as well as one special, smaller unnumbered case containing diaries discovered in the Katyn graves."[523] Presumably the work to sort and examine these records started already in the summer of 1943, on the initiative of the Polish Red Cross and Dr. Jan Zygmunt Robel, head of the

---

[521] Professor Jan Stanisław Olbrycht survived the War and in 1945 was commissioned by the Ministry of Public Security to draw up a specialist report on the findings of the German and the international forensic commissions which had worked at Katyn in 1943. The Communists sent him to West European countries to participate in international conferences during which he discredited the pronouncements of those commissions.

[522] Bratko, *Dlaczego zginąłeś prokuratorze?*, 254.

[523] Skarżyński, *Katyń. Raport Polskiego Czerwonego Krzyża*, 75.

Institute of Forensic Medicine. Also the content of the unnumbered case was examined, since at first the Poles feared that it had not been intended for their Institute.[524] Dr. Robel decided that work would be done to preserve the twenty-two diaries, and specialists made four copies of each of them. Drs. Szebesta and Robel attested they were true copies of the originals. These priceless documents were hidden away. The place was known only to the two experts and the commanders of the Home Army (presumably of its Kraków branch).

That was not the last of Szebesta's involvement in underground activities concerning the Katyn records. In late 1943 he took copies of the twenty-two diaries to Warsaw. Kazimierz Skarżyński remembered having read them overnight. He recalled that all of them stopped in the first months of 1940. "The most frequent topics were everyday matters such as the camp food and the soldiers' complaints about it etc. Many passages expressed a belief that the prisoners would be released quite soon, either due to diplomatic measures taken by the Allies or to the purported victories of the Allied forces on the front, or to the release that the Soviet authorities had promised."[525] Dr. Szebesta's wartime work for the Polish Red Cross was highly appreciated and earned him the esteem of many important persons in Kraków, such as Adam Ronikier and Archbishop Adam Sapieha. Ronikier wrote in his diary: "All of us, especially myself, knew what a good organizer Dr. Szebesta was and how dedicated he was to his work on behalf of the general public; we appreciated his immense energy and his perseverance in the face of adversity."[526] All of this made him one of the candidates considered for membership of the Board of the RGO.

In January 1945, just before the Red Army entered Kraków, the Germans evacuated the twenty-two cases of Katyn materials from the Institute of Forensic Medicine, transporting them to Breslau (now Wrocław, Poland). The Institute's Polish employees under Dr. Szebesta had prepared a plan to intercept the finds and hide them in special containers at the bottom of a lake, but the scheme did not succeed.[527] Dr. Szebesta was authorized by the Polish Red Cross to search for the Katyn records. He went to Breslau and found that the

---

[524] *Ibid.*, 76.

[525] *Ibid.*, 78.

[526] Ronikier, *Pamiętniki 1939–1945*, 280.

[527] Maresch, *Katyń 1940*, 275.

cases had been stored for some time in one of the university buildings.[528] Then the Germans transported them further west, practically at the last possible moment, in May 1945, when the city was almost completely encircled by Soviet forces. Thereafter Szebesta wanted to find Dr. Werner Beck, the German head of the Institute of Forensic Medicine, having good reason to suppose he could know the whereabouts of the Katyn materials. Yet his Breslau expedition ultimately failed, or at least that is how he presented it in his conversation with Skarżyński in 1946. He added he had to remain in hiding for many months and was not able to come out into the open until the amnesty regulations came into force.[529] We may conjecture he had September 1945 in mind. His hiding place could have been Bukowina Tatrzańska. Having gone public, Szebesta contacted Polish Red Cross associates, including Dr. Władysław Gorczycki, head of the Polish Red Cross Hospital in Warsaw. Thanks to his help, Szebesta was appointed the Red Cross' plenipotentiary in Silesia. From September 18, 1945 he lived in Katowice and held a job as a doctor in the state-owned social and health insurance institution.[530]

AFTER THE WAR IN KATOWICE

Dr. Szebesta had been a prominent figure in Katowice even before the War. After 1945, the general public became familiar with new information about him, that he had officially worked for the Polish Red Cross during the War. This is why some people thought Szebesta had collaborated with the Germans, which was not true.

Since his wartime life was known only superficially and the main fact was his involvement with the Polish Red Cross and the RGO, soon the security police in the region started to receive anonymous letters accusing Dr. Szebesta of pro-German sympathies and collaboration. On the other hand, when the security police officers interviewed Szebesta's neighbors or his subordinates at work, it turned out that his conduct had been impeccable both during and after the War. Nevertheless, the decision was to keep him under surveillance.

---

[528] Skarżyński, *Katyń. Raport Polskiego Czerwonego Krzyża*, 79.

[529] *Ibid.*, 81.

[530] AIPN Katowice, sign. no. 2/1340, Streszczenie sprawy nr 164/52 dotyczące dr Szebesty Adama [Summary of case no. 164/52 concerning Dr. Adam Szebesta], sheet 303.

One of the top officials of Department 5 of the Ministry of Public Security discussed the matter in a letter dated May 9, 1947 to the security police in Silesia,[531] putting the same questions he had already asked in a letter of November 13, 1946 which the officers in Katowice had left unanswered. The thing the Ministry was most interested in was Dr. Szebesta's work in Katyn. One of their primary concerns was whether that involvement would be enough "to suspect him of collaboration with the Germans."[532] The Ministry's extant records show that at first the opinions about Szebesta were overwhelmingly favorable. One of them reads as follows: "He is fully reliable in his duty as plenipotentiary of the Polish Red Cross, and it has to be admitted he is a good organizer. He is a member of the PPS holding centrist views (…). An acquaintance of Bishop Adamski. Has a good opinion of the public security institutions, and tries to follow the guidelines. The objections against Dr. Schebesta are that he visited Katyn during the War and is suspected of having collaborated with the Germans."[533] Another description in the security police files says Szebesta was and had always been committed to charity work. Also, he was known as a person leading a balanced lifestyle and respected by the community.[534]

Until 1948 Dr. Szebesta was on friendly relations with activists of the PPS and the PSL. The security police officers also learned that Szebesta was in touch with politicians like Arka Bożek and Jerzy Ziętek. Additionally, the list of his acquaintances included several academics from the Silesian Institute of Technology in Gliwice, as well as the British consul George Scott. Apparently Szebesta went on a skiing holiday in Zakopane with Scott. He was also visited several times by the writer Kornel Makuszyński in Bukowina Tatrzańska. I have managed to find a report that Szebesta was in touch with Franciszek Białas, one of the wartime leaders of PPS-WRN. This was a significant point for the security police. Białas was an emissary of the Polish government-in-exile and after the War managed to leave Poland as Franek (Franciszek) Góralczyk. Subsequently, all his former acquaintances were put under surveillance. Here we could look at Szebesta's story as compared to the biography of Edmund

---

[531] *Ibid.*, sheet 8.

[532] *Ibid.*

[533] *Ibid.*, sheet 11.

[534] *Ibid.*, sheet 12.

Seyfried and the circumstances of his arrest. I am led to believe that all these developments induced Dr. Adam Szebesta to join the PZPR (viz. the ruling Communists), which he did in 1948.

As a result of the Ray Madden Committee and its work, the Katyn atrocity again made the headlines in Western Europe and the United States, and therefore it became a leading political issue also on the eastern side of the Iron Curtain.[535] This is why, in my opinion, the Ministry of Public Security returned to the inquiries it had made in 1945–1946, deciding to keep under surveillance and question all those who could confirm the Soviet version of the events.

Adam Szebesta was arrested by the security police in Katowice on October 20, 1950 and put in the local jail. The records give three reasons for his arrest. The first was his suspected collaboration following his visit to Katyn in April 1943. The second concerned his contacts with the British consul George Scott, and suspected espionage. The third was Szebesta's underground activity in PPS-WRN, and later in the Polish Underground State. While the first and third issue had been investigated previously by the Ministry of Public Security and did not entail the severest consequences, the accusation of spying was a serious threat, as this offense was punishable by death. The risk was high, since the security police had collected evidence concerning intelligence activities to support the charge (including a deposition by Roman Pruchnicki, a Polish pilot who had studied architecture in Edinburgh, was wounded six times in combat missions, and returned to Poland from the United Kingdom in 1947, only to be imprisoned and charged with spying for the British).[536] However, as the materials were inconclusive, the decision was not to bring Szebesta to trial yet, and he was released on February 1, 1951. But he remained under surveillance "to clear up any confusion or ambiguity, or to prove he had acted as an enemy of People's Poland."[537] It cannot be excluded that the work on the case was temporarily discontinued for different reasons.

The medical community and inhabitants of Rabka came to Szebesta's defense, especially as the local people were full of admiration for his efforts to build a children's sanatorium in their town. As a free man, Szebesta could

---

[535] Cf. Wasilewski, 'Decyzja Politbiura,' 107–133.

[536] AIPN Katowice, sign. no 02/1340, Streszczenie sprawy nr 164/52 dotyczące dr Szebesty Adama [Summary of case no. 164/52 concerning Dr. Adam Szebesta], sheets 58–66.

[537] *Ibid.*, sheets 59–60.

prove useful to the Communists in their endeavor to obliterate the truth about Katyn. The security police could have offered a barter of favors: not harassing Szebesta for his alleged spying in exchange for the kind of public statement on Katyn the Soviet Union and Polish Communists wanted. Similar situations had occurred previously in Czechoslovakia and Bulgaria, where Drs. František Hájek and Marko Markov, who wanted to save their lives, withdrew their signatures from the 1943 German document in which they had confirmed that the Soviets were culpable of the Katyn crime, which was committed in 1940.[538]

THE KATYN CAMPAIGN OF 1952

On March 18, 1952, *Dziennik Zachodni*, the Silesian newspaper of the PZPR, which was issued in Katowice, published an interview with Dr. Adam Szebesta, "an eye witness of the propagandist provocation staged by the Nazis at Katyn."[539] There is no doubt that the text was vetted by top Communist Party officials. We now have access to irrefutable corroborating evidence for this. The interview's first reader was the deputy head of the Department of Propaganda, Education, and Culture of the Regional Committee of the PZPR in Katowice. Following his approval, on March 8, 1952 the interview was forwarded to Stefan Staszewski, head of the Press Department of the Party's Central Committee. He removed one sentence from the original text, which read: "The doctor who was showing us around presented several skulls of victims, explaining that the caliber was typical of the weapons used in the Soviet Union." No-one corrected the misspelled name of Kazimierz Skarżyński, printed "Starzyński."[540]

In this rigged text, Adam Szebesta raised several topics that were very important for the Communist propaganda. He said the Germans had forced

---

[538] M. Borák, 'Ofiary zbrodni katyńskiej w Republice Czeskiej w świetle nowych ustaleń,' 65.

[539] Wójcicki, *Prawda o Katyniu*, 186–189.

[540] AIPN Warsaw, sign. no. 00231/124, Pismo Zastępcy Kierownika Wydziału Propagandy, Oświaty i Kultury KW PZPR do Komitetu Centralnego PZPR z dnia 8 III 1952 r. [Letter from the Deputy Head of the Department of Propaganda, Education, and Culture of the Regional Committee of the Polish United Workers' Party to the Central Committee of the Polish United Workers' Party, dated Mar. 8, 1952], sheets 82–84.

him to go to Katyn and turned the inspection into a show. "Upon our arrival
at Katyn, we were assembled in a large room, where a German lieutenant gave
us a long lecture, starting with the origin and history of the graves, which, as
he said, had been discovered by chance. Then he went on to the testimonies
of some local people and findings about the site, graves, corpses, documents
etc. Later, we were taken to Katyn in a car. (…) We were shown around the
site along an established route, and we could see a number of graves which
were partly or completely open, until we reached a clearing, where we saw
rows of dead bodies in Polish uniforms. I was struck by their arrangement
according to rank. In the foreground were the bodies of two generals, then
there were colonels, and so on."[541] Dr. Szebesta answered a question about
how unrestricted the delegates were during the inspection. "We were not free
to inspect the site in any way whatsoever. First of all, we stayed at Katyn just
for an hour or so. Secondly, each of us was surrounded by several escorts and
directed to join the group if he happened to stop on the way or move away
from the fixed route. We were able to see only what they wanted to show us
and how they wanted it to be shown."[542] Toward the end, the interviewer
extorted the following conclusion from the doctor: "Although my stay in
Katyn Forest was extremely short, it gave me plenty to think about. The arti-
ficiality and theatricality in the staging of the whole event left me in no doubt
as to the motives of its designers. All the prequels, that is the lecture, the
statements by standby witnesses and experts, the presence of camera oper-
ators and photographers, stood in stark contrast to the previously declared
lack of bias on the matter, and strengthened our belief that this was a perfid-
ious propaganda scheme. Additionally, we observed several things on the site
that contradicted the German hypothesis on the time when the crime had
been committed and thus on the perpetrators. As we all know, the German
propaganda said the date of the massacre was 1940. (…) Therefore, when
I was leaving Katyn, I had no doubts who was culpable of the Katyn killings.
Unquestionably, the murderers were those whose hands had been so many
times soaked in Polish blood: Hitler's butchers."[543]

---

[541] Wójcicki, *Prawda o Katyniu*, 187.

[542] *Ibid.*, 186.

[543] *Ibid.*, 188–189.

Quite naturally, this interview with Dr. Adam Szebesta validated the Soviet version of the Katyn crime. One could even risk a statement that the Communists' plan to release Dr. Szebesta from jail paid off: they pressured him to be interviewed and then aggressively propagandized the Soviet representation of the Katyn atrocity. Szebesta was an eye witness who had personally inspected the site and then, albeit after almost a decade, cast doubt on the German allegations. But in 1952 no-one paid attention to the ten-year gap between the inspection and the interview.

THE DOUBTS HARBORED BY ALICJA BEM

I can also observe some good consequences for the Katyn case and the dispelling of the Soviet lies. After the interview with Dr. Szebesta had been published, the editors of *Dziennik Zachodni* received a letter from a person who was profoundly interested in the matter, the widow of a Polish officer who had gone missing in 1940.

"Dear Dr. Szebesta, Having seen the open graves in Katyn Forest, in your interview you describe the circumstances of the crime in much detail. Since it appears my late husband was killed there, please publish answers to the following questions: (1) My husband's last letter reached me in April 1940, when I was staying in Baranowicze [now Baranavichy, Belarus]. Previously I used to receive regular correspondence from Kozelsk once a fortnight or at least once a month. From April 1940 to the spring of 1943 I received no news whatsoever, except for an article in a reptile issued by the Germans in 1943, that my husband's body had been identified in one of the graves at Katyn. My friends and acquaintances stopped getting correspondence from their husbands at the same time. So where did the officers spend those three years? How was it they could not send any news, given that they used to write letters quite regularly before? (2) When the Germans captured Smolensk in June–July 1940, why didn't any of the 12 thousand Polish officers send any news, and why didn't any of them manage to escape from captivity, especially as a considerable number of Polish prisoners escaped from Soviet jails at that time? (3) Why were they unable to send any letters between April 1940 and July 1941? (4) Please give the month and year when they are presumed to have been killed. (5) When General Sikorski was recruiting a Polish army in Russia in August 1941, why was he not told that the officers were missing because the camps where they were imprisoned had been captured by the Germans?"[544] Alicja Bem, who sent her letter from Katowice, concluded she wanted it to be printed in the newspaper, in accordance with her constitutional rights. It seems the editors of *Dziennik Zachodni* never replied to the desperate woman, or at least I have not found a reply printed in the paper. Yet it is possible the editor-in-chief simply posted a letter to her. In my opinion, one more aspect is important regarding Capt. Józef Bem. Piotr Gontarczyk has found that during the War members of the PPR sent data to Moscow for use in the anti-German campaign concerning the Katyn crime. For instance, they provided the names of officers that the Germans said had been killed at Katyn. In 1943, one of the Communist activists coordinating the plan sent a telegram to Georgi Dimitrov, who had demanded full documentation on the matter. The text said: "regarding Captain Bem (…), whose name is on the list of victims, we know that in 1940 the Germans sent him to Auschwitz."[545]

It should be noted that Alicja Bem, the author of the letter, demonstrated great courage by speaking up publicly and asking questions about the fate of her husband. She provided her full name, showing she did not fear the consequences of sending such a letter. Countless other relatives, that is parents, siblings, wives, and children of the murdered officers, were just as stout-hearted, requesting the same information from *Fala 49*, a political propagandist program on Polish Radio; after some time they heard on the air that the Germans were the perpetrators of the Katyn crime.

---

[544] AIPN Katowice, sign. no. 02/1340, Streszczenie sprawy nr 164/52 dotyczące dr Szebesty Adama [Summary of case no. 164/52 concerning Dr. Adam Szebesta], sheet 118.

[545] Gontarczyk, *Polska Partia Robotnicza*, 225.

FROM KATYN TO REMBERTÓW. DR. KONRAD ORZECHOWSKI URGENTLY WANTED BY THE NKVD

Konrad Orzechowski's biographical note in *Polski Słownik Biograficzny* (*PSB*, the Polish biographical dictionary) does not tell us that after the War there were reprisals against him for his participation in a 1943 Katyn delegation.[546] The topic is touched upon in just one, rather enigmatic and insubstantial sentence: "As a member of the Board of the Polish Red Cross he had various additional duties which were connected with the organization's role under wartime occupation (e.g. he took part in the so-called Katyn Commission)."[547]

Orzechowski was born on February 14, 1887 to a landowning family living in Mogielnica. He attended high school in Warsaw, but was expelled because he took part in the 1905 anti-Russian school strike, and had to take his final examinations in 1906, in General Paweł Chrzanowski's private college. During the next year he worked as a private tutor in Mogielnica, saving up money to begin his university education. In 1907–1913 he studied medicine at the Jagiellonian University, and in 1913 earned his doctoral degree. Next he took up a job in Kochanówka mental hospital near Łódź. Prior to the outbreak of the Great War he was also employed for a short time in

---

[546] Z. Podgórska-Klawe, 'Orzechowski Konrad (1887–1964),' *Polski Słownik Biograficzny*, vol. 144, fascicle 101 (Wrocław, Warszawa, Kraków, and Gdańsk: Polska Akademia Nauk, 1979), 282–283. Orzechowski's biography, mainly the war years and their aftermath, has also been treated by Witold Wasilewski ('Z komisji do łagru,' *Pamięć.pl* 2015: 4, 28–31).

[547] *Ibid.*

Czerwony Bór hospital near Warsaw. In 1914–1918 he served as a military doctor in the rank of captain in the Russian army, and was head of a military hospital. When the War was over, Orzechowski settled down in Warsaw, working for the Internal Medicine University Hospital as well as the Public Health Agency (he was head physician for one of the regions and for the penitentiary in Warsaw's Mokotów district). In the early 1930s he was head of the St Stanislaus Hospital for Infectious Diseases in Warsaw. Finally he was appointed hospital inspector and head of the Hospital Care Department for the municipal authorities of Warsaw, holding the latter post until February 28, 1945.[548] Orzechowski was extremely successful in treating and preventing tuberculosis and was one of the cofounders of a TB sanatorium in Otwock. He also lectured on hygiene and germ control in the State School of Hygiene and in the School of Nursing. Before the Second World War he published a few monographs and articles on hospital care as provided in Warsaw and all over Poland. In 1938, he was awarded the Polonia Restituta Knight's Cross for his achievement in social work and medicine. His political sympathies were with the National Democrats.

THE KATYN DELEGATION

When the Second World War broke out and Warsaw was under German attack, Orzechowski was appointed medical head of the city's Civil Defense Section. On September 28, 1939 he accompanied Stefan Starzyński, Mayor of Warsaw, and General Tadeusz Kutrzeba in the capitulation negotiations held at Okęcie. Under German occupation, until 1945, Orzechowski continued to supervise all the hospitals in Warsaw. The City Council of Warsaw authorized him to take part in the first Katyn delegation of April 11, 1943. On the day preceding the departure the Germans held a meeting for the representatives of the Polish Red Cross, the RGO, the City Council, and two writers; they wanted to know who was in the delegation, as there had been continual modifications to the list. Some people (e.g. Rev. Zygmunt Kozubski, and two city councilors, Stanisław Wachowiak and Janusz Machnicki) declined to take part, offering

---

[548] I present Orzechowski's biography on the basis of the information in *PSB* and Ministry of Public Security records. AIPN BU, sign. no. 0423/4143, Życiorys z 2 VIII 1948 r. [CV dated August 2, 1948]. Some AIPN documents give an erroneous date of birth (February 19, 1887).

the names of people to replace them. During the meeting, Dr. Emil Kipa, representing the municipal authorities, said a physician, Dr. Konrad Orzechowski, would be one of the delegates.[549] Today, thanks to records in the Institute of National Remembrance, we know that Dr. Orzechowski's name was put forward by Julian Kulski, Mayor of Warsaw, who issued a special note defining the purpose of the trip: "to carry out an inspection of the Polish graves at Koziy Gory near Smolensk."[550]

Dr. Orzechowski kept a low profile in Smolensk and Katyn. He made no public statements over the open graves nor gave an interview for German radio. He did not talk to Władysław Kawecki, the Telpress correspondent, but silently observed the mass graves and victims' bodies. He listened to the comments by the German officers and doctors who were in Katyn and Smolensk at that time. If it had not been for the reptile press reports and the photograph of the delegation inspecting the site, in which Orzechowski and Grodzki are clearly visible and which was published in *Nowy Kurier Warszawski* and *Goniec Krakowski*, pretty soon after April 1943 most people would have forgotten that Orzechowski had indeed taken part in a German-organized trip to Katyn. Having returned to the GG, he never discussed the inspection in public, and just presented an oral report to Julian Kulski; regrettably, we do not know what he said. I did not manage to find a report made by Orzechowski for the top officials of the Polish Underground State and the government-in-exile. He exercised considerable restraint on the matter, so it is quite possible that he did not write such a document at all. However, his name was in the report drafted by the commanders of the Home Army and sent abroad. It reached London on April 15, 1943, but did not contain too many details.[551] In May 1943 Lt.-Col. Michał Protasewicz of the Polish Armed Forces mentioned Orzechowski's name in the Katyn report he prepared as personal advisor to General Władysław Sikorski, Polish Prime Minister and Commander-in-Chief.[552]

---

[549] The particulars of the meeting were described by Ferdynand Goetel ('Lot do Katynia,' 10).

[550] AIPN BU, sign. no. 0423/4143, Życiorys z 2 VIII 1948 r. [CV dated August 2, 1948], sheet 52.

[551] Maresch, *Katyń 1940*, 76.

[552] *Zbrodnia katyńska 1940. Polacy w Wielkiej Brytanii*, 49.

During the 1944 Warsaw Rising, Drs. Konrad Orzechowski and Edward Grodzki worked in a civilian hospital located near the Królikarnia Palace in the district of Mokotów. When the Rising fell, the Germans marched Orzechowski and a crowd of other inhabitants to the Pruszków camp. After combat operations in the neighborhood of the capital had stopped and the Red Army entered Warsaw, he settled in the nearby town of Milanówek and again worked in local hospitals.

SOVIET CAPTIVITY

Konrad Orzechowski was arrested by the political police on February 25, 1945 and handed over to the Soviets. Ministry of Public Security records say that "the detainment was a result of his participation in the Katyn [propaganda] campaign."[553] Initially he was held in the NKVD's Rembertów camp (No. 10 Soviet special prison). The security police files say Orzechowski was deported by the Soviets on March 26, 1945. According to Dariusz Rogut, for some time Dr. Orzechowski was imprisoned in camp no. 523 in the Urals.[554] He worked in the camp hospital, in exceedingly difficult conditions, and tried to provide medical assistance in every possible way. Unfortunately, 331 prisoners of the camp died from various causes. Orzechowski was one of 1,425 Poles imprisoned in that camp.[555] His internment in Rembertów and deportation to a Soviet gulag started rumors that he had not survived the reprisals. For instance, in the spring of 1946 Kazimierz Skarżyński thought he had died and put the following statement in his report: "I left Poland on May 20, 1946 and by that time several people connected with the Katyn case had already died, such as Captain Ludwik Rojkiewicz, Ferdynand Zaborzut, Col. Hugon Kassur, Count Władysław Zamoyski, as well as Dr. Władysław Gorczycki, head of the Polish Red Cross, and Dr. Konrad Orzechowski (…)."[556]

---

[553] AIPN BU, sign. no. 0423/4143, Dr K. Orzechowski i dr E. Grodzki [Dr. Konrad Orzechowski and Dr. Edward Grodzki].

[554] D. Rogut, 'Polacy w obozach dla jeńców wojennych i internowanych NKWD–MWD–ZSRR po 1944 r.,' *Łambinowicki Rocznik Muzealny* (2007: 30), 51.

[555] *Ibid.*, 51, 53.

[556] Skarżyński, *Katyń. Raport Polskiego Czerwonego Krzyża*, 81.

Orzechowski was held in the Soviet Union until November 1, 1947. According to Ministry of Public Security records the only thing he said about that period was that he had been interned in the Soviet Union, but did not name the place of his detention.[557] Several guesses may be hazarded at this point. Given that the Communists in the Soviet Union were looking for people who knew the details of the Katyn crime and might be witnesses in a show trial, held either in Poland or Nuremberg, we may assume that Orzechowski could have been an important witness. As a member of a 1943 delegation, he would have been liable to Soviet death threats and, if pressured, might have testified that the inspection had been a German hoax. This line of argumentation takes us to Moscow. If the Soviets had been lining Orzechowski up as a witness in a Katyn trial, they would have surely held him in the Lubyanka prison. That possibility cannot be excluded, even though Orzechowski was imprisoned in Camp no. 523. Actually, the chances that he was imprisoned in Moscow are quite high. Camp no. 523 was set up in April 1945 and the first group of prisoners was transported there from Sanok, south-eastern Poland, in the first two days of that month.[558] This means Orzechowski arrived in the camp later, perhaps after a period of imprisonment in the Lubyanka. This hypothesis can be supported by the date of his release from the NKVD camp. Konrad Orzechowski returned to Poland in November 1947, i.e. when the Katyn campaign was over: the proceedings were going on in Nuremberg, while the Communists definitely abandoned the idea of staging a Katyn trial in Poland. In my opinion, one more factor may be considered in Dr. Orzechowski's case, by analogy to the fate of General Jerzy Wołkowicki, who was not killed by the NKVD in 1940 thanks to his military service in the Russo–Japanese War of 1904–1905, particularly for his valor in the Battle of Tsushima. It is quite possible that Dr. Orzechowski's service in the medical corps of the Russian army in 1914–1918 earned him a modicum of good will on the part of the Soviets after the Second World War. Perhaps this is why he survived and returned home.

---

[557] AIPN BU, sign. no. 0423/4143, Życiorys z 2 VIII 1948 r. [CV dated August 2, 1948], sheet 53.

[558] Rogut, 'Polacy w obozach dla jeńców wojennych i internowanych NKWD–MWD–ZSRR po 1944 r.,' 51.

KEEPING KATYN AT BAY

Orzechowski's arrival in Poland did not mark the end of his problems; security police officers were expecting him. However, Dr. Jerzy Sawicki, the prosecutor who had been working for a Katyn trial since 1945, was not interested in interviewing Orzechowski. He had wanted to question him in July 1945, but no longer in 1947. What is interesting, though, are the opinions various doctors in Warsaw held about Orzechowski. Some thought he had received special treatment from the Germans because his wife, Wanda Julia Luniak, came from Germany. Yet many benefited from certain privileges he could enjoy in his professional life, especially under German occupation during the War, when he could obtain otherwise unavailable medicines. Ludwik Hirszfeld had a bad opinion of Orzechowski for his "unfavorable attitude to the Jewish hospitals in the ghetto."[559] On the other hand, Orzechowski was commended by those who remained faithful to the ideals of the Polish Underground State both during and after the War. They said he "came back home in an aura of martyrdom."[560] Such statements could have aroused the secret police's suspicions. Maj. Ryszard Nazarewicz became interested in Orzechowski and put him under surveillance again.[561]

Upon his return from the Soviet Union, Orzechowski approached his former employers in the hope of getting a job in Warsaw, but the attempt was unsuccessful. Therefore he decided to take a six-month health leave of absence and then, having found no stable employment, to retire at the age of 61. Eventually he received a position in the Polish Central Statistical Agency (now Statistics Poland), where he worked in 1948–1951. From 1951 on he was one of the managers of Polskie Uzdrowiska, a state-owned enterprise managing the infrastructure of the Polish health resorts. The Ministry of Public Security did not involve him in any way in the second Katyn campaign in 1952,

---

[559] AIPN BU, sign. no. 0423/4143, Pismo Naczelnika I Wydziału UBP na m.st. Warszawa do MBP Departament I, Wydział I [Letter from the Head of Division One of the Public Security Office in the Capital City of Warsaw to the Ministry of Public Security, Department One, Division One], sheet 34.

[560] *Ibid.*, sheet 35.

[561] *Ibid.*, Dr K. Orzechowski i dr E. Grodzki [Dr. Konrad Orzechowski and Dr. Edward Grodzki].

which was conducted in response to the work of the Ray Madden Committee. Orzechowski was not on the list of those who might have proved useful in the propaganda efforts concerning the Katyn case. In 1953 the secret police considered his case closed.[562]

Dr. Konrad Orzechowski died in Warsaw on March 16, 1964.

---

[562] Wasilewski, 'Z komisji do łagru,' 31.

EDMUND SEYFRIED'S INVOLVEMENT WITH THE RESISTANCE MOVEMENT, AND THE KATYN DELEGATION AS HIS MOST IMPORTANT MISSION

BEFORE THE SECOND WORLD WAR (1889–1939)

Edmund Seyfried was born in Lwów on February 15, 1889. In 1895–1899 he attended the Stanisław Staszic primary school and no. 4 high school, which he finished in June 1907. As his parents had to deal with serious financial problems, he did not continue his education, but found a job instead. At first he was employed in the Lwów revenue office, and from June 1908 until the First World War worked for a company that insured employees against industrial accidents. At the same time he studied at the Law Faculty of the University of Lwów, and graduated in 1913. During his time as a student he attended the obligatory year of military training.

When the war broke out he was drafted into the Austro–Hungarian army, joined the Second Battery of the Eleventh Regiment of Field Howitzers, and was sent to the eastern front. In the initial phase of the military operations, until December 1914, he fought at Zborów (now Zboriv, Ukraine), Lwów, Przemyśl, Gorlice, Kraków, and Mysłowice. Between December 1914 and May 1915 his unit was garrisoned at Tarnów. During that period Seyfried fell ill with typhus and was sent for treatment to a Kraków hospital, and then convalesced in

Budapest. When his leave of absence was over, he served in the Office of Aides-de-camp of the Commandant of Lwów until the end of the war in November 1918. Then he was drafted into the Polish Army in the rank of lieutenant and served in the operational group commanded by Gen. Tadeusz Rozwadowski. In March 1919 he was posted to Przemyśl as an information officer to serve under Gen. Wacław Iwaszkiewicz. After two months he was transferred to Lublin to Gen. Stanisław Haller's unit, and from there to Kraków, and eventually back to Lwów, his home town. There a Corps District Command was established, and Seyfried became head of the information service. In August 1919 he was posted to the Warsaw Corps District Command, where he participated in the establishment of Department 2 (viz. the intelligence service) of the Ministry of Internal Affairs. He took part in the 1920 war against the Bolsheviks and finished his military service on December 31, 1920 in the rank of captain.

His civilian career began in Warsaw, with Towarzystwo Aprowizacji Miast Polskich, a business which distributed foodstuffs to all parts of the country. Seyfried's task was to supply provisions to the region of Lesser Poland, which he knew well. He worked there until the spring of 1925, when the company closed down. Having moved to Lwów, he took up a job with a coal trading company owned by Jan Seles. When it was restructured in 1930 he applied for an inspector's post in a regional insurance company, which he held until July 1932. Later he worked for a few months in a social insurance company. In June 1933 he moved again to Warsaw, to work for the Ruch booksellers, and stayed in the job until the outbreak of the Second World War.[563]

Following the German invasion of September 1939, his company relocated to Lublin and then to Tarnopol (now Ternopil, Ukraine). Finally, after a short stopover in Buczacz (now Buchach, Ukraine), Seyfried and the company's employees moved to Lwów. In late October 1939 he returned to Warsaw.[564]

---

[563] I present Edmund Seyfried's biography up to 1939 on the basis of AIPN documents in Warsaw. AIPN BU, sign. no. 01251/151, Teczka Edmunda Seyfrieda i in. [Dossier of Edmund Seyfried and others]. Protokół po przesłuchaniu podejrzanego z dnia 3 I 1953 r. [Minutes of suspect's interrogation, Jan. 3, 1953], sheet 134. *Polski Słownik Biograficzny* (vol. 36, fascicle 3/150, pp. 377–378) has a brief entry on Edmund Seyfried by Zdzisław Nicman, which follows his elder brother Kamil J. Seyfried's biographical note [*Kamil J. Seyfried (1872-1960)*].

[564] AIPN BU, sign. no. 01251/151, Teczka Edmunda Seyfrieda i in. [Dossier of Edmund Seyfried and others].

In December 1939, the German authorities appointed him head of the financial department of the Ruch company.

THE RGO (1940–1945)

Seyfried resigned from his job in Ruch in December 1940 to become head of the financial department of the RGO in Kraków. From July 1, 1941 he was its director general and held the position until January 1945.[565] The RGO operated throughout the GG, and as he was in charge of the organization for several years, he was undoubtedly the right person to assess its achievements retrospectively, after a lapse of seven years, following his arrest in 1952. When interrogated by officers of the Ministry of Public Security, he said that "beside the Red Cross, the RGO was the only Polish organization that was registered and recognized by the Germans. As it conducted various activities, it was able to get an insight into the adverse circumstances in which the people of Poland had to live and, on the other hand, (…) as a result of regular contact with the German authorities, it could find out what measures they intended to introduce on Polish territories."[566] Seyfried stressed that the relations with the governing bodies of the GG had made it possible for him to obtain invaluable information on German policies on Poles and Jews. For instance, in 1941 he informed the Jewish Labor Organization in Kraków about the German plans to establish a ghetto in the city. In the same year, thanks to the efforts of the RGO, a letter of appeal was sent to the German authorities to stop the deportation of the Polish population from the region of Zamość and, though only for a short time, the ethnic cleansing program was interrupted. During his interrogation Edmund Seyfried said, "After the letter had been submitted, Ronikier and I were summoned to appear before [Hans] Frank and to witness his conversation with the recently appointed governor (…). Frank told him to adopt a less rigorous stance toward the Poles in the district of Lublin, considering that Gen. [Odilo] Globocnik, head of the Lublin Gestapo, had been dismissed. Less harsh measures were introduced, but after a few weeks the reprisals recommenced."[567]

---

[565] *Ibid.*, sheet 32.

[566] *Ibid.*, Zeznania własnoręcznie napisane przez Seyfrieda Edmunda z dnia 30 XII 1952 r. [Manuscript of Edmund Seyfried's handwritten statement, Dec. 30, 1952], sheet 37.

[567] *Ibid.*, sheet 42.

Like the [clandestine] Polish Council to Aid Jews, the RGO dispensed aid to concentration camp prisoners. From December 1943, "every week it sent supplies of provisions, such as bread, soup ingredients (e.g. vegetables, onions, noodles, and groats), special products for sick prisoners (sugar, rusks, porridge oats), margarine, jam, and sheep's milk cheese. Additionally, for Christmas, [Plaszow] prisoners received large quantities of bigos (cabbage stew) and vegetable salad. Apart from food, they also got medicines and dressings, as well as shoes and wooden clogs, coats and other clothes, as well as much needed bedding, blankets, quilts, and straw mattresses. (…) All these objects were vital necessities."[568] A portion of this aid never reached the intended recipients or was simply misdirected in the process, but the RGO did not give up supporting detainees in this way. Thanks to direct contact with certain Plaszow prisoners, some things, such as letters, money or information, were smuggled in illicitly. Also, it was possible to draw up a register of the prisoners, at least in part.[569]

In March 1943, substituting for Adam Ronikier, who was on sick leave, Edmund Seyfried protested against a German proposal to have an RGO delegation present at an event to celebrate the fact that as many as one million workers had been relocated from the GG to the Third Reich. In the presence of Lothar Weirauch, a senior German official, Seyfried announced that Poles had nothing to celebrate and added that although the RGO was obliged to accept the invitation, it did not approve of deporting Poles as a slave labor force to Germany.[570] In October 1943 the leaders of the RGO turned down an invitation to take part in a grandiose harvest festival that the Germans were staging in Wawel Castle, although Adam Ronikier, chair of the organization, had previously declared their intention to attend. Bogdan Kroll is of the opinion that the incident needs to be carefully investigated, because the representatives of the Polish Underground State had extremely divergent opinions on Polish participation in the festivities. Initially, the local representative did not raise any objections, but later the Headquarters of the Kraków Region of the Home Army actively dissuaded members of the RGO from joining the event and

---

[568] R. Kotarba, *Niemiecki obóz w Płaszowie 1942–1945* (Warszawa and Kraków: Instytut Pamięci Narodowej, 2009), 99. On Seyfried's involvement in aiding Jews and on the Council to Aid Jews, see Kroll, *Rada Główna Opiekuńcza 1939–1945*, 227–229.

[569] Kotarba, *Niemiecki obóz w Płaszowie 1942–1945*, 99.

[570] Kroll, *Rada Główna Opiekuńcza 1939–1945*, 282.

even planned to have Ronikier abducted on the day. Eventually, the leaders of the RGO including Edmund Seyfried, did not turn up at Wawel Castle.[571] In consequence, Adam Ronikier lost his position in the organization, while the RGO's protest was very well received by public opinion in the GG and the underground resistance movement. The underground *Biuletyn Informacyjny* expressed a favorable opinion and published an article entitled 'Zaszczytna dymisja' [Honorable dismissal].[572] Another RGO success, in the eyes of the Polish Underground State, was its illicit campaign to encourage Polish peasants to sabotage the obligatory provision of food supplies for the Germans.

As director of the RGO, Edmund Seyfried summed up its achievements under German occupation. In his 1945 report he enumerated the key factors that had shaped the RGO's decisions and measures. His list included stopping deportations from the regions of Radom (in 1940 and 1941), Kraków (in 1942 and 1943), and Lublin (1943). He described the wartime situation in Volhynia and Podolia and the migration of over a hundred thousand Polish people fleeing the "Ukrainian bloodbath." Finally he discussed the tragedy of the Warsaw Uprising of 1944, concluding that in the fall of that year the number of people who desperately needed humanitarian aid of any kind amounted to no less than one million.[573] He realized the RGO had not always been able to help: "One million people to feed, and provide with clothes, shoes and shelter: that was the burden the Council had to take upon its shoulders, because it was the only official voluntary welfare institution in the GG. The task was so enormous that the organization was unable to perform it adequately; no wonder we did not manage to cope with all the problems in the first months following the disaster (...)."[574] In the analysis that he prepared for the Ministry of Public Security, catering to the expectations of the Communists, Seyfried described the indifferent attitudes of the leaders of the resistance movement to his institution, claiming that the stance of the underground circles had prevented both young, talented, energetic people and experienced social workers from involvement with the RGO. He also

---

[571] *Ibid.*, 428–429.

[572] *Ibid.*, 429.

[573] AIPN Warsaw, sign. no. 1559/90, Edmund Seyfried, Opis działalności RGO na terenie byłego Generalnego Gubernatorstwa 31 I 1945 r. [Edmund Seyfried, description of the operations of the RGO in the former Generalgouvernement, Jan. 31, 1945], sheet 2.

[574] *Ibid.*

recalled that the Germans arrested as many as 392 of its social workers operating both in Warsaw and in regional branches.[575]

As one of the top officials in the RGO, Edmund Seyfried was also engaged in the resistance movement. From the very start of his appointment he was in close touch with representatives of the Polish Underground State and various political parties; the sole exception was, as he stressed himself, the Nationalist Party.[576] However, I think this lack of a connection did not result from any personal antipathy to the Nationalists, but rather from the events that affected the underground operations of the Nationalist Party in Lesser Poland: when the Germans arrested Dr. Stefan Sacha, its underground leader, it lost its ties with the RGO.

The list of Edmund Seyfried's contacts in the Polish resistance movement is impressively long. The most important was Jan Stanisław Jankowski, member of the Labor Party (Stronnictwo Pracy) and Government Delegate for Poland. He had met Seyfried much earlier, when Jankowski was working as head of the RGO's Welfare Department, which was quite understandable as they had similar responsibilities: providing aid to Polish civilians on all the occupied territories. When Jankowski was promoted to the supreme office in the Polish Underground State, Seyfried worked with Stefan Mateja, Jankowski's successor in the Welfare Department. They worked together until the 1944 Warsaw Uprising, when Mateja was killed. Another social worker who collaborated closely with Seyfried was Franciszek Białas, a member of the PPS-WRN.[577] This contact would prove vitally important in Seyfried's life after the War.

The governing bodies of the Polish Underground State (Home Army Headquarters and Bureau of Information and Propaganda, the Government Delegation for Poland, and the Regional Delegation in Kraków) received several reports from Seyfried on the reign of terror in the GG and the German reprisals against Poles.[578] In turn, the Government Delegation for Poland used Sey-

---

[575] *Ibid.*

[576] *Ibid.*, sign. no. 01251/151, Zeznanie własnoręcznie napisane przez Seyfrieda Edmunda z dnia 30 XII 1952 r. [Manuscript of Edmund Seyfried's handwritten statement, Dec. 30, 1952], sheet 37.

[577] G. Górski, *Administracja Polski Podziemnej w latach 1939–1945* (Toruń: Fundacja Inicjatyw Lokalnych Pomerania, 1995), 150–151.

[578] Kroll, *Rada Główna Opiekuńcza 1939–1945*, 443.

fried as an intermediary for the donation of large sums in US dollars to the RGO. In his later recollections, Seyfried explained the process in detail. The money in dollars was first taken to Silesia, which had a better dollar-to-reichsmark exchange rate, and only then exchanged into złoty.[579]

Seyfried's contacts also included Tadeusz Żenczykowski and Stanisław Długocki from the Home Army; Stanisław Dobrowolski from the PPS-WRN; Jan Wiktor from PSL–Roch; and Marek Arczyński from SD (the Democratic Party).[580] Unsurprisingly, they represented all the political parties and movements involved in anti-German resistance. It is quite possible they were appointed by the leaders of their respective organizations to establish ties with the top officials of the RGO. On the other hand, there is no definitive proof that Edmund Seyfried was engaged in the administrative bodies of the Polish Underground State, namely its Regional Delegation in Kraków. Marek Arczyński and Wiesław Balcerak's informative book on the Council to Aid Jews[581] does not mention Seyfried's participation in the resistance movement in Lesser Poland. Seyfried is not referred to either by Wacław Szubert, who was one of the leading officials of the Department of Labor and Welfare of the Government Delegation for Poland in 1941–1944;[582] the scope of its powers strictly corresponded to the responsibilities of the RGO. Seyfried is not mentioned in the study by Grzegorz Górski.[583] On the other hand, the invaluable monograph by Waldemar Grabowski, who discusses the civilian organizations of the Polish Underground State, names Edmund Seyfried, alongside Mieczysław Rakowski, as one of the two heads of the Department of Welfare for the Kraków Delegation in 1943.[584] The only thing I would like to add at this point

---

[579] *Idem, Opieka i samopomoc społeczna w Warszawie 1939–1945. Stołeczny Komitet Samopomocy Społecznej i warszawskie agendy Rady Głównej Opiekuńczej* (Warszawa: PWN, 1977), 305.

[580] AIPN Warsaw, sign. no. 01251/151, Zeznanie własnoręcznie napisane przez Seyfrieda Edmunda z dnia 30 XII 1952 r. [Manuscript of Edmund Seyfried's handwritten statement, Dec. 30, 1952], sheets 37–39.

[581] M. Arczyński and W. Balcerak, *Kryptonim „Żegota." Z dziejów pomocy Żydom w Polsce 1939–1945* (Warszawa: Czytelnik, 1983).

[582] W. Szubert, 'Wspomnienia o Departamencie Pracy i Opieki Społecznej Delegatury Rządu 1941–1944,' *Przegląd Historyczny* 1989: 1, 133–153.

[583] Górski, *Administracja Polski Podziemnej w latach 1939–1945*, 242–243.

[584] W. Grabowski, *Polska Tajna Administracja Cywilna* (Warszawa: Instytut Pamięci Narodowej, 2003), 348.

is that the time when he held the post is important. In my opinion Seyfried received it right after his return from Katyn, namely in mid-April 1943. His wartime efforts included one more noteworthy episode which was strongly linked with his work for the resistance, that is his trip to Smolensk and Koziy Gory to investigate the Katyn crime.

THE POLISH DELEGATION IN SMOLENSK AND KOZIY GORY ON APRIL 10–11, 1943

In the first days of April 1943 the Germans discovered mass graves of Polish officers in Koziy Gory near Smolensk. They wanted to alarm the international public opinion, as they were absolutely sure the crime had been committed by the Soviets. However, before the news reached any radio station or newspaper, the propaganda specialists of the Third Reich decided that the site should be visited by a delegation of several dozen Poles. On April 9, 1943 Richard Türk, one of the top German officials in the occupied territories, summoned Edmund Seyfried and informed him that the next day he would be going to Smolensk "to see the recently discovered mass graves of the Poles who had apparently been murdered by the Bolsheviks."[585] Türk added that the RGO should prepare a list of the members of the delegation. Seyfried returned to the RGO office with this news and the matter was discussed with the chairman, Adam Ronikier.[586] The decision was that at least for the time being it was necessary to engage in a dialog with the Germans. Moreover, it was considered necessary to involve the Polish Red Cross and to have "a clergyman for (…) the funeral rites" in the delegation.[587] So Edmund Seyfried went to see Wilhelm Ohlenbusch, head of the Main Department of Propaganda in the GG, who presented the same information and stressed that preparing a list of people to

---

[585] AIPN Warsaw, sign. no. 1559/90, Sprawozdanie z lotu do Smoleńska [Report on the flight to Smolensk]. The report was published by B. Kroll in *Życie Warszawy*, titled 'Pierwsze sprawozdanie z Katynia. Raport Edmunda Seyfrieda' (*Życie i Historia* 1989: 4 (Feb. 24), 1–3). Kroll's headline suggests Seyfried's was the first report on the inspection of the site of the atrocity, but perhaps this is not quite true, because on the same day an almost identical report was drafted by Ferdynand Goetel for the Polish Red Cross. In this book I shall be referring to the printed version of Seyfried's report.

[586] Ronikier, *Pamiętniki 1939–1945*, 233.

[587] *Ibid.*

travel to Smolensk was an absolute priority. Seyfried answered the RGO "had nothing to do with burials; they were the domain of the Polish Red Cross, whose statutory responsibilities included such tasks." He also asked Ohlenbusch to contact the Board of the Polish Red Cross in Warsaw for permission for Dr. Adam Szebesta, deputy head of the Polish Red Cross in Kraków, to make the trip too.[588] The German official considered those arguments appropriate, but nevertheless invited Seyfried to travel to the Katyn site as a visitor.[589]

Seyfried's 1945 report does not say what happened next, but later developments can be established on the basis of other Ministry of Public Security records. Edmund Seyfried returned to the RGO's headquarters and met with Marek Arczyński, one of the leaders of the SD. He gave an account of his meeting with Ohlenbusch and asked Arczyński to act as an intermediary to obtain the approval of the Polish Underground State for the RGO's final decision. He also wanted permission to participate in the trip as a visitor and stressed it was "(...) being organized by the German Department of Propaganda and that was why there was a question if it was right for Poles to take part."[590] Arczyński went out for an hour and upon his return said there was a recommendation for an RGO representative to travel to Smolensk; on his return home he would be obliged to present "as objective a report as possible to the Polish Underground State."[591]

On April 10, 1943 in the morning, a plane was waiting at Kraków airport for Edmund Seyfried and other Poles: Władysław Kawecki, a reptile press journalist working for *Goniec Krakowski*; Bruno Widera, a journalist with *Nowy Głos Lubelski*; Kazimierz Didur, a photographer; and Franciszek Prochownik, a worker from the Zieleniewski factory in Kraków. There were also three German passengers. In Warsaw the group was joined by more delegates: Dr. Konrad Orzechowski of the Polish Red Cross; Dr. Edward Grodzki of the Polish Welfare Committee; two writers, Ferdynand Goetel and Jan Emil Skiwski; and a few German press reporters.

---

[588] Kroll, 'Pierwsze sprawozdanie z Katynia. Raport Edmunda Seyfrieda,' 1.

[589] *Ibid.*, 2.

[590] AIPN Warsaw, sign. no. 1559/90, Protokół przesłuchania świadka Edmunda Seyfrieda przez prokuratora dr Jerzego Sawickiego 27 VII 1945 r. [Minutes of the hearing of witness Edmund Seyfried, conducted by Dr. Jerzy Sawicki, prosecutor, Jul. 27, 1945], sheet 1.

[591] *Ibid.*, sheet 2.

The plane landed in Smolensk in the afternoon. At the airfield the Polish delegation met a few foreign journalists who were about to fly back home. The Poles were billeted in the Wehrmacht House. During the first day, the main item on the agenda was their meeting with Col. Georg Slowenczyk, a German officer, who provided them with the basic information. He described how the graves were discovered and recalled that in October 1942 some Polish laborers working under German supervision were informed by local people about the graves of Polish officers who had been shot in Koziy Gory. The laborers apparently put up three birch crosses on the spot. Slowenczyk firmly declared the Germans had not heard of the killings until the spring of 1943. They wanted to identify the site of the Soviet crime, and so in mid-March German soldiers began digging up the area. The first mass grave discovered held bodies in Polish army uniforms. As it looked like a large-scale massacre, the German military set up a special organization to investigate the matter, including a forensic committee that had already started their fieldwork.

Following this long introduction, Slowenczyk moved on to the details, arranging them, as Seyfried remembered, in three parts. First, he stated the victims had come from the Soviet POW camp in Kozelsk. Second, he said that from late February 1940 until mid-April 1940 the Polish officers had been transported by rail to Gnezdovo station, from where they were taken to Koziy Gory. Finally, Slowenczyk listed several arguments to support the claim that the crime had been committed by the Soviets. He mentioned the documents that had been unearthed: the victims' letters, diaries and other notes, all stopping in April 1940. He described the site as a three-year pinewood. Lastly, he referred to the findings of the forensic experts, who said the bodies had been in the ground for at least three years. The delegates were shown the unearthed objects (such as photographs, military distinctions, documents etc.).[592] At the end of the meeting Slowenczyk stressed that the German army granted custody of the graves to the Poles to identify the victims. Edmund Seyfried replied that the Polish people realized what responsibilities the discovery involved and named the institution that in his opinion was best suited to handle the matter, that is the Polish Red Cross.

---

[592] Kroll, 'Pierwsze sprawozdanie z Katynia. Raport Edmunda Seyfrieda,' 2.

On April 11, 1943 the delegates were taken to the site at Koziy Gory. In his report Seyfried wrote they were greeted by a German colonel who declared that "the German army had invited over several representatives of Polish society to show them something that had no precedent in military history, namely the murder of thousands of unarmed officers who had been held prisoner by the Bolsheviks (...)."[593] Then the Poles were allowed to see the graves and bodies with hands tied behind their backs. They were shown the remains of Generals Mieczysław Smorawiński and Bronisław Bohaterewicz. Eventually they reached the place where the forensic committee headed by Professor Gerhard Buhtz from Breslau was working. Buhtz offered to perform an autopsy on any one body the Poles selected. "We chose a corpse that was buried under another layer of bodies. It was lifted out of the grave and stretched out on the examination table. During the autopsy the doctor's assistant removed the scalp from the back of the head, using appropriate instruments, and looked for a bullet hole. Also the front of the skull was exposed to find an exit hole. The body examined had both an entrance hole at the base of the skull as well as an exit hole above the right socket. Then they looked for documents, cutting open the pockets of the coat, uniform jacket, and trousers. There were no ID documents, only a wad of correspondence cards (...)."[594]

Following the autopsy and the inspection of another grave, Edmund Seyfried, acting on the suggestion of Ferdynand Goetel,[595] asked the members of the delegation to pay a tribute to the victims, saying: "I ask you to bow your heads in respect, and observe silence to commemorate these heroes, who laid down their life for their country so that Poland should live on."[596] During his short speech the German officers accompanying the Poles were standing at attention and saluting. The scene was photographed and filmed, and then put in a German documentary that showed the site of the atrocity and was being screened in the GG already in April 1943. After the inspection of the graves the

---

[593] *Ibid.*

[594] *Ibid.*

[595] Goetel, 'Katyń. Wizja lokalna,' 2.

[596] Kroll, 'Pierwsze sprawozdanie z Katynia. Raport Edmunda Seyfrieda,' 2. Seyfried put this sentence in his report for the RGO. Goetel confirmed that Seyfried had said this, and quoted him almost exactly: "I appeal to the Polish delegation to observe a moment's silence to pay a tribute to our compatriots, who laid down their lives so that their country should live" (*ibid.*).

Polish delegates were taken to a house situated about one kilometer from the site, where the Germans had collected all the documents and other belongings of the victims. In his comments concerning this item of the agenda, Seyfried said that "the correspondence was in large part illegible, as it had gotten damp in the ground; actually the postal stamps were the best preserved as the ink, which is oil-based, can resist humidity. The stamps show the correspondence stopped in early April 1940; at least no specimens we were given to examine bore a later date."[597] The members of the delegation were presented with a list of names of over thirty officers of the Polish Army who had already been identified. The group returned to Kraków on April 11, and were home in the evening, after a short stopover in Warsaw.

On the evening of April 12 Seyfried saw Marek Arczyński to present a brief oral report.[598] That shows he followed the guidelines of the representatives of the Polish Underground State. Stefan Korboński, one of the best informed members of the resistance movement, said that when they had returned from Smolensk, the delegates immediately "reported to the

---

[597] *Ibid.*

[598] AIPN Warsaw, sign. no. 1559/90, Protokół przesłuchania świadka Edmunda Seyfrieda przez prokuratora dr Jerzego Sawickiego 27 VII 1945 r. [Minutes of the hearing witness Edmund Seyfried, conducted by Dr. Jerzy Sawicki, prosecutor, Jul. 27, 1945], sheet 2. After the War, on June 19, 1945 Marek Arczyński was questioned by Dr. Jerzy Sawicki and testified as follows: "Out of the members of the Katyn delegation I know only Edmund Seyfried (…). Immediately upon his return from Katyn, I wanted to learn the particulars of his mission and told him he had a responsibility to his nation and history. Seyfried complied with my request and delivered a written report on the inspection. I believe I have it in my confidential archives and I shall do my best to submit it to the prosecution. The report was clearly written in a state of shock evoked by the sight of so many dead bodies. It is a descriptive and factual, rather than an analytical document, which stresses how pathetic the German spectacle was, given the immensity of the tragedy. It was clear to me that Seyfried was so overwhelmed by what he saw that he did not say who was culpable of the crime. With time, however, he grew more and more convinced that the Katyn victims had been murdered by the Germans, and this opinion pervaded our conversations. He arrived at this conclusion observing the political scene, analyzing the situation, and clarifying the doubts he had been harboring from the very start." Arczyński also provided Sawicki with some information about Seyfried's motives to join the Katyn delegation. Apparently Seyfried feared the Germans might retaliate if he rejected their invitation, while he wanted to continue his work for the RGO, to aid the people of Poland, and to give the Polish Underground State irrefutable evidence on the massacre. AIPN Kraków, sign. no. 303/1, Protokół przesłuchania świadka z 19 czerwca 1945 r. [Minutes of witness' hearing, Jun. 19, 1945], sheets 4–5.

institutions they represented as well as to the Polish Underground State."[599] The institutions of the latter (such as the Government Delegation for Poland, the Main Headquarters of the Home Army, and the Directorate of Civilian Resistance), used radio communication to inform the government-in-exile about each report, so Gen. Sikorski's government was very well acquainted with the background to the travel to Smolensk and the opinions and impressions the delegates brought back. One of the dispatches was a summary of Edmund Seyfried's report. The version prepared for the Polish exiles in London included information that the victims of the massacre were Polish officers. The message said that about 250 bodies had been disinterred, and Generals Mieczysław Smorawiński and Bronisław Bohaterewicz had been identified. Then it described the conduct of the Germans during the inspection on the basis of details in the reports, such as the meeting with the forensic team, the examination of the victims' belongings, and during Seyfried's speech over the graves.[600]

Next day, April 13, 1943, even before the first reptile press article on the massacre in Koziy Gory was published, Edmund Seyfried prepared a written version of his report, presumably in duplicate. One copy was passed on to the Board of the RGO, and the other to Marek Arczyński, once again acting as the representative of the Polish Underground State. In the concluding part of the document Seyfried confirmed the mass graves at Katyn contained the bodies of Polish officers from Kozelsk. He suggested that the people of Poland should assume care of the site and continue forensic investigations. These matters, in his opinion, were to be supervised by the Polish Red Cross. Considering the season of the year and the progressing decomposition of the exhumed corpses, he said appropriate measures had to be taken urgently.[601] Bogdan Kroll, a historian of Poland under German occupation, calls Seyfried's report balanced and restrained, adding that it "proved its author distanced himself off from the opinions and hypotheses voiced by the Germans, which, given the circumstances, was an act of courage."[602] I think that in the initial phase

---

[599] Korboński, *Polskie Państwo Podziemne*, 150.

[600] *Zbrodnia katyńska 1940. Polacy w Wielkiej Brytanii*, 49–50.

[601] Kroll, 'Pierwsze sprawozdanie z Katynia. Raport Edmunda Seyfrieda,' 3.

[602] Idem, *Rada Główna Opiekuńcza 1939–1945*, 292.

of the investigation Seyfried indeed distrusted the German findings. As an RGO official, he was fully aware of the enormity of the German atrocities on the Polish population. So he could have thought the Katyn massacre was yet another crime committed by the Germans, who wanted to shift the blame onto the Soviets.

On April 14, 1943 Edmund Seyfried delivered one more report on his trip to Smolensk and Koziy Gory. On the initiative of Adam Ronikier, he was received by Archbishop Adam Sapieha at a meeting with a group of individuals who were public figures in Kraków. Once again, Seyfried presented the conclusions that he had drawn from the inspection.[603] The people at the meeting already knew that the Germans had agreed to a special committee of the Polish Red Cross inspecting the Katyn site,[604] yet even during the meeting with Ronikier and Seyfried there were still voices that the Polish Red Cross team should be joined by representatives of the RGO. Ten years later Seyfried recalled that the Germans gave up these attempts about two weeks after the return of the first Polish delegation from Katyn. The decisive factor was that Adam Ronikier firmly opposed the idea.[605]

In my opinion one more fact is to be noted. Neither Seyfried's report nor similar documents prepared by other members of the first Polish delegation (e.g. by Ferdynand Goetel)[606] who saw the site of the atrocity contain the name "Katyn." The authors of the reports and the first interviews for the press (e.g. for *Nowy Kurier Warszawski* and *Goniec Krakowski*[607]) were consistent in using the name "Koziy Gory." After two days had passed, that is from April 16 onwards,

---

[603] Ronikier wrote about the event: "When Seyfried returned from Katyn on April 14, I organized a meeting, at my place, for a large number of Kraków's important figures, especially Archbishop Sapieha. Mr. Seyfried presented his report and an oral account of all his experiences in Smolensk. His suggestions were approved in a unanimous vote and appropriate steps were taken to carry them out" (Ronikier, *Pamiętniki*, 233).

[604] *Ibid.*, 234.

[605] AIPN Warsaw, sign. no. 01251/151, E. Seyfried, Sprawa Katynia ciąg dalszy [Edmund Seyfried, Katyn case continued], sheet 405.

[606] Kledzik, 'Raport z Katynia do Polskiego Czerwonego Krzyża,' 8–9.

[607] Cf. e.g. 'Kozia Góra pod Smoleńskiem odsłania swą krwawą tajemnicę,' *Nowy Kurier Warszawski* 1943: 90 (Apr. 15); 'Wstrząsający i potworny widok. Tajemnica cmentarzyska w lesie na Koziej Górze. Specjalny wywiad Agencji prasowej „Telpress" z redaktorem Wł. Kaweckim,' *Goniec Krakowski* 1943: 90 (Apr. 17).

both "Koziy Gory" and "Katyn" were used interchangeably,[608] while later the place was called just "Katyn."

In late April 1943 the Germans decided to establish a special Katyn committee in the GG. I want to stress this, because that team was to include not only Wacław Lachert, Kazimierz Skarżyński, Dr. Adam Szebesta, and Count Adam Ronikier, but also Edmund Seyfried. However, the committee operated for a very short time. By May of 1943 the German initiators complained it "had given the government [of the Third Reich] no information at all." In their reply, the committee members explained no progress had been possible due to lack of communication channels between Warsaw and Katyn. Thereafter the committee was never mentioned again.[609]

In the spring of 1943 the Germans wanted to involve Seyfried in one more operation connected with the Katyn massacre, to help their propaganda campaign with respect to Polish public opinion on the occupied territories. They hoped that due to the publicity given to the Soviet responsibility for the atrocity they could initiate some kind of alliance between the Home Army and the Wehrmacht against the Soviet Union and the Red Army. Bogdan Kroll has established that in mid-1943 Edmund Seyfried was approached by Karol Strzelczyk, a secret agent working for the Germans, with the suggestion of a "trip to Katowice to discuss confidential matters."[610] Strzelczyk was Seyfried's acquaintance: before the War both of them had worked for the Ruch booksellers. The commanders of the Home Army issued their consent, and in 1943–1944 Seyfried had two rounds of talks with the Germans. At the second meeting the Germans offered to cut down on reprisals against civilians in the GG if the Polish resistance limited its military operations against the Wehrmacht.[611] The talks stopped and in August 1944 the Gestapo put Seyfried in

---

[608] The name Katyn appeared for the first time in an article published in *Kurier Częstochowski* on April 16, 1943 ('W lasku pod Smoleńskiem wstaje groza. Cień 12000 oficerów woła z Katynia'). Next it was used in Władysław Kawecki's interview with Franciszek Prochownik ('Wrażenia krakowskiego robotnika w lesie katyńskim. Specjalny wywiad Telpressa z członkiem polskiej delegacji Franciszkiem Prochownikiem,' *Goniec Krakowski* 1943: 90 (Apr. 17). It cannot be excluded at all that the name Katyn was purposefully introduced and disseminated by Kawecki.

[609] Maresch, *Katyń 1940*, 196.

[610] Kroll, *Rada Główna Opiekuńcza 1939–1945*, 443.

[611] *Ibid.*, 444.

preventive detention. Bogdan Kroll speculates that this decision could have been made as a result of the outbreak of the Warsaw Uprising or of the attempt to assassinate Hitler on July 20, 1944.[612] Seyfried was released in October 1944, following an intervention by Archbishop Sapieha.[613]

After the War, the Communist authorities in Poland made two extensive investigations into the Katyn massacre, in 1945, and later at the turn of the 1940s and 50s, in response to the findings of the two US committees, led respectively by Arthur Bliss Lane and Ray Madden. In 1945 the Ministry of Public Security put Edmund Seyfried under close surveillance. He was detained for the first time in connection with the investigation against Ferdynand Goetel, his 1943 trip to Katyn, and his alleged wartime collaboration with the Germans.[614] In July 1945 Seyfried was questioned by the public prosecutor Dr. Jerzy Sawicki. In his answers he referred to six problems. First of all, Seyfried said he had been suspicious about the Katyn massacre because the German Department of Propaganda was one of the institutions interested in the matter, so he preferred to be cautious, distrustful, and reserved. Second, when he inspected the site of Koziy Gory, as a layman he was not able to assess the validity of the evidence of Soviet culpability produced by the Germans. By evidence he meant the state of decay of the bodies and uniforms, and the age of the trees and underbrush. Next, he stressed he issued no official statement in Katyn, although he was encouraged and even urged by the Germans to do so. "Nevertheless, I withstood the pressure because I realized that my words, supported by the authority of my name and position and yet incompatible with my inner conviction, could have become a powerful weapon in the hands of the German propaganda. I regarded it irresponsible to make any statement whatsoever; I was unable to pass any objective judgement, as I could not base it on any valid premises."[615] Then he described the working methods of the German propagandists and said they conducted the visit of the Polish

---

[612] *Ibid.*

[613] AIPN Warsaw, sign. no. 01251/151, Zeznania własnoręcznie napisane przez Seyfrieda Edmunda z dnia 30 XII 1952 r. [Manuscript of Edmund Seyfried's handwritten statement, Dec. 30, 1952], sheet 43.

[614] Jankowski and Kotarba, *Literaci a sprawa katyńska 1945*, 90.

[615] AIPN Warsaw, sign. no. 1559/90, Protokół przesłuchania świadka Edmunda Seyfrieda przez prokuratora dr Jerzego Sawickiego 27 VII 1945 r. [Minutes of the hearing of witness Edmund Seyfried, conducted by Dr. Jerzy Sawicki, prosecutor, Jul. 27, 1945], sheet 3.

delegation to Smolensk and Katyn in accordance with a prearranged scenario. The Germans presented their readymade diagnosis to the delegates, and the German explanation dominated the entire inspection. Talking to Sawicki, Seyfried argued: "Given the immense distress caused by the sight of the graves of our compatriots, it took a tremendous effort to suppress the influence of persuasion and emotional factors. On the basis of my report, I can claim I showed the utmost restraint that I was rationally able to muster in the face of the scale of the crime and the German pressure and propaganda, especially as we all knew there had been a camp for Polish POWs on Soviet territory."[616] Finally, Seyfried explained he could not have stopped the Germans from releasing the information that he had personally visited Katyn, because everybody knew it for a fact. He did not fail to underline that it had been his initiative to salute the victims at the site of the killings. Asked by Dr. Sawicki about the response of the Polish population on German-occupied territories following the discovery of the Katyn crime, he answered that on this particular issue Polish people did not believe the German propaganda. Then he added he was unable to identify the "factors that (...) contributed to the origin and dissemination of the anti-Russian version."[617]

The 1945 investigation did not mark the end of Edmund Seyfried's postwar involvement in the Katyn case. Although not of his own accord, he had to deal with the matter again in late December 1952 and early 1953. The situation was special: he was arrested on a charge of espionage. We can hardly fail to notice a connection between his arrest and the work of the Ray Madden Committee and the Communist attempts to discredit its findings. In my opinion, those factors explain the content and the ultimate sense of the statements Seyfried had to offer at that time. In 1953 he was forced by the police officers to claim it had been no secret to him that the perpetrators of the massacre at Koziy Gory were the Germans. Additionally, he had to accept the decision of the Ministry of Public Security to use that opinion in tandem with the documents that had been prepared earlier, upon his return from Katyn, in order to give even more validity to the anti-German interpretation of the Katyn events.[618] Speaking of

---

[616] *Ibid.*

[617] *Ibid.*

[618] Wasilewski, *Ludobójstwo*, 168.

the opinion Polish people had in 1943 of the crime, he unambiguously stated the response was "unanimous: it was the Germans who were held guilty of the massacre. Everybody knew all too well that the Germans were capable of committing any crime and were murdering hundreds or even thousands of people every day. So public opinion did not believe the Germans that it was the Soviet authorities who were responsible for the killings, especially as no important Polish institution or individual who was an authority for Polish people confirmed the German hypothesis. The interviews with Goetel and Skiwski, who were generally believed to be German collaborators, or with Prochownik, a completely unknown worker from the Zieleniewski factory in Kraków, had no effect on the generally held belief that the murderers were the Germans."[619] Eventually though, the Ministry of Public Security did not make use of Seyfried's new statement and arguments to any great extent in its 1952–1953 propaganda.

SEYFRIED'S INVOLVEMENT WITH THE UNDERGROUND PPS-WRN

The first time Seyfried met Franciszek Białas during the War was in October 1944. Białas (*noms de guerre* Franek Góralczyk, Szeląg, and Wysocki) was one of the main leaders of the PPS-WRN, a well-known personality both in Poland and in émigré circles.[620] However, they had actually known each other much earlier in their professional capacity, since 1933. At that time Seyfried was the director of the Ruch booksellers, while Białas was administrative manager for the Robotnik publishing house; they became acquainted with each other while handling distribution issues.[621]

In 1944 Franciszek Białas, who was head of the Welfare Department of the Government Delegation for Poland, held a meeting with Seyfried of the

---

[619] AIPN Warsaw, sign. no. 01251/151, E. Seyfried, Sprawa Katynia ciąg dalszy [Edmund Seyfried, Katyn case continued], sheets 405–406.

[620] On the work of Franciszek Białas during and after the War as an émigré, see A. Siwik, *PPS na emigracji w latach 1945–1956* (Kraków: Księgarnia Akademicka, 1998); *eadem, Polskie wychodźstwo polityczne. Socjaliści na emigracji w latach 1956–1990* (Kraków: Abrys, 2002).

[621] AIPN Warsaw, sign. no. 01251/151, Protokół przesłuchania podejrzanego z 28 XII 1952 r. [Minutes of suspect's hearing, Dec. 28, 1952], sheet 22.

RGO to discuss humanitarian aid after the Warsaw Uprising of 1944, when the city was left in ruins and its civilian population was forced to evacuate. As a representative of the Polish Underground State, Białas offered the RGO a donation of about 30–40 million złoty, which was transferred to the RGO's account between October 1944 and January 1945. This undercover transaction was handled by two clerks, Irena Dolińska for the RGO, and Maria Modlibowska for the Polish Underground State. In January 1945 Białas entrusted Seyfried with 4 thousand US dollars to be dispensed to the teachers in the Polish underground education system. Dr. Stanisław Tazbir was to act as an intermediary between Seyfried and the educators. In May 1945 Białas came to live in Kraków for a short time, as he intended to start working for the PZUW insurance company and wanted Seyfried to get a job with the same employer. Yet the plan never materialized. Somewhat later Seyfried became head of the Kraków branch of the PPS-WRN Social Welfare Committee and received 20 thousand US dollars from Białas to finance underground operations. But their contacts soon ceased, because in early 1946 Białas aka Franek Góralczyk went to London as an emissary of the Polish anti-Communist underground. During a meeting of the Polish émigré Cabinet he delivered a report on the domestic situation in Poland.[622] The money Seyfried had received was supposed to support the underground activities of PPS-WRN and to aid those party members who were subject to repressive measures. The entire amount in cash was hidden in a private apartment in Kraków. The method of distribution was unsophisticated. Every person selected by Białas to receive aid was to contact Seyfried and present a letter of recommendation which specified the sum this person was to receive, e.g. "11/2000" was two thousand dollars, and "X klg." was ten thousand dollars.[623] Yet an obstacle emerged when the money was to be paid out. In November 1946 Edmund Seyfried settled in Poznań, where he bought a foundry, while the cash was still in Kraków. Every time a person was to be given an allowance, a courier had to travel from Poznań to Kraków and return with the money after a few days. So the actual payment was always delayed by about a week.

---

[622] T. Wolsza, *Rząd RP na obczyźnie wobec wydarzeń w kraju 1945–1950* (Warszawa: Wydawnictwo DiG, 1998), 20.

[623] AIPN Warsaw, sign. no. 01251/151, Protokół przesłuchania podejrzanego z 28 XII 1952 r. [Minutes of suspect's hearing, Dec. 28, 1952], sheet 23.

Seyfried testified the resources had been used by several people e.g. to cover the lawyers' fees during the [political] trials of Adam Obarski and Kazimierz Pużak. Seyfried used the money for his own purposes a few times too. His contacts with PPS-WRN continued after 1945; he met with Zygmunt Zaremba, Józef Dzięgielewski, Adam Obarski, Dr. Stanisław Tazbir, and Aleksy Bień.[624]

He was director of the foundry until November 1951. Later, as his health had badly deteriorated, he retired on a disability pension. In 1952 he was arrested a second time by the security police. The Communists carried out an operation codenamed Urszula, in the course of which they conducted a thorough investigation and charged Seyfried with espionage. The prosecution indicted him for his cooperation with Franciszek Białas in 1945–1952, which apparently was detrimental to the Polish State, as well as for illegally possessing and using the sum of 33 thousand dollars. The latter part of the record of Seyfried's interrogation says that Edmund Seyfried illegally kept 24 publications "with false and defamatory opinions about the Soviet Union (…)."[625] Another accused party in the same trial was Irena Dolińska, Seyfried's "accomplice" during and after the War. The trial was held in 1953 and Edmund Seyfried was sentenced to ten years' imprisonment.[626]

He was released after the political thaw of 1956. In April 1957 he took up a managerial job with *Tygodnik Powszechny*, a Catholic weekly. The next year he was officially rehabilitated. He died in 1968.[627]

---

[624] *Ibid.*, sheet 25.

[625] *Ibid.*, sheet 298.

[626] *Polski Słownik Biograficzny* is wrong on the date of the sentence, which it gives as 1948.

[627] Nicman, 'Kamil J. Seyfried (1872–1960),' 378.

THE COMPLICATED LIFE OF DR. EDWARD GRODZKI, DELEGATE OF THE WARSAW BRANCH OF THE RGO, AFTER HIS VISIT TO KATYN IN APRIL 1943

26. Edward Grodzki

Dr. Edward Grodzki was the representative of the Health Section of the Warsaw branch of the RGO on a Katyn delegation.[628] His appointment did not stir controversy or incite debate. What is more, we may assume he had a personal motive to take the trip, although after the War, when he was questioned by People's Republic security police officers, he testified otherwise, and even spoke of having been forced to participate.[629]

---

[628] Edward Grodzki was born on February 17, 1905 (some documents say February 12) in Mińsk Litewski (now Minsk, Belarus) to a landowning family. In 1931 he graduated from the Medical Faculty of the University of Warsaw. Until the outbreak of the War he worked for Ubezpieczalnia Społeczna, a social insurance company in Warsaw.

[629] AIPN Warsaw, sign. no. 00231/124, vol. 2, Notatka informacyjna [Memo], sheet 11.

```
        Nadaję pośmiertnie

doktorowi EDWARDOWI GRODZKIEMU

     KRZYŻ ARMII KRAJOWEJ

za pracę na stanowisku lekarza
  Polski Podziemnej w latach
        1939-1945

              Antoni Sanojca
      /-/ pułk.Antoni Sanojca
              ps."Kortum"
              Szef Oddziału I
  Warszawa       Komendy Głównej
  21 kwietnia    Armii Krajowej
        1987
```

27. Certificate issued by Col. Antoni Sanojca, for the posthumous conferral of the Home Army Cross on Dr. Grodzki for his work as a Polish Underground State physician in 1939–1945

PHYSICIAN AND SOCIAL ACTIVIST

Under German occupation Grodzki was not a well-known figure outside medical circles and the groups of beneficiaries of the Warsaw SKSS (Stołeczny Komitet Samopomocy Społecznej, the Warsaw Social Self-Care Committee). He joined the organization immediately after the German invasion and became deeply involved in welfare and charity work for those inhabitants of the capital who fell victim to the horrors of war, and for those who were forced to resettle and lived in Warsaw following the turmoil of September 1939. Grodzki was head of the Committee's Health Section and continued to hold the post until the 1944 Warsaw Uprising. His section dispensed various treatments and medical assistance to over 13,000 inhabitants.[630] Grodzki was one of the co-founders of a children's TB preventorium and sanatorium at Otwock and

---

[630] H. Drozdowski, *Stołeczny Komitet Samopomocy Społecznej. Fragmenty dotyczące Sekcji Zdrowia* [The Warsaw Social Self-Care Committee. Passages concerning the Health Section], sheet 148. (I used the copy owned by Dr. Mirosław Grodzki.)

229

Skolimów near Warsaw. This development proved to be quite significant later on in his life. One of the employees of the Otwock institution was Edward Osóbka-Morawski, a prewar member of the PPS, and the Prime Minister in the 1944 Provisional Government of National Unity (viz. the government established by the Soviets).[631] Grodzki worked for the Polish Underground State as a physician and also became engaged in its political activities.[632]

THE KATYN DELEGATION

Ferdynand Goetel recalled that in 1943, as the delegation was setting off for Katyn, there were two doctors present at the airport: one "from the city council, the other from the RGO."[633] The former was Dr. Konrad Orzechowski, and the latter Dr. Edward Grodzki. Both knew each other well.

In Katyn, Grodzki carefully scrutinized the site of the crime. He listened patiently to the German comments on the date and other circumstances of the killings, paying attention to the fact that victims' hands were tied up with paper rope, and on his return home referred to that in several private conversations concerning his Katyn inspection. Neither reports by other participants (such as Ferdynand Goetel or Edmund Seyfried) nor publications in the reptile press, written mainly by Władysław Kawecki, signal that Grodzki was very deeply engaged in the careful examination of the case. He voiced no opinions and asked no questions. But he did take photographs of the site and victims, using his private camera.

On his return to the GG he prepared his report, just like many other members of the delegation. The document was submitted to Janusz Machnicki, Deputy Chair of the RGO and Chair of its Warsaw branch.[634] Unfortunately, we do not know its content, neither can we be sure that Grodzki said the same

---

[631] Information from Dr. Mirosław Grodzki.

[632] In 1987, on application from Col. Antoni Sanojca aka Kortum, Grodzki was posthumously awarded the Home Army Cross. Henryk Drozdowski, secretary general of the Warsaw Social Self-Care Committee, often spoke of the work of the Health Section for the Polish Underground (*Stołeczny Komitet Samopomocy Społecznej*, sheets 74–75, 122–123).

[633] Goetel, 'Lot do Katynia,' 10.

[634] AIPN Warsaw, sign. no. 00231/124, vol. 2, Dr Grodzki Edward, Oświadczenie w sprawie Katynia z dnia 18 III 1952 r. [Dr. Edward Grodzki, statement re Katyn, dated March 18, 1952], sheet 2.

in his later statements for the Ministry of Public Security. His 1943 report appears to have differed from the statements he made in 1946 and 1952; most probably the earliest document identified a different perpetrator. So we should take a closer look at the postwar documentation. In his statement for the Ministry of Public Security Grodzki observed that the corpses and clothes had not been decomposed to a very great extent, and that the Germans controlled the course of the inspection and showed the delegates only what they wanted them to see.[635] He also expressed his opinion on the work of the German Medical Commission: "When the neighboring area, which was under grass, was to be dug up 'upon request,' they insisted corpses would be found there as well (how could they have known?). Indeed, as soon as they dug up the soil bodies were immediately discovered – both of officers and other ranks (as we could judge by the uniforms). The corpses were fresh, so you could even distinguish the facial features on some. The uniforms were in fairly good condition too, and the soft tissue and joints were still integral parts of the bodies." When questioned by a secret police officer, Grodzki offered his explanations so as to persuade him he had never had any doubts as to the intentions of the German organizers of the inspection. To round up he added: "During the demonstration autopsy performed by a German doctor who was addressed as 'Herr Professor,' he informed me that we'd find a bullet hole under a flap of skin in the occipital area (and, again, how did he know?). We did indeed. After about two hours we were taken back (…) to the airport."[636] In conclusion, Grodzki stressed the Katyn massacre was a German frame-up: "Bodies buried in a sandy soil for three or four years (and sandy it was, as they have coniferous forests there), would not have been so well-preserved. The evidence, such as the photographs and the dates, which were written on them by the Germans, demonstrated they were most likely *ad hoc* fabrications for propaganda purposes, so that the site could be shown to visitors."[637] When interrogated in the Ministry of Public Security nearly ten years after the inspection, Grodzki said that in accordance with Janusz Machnicki's instructions, he had refused to be interviewed by the reptile press (probably he meant *Nowy Kurier Warszawski*) on his visit

---

[635] *Ibid.*, Notatka informacyjna [Memo], sheet 11.

[636] *Ibid.*, Dr Grodzki Edward, Oświadczenie w sprawie Katynia z dnia 18 III 1952 r. [Dr. Edward Grodzki, statement re Katyn, dated March 18, 1952], sheet 2.

[637] *Ibid.*, sheet 3.

28. One of the photographs taken by Edward Grodzki at Katyn in April 1943

to Katyn.[638] That was actually true, but some press publications (e.g. in *Nowy Kurier Warszawski* and *Goniec Krakowski*) named him as a delegation member representing Warsaw organizations.

Grodzki's Katyn visit was significant for one more vital reason. The main author of the pictorial records of the crime was Kazimierz Didur, a "photographer-in-ordinary" to Hans Frank and, as it turned out recently, a Home Army soldier who handed in copies of his photos to representatives of the Polish Underground State. He performed such services on several occasions, not only in connection with the Katyn delegation. The other person who brought his camera to the site of the atrocity was Edward Grodzki.[639] Other members of the delegation later recalled the fairly few photographs he had taken, but they did not mention his name. This priceless evidence was sent to London to be used by the Polish government-in-exile, and Grodzki kept just a few prints.

The Polish government was informed already in April 1943 that the Germans had invited two delegations from the GG to visit Smolensk and Katyn. The first ciphertext, sent from Home Army Headquarters in Warsaw on April 19, 1943, listed a Grodzki as one of the delegation members.[640] A week or so later, Lt.-Col. Michał Protasewicz wrote a report for Gen. Władysław Sikorski, Commander-in-Chief of the Polish Armed Forces, in which Grodzki was described as "a physician representing the Warsaw branch of the Polish Welfare Committee."[641]

Several enigmatic, and sometimes genuinely dramatic events occurred in the later years of Grodzki's life, both during and after the War. Ferdynand Goetel, who remembered Grodzki as one of the Katyn delegates, thought he must have died a tragic death, saying: "To the best of my knowledge, though I cannot confirm the truth of this information, Dr. Grodzki was killed by a Communist squad in the woods near Jabłonna still in 1943."[642] This information proved wrong, although we know Grodzki did have serious problems during the War. If the statement he gave the Ministry of Public Security in 1952 is to be believed, Grodzki did not want to be involved in the German

---

[638] *Ibid.*

[639] Information from Dr. Mirosław Grodzki.

[640] Maresch, *Katyń 1940*, 74.

[641] *Zbrodnia katyńska 1940. Polacy w Wielkiej Brytanii*, 49.

[642] F. Goetel, 'Zachód i Katyń,' *Wiadomości* (1951: 27) (July 8, 1951), 1.

propaganda campaign regarding the Katyn massacre and therefore had to live under an assumed name. He worked in the Otwock sanatorium as Stanisław Kamiński until the end of the War.[643] The person who provided the necessary help was Franciszek Jóźwiak aka Comrade Witold, a member of the PPR [viz. a card-carrying Communist]. This was an important episode, for Dr. Grodzki used this name again, in a slightly modified form, on another occasion.

LOOKING FOR PEACE AND SAFETY

When the military operations in the area of Warsaw were over, Grodzki promptly left Otwock, moving to Milanówek. For a time he was in touch with Dr. Konrad Orzechowski, then his neighbor, until the latter's arrest on February 28, 1945. At that time Grodzki was already being sought by the secret police, too, on suspicion of wartime collaboration with the Germans, and was soon arrested, on April 7, 1945. After being questioned he was released, as the evidence against him proved insufficient. Considering what transpired later on, one can assume that in April 1945 the security police officers had no background knowledge concerning the Katyn crime or Grodzki's participation in the 1943 German-organized inspection of the site. After the Polish secret police released him, Grodzki was shortly held for questioning by the NKVD,[644] which was a clear signal what could happen to him in the near future.

Hastily, he took the simplest, obvious decision – to leave Milanówek. The Ministry of Public Security records say that Grodzki and his family secretly moved to the region of Silesia. Prior to their departure, his neighbors were given to understand that Grodzki was just looking for a new job and would soon return home. He seems to have wanted to mislead those who could have informed the secret police about his departure. He left Milanówek on May 11 or 14, 1945. His first destination was Katowice and subsequently Włocławek in the region of Kujawy (Central Poland). Initially Grodzki traveled south, so perhaps he wanted to cross the border illegally and head for Western Europe via Czechoslovakia. On the basis of his itinerary we can guess he wanted to

---

[643] AIPN Warsaw, sign. no. 00231/124, vol. 2, Dr Grodzki Edward, Oświadczenie w sprawie Katynia z dnia 18 III 1952 r. [Dr. Edward Grodzki, statement re Katyn, dated March 18, 1952], sheet 3.

[644] Information from Dr. Mirosław Grodzki.

make the secret police lose his trail. On the other hand, Edward Grodzki's son claims his father never planned to flee and never took that journey to Silesia.[645] Mirosław Grodzki says instead the family traveled straight to Kujawy, as they intended to take up residence in Nieszawa. They happened to spend the night in Włocławek, where they stayed for good and Edward Grodzki started working as a doctor.

It is not clear how they traveled, but it is evident that Grodzki was wanted by the secret police and subsequently put under surveillance by the Ministry of Public Security. As of July 1945, prosecutor Jerzy Sawicki wanted to find and question him as well. It is quite probable that the police identified the Grodzkis' whereabouts in Włocławek on information they received in 1946 from a friend of Grodzki's sister.[646]

Grodzki was questioned on the Katyn atrocity again. Later, although he was allowed to practice as a gynecologist,[647] he was constantly under surveillance and would have to report to the police if summoned. Paradoxically, he was never questioned about his involvement with the Polish Underground State and the Home Army.

THE POSTWAR KATYN PROPAGANDA CAMPAIGNS

In Włocławek Grodzki was urged by the secret police and the PPR to settle his account with the past, especially the Katyn episode, and he decided to do that by taking an unambiguous stance on the German revelations of April 1943. Using a pen name, he published an article in the local press identifying the Germans as the perpetrators of the Katyn massacre. On February 9, 1946, *Gazeta Kujawska* printed his text entitled "Katyń 1943 r." [Katyn, 1943]. At that relatively low cost, Edward Grodzki presumably satisfied the Communists' desire to publicize "appropriate" commentaries on the events of 1943. Prior to publication the text was read, modified, and ultimately approved by

---

[645] Information from Dr. Mirosław Grodzki.

[646] AIPN Warsaw, sign. no. 00231/124, vol. 1, Informacja nr 1 dotycząca dowodów prowokacji niemieckiej w sprawie Katynia z 3 IV 1952 r. [Information no. 1 concerning evidence for the German provocation regarding Katyn, dated April 3, 1952], sheet 14.

[647] AIPN BU, sign. no. 0423/4143, Dr Konrad Orzechowski i dr Edward Grodzki [Dr. Konrad Orzechowski and Dr. Edward Grodzki].

Władysław Dworakowski, First Secretary of the Municipal Committee of the PPR. Grodzki's *alter ego*, Dr K. Miński (cf. his wartime false name) said the Germans had organized many trips to Katyn, forcing "volunteers" to participate, so that they could personally assess the horror of the crime. "And indeed I saw with my own eyes that, although the plugging had been faultless, the performance was botched, and some positive evidence and details pointed immediately to the real perpetrators and the real purpose of the crime."[648] To expose the Germans' culpability, Grodzki asked why they had remained silent for so long, the crime having apparently been committed in the spring of 1940 and discovered already by 1941. He hastened to answer that they needed time to remove the evidence. Further, he challenged the claim that the bodies had lain in the ground for almost four years, yet they were so well preserved. He argued: "Forensic science does not know of any cases of corpses interred for four years being so intact as to still have recognizable facial features."[649] Finally, he referred to one more fact which he considered important: the concurrence of the dates when the Katyn atrocity was made public and when the Warsaw ghetto was cleared. The first Katyn article was published in *Nowy Kurier Warszawski* on April 14, 1943, and the Germans started to close down the ghetto on April 19, 1943. According to Grodzki, it was not a coincidence that on the previous day the reptile press had published a text which said that the massacre near Smolensk had been the work of Jewish killers.[650] In his 1946 article he wrote: "The windows of my apartment looked out onto the ghetto, where I could see many pools of blood in which the Germans waded!"[651] For Grodzki Katyn, Auschwitz, and Treblinka should be mentioned in the same breath.

---

[648] Dr K. Miński, 'Katyń w 1943 r.,' *Gazeta Kujawska* (Feb. 9, 1946), 1. Prior to publication, the typescript of the article was submitted to the First Secretary of the Municipal Committee of the PPR for approval, with a note explaining Dr K. Miński was really Dr. Edward Grodzki (AIPN Warsaw, sign. no. 00231/124, vol. 2, Dr Grodzki Edward, Oświadczenie w sprawie Katynia z dnia 18 III 1952 r. [Dr. Edward Grodzki, statement re Katyn, dated March 18, 1952], sheet 4).

[649] Dr K. Miński, 'Katyń w 1943 r.,' *passim*.

[650] 'Potworną zbrodnią kierowali żydzi,' *Nowy Kurier Warszawski* 1943: 92 (April 18, 1943), 1.

[651] *Ibid.*

Thanks to the article Grodzki led a relatively peaceful existence, if only for a while. The situation changed after a visit paid by his old friend, Dr. Konrad Orzechowski, who had just returned from deportation in the Soviet Union.[652] Their get-together triggered an alert in the Ministry of Public Security. On December 19, 1947 Grodzki was put under close surveillance.[653] In 1952 he was again being invigilated, as I have said above. On that occasion the officers reminded him of what he had declared in his statements in 1946. He was also put on the list of people who were expected to testify on demand that the Germans were the perpetrators of the Katyn crime. The relevant note reads as follows: "Dr. Edward Grodzki of Włocławek deposes and says that as Head of the Health Section of the RGO in Warsaw he was forced by the Germans to join the Katyn delegation. Inspecting the site, he saw that the bodies and the clothes had not decomposed to any great extent, which means they had been in the ground for a fairly short time. He observed that the Germans had prepared whatever they wanted to show the delegation and did not permit any inspection of other graves."[654]

Dr. Edward Grodzki lived in Włocławek until his death in 1960.

---

[652] Information from Dr. Mirosław Grodzki.

[653] AIPN BU, sign. no. 0423/4143, Dr Konrad Orzechowski i dr Edward Grodzki [Dr. Konrad Orzechowski and Dr. Edward Grodzki].

[654] AIPN Warsaw, sign. no. 00231/124, vol. 1, Informacja nr 1 dotycząca dowodów prowokacji niemieckiej w sprawie Katynia z 3 IV 1952 r. [Information no. 1 concerning evidence for the German provocation regarding Katyn, dated April 3, 1952].

SELF-CONTRADICTORY VIEWS ON THE KATYN MASSACRE. GEN. STEFAN MOSSOR ON KATYN DURING AND AFTER THE WAR

A DELEGATION OF POLISH PRISONERS IN KATYN

Polish Army officers were members of one of the delegations visiting Katyn in 1943. They were prisoners-of-war held by the Germans in several oflags since the cessation of armed combat. At the time the Germans publicized the Katyn massacre the oflags in question were in Neubrandenburg, Woldenberg and Gross-Born. Initially, there were seven delegates: Gen. Jan Chmurowicz, Lt.- Col. Stefan Mossor, Maj. Aleksander Nowosielski, Capt. Stanisław Cylkowski, Capt. Konstanty Adamski, Capt. Eugeniusz Kleban, Plt. Off. Zbigniew Rowiński, and 2nd Lt. Stanisław Gostkowski. Later, during the voyage itself, two officers left the delegation. Jan Chmurowicz never left Berlin, where the flight to the East was to start, because of his serious health condition certified earlier by a doctor in the oflag at Murnau. While waiting for the return of the delegation, the Germans suggested he should meet with Professor Leon Kozłowski, an ex-prime minister of interwar Poland, to discuss Katyn. He categorically rejected the offer.[655] Maj. Aleksander Nowosielski, another member of the delegation, reached Warsaw, where the first stopover had been planned, but did not continue the journey. According to extant documents he had a "severe heart condition," that is, he was on the verge of a heart attack,

---

[655] AIPN BU sign. no. 00199/297.

238

which was the reason why he stayed behind at Okęcie airport.[656] The absence of Gen. Chmurowicz made Lt.-Col. Stefan Mossor the highest ranking officer in the delegation. Probably he did not anticipate at the time that the Katyn massacre would leave an imprint on his wartime, and especially his postwar life.[657]

The members of the delegation were selected only from those imprisoned in the oflags in the 3rd Wehrmacht Military District in Stettin. As the Germans explained, the hurry was due to the fact that "because of the rapid rate of decomposition of the bodies in the open air only officers from the Stettin corps were selected, as it was closest to Berlin, with which it had the best rail connections."[658] Although this makes sense, I suspect there were other reasons as well. The decomposition of the bodies removed from the ground was not imminent, as in April it was still cold in Katyn forest. The German were in a hurry because they wanted to present as many eyewitnesses as possible as fast they could, of course for propaganda purposes only. Thus the Polish officers still alive held as POWs by the Germans were much better evidence than the dead officers once kept by the Russians.

The Polish officers reached Smolensk on April 16, 1943. After the two earlier delegations from the GG, they were the third consecutive delegation to visit the site of the Katyn massacre. They were housed in the quarters of the military gendarmerie and that night they browsed photographs, documents, and other evidence of the massacre. Capt. Stanisław Cylkowski called this phase of their stay "a grim foretaste of the tragedy."[659] On the next morning the Germans took them to Katyn forest. At this time only the German medical commission led by Gerhard Buhtz was carrying out autopsies on victims. This was one of the observations Lt.-Col. Mossor made in his report. On the same day, though a little bit later, the first group of the Technical Commission of the Polish Red Cross, consisting of Ludwik Rojkiewicz, Stefan Kołodziejski,

---

[656] A. Toczewski, 'Raport ppłk. dypl. Stefana Mossora o wizycie polskich oficerów z niemieckich oflagów w Katyniu,' *Niepodległość* 45 (new edn.25): 1992,79

[657] This was noted by the general's biographer: J. Pałka, *Generał Stefan Mossor (1896–1957). Biografia wojskowa*, (Warszawa: Światowy Związek Żołnierzy Armii Krajowej: Oficyna Wydawnicza Rytm: Fundacja «Historia i Kultura,» 2008), 153–157, 181–184.

[658] Toczewski, *Generał Stefan Mossor*, 85.

[659] H. Tomiczek, 'O Katyniu – z oflagu.' *Tygodnik Demokratyczny* 1989: 34 (Aug. 20), 20.

and Jerzy Wodzinowski, reached Katyn.[660] The first meeting of the two Polish groups took place in a climate of mutual distrust. As Stanisław Gostkowski writes, "We were told that a delegation sent by the Polish Red Cross or the RGO – I really don't remember which – had arrived from Warsaw. We exchanged cold greetings, we didn't know who they really were. Volksdeutsche, possibly? They must have thought the same about us, so we started small talk about the weather, as if turning a blind eye to Katyn."[661]

The Germans strove to publicize the visit of the Polish POWs in Katyn. German newspapers, like *Pommersche Zeitung* and *Berliner Nachtausgabe* of April 18 and 19, 1943, reported their arrival in Katyn. From the outset the Germans urged the prisoners to comment on the developments and to share their thoughts on the matter. One of them, 2nd Lt. Stanisław Gostkowski, remembered that there were radio employees and projectionists present, and witnesses wearing sheepskin coats "whom Mossor was keenly interviewing."[662] This was probably the time when Lt.-Col. Stefan Mossor protested that the only organization which was authorized to produce official announcements on the matter was the International Red Cross. Moreover, in Katyn he told German officers that in Berlin he had been assured that the Poles would not be forced to give press and radio interviews or make any public statements. As far as photographic documentation was concerned, the organizers of the visit had insisted it would be designated only for the command of the Wehrmacht Military District.

Immediately upon their arrival in Katyn the delegation of Polish POWs and three members of the Technical Commission of the Polish Red Cross examined the mass graves and documents found on the victims, which the Germans had collected earlier. Gostkowski writes, "We began surveying the area. Exhumed and identified corpses lay in the field according to the rank. Gen. Smorawiński on the right wing, with Gen. Bohatyrowicz close by (. . .), all in all about two hundred corpses. Next we examined the "exhibit" of objects found by the corpses: small medallions, gorgets, medals, regiment badges, family letters and notebooks – memoirs, which stopped in March to April 1940. One had

---

[660] Maresch, *Katyń 1940*, 204.

[661] S. Gostkowski, 'Week-end,' *Kultura* 1965: 3, 83.

[662] *Ibid.*

a message entered as late as Gnezdovo station, that is not long before he was shot."[663] The officers were also told about the circumstances in which the graves had been found and about the exhumations, and they were given preliminary lists of the identified victims. With the consent of the Germans one of the Poles extricated a corpse. "I entered the grave, in which the poor wretches had their hands tied up behind their backs with a thick rope – they must have resisted. To make sure they had not been murdered recently, I dug out a corpse – actually, I used a pickaxe to chop out a body entangled with others. Yes.

29. Col. Stefan Mossor in Oflag II E Neubrandenburg

They had been lying here for long. For how long, though?"[664] Stanisław Gostkowski also talked briefly to Georg Slowenczyk, the German officer in charge of the site, whose second name Gostowski rendered as "Jeschonek." In conclusion, Georg Slowenczyk admitted quite bluntly that "if we had done it, it would have been a totally different job."[665] A final report prepared by Kazimierz Skarżyński in June 1943 says that "the Polish officers distanced themselves off from the Germans and behaved with dignity. During a brief private conversation they were evidently relieved to learn that the Polish Red Cross was taking care only of the technical aspect of the exhumation work, and entirely dissociating itself from its political aspect."[666]

---

[663] *Ibid.*, 84.

[664] *Ibid.* Capt. Stanisław Cylkowski admitted he did the same: "we are digging out a corpse on our own. We are removing the shackles – the rope – from its cold hands. It was a rope, thin but strong, that I brought back from Katyn." Tomiczek, 'O Katyniu – z oflagu,' 20. 2nd Lt. Zbigniew Rowiński also brought back a rope from Katyn.

[665] Gostkowski, 'Week-end,' 85.

[666] Quoted after Maresch, *Katyń 1940*, 205.

LT.-COL. STEFAN MOSSOR'S REPORTS

After the visit Lt.-Col. Stefan Mossor prepared a report, which he intended to hand over to Col. Tadeusz Trapszo, the highest ranking Polish officer detained in Oflag II E Neubrandenburg. The report was to a large extent a reflection of the thoughts and opinions of all the members of the delegation. To collect them, the Polish officers held a meeting after returning to Berlin. The document signed by Lt.-Col. Mossor was written on April 21, 1943 and included information on the state of the corpses and the uniforms, the time for which they had been interred, the number of victims and of those who had been identified, the way they were killed, the documents and artifacts found on the victims and the likely duration of the exhumation. Mossor produced interesting comments on each of these aspects. He wrote that the corpses which had been exhumed had already decomposed to a considerable extent and were partly mummified, whereas "most of their facial features were unrecognizable (their eyes, eyelids, and nostrils were damaged, almost all the mouths were open due either to shouting or postmortem spasm, lips tight or generally damaged, teeth bared)." This is his description of an opened up grave: "it gives the impression of something like a terrible box of pressed dates, with corpses lying next to, crosswise, or slantwise to each other, in many different positions, as if they had fallen or been dumped into the pits. Here and there arms, legs and heads are strangely intertwined."[667]

In his description of the state of the uniforms, the documents found on the bodies, and their personal belongings, he wrote that "the degree to which the uniforms have decayed matches the decomposition of the corpses. The uniforms, one may say, fit the corpses like a glove, they adhere to the skin like they were glued on, they have dried out in the shape of the bodies."[668] The documents, photographs, cigarette cases and money found in the victims' pockets had survived in a good or even excellent state of preservation. Following German estimates, he thought there were 10-12 thousand bodies buried in Katyn Forest, though he was not sure about the ultimate count. He attached a list of 158 identified corpses.

---

[667] Quoted after Toczewski, *Generał Stefan Mossor*, 80.

[668] Quoted after Toczewski, *Generał Stefan Mossor*, 80.

As far as the method of the execution was concerned, he noted that the skulls "were riddled with large-caliber, handgun bullets. As a rule, the bullet entrance was situated at the base of the skull, whereas the location of the exit varied – at the crown, at the temples or the orbits – depending on the position of the head at the time of the shot." Mossor considered the documents retrieved (postcards, notebooks and memoirs) important evidence, which testified to the chronology of the events. None of the documents was dated later than January-March 1940.[669] In his evaluation of Mossor's report, his biographer wrote that it was "extremely detailed and matter-of-fact, it focused only on the facts Mossor had learned in Katyn Forest and was devoid of digressions. Mossor's account was detached, devoid of any stylistic ornamentation or emotional expressions."[670]

Intended first for Col. Tadeusz Trapszo, the report was subsequently put on display on the oflag board freely accessible to all prisoners. But this was by no means the end of Lt.-Col. Stefan Mossor's activities related to the Katyn massacre. In Berlin he was urged by some high-ranking Germans to make a public announcement on the matter, either a radio broadcast or a newsreel item. Mossor maintained he had firmly refused. Later the Germans took him to places in the environs of Berlin to meet a few groups of Poles doing forced labor or incarcerated in the oflags and talk to them about Katyn. Next he was transferred to Frauenberg, a prison camp with a less rigid regime.[671] Taking into consideration the fact that soon he was back in Neubrandenburg, we may assume he had never fully met the German expectations. Perhaps he was not committed enough to the task. In Oflag II E he continued to refuse to speak in public on the Katyn massacre. As he himself claimed, he avoided the subject in private exchanges as well.[672] However, in August 1943 he prepared a report for Gen. Kazimierz Sosnkowski in London. In October 1943 the report was sent to the Home Army military command in Warsaw and then to Sosnkowski by hitherto unknown means. It reached the Poles in London in December 1943.

---

[669] Quoted after Toczewski, *Generał Stefan Mossor*, 83–84.

[670] Pałka, *Generał Stefan Mossor,* 156.

[671] AIPN Warsaw, sign. no. 0298/382, Notatka z rozmowy z członkami Kontroli Partyjnej i prokuratury z 18 I 1955 r. [Record of a talk with members of the Internal Party Control Unit and the prosecutors, Jan.18. 1955], sheet 10.

[672] *Ibid.*, 9.

In his report he included a passage on the Katyn massacre: "The Katyn propaganda project started in May 1943. I was one of the officers transported to the place to see the graves and the exhumed corpses. There is no doubt that thousands of Polish officers were summarily shot in Katyn Forest in the spring of 1940. We were urged to take part in radio, press and newsreel propaganda, which I categorically and effectively refused to do. The only thing I agreed to was to share our impressions directly with other Polish POWs."[673] At the same time, he notified the commander-in-chief that the Germans were getting ready to form a Polish military unit to be used against the Red Army. He mentioned Oflag VIII and his short stay there. He also stressed that the German initiative was likely to fall on deaf ears. In his report he put it succinctly: "extremely lenient treatment. Negligible results. Only worthless characters accepted the offer of release."[674]

Other members of the delegation shared their impressions on Katyn during special meetings upon their return to their oflags. We know what the situation was like in Oflag Woldenberg, from which four officers (Gen. Jan Chmurowicz, Maj. Aleksander Nowosielski, Capt. Konstanty Adamski and 2nd Lt. Zbigniew Rowiński) were sent to Katyn. On their return to the oflag "the captain and the second lieutenant presented their report to the Senior Prisoner [Col. Wacław Szalewicz – T.W.]. When asked to visit other barracks, they shared their thoughts on Katyn, and 2nd Lt. Rowiński showed the rope with which the hands of one of the victims had been tied and which the Germans did not notice that he had taken. The visiting officers and all of their listeners were shocked at the enormity of the genocide. Although most of them had seen corpses of those killed in war, sometimes even heaps of them, a massacre committed in such circumstances was unimaginable. "We were all devastated, physically and psychologically at the end of our tether."[675] Capt. Stanisław Cylkowski described the atmosphere in Oflag Neubrandenburg in two letters of April 26 and May 7, 1943 to his wife and children. This is how he begins his account: "I locked myself up in the canteen because I could not cope with

---

[673] *Ibid.*, Lt. Col. Stefan Mossor's personal report for Gen. Sosnkowski in London, sheet 112.

[674] *Ibid.*

[675] H. Tomiczek, 'Woldenberski oddźwięk Katynia,' *Tygodnik Demokratyczny* 1989: 14 (Apr. 2), 21.

the questions my colleagues asked about Katyn."[676] Next he wrote how deeply shattered he was by what he had seen on the site of the massacre. He recalled seeing thousands of unidentified soldiers in the death pits. His second letter may certainly be treated as a report on his stay in Katyn. As I have already said, it shows that all the members of the delegation worked together on the final report. Cylkowski makes frequent references to conclusions drawn by the whole group, which we have read in Mossor's report, as may be seen in the following extract, in which he writes, "Ahead of us there is a sparse wood growing on a sandy soil. We turn left and get out of the vehicle. We are taken aback by an exceptionally foul smell – well, this is the smell of decomposing corpses. We cannot bear it, really. Bodies thrown into deep trenches, one upon and next to another, hands and fists clenched in their death throes, hands bound, terrible, empty eye sockets, bare teeth and jaws as if in a death scream. (...) Uniforms, shoes, belts, etc. still in a good condition. And everywhere this treacherous shot in the back of the head."[677] Finally he dates the crime, thereby implying who the culprit was. "How sad and tragic are those letters and postcards addressed to loved ones. And those memoirs! Poor wretches! Everything stops after March 1940."[678]

KATYN AND GEN. MOSSOR'S POSTWAR STORY

Lt.-Col. Stefan Mossor was kept in Oflag II Neubrandenburg until January 1945. During the oflag's evacuation he and hundreds of other Polish and Yugoslavian prisoners deliberately postponed marching out west. The delay paid off, because they remained in the camp. Even a Latvian SS company sent by the Germans was not able to force the Poles to evacuate. Eventually it was the approaching Red Army that solved all the problems. Mossor and a few other officers crossed the front line and joined the First Polish Army. Straightaway he signed up for military service.[679] Already at his first meeting with its officers, including Lt.-Col. Zygmunt Okręt, Mossor told them and then confirmed

---

[676] Tomiczek, 'O Katyniu – z oflagu,' 20.

[677] *Ibid.*

[678] *Ibid.*

[679] This is more thoroughly discussed by Jarosław Pałka (*Generał Stefan Mossor*, 170–171).

[**30.** Stefan Mossors's article, 'Palmiry – Katyń' in *Polska Zbrojna* 1946: 176

in writing that in 1943 he had been to Katyn and had talked about this experience. Later he passed the information on to Col. Stanisław Zawadzki from the Department of Military Personnel of the Polish Army.[680] As for some time three prosecutors, Dr. Jerzy Sawicki, Dr. Roman Martini and Karol Szwarc, had been looking for members of the 1943 Katyn delegations, he was interrogated on the matter. During the War he had been in no doubt that the Soviets were responsible for the Katyn massacre, but on July 26,1945, in the presence of Jerzy Sawicki, he said, "the whole show was staged by the Germans with their characteristic scientific rigor, which could have misled even the most incredulous man, making him believe that the massacre had not been carried out by the Soviet Union as such, as other camps had remained intact, but that it was due to the willfulness of a local commandeer. (...) When I got through

---

[680] AIPN Warsaw, sign.no. 0298/382, record of a talk with members of the Internal Party Control Unit and the prosecutors, Jan. 18,1955, sheet 11.

to the Polish side in February this year I learned the details of the mass murders in Auschwitz, Majdanek and Treblinka. I can testify now that when you compare these camps with Katyn you can see the same, scientifically precise hand of the executioner at work in all of them."[681]

In 1946 Mossor presented his new perspective on the Katyn crime during his first public appearance on the case. As he stressed a few years later when interrogated by a prosecutor, in the spring of 1946 he had the opportunity to visit the village of Palmiry near Warsaw during the exhumation work carried out by the Polish Red Cross there.[682] After the visit he came to the conclusion that "in respect of the method of killing used, the mass murders committed there were identical with those in Katyn."[683] He used the same argument to explain how he came to write his article 'Palmiry – Katyń,' first published in the weekly *Polska Zbrojna* and later reprinted in the daily *Głos Ludu* and local papers published by the PPR. The article opens with an evocative analogy: "as I was entering the tragic field [the village of Palmiry – T.W.] I was surprised how strikingly similar the landscape was to that of Katyn. The same type of isolated area, pine forest, the same type of sandy hills overgrown with a sparse heath and anemic pines planted quite recently." Next he tried to persuade the reader that the Katyn and Palmiry atrocities had been committed by the same hand. So he wrote: "The staging of the macabre show [in Katyn in 1943 – T.W.] was precise, in a truly German manner. The 'material evidence', the selection of witnesses and expert opinions were presented as an overpowering proof. They convinced many experts, carefully chosen in the first place. (...) It should be noted that during the terrible journey the people who for 20 years had been fed on propaganda about the 'Bolshevik hell' thought that this could not have been done by any central agency of the Soviet government, because the captive officers killed came from one camp only (...) , whereas all in all there were more than ten camps. Thus it could have been a horrendous whim of the local authorities of Smolensk, for which there is no rational explanation. Further

---

[681] Jankowski and Kotarba, *Literaci a sprawa katyńska 1945*, 113–114.

[682] Palmiry – a place about 30 km (23 miles) northwest of Warsaw, site of a Nazi German WW2 atrocity, the mass execution and burial of about 1,700 Polish citizens.

[683] AIPN Warsaw, sign.no. 0298/382, Notatka z rozmowy z członkami Kontroli Partyjnej i prokuratury z 18 I 1955 r. [Record of a talk with members of the Internal Party Control Unit and the prosecutors, Jan.18. 1955], sheet 9.

in the article he got to the heart of the matter: "sooner or later the truth must come out. Toward the end of our captivity now and then we would learn that some officers, whose names were put on the list of those exhumed in Katyn on the basis of the documents that had been found on them, were alive in Poland or abroad. When we got to Poland we learned all the details about the terrible, equally precise murders that had taken place in the camps of Auschwitz, Majdanek, Treblinka, etc. We recognized the same, devil-like hand of the German executioners. All these mass murders, of the same systematic and precise character, calculated in cold blood and carried out scientifically, were executed by the same apparatus of oppression, divided into many teams or units, which carried out their bloody business in Katyn, Vinnitsia, Auschwitz or Buchenwald, always accompanied by inhuman sadism." In conclusion he wrote, "Buchenwald has many common features with Auschwitz, and Katyn is an enhanced version of Palmiry. (...) Those who are still under the influence of what is left of Goebbels' propaganda about Katyn that spread around the world should realize that Palmiry is incontrovertible evidence testifying against the German executioners in Katyn."[684]

Jarosław Pałka was right to comment that the Communists needed Stefan Mossor's testimony on Katyn, which he treated as a security for his service in the Polish Army and perhaps as a guarantee of his personal immunity. More or less at the same time he approached the Ministry of Propaganda and Information, offering to draft a leaflet on Polish–Russian relations, in which he would explain the Katyn issue.[685] Presumably the explanation would have been like the one he published in the soldiers' weekly *Polska Zbrojna*. He also suggested that a memorial plaque bearing the inscription "Smoleńsk" with no specific date should be put up on the Tomb of the Unknown Soldier. However, the idea did not appeal to Gen. Marian Spychalski.[686] The arguments against such a plaque are understandable, even though the proposal was made in 1946. For the Communists, who knew very well what had happened in Katyn – just like for the majority of the Poles living in Poland and abroad – the plaque would have commemorated officers murdered by the NKVD. That is why the

---

[684] S. Mossor, 'Palmiry – Katyń,' *Polska Zbrojna* 176 (Jul. 26, 1946), 3.

[685] Pałka, *Generał Stefan Mossor*, 183.

[686] *Ibidem*.

Communist elites could not accept such an idea. Now it is difficult to speculate what made Mossor submit such a proposal. Perhaps he just made a blunder and did not take into account all the possible ramifications. Or maybe he wanted to make the bad aftertaste of his postwar enunciations and publications on Katyn less conspicuous. The ambiguity of the plaque's inscription could have served that purpose well.

Mossor's visit to Katyn in 1943 was a major stumbling block, especially in view of his evolving military career. I believe he was fully aware of the problem and was trying to deal with it by finding the most convenient solutions, such as appropriate publications and joining the PPR. In the latter case it was necessary for Mossor to discuss his intentions with Jakub Berman, a very close associate of Bolesław Bierut. The meeting took place at the turn of 1945 and the decision was made that Mossor could join the Party after he became better versed in the ideology. Indeed, he joined the Party on October 23, 1946.

His military career stalled when he was arrested on May 13, 1950. It was the beginning of an exceptionally difficult time in his life, which lasted five and a half years.[687] During prolonged interrogations he would come back to the issue of Katyn, which, as he believed at least for some time, was the reason for the problems emerging in his life. Only some time later did he understand that Katyn was just an element of the game and not the most important one. He was discharged from Wronki prison on December 13, 1955 as a seriously sick man. He died of a heart attack on September 22, 1957.

Of the other members of the delegation, Jan Chmurowicz settled in Kraków after the War. Here in the fall of 1945 he was interrogated by one of the prosecutors appointed for the Katyn case. At the time he acknowledged that the report prepared by Lt.-Col. Stefan Mossor was in line with what the Germans wanted. He wanted to join the Polish Army but was rejected. He worked as a warehouse attendant and traded in apples. He died in 1965.[688] Zbigniew Rowiński remained in exile abroad after the War and on numerous occasions confirmed Soviet culpability for the crime. I shall discuss this point elsewhere. Also Stanisław Gostkowski remained in exile and in 1965 published an

---

[687] A detailed description of this period is in Pałka's biography of Gen. Stefan Mossor.

[688] J. Kutta, 'Chmurowicz Jan Władysław (1887–1965),' *Bydgoski Słownik Biograficzny*, vol. 6, ed. J. Kutta (Bydgoszcz: Kujawsko-Pomorskie Towarzystwo Kulturalne, 2000), 26–28. Kutta does not mention the Katyn episode in Chmurowicz's life.

account of his visit to Katyn in the Paris-based Polish émigré magazine *Kultura*. Eugeniusz Kleban (born in 1909 near Stanisławów, now Ivano-Frankivsk, Ukraine) was detained in several oflags, Hohnstein, Arnswalde, Grossborn, and Sandbostel. Upon his release, for a short period of time he served in the Polish Second Corps in Ancona, Italy. Later he left for the USA and was an active member of the Polish Army Veterans of America (SWAP). At the same time he took up university studies and earned a master's degree and doctorate in sociology at a university in New York. Later he joined the faculty of the Sociology and Anthropology Departments at Wagner College in New York. His academic interests evolved around the Polish Diaspora in the United States. Finally he became the director of the Polish Institute of Arts and Sciences in the United States. I was not able to find any trace of his pursuit of the Katyn issue after the War. His visit to Katyn is mentioned in his military CV which he prepared for SWAP. He wrote that he had been a member of "a group of officers – Polish, British and American POWs sent to see the graves of Katyn." He died in Manhattan on September 9, 1987.[689] Stanisław Cylkowski returned to Poland on February 14, 1945. He took a job with the Gdynia Chamber of Commerce and Industry and never faced any problems because of his visit to Katyn. He died in 1952.[690] I was not able to obtain any detailed information on the postwar lives of the other members of the delegation.

In conclusion it should be noted that after the War it was Gen. Stefan Mossor who in comparison with other members of the Katyn delegation bore most of the brunt for the visit.

---

[689] I was able to collect biographical data on the basis of the extant records (SWAP membership application form, war records, a new director of the Polish Institute of Arts and Sciences in the United States) related to Eugeniusz Kleban kept in the SWAP Archives in New York. I received copies of these invaluable documents from Dr. Krzysztof Langowski, to whom I am very grateful. On Eugeniusz Kleban see also P. Kardela, *Stanisław Gierat 1903–1977. Działalność społeczno-polityczna*, (Szczecin: Wydawnictwo Promocyjne „Albatros"), 2000, 462.

[690] S. Błażejewski, 'Cylkowski Stanisław Teodor (1892–1952),' *Bydgoski Słownik Biograficzny*, vol. 4, 33–34.

KATYN AND WHAT HAPPENED AFTER THE WAR TO REPTILE JOURNALIST MARIAN MAAK

During the German occupation of Poland the Germans employed the services of a group of Polish journalists and technicians to target a few newspapers and professional magazines at the Poles living in the GG. These papers were first and foremost *Nowy Kurier Warszawski, Goniec Krakowski, Kurier Kielecki, Goniec Częstochowski* (*Kurier Częstochowski* as of November 1939), *Kurier Radomski* (as of March 1940 renamed *Dziennik Radomski*), *Nowy Głos Lubelski, Gazeta Lwowska, Goniec Codzienny,* and *Nowy Czas* in the town of Jędrzejów. There were also professional magazines addressed to selected groups of readers: *Ilustrowany Kurier Codzienny, 7 Dni, Fala, Gazeta Ogłoszeń, Siew, Rolnik, Pszczelarz, Kolejowiec, Zawód i Życie, Ster, Mały Ster,* and *Co Tydzień Powieść.* According to German figures 10 dailies with a total press run of 700 thousand copies, 11 weeklies with a total press run of 410 thousand copies, 10 monthlies with a total press run of 210 thousand copies, and 25 professional magazines were published in Polish in the GG, making up what the Poles called the reptile press.[691]

Naturally, Polish journalists and men of letters did not collaborate with the Germans only by publishing in the reptiles. A few of them worked for Wanda, the German radio station broadcasting to the Polish Second Corps in Italy.[692]

---

[691] I discuss this aspect elsewhere in the present volume.

[692] For more on the Wanda radio station see Habielski, 'Radiostacja „Wanda"'; also the large collection of documents on the Poles collaborating with the Germans by working for Wanda, acquired by the Ministry of Public Security of the People's Republic, now available at AIPN GK in Warsaw (164/100). They concern Maria Kałamacka, Władysław Kawecki, Jan Maleszewski, Mieczysław Dunin-Borkowski and his wife Maria, Alfred Wysocki, and others.

251

Yet most of these journalists and announcers had first worked for the reptiles. The reptile journalists included a few who published fake (in reality German-sponsored) samizdats with an anti-Soviet, anti-British and anti-American agenda. Finally there were the prose writers – authors of novels, romance novels and short stories circulated either in book format or published in installments in the reptiles. There were other cases as well, but all in all those who collaborated and acted to the detriment of the Polish state belonged to the categories mentioned above.

The most notorious collaborators were Zenon Antoni Opęchowski from Kraków; Stanisław Brochowicz-Kozłowski; Eugeniusz Świerczewski from Warsaw, who was also involved in the betrayal of General Stefan Grot-Rowecki and the disclosure of his whereabouts to the Germans; Aleksander Kiedrowski from Bydgoszcz; Antoni Mikulski; Czesław Ancerewicz of Wilno; Zygmunt Ipohorski-Lenkiewicz; Władysław Kawecki of the Kraków-based Telpress agency; Jan Emil Skiwski and Feliks Burdecki, publishers of *Przełom*; Piotr Paliwoda-Matiolański; Ewa Smolka, one of the editors of *Siew*; Stanisław Jucha; Orest Marian Kałużniacki; Zdzisław Józef Stanisz; Helena Wielgomas, a record-holder for the number of poems, short stories and plays she published in the reptiles;[693] as well as Maria Kałamacka and Jan Godziemba-Maleszewski of the Wanda radio station.[694]

I have omitted the names of two journalists who for some time stood accused of collaboration. I will discuss the issue separately, as it demands a detailed and accurate explanation. It concerns Józef Mackiewicz, who spent some during the War in Wilno, and Ferdynand Goetel from Warsaw – they were both sentenced during the War by the Polish Underground State through its Special Military Courts (WSS). Mackiewicz was actually sentenced to death for publishing articles in *Goniec Codzienny* and for his contacts with the Germans. However, the sentence was annulled because it was

---

[693] AIPN Warsaw, sig. no. 0207/6864, Sentencja wyroku Heleny Wielgomas z 7 IX 1948 r. [Sentence of the verdict of Sep. 7, 1948 against Helena Wielgomas] sheets 106–117.

[694] For more on this see Gondek, *Polska karząca 1939–1945*, 117–118; T. Wolsza, 'Aparat bezpieczeństwa wobec polskich dziennikarzy wizytujących w 1943 roku miejsce sowieckiej zbrodni w Katyniu. Przypadek Władysława Kaweckiego,' in *Dziennikarze władzy, władza dziennikarzom. Aparat represji wobec środowiska dziennikarskiego 1945–1990*, T. Wolsza and S. Ligarski eds. (Warszawa: Instytut Pamięci Narodowej. Komisja Ścigania Zbrodni przeciwko Narodowi Polskiemu, 2010), 383–384, 389–390.

not only unfair and wrong, but also because the allegations had been fabricated by his political opponents. While he was still in occupied Wilno and later in exile he proved he was innocent of the charge of collaborating with the Germans.[695] Ferdynand Goetel, a member of the Polish Academy of Literature, was accused of being pro-German. Just like Józef Mackiewicz, after some time Goetel's name was cleared of these allegations.[696] They were both helped by their visit to Katyn in 1943 along with other members of the delegation organized by the Germans. If they had not received a go-ahead from the authorities of the Polish Underground State, they would have suffered severe consequences in the form of even harsher sentences passed by the underground military courts, including death sentences, which would not have been annulled or temporarily suspended.

Is it possible to find a common factor in the biographies of Marian Maak and, for instance, Ferdynand Goetel and Józef Mackiewicz? For one, they were all journalists and men of letters who were involved in some way with the propaganda machine run by the Third Reich during the War. And in addition, just like Goetel and Mackiewicz, Maak visited Katyn in 1943 as a member of one of the delegations organized by the Germans.

MAAK'S WARTIME LIFE

Marian Maak was born on May 24, 1917 in the town of Brzesk, in the Powiat of Tarnów. In the mid-1930s he graduated from the Władysław Jaworski high school in Kraków. Next he took up university studies in physical education, which he did not complete. In 1936 he did his military service in the 16th Infantry Regiment in Ostrów Mazowiecka, attending the Komorów military college. He left the service as a second lieutenant. At the same time he became a driving instructor. Following the German attack on Poland he became a company commander and fought in the combat route from Częstochowa

---

[695] For a full explanation of the case see Malewski (W. Bolecki), *Wyrok na Józefa Mackiewicza*, 64–66, 77–83.

[696] Polechoński, 'Ferdynand Goetel w Katyniu'; *idem*, *Pisarz w czasach wojny i emigracji. Ferdynand Goetel i jego twórczość w latach 1939–1960*, (Wrocław: Wydawnictwo Uniwersytetu Wrocławskiego: Wydział Filologiczny Uniwersytetu Wrocławskiego, 2012); Zamorski, *Dwa tajne biura 2. Korpusu*, 252.

(now Central Poland) to the town of Uściług (now Ustyluh, Ukraine).[697] After the cessation of combat and the capitulation his unit returned to Kraków. Here Maak remained for some time – he was jobless and, as he himself stressed a few years later, suffering poverty.[698]

As he wrote in the documentation he prepared for his military service in 1945, under wartime occupation initially he worked at a coal depot in Wieliczka (1941–1942). Next he was a driving instructor in Kraków (1942–1943). What he omitted was a mention of a different job he had held and tried to conceal from the Poles and Soviets in the Polish Army. The job was his collaboration with the reptile press.

Marian Maak's first job for a German employer was as a driver with a German press agency. Later he became an editor of a local news section for Polskie Wiadomości Prasowe, which subsequently changed its name to Telpress. His job was to prepare local news and copy edit regional correspondence.[699] Hans Fenske, the head of the Telpress agency, who incidentally came from Bydgoszcz, officially addressed Maak as a chief editor managing a team of editors.[700] Maak would sign his articles in the reptile press and other publications "K. Szarota", "A.K." or he would use his full first name and surname.[701]

In the spring of 1943 the Katyn massacre became known world-wide. The Germans made a public announcement about the mass graves of the Polish officers and blamed the massacre on the Soviet Union. At the same time the German propaganda machine made a concerted effort to spread the news in the GG in the hope of making at least some of the Poles change their hostile attitude to Germany. One of the measures the Germans used to achieve this purpose was to organize visits to Katyn for Polish delegations. The first delegation reached the site near Smoleńsk on April 11, 1943. It included Dr. Edward

---

[697] AIPN Kraków, sign. no. 1847/79, Teczka akt personalnych Mariana Maaka (ur. 1917 r.) [Personal dossier of Marian Maak, b. 1917].

[698] *Ibid.*

[699] 'Od endecji do kolaboracji. Trzeci dzień procesu Burdeckiego, Skiwskiego i towarzyszy,' *Dziennik Polski* 1949 (Jun.10), 3.

[700] 'Na pozycjach zdrady,' *Dziennik Polski* 1949 (Jun. 9),.

[701] AIPN Kielce, sign. no. 127/268, vol. 1, Akta w sprawie karnej Oresta Mariana Kałużniackiego [Documents on file relating to the criminal case against Orest Marian Kałużniacki], sheet 221.

Grodzki; Dr. Konrad Orzechowski; Edmund Seyfried of the RGO; writers Jan Emil Skiwski and Ferdynand Goetel; Franciszek Prochownik, a laborer from Kraków; Władysław Kawecki, a reptile editor; and Kazimierz Didur, a photographer.[702] A few days later, on April 14, 1943, a second delegation was sent to Katyn, with Marian Maak as a driver, interpreter, and an observer affiliated with the Polish Red Cross delegation, most likely on the bidding of his boss Hans Fenske. The other members of the second delegation were Fr Stanisław Jasiński ; Kazimierz Skarżyński, secretary general of the Polish Red Cross; Dr. Adam Szebesta; Dr. Tadeusz Pragłowski; Dr. Stanisław Plappert; Dr. Hieronim Bartoszewski; and a few Polish Red Cross technicians.[703] Many years later Maak admitted in his interrogation statement for the functionaries of the Ministry of Public Security that he never did the job he had been supposed to do in Katyn, because Kazimierz Skarżyński, who headed the Polish Red Cross delegation, was fluent in German. Additionally, he stressed that upon his return to Kraków he did not discuss his Katyn visit publicly.[704] The claim seems to be true, because so far all the attempts to find a text on Katyn published in the reptiles under his name or pseudonym have failed. However, he could have published something anonymously, the more so as after mid-April 1943 the Katyn issue dominated the propaganda press for more than two months and the number of articles of various types, interviews and comments went into the hundreds. Most were anonymous.

On his return from Katyn, Maak took part in another German propaganda event, Hans Frank's infamous harvest festival at Wawel Castle in Kraków in October 1943. The Germans held the festival to celebrate the fourth anniversary of the GG. Maak welcomed delegations of peasants arriving in the city and escort them to the castle. The ceremony itself was widely publicized in the reptiles and in German-language papers and magazines published on the territories of occupied Poland.[705] To make Polish peasants appreciate

---

[702] On the first delegation see Madajczyk, *Dramat katyński*, 36–37; Wolsza, *„Katyń to już na zawsze katy i katowani,* 32–33.

[703] On the delegation see Madajczyk, *Dramat katyński*, 40; T. Wolsza, *„Katyń to już na zawsze katy i katowani,* 33.

[704] 'Proces zdrajców narodu polskiego,' *Dziennik Polski*, 1949 (Jun. 8), 3.

[705] The celebrations of the fourth anniversary of the establishment of the GG were extensively discussed by Adam Ronikier in *Pamiętniki 1939–1945*, 267–280.

the German authorities, they let them visit Marshal Józef Piłsudski's crypt. As the reptile weekly *7 Dni* reported, "Following a special request from the delegates, the Governor General gave an order that the crypt with the body of Marshal Piłsudski, which had been closed to the public since the outbreak of the War, should be reopened. Moved by the experience, delegates attended the Marshal's sarcophagus for a long time and expressed their feelings by saying prayers aloud."[706]

According to available data, another form of Maak's wartime collaboration with the Germans was his participation in several German radio broadcasts and the publication of a short story in *Goniec Krakowski*.[707] In 1944 he reduced the number of his visits to the Telpress agency, though he did not sever all his connections with its editorial board.

However, in June 1944 he quarreled with Hans Fenske and was fired from Telpress. When the War was over he claimed that in mid-1944 the Germans had threatened to deport him to Auschwitz-Birkenau or Plaszow. Apparently, they accused him of collaborating with Tadeusz Hołuj on the editing of *Gazeta Pansłowiańska*. Years later Maak said in court that he had been a member of the Home Army and had been involved in issuing false ID documents.[708] However, I have not been able to verify this claim.

It is likely that initially Maak's Katyn visit as a member of the official delegation saved him from serious repressive measures at the hands of the Germans. When toward the end of the War his German employers barred him from practicing journalism, he went into hiding. It is likely, though, that Maak considered his future prospects and came to a conclusion that further collaboration with the Germans would no longer pay off and was quite risky. He must have anticipated that sometime in the future he could be accused of collaborating with the enemy. So he decided to go into hiding till the end of the War.

---

[706] 'Dożynki,' *7 Dni* 1943: 44, 11.

[707] (jk), 'Świadkowie o roli prasy gadzinowej,' *Dziennik Polski* 1949 (Jun. 11), 3.

[708] AIPN Kielce, sign. no. 127/268, Vol. 1, Akta w sprawie karnej Oresta Mariana Kałużniackiego [Documents on file relating to the criminal case against Orest Marian Kałużniacki], sheet 221.

BEFORE COMMUNIST COURTS
IN PEOPLE'S POLAND

When military operations ended on the Polish territories Maak made an attempt to prove his military rank with a special Ministry of National Defense military recruiting office, hoping that not much evidence could be found against him on his former collaboration with the Germans. He started the procedure already in April 1945. The recruiting officers confirmed his military service as an ensign, and he resumed military service, joining a regiment at Rembertów. At this time a sketch of his character and personality was produced by Lt.-Col. Pavlov, the regiment's commanding officer: "During his short period of service with the regiment Ensign Maak has proved an able officer (...). His demeanor is very good, he is talented and ambitious, he has a good reputation with officers and his superiors. His ethics and morality are impeccable, he is dutiful and disciplined. He is not listed in the register of penalties, instead he has received commendation for his good work. Ensign Maak meets the requirements for the post of the regiment's physical education officer and in future he promises to be very successful in the job."[709] As we can easily guess, a few days later he was promoted to second lieutenant and continued his service in the 2nd Motorized Training Regiment at Legionowo. This must have allayed his fears. He came to the conclusion that his wartime engagements were no longer of any consequence. However, he did not expect that the special intelligence services of the Ministry of Public Security of People's Poland were already singling out those Poles who had collaborated with the Germans in any way at all, especially those who could challenge the official interpretation of the Katyn massacre.

On September 20, 1945 Lt. Marian Maak was unexpectedly summoned to Warsaw to see Prosecutor Karol Szwarc to talk about his visit to Katyn as a member of a 1943 delegation. Other members of the delegation had already been interrogated, so it was likely they had mentioned his participation in the second Polish delegation to Katyn. Presumably Marian Maak had never about talked his visit to Katyn in public, which would have made things quite awkward for him. At the prosecutor's office he provided a detailed account of his

---

[709] AIPN Kraków, sig. no. 1847/79, Teczka akt personalnych Mariana Maaka (ur. 1917 r.) [Personal dossier of Marian Maak, b. 1917].

Katyn experience. He said that to the best of his knowledge everything that had happened there was stage-managed by the Germans. Neither the meetings with Smolensk inhabitants nor their testimony were accidental. He quoted a few examples, which from the prosecutor's point of view could be used in the Katyn trial for which preparations had been going on for some time. "An old man – a Russian the Germans had brought to Katyn at gunpoint to say what he knew (...) was shaking with fear and staring at the Germans so intensely that he looked insane. The Germans claimed he had witnessed the transport of the Polish officers by the Soviet authorities to the village of Koziy Gory." Next he recalled a passage from a speech given by a German officer who accompanied the delegation: "he told each of us that you couldn't find a single watch on the corpses, which he thought incriminated the Soviets, as they were known to be fond of watches." He commented that the Germans made a big effort to convince the Poles of the truthfulness of their claim.[710]

Probably trying to save his freedom, Maak said that in a conversation with a Russian woman he had heard that it had all been done by the Germans.[711] What is more, at the end of his statement he evaluated the veracity of what some other Russian witnesses had said about the crime while facing armed German soldiers, and concluded that they must have been briefed to provide the right kind of answers. What he also found problematic was the conduct of the German officers supervising the exhumation work. He went as far as to suggest that the Germans had fabricated the evidence that implicated the Soviets, and gave examples to support his claim. He said that occasionally double sets of identity documents (e.g. military IDs) had been found on the exhumed officers, thus implying that perhaps someone (meaning the Germans) had planted them there. He also claimed that the German SS officers who had forced Russian prisoners to excavate the graves, always seemed to know beforehand where to dig to find buried Polish officers.[712] Maak's testimony turned out to be exactly what Prosecutor Szwarc had been waiting for, because Maak did his best to adopt a communist version of the events. At the same time, he was quite credible, as what he said might have actually taken place.

---

[710] *Ibid*, sign. no. 303/8, Protokół przesłuchania świadka w Warszawie dnia 20 IX 1945 r., [Minutes of witness's hearing, Warsaw. Sept. 20, 1945], sheets 4–5.

[711] *Ibid*, sheet 4.

[712] *Ibid*.

Not having an inkling of what awaited him, Maak told the prosecutors that he would be moving to Kraków. His decision to move was probably due to the fact that the army had decided to demobilize him and send him to university in Kraków to study physical education.[713] Perhaps it was dictated by the developments related to Katyn and Maak's dubious relations with the Germans during the War. Until 1948 he was also seen in the Lower Silesian region and he stayed for a short spell in the towns of Gryfów Śląski and Mirsk. In the latter place he even opened a drivers' school. Perhaps his move to Lower Silesia should not be seen as going into hiding but rather as an attempt to avoid publicity and encounters with Ministry of Public Security functionaries. However, documents relating to the activities of the security forces in the administrative area of Lwówek Śląski, to which Gryfów Śląski and Mirsk belonged, do not indicate that Maak was under surveillance.[714] Ultimately, his plan did not work out and again he became a target of interest for security agents.

Maak's 1943 Katyn visit was not his only form of collaboration with the Germans – after all, he had worked for the Telpress agency, published in the reptile press, and given radio interviews. When the temporary lull in the Katyn investigation and plans for a trial was over, Communist functionaries arrested Maak, for the first time on November 24, 1948. He and some other newspaper men were rounded up in connection with their work for reptiles such as *Goniec Krakowski, Dziennik Radomski*, and *Kurier Kielecki*, which the Germans had published in the GG during the War. The following editors stood trial in Kielce between March 22 and 28, 1949: Dr. Orest Marian Kałużniacki, Józef Kondek, Zbigniew Strzębalski, Józef Głogowski, Zdzisław Tranda, Wiktor Smenda, Anna Kozłowska, Jan Wierzbówka, Maria Hessel, and Marian Maak.[715] The accused pleaded not guilty though they admitted they had collaborated with the Polish-language newspapers and magazines published by the Germans. They defended what they had done by claiming they had not realized they

---

[713] *Ibid.*, sig. no. 1847/79, Teczka akt personalnych Mariana Maaka (ur. 1917 r.) [Personal dossier of Marian Maak, b. 1917].

[714] R. Klementowski, *Służba Bezpieczeństwa w powiecie Lwówek Śląski (1945–1956)*, (Wrocław: Oddział Instytutu Pamięci Narodowej – Komisji Ścigania Zbrodni przeciwko Narodowi Polskiemu, 2009).

[715] W. Sztejn, 'Proces redaktorów gadzinówek,' *Kielecka Trybuna Robotnicza* 1949 (Mar. 24).

were acting against the Polish nation.[716] The Kielce Regional Court sent 8 of the 10 defendants to prison, with sentences ranging from three to five years. Marian Maak was sentenced to four years in prison, with disenfranchisement for three years and the confiscation of his property.[717]

The Kielce trial did not put an end to Maak's problems. He stood a second trial in Kraków a couple of months later, when he joined four other Poles accused in the local and national press of collaboration with the Germans. Security functionaries arrested two of them, Ewa Smolka and Piotr Paliwoda-Matiolański, and issued an arrest warrant for Dr. Feliks Burdecki and Jan Emil Skiwski. Maak's indictment in the company of Skiwski and Burdecki, the publishers of the pro-German *Przełom*, did not augur well for him, as they were considered out-and-out collaborators.[718] In fact, a joint trial was all the more dangerous for the defendants who were rounded up, because Skiwski and Burdecki had long since left the country. Harsh sentences were handed down on those who actually stood in the dock. In June 1949 the trial came to an end. The prosecutor had charged Marian Maak with a number of serious offenses, especially his work for the Polskie Wiadomości Prasowe agency, and later for Telpress. Additionally, he was liable for "weakening the spirit of resistance in Polish society," and hence for acting to the detriment of the Polish State. Also his books, the novels *Powrót Krzysztofa Szaroty* (1941) and *Trzy kwadranse na mężczyznę* (1944), and a number of columns published in reptiles like *Goniec Krakowski*, *Ilustrowany Kurier Polski*, and *Rolnik* were taken against him. However, contrary to some claims,[719] he does not seem to have authored the novel *Ludzie z kawiarni* (1943), published under the pen-name of "Marian Makowski". The extant court records do not imply that he ever used such a pen-name.

---

[716] 'Pierwsze dni procesu współpracowników „gadzinówek" okupacyjnych' *Kielecka Trybuna Robotnicza* 1949 (Mar. 29).

[717] 'Wyrok w procesie redaktorów „gadzinówek",' *Kielecka Trybuna Robotnicza* 1949 (Apr. 1).

[718] Incidentally, earlier these two defendants got a bad character reference from Stefan Korboński, one of the leaders of the Polish Underground State (*W imieniu Rzeczpospolitej...*, 159). He put it in the chapter on collaboration, where he wrote, "Some of the most active collaborators in Kraków were Feliks Burdecki and Jan Emil Skiwski, editors of *Przełom*, a 1944/45 Polish-language fortnightly serving the German propaganda. They were condemned in the Polish underground press. After the War they managed to flee Poland" (*ibid*).

[719] Woźniakowski, *W kręgu jawnego piśmiennictwa*, 410.

The critic Krzysztof Woźniakowski has analyzed the literary value of Maak's novels and come to the conclusion that Maak pioneered the writing of romance novels in the GG and was counted among an "elitist" group of the "GG writers" who were allowed to publish their novels in *Ilustrowany Kurier Polski*.[720] He published his work with Księgarnia Powszechna publishing house, which was under a Polish Underground State ban and Polish writers had been warned not to publish with it. Woźniakowski comments that Maak's two novels turn a blind eye to the reality of the GG. They don't show either the War or the German repressive measures – life is idyllic. Although the GG is presented "under a vague Third Reich tutelage and is affected by certain inconveniences of war, this has no serious impact on the quiet lives of well-to-do residents, whose attention is fully focused on their everyday business, undisturbed by the German authorities, the latter being absent from the pages of this peculiar above-board literary product."[721] Woźniakowski is right to observe that Maak and writers like him invited their readers to "escape into another world."[722] Although in *Powrót Krzystofa Szaroty* the September 1939 attack on Poland is mentioned, it is hard to find out who the actual invader was. Instead, the reader learns that the Poles kept losing and retreating. Wartime resettlements and displacements boil down to automobile rides from country house to country house, social gossip, banquets, and gambling. The only petty annoyances concern stealing gasoline from one another.[723]

The court sentenced Marian Maak to 10 years in prison, five-year disfranchisement and forfeiture, whereas Skiwski and Burdecki were given life sentences.[724] The other defendants received the following sentences: Ewa Smolka 7 years in prison, and Piotr Paliwoda-Matiolański 4 years in prison. The court rejected the defense's argument that the Polish Underground State had permitted some forms of collaboration with the Germans, as it found the activities of Telpress particularly detrimental to the Polish national interest. The court maintained that the permission had been issued by unauthorized agencies.

---

[720] *Ibid.*, 90, 325.

[721] *Ibid.*, 309.

[722] *Ibid.*

[723] *Ibid.*, 326.

[724] 'Winni są zdrady narodu. Motywy wyroku na kolaborantów prasy gadzinowej,' *Dziennik Polski* 1949 (Jun. 15), 3.

Remarkably, the court was not at all interested in Maak's revelations about Katyn. Maak might have been hoping that his detailed statement of September 20, 1945 would help establish his line of defense and radically change his situation, but that never happened. The Katyn issue was raised many times during the interrogations, but it was not mentioned in court in 1949. This was before the Madden Committee report was published in the United States. In my opinion the Communist propaganda functionaries did not find Maak's account to be of any value. Later, when the Soviet Union and other Communist countries launched a propaganda campaign on Katyn, Maak was already in prison.

The 1949 sentence did not put an end to Maak's case. His defense attorney appealed it and the case was sent back to the court. In March 1950 the appellate court reduced the sentence to 4 years in prison. In 1952 the Kraków appellate court summed up Maak's multiple sentences and "in place of the imposed sentences sentenced Maak to 4 years and 6 months in prison."[725] He left prison on September 1, 1953 and never took up writing and journalism again. He died in Kraków on October 31, 2005.

---

[725] AIPN Kraków, sig. no. 1847/79, Teczka akt personalnych Mariana Maaka (ur. 1917 r.) [Personal dossier of Marian Maak, b. 1917].

TARGETED BY THE MINISTRY OF PUBLIC SECURITY. THE POSTWAR LIVES OF THREE LABORERS WHO VISITED KATYN IN 1943

Three of the delegations the Germans brought to Katyn in 1943 appear to have comprised 14 Polish blue-collar workers from a few companies located in the Generalgouvernement and in the Reichsgau Wartheland. The three delegations arrived on April 10, April 17, and May 20, 1943. Other members of the third delegation included the Vilnian writer Józef Mackiewicz, and journalist Władysław Kawecki, who worked for Telpress and *Goniec Krakowski* and had visited Katyn on April 10, 1943, and four journalists from Portugal and Sweden.

So far it has been possible to ascertain the names of 12 workers and their workplaces. They were: Włodzimierz Ambroż from a Warsaw optics company (Zakłady Optyki Precyzyjnej); Dr. Zygmunt Giżycki, a dentist employed in the Poznań streetcar company; Władysław Herz from Fabryka Baterii Centra (a Poznań battery factory); Edmund Kiler aka Killer, an engineer from the Warsaw branch of the Steyr-Daimler-Puch engineering company; Leon Kowalewicz, an engineer from the Avia engineering works, Warsaw; Stanisław Kłosowicz from the Radom branch of Steyr-Daimler-Puch; Hieronim Majewski of the Sieradz railroad works; Mikołaj Marczyk from the Stalowa Wola steelworks; Leon Nowicki, an engineer employed in the Cegielski heavy engineering works in Poznań; Jan Symon aka Szymon from the F.S.W. automobile works in Warsaw; Franciszek Prochownik from Zieleniewski's engineering factory, Kraków; and Bolesław Smektała from the Poznań branch of the Focke-Wulf aviation company. There were two more unidentified employees of Łódź companies. Thus, besides the Polish Red Cross employees, Polish blue-collar workers were the most numerous members of the Katyn delegations.

As I have already pointed out elsewhere, during the War some of them did not meet the expectations of the Germans as regards their visit in Katyn. To put it briefly, upon their return they refused to engage in any form of collaboration with the Germans and did not participate in any propaganda events (such as, for example, meetings in workplaces, talks preceding the German documentary film, press interviews, setting up exhibitions, etc.). Some of them kept a low profile or went into hiding, thus presumably saving their lives with the prospect of prosecution by the Germans or Soviets looming ahead of them. After all, in a few cases underground communist agencies imposed death sentences on some of the delegates. But there were also those who joined German propaganda efforts in their hometowns or workplaces. They attended the Germans on visits to nearby villages and towns. After the War they were the ones who were most at risk of repressions, though initially their fate was not sealed. With a few exceptions, such as Franciszek Prochownik, for some time the Communist security functionaries were not able to collect enough evidence against them. In Prochownik's case they examined materials printed in reptiles like *Nowy Kurier Warszawski* and *Goniec Krakowski*, which contained interviews given by Franciszek Prochownik[726] and Włodzimierz Ambroż,[727] and recorded by Władysław Kawecki; the information that the delegates had laid a bouquet of flowers bearing the message "For the Polish Army officers murdered by the Bolsheviks. From their fellow countrymen," and that Mikołaj Marczyk[728] had delivered an address on the occasion. It is also certain that another matter made the investigation difficult. Sometimes delegates' names were misspelled in the reptiles and have come down to us in different versions. However, according to the records kept by the Ministry of Public Security, from 1945 on for some delegates there were consequences of their Katyn visit, either (for Prochownik, Majewski and Marczyk) in

---

[726] 'Wrażenia krakowskiego robotnika w lesie katyńskim. Specjalny wywiad „Telpressu" z członkiem polskiej delegacji Franciszkiem Prochownikiem,' *Goniec Krakowski* 1943:90 (Apr. 17), 1. This interview was reprinted in *Dziennik Radomski* with a new headline, 'Ręce złożyć w pięść. Robotnik polski na miejscu krwawej zbrodni. Żydzi z GPU mordowali polskich oficerów,' *Dziennik Radomski* 1943: 91 (Apr. 18), 1.

[727] 'Sosnowe krzyże na bratnich mogiłach w Katyniu. Wywiad z uczestnikiem delegacji polskiego*świata pracy*,' *Nowy Kurier Warszawski* 1943: 127 (May 29–30), 2.

[728] 'Delegacja polskiego świata pracy w Katyniu,' *Nowy Kurier Warszawski* 1943: 126 (May 28), 1.

outcome of the Ministry of Public Security investigation; or (for Smektała and Kłosowicz) due to the NKVD. Below I will focus on the fate of the former three. It is worth noting here that in the case of a few others (e.g. Ambroż, Kowalewicz, Kiler, and Symon) no information has ever been found on their postwar doings. The extant records suggest that after the War the Ministry of Public Security did not search for them. Neither have I found their names on any of the lists compiled by the Ministry of Public Security in 1945–46 and in the early 50s of those who in one way or other had been implicated in the Katyn case. This has been confirmed by fairly recent research done by a number of historians, such as Joanna Żelazko, Stanisław M. Jankowski, Przemysław Gasztold-Seń, Mirosław Golon, and Wojciech Materski.[729]

THE CASE OF FOREMAN FRANCISZEK PROCHOWNIK

The first to draw the attention of the Ministry of Public Security was Franciszek Prochownik, a foreman from Zieleniewski's and the best known of the blue-collar delegates. His name appeared in Edmund Seyfried's report, though it was not in Goetel's report.[730] It became known in the Polish community in London thanks to a report prepared by the authorities of the Polish Underground State. The Communist security service was probably not aware

---

[729] S.M. Jankowski, 'Pod specjalnym nadzorem przy drzwiach zamkniętych. Wyroki sądowe w PRL za ujawnienie prawdy o zbrodni katyńskiej,' *Zeszyty Katyńskie* 20 (2005) 95–135; P. Gasztold-Seń, 'Siła przeciw prawdzie. Represje aparatu bezpieczeństwa PRL wobec osób kwestionujących oficjalną wersję Zbrodni Katyńskiej,' *Zbrodnia katyńska. W kręgu prawdy i kłamstwa*, ed. S. Kalbarczyk, (Warszawa: Instytut Pamięci Narodowej, 2010), 132–153; Golon, 'Kary za prawdę o zbrodni Stalina,'; Materski, *Mord katyński; Zbrodnia katyńska. Kryzys prawdy 1940–2010*, Warszawa 2010, s. 45–54; M. Tarczyński (ed.), Zbrodnia katyńska. Kryzys prawdy 1940–2010, (Warszawa: Niezależny Komitet Historyczny Badania Zbrodni Katyńskiej: Polska Fundacja Katyńska, 2010), 45–54; J. Żelazko, 'Dzieje sprawy katyńskiej na przestrzeni siedemdziesięciu lat historii,' in *Jeńcy wojenni z Łódzkiego – ofiary zbrodni katyńskiej*, J. Żelazko and P. Zawilski, (eds.), (Łódź: Instytut Pamięci Narodowej – Komisja Ścigania Zbrodni przeciwko Narodowi Polskiemu; Archiwum Państwowe w Łodzi, 2011), 35–62.

[730] Even after a few years Ferdynand Goetel did not mention Franciszek Prochownik as one of the delegates. This is what he wrote about those who visited Katyn: "Dr. Edmund Seyfryd (name misspelled), the head of the board of the RGO, arrived from Kraków by plane, as did Polish factory workers" (Goetel, *Czasy wojny*, 156).

of this last fact. According to the latest findings Prochownik, a member of the underground PPS-WRN, was put on the list of delegates at the last minute thanks to his popularity with his workmates at Zieleniewski's.[731] Subsequently he avoided contact with the Germans, fearing for his life. He went into hiding because apparently the Communists had passed a death sentence on him.[732] After the War he was arrested for the first time on June 7, 1945. Dr. Jerzy Sawicki, the prosecutor conducting the Katyn investigation, then consulted his superior, Dr. Roman Martini, over what further steps should be taken. He suggested a close investigation of the case on the one hand, but on the other restraint in bringing charges: "We want to acquire a detailed characteristic of this worker. It may well be that he was exploited by the German propaganda. All the evidence in his favor and against him should be weighed up carefully."[733] The documentation collected on Franciszek Prochownik confirmed that he was not only a popular worker and a PPS activist, but also that after 1943 he refused to be exploited by the Germans. The fact that his son was a member of the anti-German resistance and was murdered in KL Auschwitz in 1941 also spoke in his favor. His wife, Wiktoria Prochownik, interceded on his behalf and sent a letter requesting clemency to Bolesław Bierut, President of the National Council of People's Poland. Martini gave Prochownik's Katyn visit with the delegation and his interview for a reptile as the reason for his arrest. He also noted that Prochownik enjoyed a good reputation in his workplace. Nevertheless, Prochownik remained in detention until October 2, 1946, and his release occurred after Prosecutor Martini's death, when the Communists decided to abandon the Katyn trial in Poland, and after the Nuremberg debacle sustained by the Soviets over Katyn. It seems he was no longer needed as an intimidated witness. However, he made a promise to the Communists to collaborate on the Katyn massacre in future. He was also put under police surveillance. In 1948 he was arrested for shouting "Down with democracy, to hell with it!" in public.[734]

---

[731] Jankowski and Kotarba, *Literaci a sprawa katyńska 1945*, 96.

[732] *Ibid.*

[733] *Ibid.*

[734] K. Siemaszko, „*W trudnym okresie odbudowy państwa*". *Tak zwany Mały Kodeks Karny w świetle orzecznictwa Sądu Okręgowego w Krakowie w latach 1946–1950* (Warszawa: Instytut Pamięci Narodowej. Komisja Ścigania Zbrodni Przeciwko Narodowi Polskiemu, 2015), 199.

In 1952 the Ministry of Public Security recollected its encounter with Franciszek Prochownik and his suitably molded opinions on Katyn. In one of the Ministry of Public Security documents he was listed among "the members of the 'commission' sent by the Germans, who acknowledged that what they had seen in Katyn was a German provocation."[735] On March 22, 1952 Prochownik was detained by the internal security functionaries for a second time. He now made a report on his visit to Katyn.[736] He claimed he had been misled by the Germans before the journey, because apparently they told him he would attend the funeral of Polish workers who had died during earthworks somewhere in the East. Next he stressed that the only delegate he knew in the group was Ferdynand Goetel. They learned more once they reached Smolensk. A German officer told them about the atrocities committed by Soviet soldiers on Polish officers. "Next morning they put us on a bus and drove us to the site of the massacre where we saw a horrible sight. A commission of German experts kept saying it had been done by the Soviet Union. Dr. Buhtz, a German physician, performed autopsies and characteristically, the hirsute parts of the corpses were in a good state of preservation, the skin on the faces and hands was very well preserved, and each of us smiled to himself when they said it had been done in 1940; looking carefully at the corpses you could see well-preserved shoes, belts, buttons and belt buckles; besides, various personal documents indicated that the corpses could not possibly have lain on each other for three years; "to prove this I took a 50 złoty bill I had found there – it was brand new, there was no trace of a decomposing body on it despite the fact that I pulled it from a side pocket of an army jacket, where it was tucked in with only two postcards next to it," said Prochownik.[737] Next he said that the Germans had shown the delegates many different documents found on the victims. He thought the large number of documents was quite striking: "There were about 25 corpses pulled out of the graves, but the letters, postcards, and tokens found there must have belonged to 150 or 200 people, though those corpses

---

[735] AIPN, Warsaw, sign. no. 00231/124, vol. 1, Informacja nr 1 dotycząca dowodów prowokacji niemieckiej w sprawie Katynia z 3 IV 1952 r., [Information no. 1 related to the evidence proving the German provocation in the Katyn case, Apr. 3, 1952] sheet 3.

[736] *Ibid.*, vol. 2, Oświadczenie Franciszka Prochownika z 22 III 1952 [Franciszk Prochownik's statement of Mar. 22, 1952], sheets 1–2.

[737] *Ibid.*, sheet 1.

had not been touched."[738] Prochownik also said that upon his return he was pestered by a *Goniec Krakowski* editor, who asked him about his Katyn experience. He added that the conversation they had was published in the reptile in a very distorted way. Prochownik also claimed the Germans urged him to give a talk before the showing of their documentary film on Katyn. He refused and explained that he was a poor speaker and drank too much, which made him ill-suited for the job.[739] He remained under surveillance till the mid-50s.

A DELEGATE FROM THE REICHSGAU WARTHELAND

The delegates from the Reichsgau Wartheland were blue-collar workers and craftsmen from Poznań, Łódź, and Sieradz, as well as a dentist. There were seven of them, five of whom including Hieronim Majewski have been identified. They traveled via Poznań and Warsaw, reached Katyn on April 17, 1943, and were shown around the site. They saw the work of the German medical commission and listened to a detailed lecture on the massacre and its timing. Majewski, who was fluent in German, learnt a lot during the visit and became convinced that the Soviets had carried out the massacre in the spring of 1940. He must have been a keen observer, as he remembered a number of details pertaining to the bodies. He took home a packet containing many mementos provided by the Germans, such as epaulettes and uniform buttons, photographs belonging to the murdered officers, and their letters.

After the War Hieronim Majewski was put under close surveillance.[740] This was due to two causes. The first concerned the time just after the War, when he

---

[738] *Ibid.*, sheet 2.

[739] *Ibid.*

[740] Hieronim Majewski was born in Chełmża on August 8, 1914. In 1936 he did his military service with the Officer Cadet Corps at Zambrów. Next he became a member of the railroad guards in Grudziądz. In 1939 he was a second lieutenant in the combat operations for the defense of the Polish coast. Subsequently he was in German captivity, but was released from the POW camp in 1940 on account of illness. He joined his family at Karsznice and got a railroad job, first in an engine house and later as an office worker. He worked in Karsznice till January 1945 and then moved to Pomerania. He still held a railroad job (as a railroad guard) in Kwidzyń, Iława, Tczew, and other places. In 1947 he joined the PPR and later became a member of the PZPR. M. Zemła, 'Świadek ekshumacji w Katyniu,' *Sowiniec* (Dec. 2006), 135–137. See also S.M. Jankowski, 'Sprawa Hieronima Majewskiego. Wyroki sądowe w PRL za ujawnienie prawdy o zbrodni katyńskiej,' *Zeszyty Katyńskie* 21: 2006, 83–107.

was in favor of a boycott of the First of May celebrations and wanted an active observance of the Third of May national holiday. Moreover, he supported the PSL and was quite open about his hostility to the Communists and their vision of the postwar reality. His problems with the Ministry of Public Security began in March 1947,[741] but at the time he did not suffer any serious consequences yet, and did not mention his 1943 visit to Katyn in the CV he compiled for the Ministry of Public Security. This was the second cause responsible for his problems. Soon it turned out that he had not managed to expunge his Katyn visit from his biography.

For the first time the visit impacted seriously on his postwar life in October 1949. The Ministry of Public Security suspected that Majewski had collaborated with the Gestapo in the Karsznice area. Somewhat later it turned out his collaboration had been more extensive. A number of witnesses confessed that between the spring and fall of 1943 Majewski delivered about twenty talks on Katyn and interpreted the soundtrack of the German documentary film for Polish audiences. The court records show he had spoken in the towns of Zduńska Wola, Karsznice, Sieradz, Kutno, Turek, Uniejów, Pabianice, Żychlin, Wieluń, and Ostrów Wielkopolski.[742] At all times he was accompanied by Gestapo officers, who cross-checked what he had said. Considering the duration and intensity of his engagement in the propaganda work – he visited ten towns and villages in six months – we can conclude that in this respect he was the record-holder among all the fifty Polish delegates who had visited Katyn.

At these rallies he spoke persuasively about his meetings with the locals of Katyn, who had told him about the perpetrators of the massacre and the time it had taken place. He had no doubt the Bolsheviks were responsible, and to cover up the crime they had planted a copse on the graves. His talks were accompanied by the showing of the German documentary.

At the trial he defended himself by saying the Germans had forced him to go to Katyn and that he had never been paid for the talks he delivered, which was confirmed by some of the witnesses. There were also some (just two witnesses) who said that in private conversations he had put the blame for the massacre on the Germans.[743] The court sentenced him to six years in prison.

---

[741] Zemła, 'Świadek ekshumacji w Katyniu,' 136.

[742] *Ibid.*, 138.

[743] *Ibid.*, 139.

The Łódź appellate court confirmed the sentence.[744] Majewski spent four years in Sieradz prison and was discharged in 1954.[745]

A KPP ACTIVIST ON THE KATYN MASSACRE

One of the blue-collar workers from the GG who visited Smolensk and Katyn on May 20-21, 1943 was Mikołaj Marczyk, a blue-collar worker from the Stalowa Wola steelworks. If I am not mistaken he was the only member of the KPP, the prewar Communist Party of Poland, who saw the site in the spring of 1943.

Mikołaj Marczyk was born on December 11, 1905 in Warsaw.[746] His father was a janitor at the Warsaw Polytechnic. His family was evacuated to Russia during World War 1. They stayed in Vitebsk and Gorki. Marczyk returned to Poland in 1921. As he was unemployed and in a difficult family situation, he made an attempt to leave for Soviet Russia and contacted the Soviet legation in Warsaw for help. However, as he claimed, an official from the legation encouraged him to stay in Poland and start cooperating with the Communists, which eventually he did. He did his military service in Lida (now in Belarus) in the 77th Infantry Regiment. In the army his communist sympathies continued, especially for Hramada, the Belarusian Peasants' and Workers' Union. Upon his discharge from the army he returned to Warsaw and thanks to a good word from an acquaintance landed a job at the Gerlach Factory as a fitter. From 1931 on he was a member of the KPP and the head of the Communist cell in Gerlach's. In 1938 he left for Stalowa Wola in the Central Industrial District, where he took up a job. When World War 2 broke out he initially wanted to get across to the Soviet Union, but when he reached Kowel (now Kovel', Ukraine) he turned back to Stalowa Wola. As he admitted during his 1950 interrogation, he was still thinking of leaving for the Soviet Union. In November 1939 he was issued appropriate documents by the Soviet mission in Jarosław (then in the Soviet-occupied part of Poland), thanks to which he

---

[744] AIPN Łódź, sign. no. 5657/VII, Sentencja wyroku z dnia 1 VIII 1950 r., [Sentence of the judgment of Aug. 1, 1950], sheet 1.

[745] Gasztold-Seń, 'Siła przeciw prawdzie,' 134.

[746] In the CV Marczyk's date of birth is given as December 11, 1905, whereas the court records give November 11, 1905.

and his family could leave for the Soviet Union at any time. He resolved to go, but for reasons unknown did not. The Soviets canceled the visas issued to his family. He remained in Stalowa Wola, where he learned that the Germans had attacked the Soviet Union.[747]

As far as his Katyn visit was concerned, he had been selected by the Germans. It is impossible to ascertain whether this explanation was actually true. Apparently, a German official who talked to him acknowledged they knew very well he was a communist and a supporter of the Soviet Union. He added they would send him to Katyn "to make him see that the Russians murdered Poles."[748] He had traveled to Warsaw by train via Radom. In Warsaw he was joined by Stanisław Kłosowicz (whom Marczyk called "a certain gentleman").

In Warsaw they stayed at the Volksdeutsch House in Aleje Ujzdowskie. Next they were flown to Smolensk, where Marczyk shared a room with the writer and journalist Józef Mackiewicz. He also named two other delegates: the editor Władysław Kawecki, and Leon Kowalewicz, an engineer. During his visit in Katyn he was convinced the massacre had been carried out by the Soviets.[749] The Germans gave him a packet containing uniform tabs and a major's epaulettes, uniform buttons, a medallion, Polish bills, a gorget with an image of the Blessed Virgin Mary, a cigarette case, an eagle badge from a Polish army cap, and a set of photographs showing the work of the medical commission and the Polish delegations, including the blue-collar delegation. Additionally, he had a list of the names of Katyn victims and he was knowledgeable about the findings made by the members of the Technical Commission of the Polish Red Cross who had worked on the site. The Germans hoped every delegate would go back to his hometown and workplace equipped with such a packet and knowledge, and organize an exhibit in a factory or company showcase with some help from local German officials. In the steelworks the showcase was black and displayed "epaulettes, Polish

---

[747] AIPN Rzeszów, sign. no. 046/1197, Vol. 1, Akta kontrolno-śledcze dotyczące Mikołaja Marczyka, [Documents obtained during the investigation against Mikołaj Marczyk], sheets 1–14.

[748] *Ibid.*, sheet 14.

[749] *Ibid.*, sign. no. 108/6521, Akta kontrolno-śledcze dotyczące Mikołaja Marczyka. Akt oskarżenia, [Documents obtained during the investigation against Mikołaj Marczyk. Charges against the accused], sheet 3.

military uniform buttons, a key ring, some carved wood and many other things."[750] Moreover, Marczyk gave a few talks in which he concluded that the massacre had been done either by the Red Army or "Judeo-Communists." Many of his talks preceded a showing of the documentary film. If a need arose, he would travel to neighboring villages and towns in the company of Germans, to speak on Katyn.

Marczyk turned out to be fairly conscientious in all he did at the behest of the Germans. According to the count established by Ministry of Public Security officers, he had given at least nine talks in Stalowa Wola. He was always attended by Gestapo officers, who controlled what he was saying. In 1944 he went into a Warsaw hospital for treatment for a duodenal ulcer. In 1949 he admitted it had been a ruse on his part, as he had decided to stop his relations with the Germans and wait for the arrival of the Red Army. When Soviet forces entered Warsaw he returned to Stalowa Wola, where he reported to the mayor and told him of his Katyn experience. Next he was subjected to a thorough interrogation by an NKVD officer and, much to his surprise, released.[751] He reached a conclusion that now he could join the Polish Army. Many years later he explained that by doing this he had wanted to make amends for his past mistakes. He served in the 27th infantry regiment and took part in the crossing of the Lusatian Neisse and the Spree. In November 1945 he left the army as a sergeant. He stayed in the Western Territories of Poland and settled in Skarbków near the town of Mirsk. Soon his family joined him there.[752] Incidentally, the editor Marian Maak, another member of the Polish Katyn delegations, settled in Mirsk. Both of them must have feared that if they had remained in their former places of residence (Stalowa Wola and Kraków respectively) they would have had still more trouble in connection with their Katyn visit. In the Western Territories no one knew them and as long as they kept a low profile they expected to be safe there.

---

[750] *Ibid.*, sign. no. 046/1197, Vol. 1, Akta kontrolno-śledcze dotyczące Mikołaja Marczyka. Protokół przesłuchania Obwisło Stefana [Documents obtained during the investigation against Mikołaj Marczyk. Minutes of the statement made by Stefan Obwisło], sheet 3.

[751] *Ibid.*, Akta kontrolno-śledcze dotyczące Mikołaja Marczyka. Protokół przesłuchania Woźniczki Jerzego z 25 I 1950 r., [Documents obtained during the investigation against Mikołaj Marczyk. Minutes of the statement made by Jerzy Woźniczka on Jan. 25, 1951], sheet 21.

[752] *Ibid.*, sheet 19.

In Skarbków and Mirsk Mikołaj Marczyk proved himself a professionally and socially active person. He set up a workshop and was appointed chairman of the local branch of ZBoWiD (a Polish postwar veterans' association) and the TPPR (Polish-Soviet Friendship Society). In 1948 he joined the PZPR.[753] His postwar life resembled the lives of a few other members of the Katyn delegations and reptile editors who found a haven in the Northern and Western Territories, where some of them became Communist Party activists and local administrators.

The security service discovered Marczyk in 1949, though publications on the security service agency of the *powiat* of Lwówek Śląski do not imply he was under surveillance prior to his arrest.[754] Perhaps what turned the scales against him was a vetting process of Party members that took placed at the time of the fusion of the PPR and the PPS, or a tip from someone who knew his past.

He was put in custody in Rzeszów prison on October 7, 1949, and indicted on the grounds of the decree of August 31, 1944. The charge was "collaboration with the Germans; (...) at Stalowa Wola in the spring of 1943 to accommodate the authorities of the German state in their attempt to weaken the spirit of defiance of the Polish Nation in the battle against the enemy, he disseminated fake news at meetings organized specifically to uphold the Fascist propaganda on the crime of Katyn."[755] Marczyk defended himself by claiming that he had been forced to go to Katyn and that upon his return his talks had been monitored by the Gestapo. He added that the content of his talks was questioned and doctored by the Germans, who added information on Soviet atrocities. During his interrogations he said many times that he made his colleagues secretly aware of the fact that it was the Germans who had committed the crime.

On February 14, 1951 Rzeszów Voivodeship Court sentenced Marczyk to two years in prison. In the grounds for the sentence the court said it had taken extenuating circumstances into consideration and passed the lowest possible sentence: "despite the fact that the defendant had been a Communist since

---

[753] *Ibid.,* sheets 20–21.

[754] See, for instance, Klementowski, *Służba Bezpieczeństwa w powiecie Lwówek Śląski (1945-1956)*.

[755] AIPN Rzeszów, sign. no. 108/6521, Akta kontrolno-śledcze dotyczące Mikołaja Marczyka. Akt oskarżenia, [Documents obtained during the investigation against Mikołaj Marczyk. Charges against the accused], sheet 2.

1925 and was a vigorous political activist, when he and his family were threatened with death, he succumbed to the German demands and delivered the aforementioned talks, though now and again he confided to colleagues that the Katyn massacre had been done by the Germans."[756]

---

[756] *Ibid.*, sheet 3.

FATHER TOMASZ RUSEK'S SERMONS AND STATEMENTS ON THE KATYN MASSACRE AND HIS POSTWAR PROBLEMS

REACTIONS TO THE KATYN MASSACRE IN THE CITY OF LUBLIN UNDER GERMAN OCCUPATION

In April 1943, when the Germans spread news of the Katyn massacre, the issue was taken up in Lublin by *Nowy Głos Lubelski*, the local reptile paper, which followed the propaganda strategy prepared beforehand by the Germans. The task was entrusted to Bruno Widera, one of its editors[757] and a member of the first GG delegation to visit Smolensk and the site of the Soviet atrocity. Upon his return he wrote a number of articles for *Nowy Głos Lubelski*, in particular 'Lubliniacy wśród ofiar bolszewickich,' on Lublin inhabitants among the victims killed by the Bolsheviks.[758]

The Germans made priests from local parishes, including Fr Tomasz Rusek from the Lublin Parish of St Paul, join in the campaign. Documents collected by the Communist security service straight after the War show that the initiative to celebrate a solemn mass for the victims of Katyn had been prompted by German propagandists. Lublin's district public prosecutor informed Dr. Arnold Gubiński, plenipotentiary for the prosecution of German collaborators, that Fr Józef Kruszyński, wartime vicar-general for the

---

[757] For the headlines of a number of articles on the Katyn massacre in *Nowy Głos Lubelski* see Wolsza, *„Katyń to już na zawsze katy i katowani”*, 30.

[758] B.W., 'Lubliniacy wśród ofiar bolszewickich,' *Nowy Głos Lubelski* 1943: 91 (Apr. 18/19), 3.

31. Father Tomasz Rusek

diocese of Lublin, had been involved in the matter. He was the priest the Germans pressurized into making arrangements for the mass.[759] There are more details in the district prosecutor's letter: "the representatives of the German occupying authorities ordered Fr Kruszyński to have a mass said (…). Fr Kruszyński agreed under pressure, but contrary to the German demands he assigned one of the minor churches for the mass and justified his choice by claiming that for technical reasons it was impossible to celebrate it in the cathedral."[760] At the same time Fr Kruszyński asked Fr Tomasz Rusek of the Parish of St. Paul to make the arrangements for the mass and preach the sermon (at the time the parish priest, Fr Paweł Dziubiński, was out of town, staying in Nowy Sącz). The Germans ordered the final version of the sermon sent to them for approval before it was delivered. The sermon's outline and main points were prepared by the Germans themselves (the documents in the security service's holdings suggest that apparently it was done by one Zeiperk, an employee of the Department of Propaganda in the district of Lubin) and then handed over to the Polish clergy. Fr Józef Kruszyński and Fr Tomasz Rusek modified the text slightly and sent it back to the Germans for final approval. However, their version was not accepted, so they received yet another version, edited and modified by German propagandists to highlight Soviet involvement. Apparently Fr Kruszyński was highly critical of these new German modifications. However, it is difficult to speculate if or to what extent his dissatisfaction had an impact on the final version of the

---

[759] AIPN Lublin, sign. no. 015/432, Prokurator sądu okręgowego w Lublinie do ministerstwa sprawiedliwości w Warszawie, 15 X 1948 r. [The prosecutor of the Lublin District Court to the Ministry of Justice in Warsaw, Oct. 15, 1948].

[760] *Ibid.*

sermon, because there is no full record extant of what was actually delivered. Years later, when Tomasz Rusek was charged with collaborating with the Germans, he told a prosecution officer from the Gdańsk District Office of Public Security that Fr Kruszyński had forced him to deliver an anti-Soviet sermon.[761] Perhaps it was his only defense strategy, but it had nothing to do with the real events that occurred nine years before.

We have a press report of the church ceremony held on June 11,1943.[762] There is no doubt the Germans treated it as an important event and had high expectations of concrete, palpable benefits. The church was equipped with state-of the-art speakers, "moving cameras," and microphones. The mass was broadcast outside the church and could be heard on the radio and propaganda loudspeakers in the streets. The Germans made an effort to spread rumors that thanks to radio transmission the mass would be heard all over the world. There was a delay of half an hour caused by a power failure – and power was essential to conduct all the points on the agenda efficiently. Considering the fact that the events occurred in June 1943, that is well over 70 years ago, it is clear that the Germans did their best to use all the propaganda means available to publicize the occasion. Their commitment to have the Lublin memorial service run smoothly was like the propaganda effort they had made in April 1943 at Katyn, where visiting delegations were constantly attended by microphones, moving cameras, loudspeakers, and photojournalists. Why did German propagandists go to such incredibly great lengths in Lublin? The answer seems simple. It was the last chance to present their anti-Soviet propaganda materials, because the work of the German Medical Commission and the Polish Red Cross Technical Commission was coming to an end and because the Red Army was advancing on the Eastern front. It is enough to note here that the Polish Red Cross team led by Dr. Marian Wodziński worked in Katyn for five weeks, until June 3, 1943, whereas the Soviets reached Smolensk on September 25, 1943.

It is also quite understandable that the organizers made an effort to ensure the proper attendance. All the administrative staff and employees of Lublin

---

[761] *Ibid.* Protokół przesłuchania podejrzanego Tomasza Ruska z 9 IX 1952 r., [Minutes of interrogation of the accused Tomasz Rusek, Sept. 9,1952], sheet 146.

[762] 'Nabożeństwo żałobne za dusze polskich żołnierzy pomordowanych w Katyniu,' *Nowy Głos Lubelski* 1943: 136 (Jun. 13–14), 3.

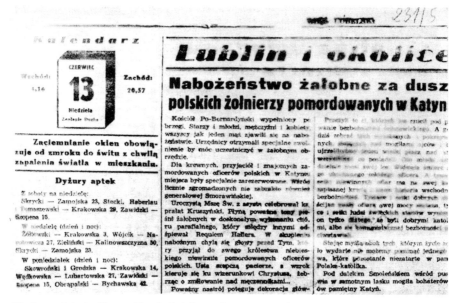

32. An article in *Nowy Głos Lubelski* on the memorial mass, June 1943

offices, companies and factories were given leave of absence to attend the mass, and schools were closed. Evidently the Germans attached great significance to the occasion. To obtain the required propaganda effect they wanted as big a congregation as possible of Poles living in Lublin and its vicinity.

It is difficult to say exactly what the response of the Lublin townspeople was, because the extant sources show this in different ways. According to the reptiles the occasion was a propaganda success: "The church (…) was filled to the brim with people. Young and old, men and women, they all came in large numbers to the mass (…). The relatives, friends and acquaintances of the officers murdered in Katyn had specially reserved seats. The wife of General Smorawiński was in the huge congregation."[763] On the other hand, five years later Czesław Skorupski, a district prosecutor, viewed the event as a complete failure: "Lublin townspeople did not attend the mass, as they saw it as a German propaganda event rather than as a religious ceremony. In particular, the widow of General Smorawiński, commander-in-chief of the Lublin Corps District Command, who died in Katyn, refused to attend despite the

---

[763] *Ibid.*

pressure."[764] What is certain, though, is that the mass and the sermon could be listened to outside the church. This was what Fr Tomasz Rusek was told by his friends and acquaintances. The Germans were pleased with the outcome.

Nowy Głos Lubelski provided a detailed account of the mass, which was celebrated by Fr Kruszyńki. The parish choir sang funeral hymns. The solemn character of the ceremony was highlighted by the church décor, especially the catafalque festooned with spruce branches, wreaths and ribbons. Funeral honors were given by State Police officers and petty officers. In his sermon Fr Rusek highlighted the Soviet responsibility for the mass murder of the Polish officers. He took his time before reaching the concluding part and gradually heightened the emotions and suspense. This is just a sample: "A dragon bloated with the blood of its own children threw a noose round the necks of Polish soldiers. New graves were dug, widows' and orphans' tears flowed, thousands of broken families and forsaken children were doomed to exile and misery in a foreign country (…). Standing in spirit by those whose life was ruined, we cannot pass over one word which is still fresh in the memory of the Polish Catholic. Out in the middle of nowhere, in the environs of Smolensk, in a desolate forest, there is a heroes' grave, that notorious Katyn. It is with deep sorrow that we remember those brave men, whose blood has mingled with that of the martyrs of the Catholic Church (…)."[765] In the last part of the sermon Fr Rusek named the perpetrators in a poignant conclusion: "In our thoughts we are in Katyn, grieving over the desecrated bodies, which we embalm with the tears of the grief-stricken families and kiss on the tormented temples pierced by the bullets of Bolshevik executioners."[766] The ceremony was concluded by Fr Józef Kruszyński, who urged the congregation to pray for the repose of the souls of those murdered by the Bolsheviks and laid to rest in Katyn.

The sermon Fr Tomasz Rusek delivered was recorded on a phonograph record.[767] As he later observed, the record was of an inferior quality and broke

---

[764] AIPN Lublin, sign. no. 015/432, Prokurator sądu okręgowego w Lublinie do Ministerstwa Sprawiedliwości w Warszawie, 15 X 1948 r. [The prosecutor of the Lublin District Court to the Ministry of Justice in Warsaw, Oct. 15, 1948].

[765] 'Nabożeństwo żałobne za dusze polskich żołnierzy,' 3.

[766] *Ibid.*

[767] AIPN Lublin, sign. no. 015/432, Protokół przesłuchania podejrzanego z 11. IX 1952 r. [Minutes of interrogation of the suspect, Sept.11, 1952], sheet 152.

quite soon, apparently right after the first time it was played.[768] Undoubtedly the idea of recording a sermon was a novel propaganda idea for the Germans in the Katyn case. As far as I know, they had never used such a propaganda tool before. What they usually did – and the Lublin ceremony was no different in this respect – was to produce materials for a newsreel to be screened in cinemas and out of doors.

The memorial held in St. Paul's was commented upon by the local underground political activists. The Communists called it "outrageous buffoonery" and a "propaganda comedy, ill devised at that." In conclusion they wrote: "The effect of that buffoonery was the opposite of what the Germans wanted. Saying prayers for those killed in Katyn precisely in Lublin, so close to the infamous Majdanek concentration camp, proves how callous the Germans are (…)."[769] This comment was no different from other Communist opinions on the subject.[770]

The Germans were planning more events of this kind in Lublin. They organized several meetings with Fr Kruszyński and Fr Rusek to make them participate in other propaganda activities on the Katyn massacre and the threat posed by the Soviet Union and the Red Army.[771] Evidently their efforts were at least partly successful, as in February 1944 Fr Rusek spoke at an official public rally organized by the Germans on Katyn and the Soviet threat. The date was not coincidental, as it was a response to the communiqué issued by the Burdenko Commission in January 1944, in which the Soviets charged the Germans with responsibility for the Katyn massacre and made sure the news circulated internationally, especially in the English-speaking countries. The rally was held in the Apollo cinema. Fr Rusek obtained the text of his talk on the Soviet Union as the enemy of the Western culture ('Związek Sowiecki wróg kultury zachodniej') directly from the German organizers. An important component of the event supplementing Fr Rusek's talk was the appearance of two Polish soldiers

---

[768] *Ibid.*, sign. no. 326/132, Protokół przesłuchania podejrzanego z dnia 21 IX 1952 r., [Minutes of interrogation of the suspect, Sept. 21, 1952], sheet 38.

[769] *Ibid*, sign. no. 015/432, Oburzające błazeństwo [Outrageous buffoonery], 206.

[770] See Gontarczyk, *Polska Partia Robotnicza.* 222–233; K. Sacewicz, *Centralna prasa Polski Podziemnej wobec komunistów polskich 1939–1945*, (Warszawa: Instytut Pamięci Narodowej – Komisja Ścigania Zbrodni przeciwko Narodowi Polskiemu, 2009).

[771] AIPN Lublin, sign. no. 015/432, Protokół przesłuchania podejrzanego Tomasza Ruska z 9 IX 1952 r., [Minutes of interrogation of the suspect Tomasz Rusek, Sept. 9,1952], sheet 146.

the Germans had taken prisoner in the Battle of Lenino. Fr Rusek's commitment to the Katyn issue caught the attention of the local Communists on this occasion as well, quite apart from the details and circumstances of the sermons and public addresses. For instance, an underground PPR bulletin commented on what he said.[772] Tomasz Rusek himself made the following comment: "the underground organization was critical of my address."[773]

It is very likely that the Communists put Fr Rusek on their list of dangerous persons engaged in collaboration with the Germans. According to his statements, at the time he felt threatened and helpless. He sought help in the diocesan curia, but in vain. Out of desperation he decided to leave the priesthood. This is how the Lublin chapter of his life came to the end. The only viable option he had was to leave the area.

TO THE BALTIC COAST VIA THE WARSAW UPRISING

Tomasz Rusek left for Warsaw. He got there in April 1944 and changed his name to Tomasz Reszta. He married and found a job as a supplier in a toy warehouse. As he said during an interrogation in 1952, when the Warsaw Uprising broke out he reported to the Baszta regiment and took part in raising barricades, but did not engage in further military activities. After the Uprising he ended up in a transition camp in Pruszków. There he was declared fit for forced labor in Germany. He escaped from the deportation train between Radom and Skarżysko rail stations and found a hideout in the village of Długosz near Radom, his father's family village. He spent the last months of the War in Radom. He took up a job, first at the rail station and when the War was over, at the local art school. In August 1945 he was an employee of the State Repatriation Office and moved first to Miastko and later to Sopot on the Baltic coast. When the office was closed down he moved to Gdynia and got a job in the secretaries' office of the College for Maritime Trade. When the college was closed he found a job with the Chamber of Industry and Commerce and later moved to the fish marketing board. In the early 50s he started working at a vocational school for statisticians in Gdynia. Occasionally he had taught

---

[772] *Ibid.*, sign. no. 015/432, Protokół przesłuchania podejrzanego z 11. IX 1952 r., [Minutes of interrogation of the suspect, Sept.11, 1952], sheet 152.

[773] *Ibid.*

statistics at the College for Maritime Trade as well. In February 1952 he started a job in the Gdynia shipyard. He was never engaged in the activities of the PPR or the PZPR.[774]

As Rusek often changed jobs and his place of residence, and for some time used a false name, it is likely he was afraid that his Lublin engagements in 1943-1944 would catch up with him. His fears were justified, because Ministry of Public Security agents had been looking for him since 1945, on two counts. The first was related to the sermons and addresses he had delivered and the second was collaboration with *Nowy Głos Lubelski*. However, the latter involvement had been negligible. He had never written anything for the reptile press, unlike Fr Józef Kruszyński, who had published an article in late February 1943 on the clergy's position on communism ('Stanowisko duchowieństwa wobec komunizmu'). Nevertheless, his name had appeared in some other articles, but they were reports on various events organized by the Germans in which he had participated. However, just like Kruszyński, he was on the wanted bulletin (a news-sheet tantamount to an arrest warrant) the Ministry of Public Security set about publishing already in 1945.[775]

The question of punishing the *Nowy Głos Lubelski* journalists did not emerge until 1948, when the Ministry of Public Security was collecting evidence of collaboration by journalists writing for *Kurier Kielecki* and *Dziennik Radomski*. However, progress was very slow and rather chaotic, without the required expertise and methodology. The Ministry did not even manage to establish the names of the journalists to be found and interrogated. Only after some time did the Lublin prosecutors send formal inquiries concerning the whereabouts of Hipolit Szczotecki, Bernard Górecki, Tadeusz Marcinkowski, Bruno Widera, Kazimierz Bąkowski, Zofia Musielak, and Krystyna Szarska to the District Offices of Public Security in Kielce, Radom and Kraków. However, none of the listed persons were found and detained. The Germans had killed

---

[774] My survey of the particular stages in Tomasz Rusek's life is based on AIPN Lublin, sign. no. 015/432, Protokół przesłuchania podejrzanego Tomasza Ruska z 9 IX 1952 r., [Minutes of interrogation of the suspect Tomasz Rusek, Sept. 9,1952], sheets146–147; and *Ibid.*, Życiorys [Curriculum Vitae], sheet 137.

[775] *Ibid.*, Pismo szefa Wojewódzkiego Urzędu Bezpieczeństwa Publicznego w Gdańsku do szefa Wojewódzkiego Urzędu Bezpieczeństwa Publicznego w Lublinie z 30 IX 1952 r., [Letter from the Head of the Gdańsk Voivodeship Public Security Office to the Head of the Lublin District Public Security Office, Sept. 30, 1952], sheet 134.

off some of the Lublin reptilians still during the War. Kazimierz Bąkowski served in the Polish army until he was demobilized in 1946; thereafter he vanished into thin air. Bruno Widera, the editor-in-chief, who was at the top of the most wanted list, had fled the city just before the Red Army entered. In 1945 the Ministry of Public Security sent out an arrest warrant for him. As late as 1953 his name was still on the Ministry's wanted list. The only Lublin editor who was arrested was Jan Pelczarski; he was detained in a Kraków prison. So there were good reasons to abandon the trial of the *Nowy Głos Lubelski* journalists that had been planned for 1949.

More or less at the same time the Ministry of Public Security tried to establish the basic facts on the Katyn memorial events held in Lublin in 1943-1944, so as to bring the organizers of the masses and meetings to justice. In his first dispatch sent to the Regional Court Public Prosecutor's Office, Maj. Franciszek Zalewski, head of the Lublin Regional Office of Public Security, mentioned three persons: Fr Paweł Dziubiński, Fr Franciszek Dobrucki, and Fr Tomasz Rusek.[776] Later Fr Józef Kruszyński was also put on the list, while Fr Paweł Dobrucki was crossed off because he had died.[777] The list of suspects was further adjusted on the basis of new findings. Fr Rusek was singled out as the main suspect.[778] At the same time the security service learned that Tomasz Rusek

---

[776] *Ibid.*, Pismo mjr Franciszka Zalewskiego do Prokuratury Sądu Okręgowego w Lublinie z 11 VIII 1948 r. [Letter from Maj. Franciszek Zalewski to the Lublin Regional Court Public Prosecutor's Office, Aug. 11,1948], sheet 11.

[777] *Ibid.*, Pismo prokuratora Cz. Skorupskiego do Pełnomocnika do Spraw Ścigania Osób Podejrzanych o Kollaborację z Niemcami z 15 IX 1948 r. [Letter from Public Prosecutor C. Skorupski to the Plenipotentiary for the Prosecution of Persons Suspected of Collaborating with the Germans, Sept. 15, 1948], sheet 15.

[778] Tomasz Rusek was born in the village of Koszorów near Radom on December 20, 1910. During the First World War his family lived in Kiev. They returned to Poland in 1922. He attended high school in Lublin and Kowel [now Kovel, Ukraine]. He did his military service in 1932–1933 in the 24th Infantry Regiment in Łuck [now Lutsk, Ukraine]. He was a second lieutenant in the military reserve force. In 1934 he enrolled in Theology at the Lublin seminary, but his studies were interrupted when the War broke out in September 1939. In 1939–1941 he worked in a laundry, and as of 1940 attended special courses leading up to Holy Orders. He was ordained in 1941 and the Lublin Curia sent him to the Parish of St Paul. *Ibid.*, Kwestionariusz personalny [Personal questionnaire], sheets 260–262; *Ibid.*, Raport naczelnika Wydziału IV MBP w Gdańsku z 6 IX 1952 r. [Report of the Head of the 4th Department of the Gdańsk Branch of the Ministry of Public Security, Sept. 6, 1952], sheet 144; *Ibid.*, sign. no. 326/132, Protokół przesłuchania podejrzanego z 9 IX 1952 r., [Minutes of interrogation of the suspect, Sept. 9,1952], sheets 19–28.

had left Lublin in March or April 1944, probably for the Retrieved Territories, having quit the priesthood. The first search for him was carried out in 1945-1946 and 1948, and was unsuccessful, so the investigation was shelved until such time as Rusek's whereabouts could be established.

IN THE CROSSHAIRS OF THE MINISTRY OF PUBLIC SECURITY

The District Office of Public Security did not discover his whereabouts until 1952. Tomasz Rusek's detention coincided with the vigorous campaign orchestrated by the Communist mass media to discredit the Madden Committee's report. It occurred at the time the Ministry of Public Security ordered its local offices to find all those who had had anything to do with Katyn. The order entailed a wanted list, albeit a very inaccurate one, with names of those who had died, those who had long since left the country, and even people with no connection at all to the Katyn question. It is likely that had it not been for the heightened vigilance of the security service agents in 1952, Rusek might have evaded all responsibility and could have lived undisturbed for the rest of his life. The fact that he was mostly known as a clergyman and that the public security functionaries were looking for him in the ecclesiastic milieu helped him remain free for a quite a long time.

On September 6, 1952 the Gdańsk District Office of Public Security came across the first clue to Rusek's whereabouts. Although its agents were not entirely sure that the person under their surveillance who worked in the supply department of the Gdynia shipyard was the ex-priest from Lublin, nevertheless they painstakingly examined his biography and interviewed those who knew him. Their diligence was due to the fact that the documents that had been sent out from Lublin to all the district offices still in 1945 emphasized Rusek's contacts with the Gestapo, which was a serious matter. When the head of the Gdańsk office compared the materials sent from Lublin with the CV Tomasz Rusek had submitted at his workplace he came to the conclusion it was the same person.

Rusek was detained in Gdynia on September 9, 1952 and taken into custody by the Lublin District Office of Public Security. He was not the first postwar victim of repressions by public security functionaries against those who had been responsible for spreading the truth about Katyn and had stayed in Poland after the War. According to Przemysław Gasztold-Seń's and Mirsław Golon's research, there were 25 people subjected to repressive measures in 1945–1956. They included three priests: Fr Leon Musielak, a Kozielsk survivor; Fr Bernard Pyclik of Lwówek Śląski; Fr Tomasz Sapeta of Bardo Śląskie; as well as the ex-priest Tomasz Rusek.[779]

In March 1953 Rusek was committed for trial. He was charged on the grounds of the decree of August 31,1944 with "collaborating with the German occupation authorities in June 1943 and February 1944, to the detriment of the people of Poland by spreading defeatism in a sermon he preached at St. Paul's Church on the Katyn massacre and giving a public address at the Apollo cinema on Socialism as a political system. He discussed the alleged threat of Bolshevism and urged his listeners to join forces with the Hitlerite occupation authorities."[780] At the same time the public prosecutor launched an attack on all the Lublin Roman Catholic clergy. He mentioned Fr Józef Kruszyński as "the staunchest supporter of the pro-Nazi option" and generally accused the clergy of conducting harmful activities during the German occupation of Poland and after 1945, "(…) so it is not surprising that because of such criminal activities carried out against the Polish nation by the Polish reactionary clergy and because the clergy has brought up reactionary social outcasts, during the War we experienced and are still experiencing fratricidal killings, acts of sabotage, and espionage against the Polish People's Republic. One of the reactionary clergymen who collaborated with the Nazi state in Lublin was Fr Kruszyński's disciple, Fr Tomasz Rusek (…)."[781] For the sake of contrast the indictment also contained information on the crucial role and significance of the Soviet Union and the PPR in defeating the Third Reich.

The defendant acknowledged his guilt and explained that indeed he had delivered a sermon and a talk on Katyn in the Apollo cinema, in which he provided a distorted interpretation of the massacre and the role of the Soviet

---

[779] Gasztold-Seń, 'Siła przeciw prawdzie,' 135; Golon, 'Kary za prawdę o zbrodni Stalina,' 230–231, 233.

[780] AIPN Lublin, sign. no. 015/432, Akt oskarżenia przeciwko Ruskowi Tomaszowi s. Michała z 31 III 1953 r., [Indictment of Mar. 31, 1953, against Tomasz Rusek, son of Michał], sheet 231.

[781] *Ibid.*

Union. He blamed the Church hierarchy for the words he had used, as apparently it had been particularly keen on spreading Nazi propaganda. Initially the court sentenced Tomasz Rusek to one year in prison. According to Judge J. Różycki the sentence was relatively short because almost ten years had passed since the offense and the accused had acknowledged his behavior as reprehensible and made amends still during the War. This was demonstrated by the fact that Rusek had left the priesthood and contributed to the effort of building the new Polish reality.[782] The public prosecutor appealed the sentence and as a result the Supreme Court headed by Judge Gustaw Auscaler increased it to three years in prison. In comparison with other sentences passed on clergymen this was relatively low. The highest sentence – five years in prison – was passed on Fr Leon Musielak (he left prison in 1955, after serving three years) and the lowest on Fr Tomasz Sapeta – two years in prison. In 1954, following Tomasz Rusek's appeal, the Lublin Voivodeship Court reduced the sentence to half the term.[783]

---

[782] *Ibid.*, sign. no. 326/132, Sentencja wyroku z 22 VIII 1953 r. [Sentence of the verdict of Aug. 22, 1953], sheet 87.

[783] *Ibid.*, Postanowienie z 3 V 1954 r. [Decision of May 3, 1954], sheet 161.

KATYN IN THE REPTILIAN TRIALS
(1946-1948)

The Katyn atrocity was a regular issue raised by the prosecution in the postwar proceedings against about a dozen or so editors of the reptile press published in the GG and in Lwów, either as part of the indictment or during interrogations. It happened in the trial of Stanisław Wasylewski, editor of *Gazeta Lwowska*; and in the Kraków trial of Jan Emil Skiwski, Dr. Feliks Burdecki and additionally with Marian Maak, all of whom were charged with collaboration with the reptiles. It is worth noting that the public prosecutors were seriously thinking of bringing charges against Ferdynand Goetel.

Reptilian journalists and associates published in papers like *Nowy Kurier Warszawski*, *Goniec Krakowski*, *Gazeta Lwowska*, the Vilnian *Goniec Codzienny*, and a number of local spin-offs of the first two papers, issued by the Telpress agency. As we know, Katyn made the headlines in the spring of 1943.[784] The urgent demand for any news about the Katyn massacre at that time made the Poles living under the German occupation by and large accept the information provided by the reptiles as reliable – sometimes it was the only source of information available.[785] After the War this created a formidable challenge for the Communists. They were of the opinion that bringing the reptilians to justice in postwar trials was tantamount to condemning a host of publications on the Katyn massacre and exposing them as false and exceptionally

---

[784] Głowiński, 'Sprawa katyńska w oficjalnej polskojęzycznej prasie,' 135–167.

[785] Tomasz Głowiński is right to observe that "In the reptile press the Katyn massacre turned into a propaganda drive on an unprecedented scale. Practically for three months on end it was front-page news, fanned by new revelations and new considerations. Beyond all doubt the facts related to what had been found in Katyń were reported in an accurate and practically undistorted way," (*Ibid.*, 164).

malevolent. This I would take as the reason for the issue of arrest warrants for the most notorious collaborators and for repressive measures against reptile journalists, even though the Katyn issue was not a prominent feature in the mass media at the time.

THE REPTILE PRESS
IN THE GENERALGOUVERNEMENT AND DISTRIKT
GALIZIEN: EDITORS AND JOURNALISTS

To begin with, it will be worthwhile examining the significance and growth of the reptile press in Poland under German occupation. While the research on the Polish-language propaganda press published by the Germans and the Soviets in occupied Poland after 1939 has produced quite a number of mostly high-quality publications,[786] the same cannot be said about the research on the postwar prosecution of Poles who had collaborated with "the reptile press,"[787]

---

[786] L. Dobroszycki, *Reptile Journalism: The Official Polish-Language Press under the Nazis, 1939–1945* (Yale University Press: New Haven and London), 1994; T. Szarota, 'Jawne wydawnictwa i prasa w okupowanej Warszawie,' *Studia Warszawskie. Warszawa lat wojny i okupacji* 1972 (Series no. 2): 139–165; W. Chojnacki, 'Jawna prasa polskojęzyczna na terenach włączonych do Rzeszy i w Niemczech w latach 1939–1935,' *Dzieje Najnowsze* 1985: 1, 101–147; S. Lewandowska, *Prasa okupowanej Warszawy 1939–1945* (Warszawa: Instytut Historii PAN, 1992); E. Cytowska-Siegrist, *Szkice z dziejów prasy pod okupacją niemiecką (1939–1945)* (Warszawa and Łódź: PIW, 1986); W. Wójcik, *Prasa gadzinowa Generalnego Gubernatorstwa 1939–1945* (Kraków: Wydawnictwo Naukowe WSP, 1988); G. Hryciuk, *„Gazeta Lwowska" 1941–1944* (Wrocław: Wydawnictwo Uniwersytetu Wrocławskiego, 1992); T. Głowiński, *O nowy porządek europejski. Ewolucja hitlerowskiej propagandy politycznej wobec Polaków w Generalnym Gubernatorstwie 1939–1945* (Wrocław: Wydawnictwo Uniwersytetu Wrocławskiego, 2000); M. Okułowicz, '„Kurier Białostocki" jako przykład hitlerowskiej prasy gadzinowej, wydawanej w okręgu białostockim w 1944 r.,' *Studia Podlaskie* 2006: 16, 209–260; E.C. Król, 'Niemieckie czasopisma w języku polskim w Generalnej Guberni („Ster", „Mały Ster", „Zawód i Życie"),' *Kwartalnik Historii Prasy Polskiej* 1978: 1; Woźniakowski, *W kręgu jawnego piśmiennictwa*; Idem, '„7 Dni" (1940–1944). Quasi-kulturalny gadzinowy tygodnik warszawski,' *Zeszyty Prasoznawcze* 1994: 1/2; B. Gogol, *Czerwony Sztandar. Rzecz o sowietyzacji ziem Małopolski Wschodniej, wrzesień 1939 – czerwiec 1941* (Gdańsk: Wydawnictwo Uniwersytetu Gdańskiego, 2000); L. Jockheck, *Propaganda im Generalgouvernement. Die NS-Besatzungspresse für Deutsche und Polen 1939–1945*, (Osnabrück: fibre Verlag, 2006).

[787] The Polish underground weekly *Biuletyn Informacyjny* 1941 (Jan.9) gave a good description of the German-controlled propaganda press published in Polish (viz. the reptiles): "The German propaganda papers are like reptiles – they treacherously clad themselves in the skin

as the papers sponsored by the occupying powers were called, [788] though there have been several publications in which the issue has been treated fairly cursorily.[789]

There is another important aspect to these papers and periodicals, which apart from being called "the reptile press", were also referred to as *szmatławce* (raggish newspapers); *szmaty* (rags) or *kurwary* (pimps) used of *Nowy Kurier Warszawski*,[790] the latter sobriquet being a pun on the paper's title; or *podogońce* (underlings, literally "what hangs under an animal's tail" – a punning epithet for *Goniec Krakowski*).[791] That aspect is their place in the historical research on the 1939–1945 period. According to Tomasz Szarota, Andrzej Chwalba, Grzegorz Hryciuk, Anna Czocher, Sebastian Piątkowski, Adam Massalski and Stanisław Meducki, dailies such as *Nowy Kurier Warszawski, Goniec Krakowski, Gazeta Lwowska, Dziennik Radomski, Kurier Kielecki, Kurier Częstochowski, Nowy Głos Lubelski* and *Nowy Czas*, are important sources of information on

---

of the Polish language to poison the body of the Polish Nation with their venomous content. Their words are printed in Polish, but the mind and hand that control them are German. They are doing their job for Germany." See Szarota, *Okupowanej Warszawy dzień powszedni*, 319.

[788] So far (I believe) there have been only two studies published on the postwar stories of the Warsaw reptilians working for *Nowy Kurier Warszawski, Fala*, and *7 Dni* – Tomasz Szarota's study 'Trudny temat – kolaboracja' in *Karuzela na Placu Krasińskich. Studia i szkice z lat wojny i okupacji* (Warszawa: Oficyna Wydawnicza Rytm: Fundacja Historia i Kultura, 2007), 71–147, especially a trail-blazing passage, 'Kolaboracja z okupantem niemieckim i sowieckim w oczach Polaków – wówczas, wczoraj i dziś,' pp. 71–92; and an important article by Zuzanna Schnepf ('Losy pracowników niemieckiej gadzinówki „Nowy Kurier Warszawski" w świetle powojennych procesów z dekretu sierpniowego," in *Zagłada Żydów. Studia i Materiały* 2006:2, 132–159).

[789] Piątkowski, *Okupacja i propaganda. Dystrykt radomski Generalnego Gubernatorstwa*, 60–62; T. Wolsza, 'Aparat bezpieczeństwa wobec polskich dziennikarzy wizytujących w 1943 r. miejsce sowieckiej zbrodni w Katyniu. Przypadek Władysława Kaweckiego,' in *Dziennikarze władzy, władza dziennikarzom. Aparat represji wobec środowiska dziennikarskiego 1945–1990*, T. Wolsza and S. Ligarski, eds. (Warszawa: Instytut Pamięci Narodowej. Komisja Ścigania Zbrodni przeciwko Narodowi Polskiemu, 2010), 381–393; T. Wolsza, 'Los dziennikarza z tzw. gadzinówki w powojennej Polsce (Przypadek Mariana Maaka),' in *Nie tylko niezłomni i kolaboranci... Losy dziennikarzy w kraju i na emigracji w latach 1945–1990*, T. Wolsza and P. Wójtowicz, eds., (Warszawa: Instytut Pamięci Narodowej. Komisja Ścigania Zbrodni przeciwko Narodowi Polskiemu, 2014), 134–142. For reasons unknown to me, this subject was not discussed by Leszek Olejnik in *Zdrajcy narodu? Losy volksdeutschów w Polsce po II wojnie światowej* (Warszawa: Wydawnictwo Trio, 2006).

[790] Szarota, *Okupowanej Warszawy dzień powszedni*, 319.

[791] Quoted after Jockheck, *Propaganda im Generalgouvernement*, 129.

everyday life under German occupation.[792] I would also emphasize the importance of the reptiles for research on the Katyn massacre, especially in the context of the events that took place in the spring of 1943, when the German propaganda machine publicized the massacre on an unprecedented scale.[793]

During the occupation of Poland the Germans published about 60 press titles (including 10 dailies, 11 weeklies, 10 monthlies and 25 professional magazines) with a maximum circulation of over 1.32 million copies in 1944 (including 700,000 for the dailies, 410,000 for weeklies, and 210,000 for monthlies). On top of this there were 1.22 million copies of professional and trade journals. In his analysis of such publications Hans Frank wrote that it was an "endemic press."[794] In 1939 the press-run of all these periodicals numbered about 80 thousand copies,[795] gradually rising over the next years. Contemporary estimates put the edition data for Polish-language dailies published in 1940 at 275 thousand copies (some sources give 380 thousand copies as the correct figure),[796] over 392 thousand in 1941, over 363 thousand in 1942, and 400 thousand copies in 1943 (the holiday press-run was as much as 500 thousand copies).[797] By 1944 a record 620 thousand copies had been published.[798] A similar increase in press-run figures was observed for the trade, professional and propaganda journals. In 1942–1943 the Germans published

---

[792] Szarota, *Okupowanej Warszawy dzień powszedni, passim*; A. Chwalba, *Dzieje Krakowa*, vol. 5: *Kraków w latach 1939–1945* (Kraków: Wydawnictwo Literackie, 2002); A. Czocher, *W okupowanym Krakowie. Codzienność polskich mieszkańców miasta 1939–1945* (Gdańsk: Wydawnictwo Oskar: Muzeum II Wojny Światowej, 2011); Piątkowski, *Okupacja i propaganda. Dystrykt radomski Generalnego Gubernatorstwa, passim*; G. Hryciuk, *Polacy we Lwowie 1939–1944. Życie codzienne* (Warszawa: Książka i Wiedza, 2000); A. Massalski and S. Meducki, *Kielce w latach okupacji hitlerowskiej 1939–1945* (Kielce: Kieleckie Towarzystwo Naukowe; Wrocław: Zakład Narodowy im. Ossolińskich – Wydawnictwo).

[793] Głowiński, 'Sprawa katyńska w oficjalnej polskojęzycznej prasie,' *passim*; C. Madajczyk, *Dramat katyński*; Wolsza, *„Katyń to już na zawsze katy i katowani"*; Szarota, *Okupowanej Warszawy dzień powszedni, passim*.

[794] AIPN Kraków, sign. no. 1/1394, Akta oskarżenia przeciwko Janowi Skiwskiemu, F. Burdeckiemu i innym [Indictment against Jan Skiwski, F. Burdecki and others], sheet 40.

[795] J.A. Młynarczyk, 'Pomiędzy współpracą a zdradą. Problem kolaboracji w Generalnym Gubernatorstwie – próba syntezy,' *Pamięć i Sprawiedliwość* 2009: 1, 125.

[796] Jockheck, *Propaganda im Generalgouvernement*, 351.

[797] *Ibid.*, 127.

[798] *Ibid.*

as many as 700 thousand copies of professional journals for Polish readers.[799] The authorities of the Polish Underground State kept an eye on the press-run of the reptiles. Already in 1941 the underground *Biuletyn Informacyjny* wrote about the magnitude of the phenomenon, giving the example of "the most pernicious *Nowy Kurier Warszawski*, the largest propaganda daily in the GG, with a daily press-run of over 150 thousand copies and a holiday and Sunday press-run over 300 thousand copies (...)."[800]

Of all the dailies published in the GG, the Germans attached most significance to *Nowy Kurier Warszawski*, so it had a press-run of about 200 thousand copies. The press-run of other dailies with the same profile was much lower: for instance, 65 thousand copies for *Gazeta Lwowska*, 60 thousand for *Goniec Krakowski*, 50 thousand for *Nowy Głos Lubelski*, and 40 thousand for *Kurier Częstochowski*. With the weeklies, the biggest press-run was for *Ilustrowany Kurier Codzienny*, 50 thousand copies; followed by *7 Dni* with 40 thousand, and *Fala* with 10-30 thousand copies. There were also professional and trade magazines, addressed to a specifically targeted reader, with press-runs between a few hundred and a few thousand copies. They included *Nowiny, Co miesiąc powieść, Siew, Kolejowiec, Spółdzielca, Rolnik, Pszczelarz, Ogrodnictwo, Las i Drewno, Rzemiosło, Wiadomości Aptekarskie dla Generalnego Gubernatorstwa, Poradnik. Miesięcznik Służby dla Wójtów, Straż nad Bugiem, Biuletyn Kasyna Gry w Warszawie, Miesięcznik Teatru m. Warszawy, Wiadomości Chełmskie, Wzorowa Gospodarka, Strażnica, Mały Ster,* and *Zawód i Życie.*[801] In addition there was the monthly *Ster* addressed to young people, which in 1943 had an impressive press-run of 600 thousand copies.[802] Naturally, the authorities the Polish Underground State were aware of this. A 1941 issue of *Biuletyn Informacyjny* wrote that "the campaign of *Nowy Kurier Warszawski* has been strengthened by 'literary' and special-purpose periodicals. The press-run of the pornographic fortnightly *Fala* is 10 thousand copies, and in

---

[799] P. Majewski, 'Kolaboracja, której nie było... Problem postaw społeczeństwa polskiego w warunkach okupacji niemieckiej 1939–1945,' *Dzieje Najnowsze* 2004: 4, 65.

[800] 'Gadzinowa farsa,' *Biuletyn Informacyjny* 1941 (Jan. 9).

[801] Dobroszycki, *Reptile Journalism*; Cytowska-Siegrist, *Szkice z dziejów prasy pod okupacją niemiecką (1939–1945)*; Wójcik, *Prasa gadzinowa Generalnego Gubernatorstwa 1939–1945*; Piątkowski, *Okupacja i propaganda. Dystrykt radomski Generalnego Gubernatorstwa*, 53.

[802] T. Głowiński, 'Kolaboracja do końca. Wystąpienia radiowe dr Feliksa Burdeckiego w Krakowie jesienią 1944 r.,' *Śląski Kwartalnik Historyczny Sobótka* 2003: 3, 298.

the past three months it has risen by 2,800 copies. *Co miesiąc powieść*, a worthless monthly that publishes translations from German tabloids, has a press-run of 10 thousand and has increased by 4,500 copies; *Ilustrowany Kurier Polski* has a press-run of 11,900 copies in the Warsaw and Lublin regions and in parts of the Radom region (we do not have the figures for the GG as a whole), *Siedem Dni* also has a press-run of 11,900 copies; *Siew*, a reptile for country people, has not been selling well, whereas *Ster*, a magazine for children and youngsters, has a press-run of 100 thousand copies, because it has been disseminated mostly via compulsory school acquisitions."[803]

Understandably, the business of publishing so many titles required the services of many employees for many different jobs. Each publication employed several Polish journalists and a number of contributors. Poles outnumbered other employees in technical departments, working as typesetters, proofreaders, translators, and editors. The majority of the lower managerial positions were also held by Poles. For instance, in the GG the top managerial positions in Zeitungsverlag Krakau-Warschau G.m.b.H., a company that employed about a thousand people, or in Telpress, a much smaller company, all the chief editors' appointments were held by highly trusted Germans transferred from other parts of the Third Reich (like Silesia or Pomerania), or Posen, Kattowitz or Bromberg Volksdeutsche. The editor-in-chief of *Nowy Kurier Warszawski* was Kurt Seidel, a German who had worked for Łódź newspapers before the War. The editorial board of *Goniec Krakowski* was controlled by Karl L. Reischner, who had been the editor of *Beskidenländische Deutsche Zeitung* in the interwar period.[804] In 1943 the position of its chief editor was entrusted to Włodzimierz Długoszewski, a well-known sports journalist working for the prewar *Ilustrowany Kurier Codzienny*; subsequently the Germans arrested him and sent him to a concentration camp. He was replaced by Dr. Orest Marian Kałużniacki. The German historian Lars Jockheck has written about the important role played by Władysław Kawecki on the editorial board of *Goniec Krakowski*.[805] The editor-in-chief of *Ilustrowany Kurier Polski* was Hans Apfel (he was also responsible for

---

[803] 'Gadzinowa farsa,' *passim*.

[804] Jockheck, *Propaganda im Generalgouvernement*, 132.

[805] *Ibid.*

the graphics department at *Goniec Krakowski*). The most important Polish editor was Jan Maleszewski, and later, in 1942–1944, Piotr Paliwoda-Matiolański. Helena Wielgomas was head of an editorial board for a short time in January 1945. *Kurier Kielecki* was edited by Józef Kloesel a *Volksdeutscher* from Częstochowa, along with Julian Banaszek, a Bromberg *Volksdeutscher* teacher. The chief editor of *Dziennik Radomski* was Karl L. Reischner, and Count Mieczysław Dunin-Borkowski was the acting editor-in-chief. His successor in the post was Zdzisław Koss. Georg M. Machura became the editor-in-chief of *Kurier Częstochowski* and in mid-1944 he was replaced by Józef Stanisz. *Gazeta Lwowska* was edited by Feliks Rufenach, a *Volksdeutscher* from Łódź, and later by Aleksander von Schoedlin-Czarliński, a prewar editor of the PAT Polish Telegraphic Agency. Finally, the post was taken over by Georg Lehmann, who used the pen-name Jerzy Zwoliński.[806] In Warsaw the job of administrative director of all the papers published by the Germans in Polish was held by Eugeniusz Riedl, a *Volksdeutscher*. One of the most prominent roles in the Telpress agency was played by Karol Fenske from Bromberg, who had studied in Wilno before the War and worked as a Poznań correspondent for German newspapers.

All in all, according to Polish and German researchers, between 67 and 100 authors regularly published in the reptiles, not to mention about 500 freelancers.[807] The index of authors writing for the Polish-language German papers contains 700 names.[808] Evidently, the number of authors collaborating with the reptiles in the GG was much higher than the number of journalists who registered as such in German–occupied Poland. The registration obtained by 165 journalists, writers and editors, enabled them to take up legal jobs in publishing or periodicals such as the reptiles.[809] About 300 journalists refused to register and collaborate. They survived the German occupation thanks to a cooperative, which provided about 70 of them with a job, usually a blue-collar

---

[806] Hryciuk, „*Gazeta Lwowska*" *1941–1944*, 37. Wójcik, *Prasa gadzinowa Generalnego Gubernatorstwa 1939–1945* provides a lot of invaluable details on the human resources of particular editorial boards.

[807] Młynarczyk, 'Pomiędzy współpracą a zdradą. Problem kolaboracji w Generalnym Gubernatorstwie – próby syntezy,' 125.

[808] Majewski, 'Kolaboracja, której nie było…,' 66.

[809] *Ibid.*, 65.

job.[810] Summing up the problem of prewar Polish journalists' collaboration with the German papers published in Poland, Tomasz Szarota came to a conclusion that "despite the pressure they exerted, the German authorities failed to ensure collaboration on the part of well-known Polish journalists. It took some time before some renegades, usually of little professional distinction, strayed from the straight and narrow."[811]

Apart from the reptiles, the Germans also published Kraków- and Warsaw-based papers in German, for the Germans living in the GG, for instance *Krakauer Zeitung* and *Warschauer Zeitung*, which had a print-run of about 160 thousand copies each. Here I should also mention other German initiatives related to publishing papers for Poles. For instance, there were periodicals published by Polish journalists and politicians, such as the fortnightly *Przełom. Dwutygodnik Polityczny*, inspired by Dr. Feliks Burdecki and Jerzy de Nissau, which in reality were financed by the Germans.[812]

Specialists who have studied the Polish-language papers published by the Germans in Poland under German occupation from 1939 have singled out a dozen or so well-known journalists and men of letters who started their professional career between the wars, sometimes even earlier and had achieved a significant reputation, and then fell into temptation. Among them were: Witold Horain, a well-known sports journalist for *Ilustrowany Kurier Codzienny*, Zygmunt Kawecki of *Kurier Warszawski*, Józef Antoni Dąbrowa-Sierzputowski of Polish Radio, Helena Wielgomas of *Dziennik Łódzki*, Stanisław Mróz of the Katowice *Polonia*, Tadeusz Jackowski of *Tygodnik Kielecki*, Stanisław Homan of *Dziennik Poznański*, Zdzisław Stanisz of *Kurier Poranny*, Władysław Kawecki of *Ilustrowany Kurier Codzienny*, Jan Maleszewski of *As*, Stanisław Wasylewski of *Słowo Polskie*, Józef Mackiewicz of the Vilnian *Słowo*; Zygmunt Szargut, Piotr Paliwoda-Matiolański as well as Jan Emil Skiwski, Feliks Burdecki, and Alfred Szklarski. Szklarski's career did not reach its peak until after the War, after his release from prison. But most of the reptile journalists, correspondents, and collaborators launched their careers after 1939 in

---

[810] AIPN Kraków, sign. no. 1/1392, Zeznania świadków druzgocą kłamliwą obronę oskarżonych [Witnesses' statements demolish defendants' mendacious defense].

[811] Szarota, *Okupowanej Warszawy dzień powszedni*, 319.

[812] Głowiński, 'Kolaboracja do końca,' 297–302; see also Jockheck, *Propaganda im Generalgouvernement*, 124.

newspapers and periodicals published by the Germans in Polish. Sometimes it was their first job which they took up to earn a living, to launch or continue their career. Among them there were also individuals designated by the authorities of the Polish Underground State to infiltrate the reptile press. The extant records show that some journalists and writers decided to collaborate with the Germans fully aware of what they were doing, and not caring at all about the great harm they would inflict on Poland and its people.

They bore the consequences of their decision in their wartime and postwar lives. Some of them, expecting strict retribution for their collaboration with the enemy or fearing the impending Sovietization of Poland and their potential deportation to the Soviet Union, decided to flee the country. These included Jan Emil Skiwski, Feliks Burdecki, Ferdynad Goetel, Józef Mackiewicz, Władysław Kawecki, and a few other journalists and editors who succumbed to German incentives and joined the staff of the Wanda propaganda radio station operating in Italy, hoping to indoctrinate the soldiers of Gen. Anders' Second Corps. In 1944 Wanda hired the services of Jan Maleszewski, a prewar columnist of *Ilustrowany Kurier Codzienny* and *As*; Joanna Czarkowska-Bekierska from the Lwów branch of Polish Radio; Mieczysław Dunin-Borkowski of *Dziennik Radomski*; Maria Kałamacka, a radio announcer; and Władysław Kawecki of the Telpress agency.[813] For them the decision not to return home upon the termination of their shameful mission with Radio Wanda was perfectly logical. They chose the life of émigrés, and according to the extant records were kept under constant surveillance by the Polish Communist secret service.[814]

On the other hand, for a number of months after the War those who decided to return to Poland did not face any reprisals for their collaboration with the Germans. Eugeniusz Riedl was pardoned for signing the Deutsche Volksliste, and joined the *milicja obywatelska* (citizens' police force).[815] In 1945 an investigation was launched to examine Tadeusz Trepanowski's collaboration with the Germans but was dropped pretty soon "due to insufficient grounds for

---

[813] 'Radiostacja „Wanda",' 169; Wolsza, 'Aparat bezpieczeństwa,' 381–393.

[814] AIPN GK, sign. no. 164/100, Sprawa prohitlerowskiej radiostacji „Wanda"; Spis współpracowników prohitlerowskiej radiostacji „Wanda"; Radiostacja „Wanda". [The Wanda pro-Nazi broadcasting station; roster of collaborators; Wanda broadcasting station.]

[815] Schnepf, 'Losy pracowników niemieckiej gadzinówki,' 135.

charges."[816] Helena Wielgomas and three other Warsaw journalists who had collaborated with the reptiles, Adam Królak,[817] Leonard Muszyński,[818] and Alfred Szklarski,[819] launched their careers as card-carrying members of the PPR, respectively in Głogów and Olsztyn, Silesia, and Kraków. This must have convinced them that henceforth no one would hold them accountable for their work as reptile journalists and administrative staff.

On 6 April 1945 Zdzisław Tranda, an editor who worked for the reptile *Dziennik Radomski,* successfully reactivated the paper as *Głos Ziemi Radomskiej,*[820] while Józef Głogowski joined the staff of *Dziennik Ludowy,* a paper published by the PSL. Such developments must have alleviated the fear of the retribution that they all expected, as illustrated by the behavior of ex-reptilians like Marian Maak, who despite his former involvement with the Germans had no misgivings about resuming his career with the Polish Army, in which he served before the outbreak of the War and during the military campaign of September

---

[816] *Ibid.*

[817] Adam Królak was a prewar journalist. From 1939 he worked in Warsaw. After the Warsaw Uprising he left for Jaworzno. In May 1945 he joined a Communist operation unit which moved to Głogów. There he became first secretary of the local PPR, deputy mayor of the town and head of the local Socio-Cultural Society. L. Lenarczyk, 'Marian Borawski prezydent Głogowa (1982–1988) z wizją i charyzmą,' in *Głogów w latach 1945–1990. Studia z dziejów miasta,* R. Klementowski and K. Szwagrzyk, (eds.), (Wrocław: Oddział Instytutu Pamięci Narodowej – Komisja Ścigania Zbrodni przeciwko Narodowi Polskiemu, 2014), 130.

[818] Leonard Muszyński joined the PPR in 1945. Next at the behest of the Central Committee of the Party he moved to Olsztyn, where in 1945 he became head of the Department of Propaganda for the Voivodeship Committee of the Party. He was a Party activist until his arrest in 1948. Archiwum Państwowe Olsztyn, KW PPR w Olsztynie, sygn. 1073/236, Karta personalna [The State Archives in Olsztyn, Olsztyn Voivodeship Committee of the PPR, sign. no. 1073/236, personal sheet], sheets 260–261. I would like to thank Mr. Dominik Krysiak of the Olsztyn branch of the Institute of National Remembrance for the records on L. Muszyński.

[819] M. Urbanowski, *Alfred Szklarski (1912–1992), PSB,* vol. 48 (Warszawa and Kraków: Wydawnictwo Towarzystwa Naukowego Societas Vistulana, 2012), ed. A. Romanowski, 319. Alfred Szklarski's wartime and postwar life was full of sudden and surprising changes. Before the Warsaw Uprising he worked for the reptiles. When the Uprising broke out he joined the Polish insurgent forces. Then thanks to the help of the Germans he reached Kraków via Pruszków and Radom. He started writing for the reptiles again and continued till December 1944. After the War he settled in Katowice and found a job with the Bureau of Information and Propaganda of the Voivodeship Office. Later he worked for a number of journals. In 1949 he voluntarily reported to the public prosecutor's office and admitted he had collaborated with reptiles during the War.

[820] A. Ławrynowicz, 'A zaczęło się tak…,' *Życie Radomskie* 1948: 60 (Mar. 1).

1939. Initially, his military service was very highly regarded.[821] However, in 1946 things unexpectedly took a turn for the worse, both for him and dozens of other Old Reptilians.

POSTWAR PROCEEDINGS AGAINST REPTILE COLLABORATORS: A REVIEW

According to the documents generated by the Ministry of Public Security, already in 1945 the Communist authorities were addressing the problem of collaboration with the German administration and the Gestapo in which some Poles had engaged. To facilitate the proceedings, they instituted the office of a plenipotentiary for prosecuting collaborators. Public prosecutor Arnold Gubiński became its head and ordered his subordinate prosecutors to start investigating cases of collaboration with the reptile press by collecting and examining sets of particular newspapers. However, contrary to what we might expect, this turned out difficult to accomplish. Some prosecutors went so far as to advertise their search of the particular periodicals required for their work. They guaranteed they would return the newspapers immediately upon the closure of the case. For instance, such an advertisement was published by the prosecutor investigating the case against *Dziennik Radomski*.[822] Occasionally, the defendants themselves would submit paper clippings of the texts they had published in the reptiles. Some time later it transpired that complete sets of the most important reptiles were kept at the National Library in Warsaw and at the Jagiellonian University Library in Kraków. This information, fairly insignificant from the present-day point of view, made the prosecutors' job considerably faster.

On the basis of Ministry of Public Security records we can conclude that initially the reptile collections borrowed from the Jagiellonian Library and the National Library were circulating in courts all over the whole country. Using these collections, as well as witnesses' statements and the documents of the Polish Underground State kept in the Ministry of Public Security, prosecutor Arnold Gubiński made an attempt to produce a preliminary list of journalists and editors collaborating with the reptile press. His handwritten notes

---

[821] Wolsza, 'Los dziennikarza,' 139.

[822] AIPN Kielce, sign.no. 127/308, List do redakcji „*Życia Radomskiego*" [A letter to the editors of Życie Radomskie], sheet 108.

indicate that initially the list contained the following periodicals: *Nowy Kurier Warszawski, Goniec Krakowski, Ilustrowany Kurier Polski, Gazeta Lwowska, Siew, Ster, Przełom*, and the editorial board of the Telpress agency (which consisted of three departments: a daily service of dispatches and articles, a news service for broadcasts through loudspeakers installed in the streets, and wall newspapers for the countryfolk). The list bore the prosecutor's annotation, "to be prosecuted." It also contained the names of 26 journalists, accompanied by their permanent addresses or information on their likely whereabouts. Feliks Burdecki, Jan Emil Skiwski, and Jan Maleszewski were marked as absent. Some other journalists on the list were marked as already in prison. Some time later the prosecutor prepared another list, which comprised the names of 23 journalists from *Gazeta Lwowska, Nowy Kurier Warszawski*, and *Fala*. Additionally he compiled a list of books by Polish authors who had collaborated with the German reptile press published under German occupation.[823]

At the same time, doubtless at the behest of the Soviet authorities, a special task team consisting of three prosecutors, Dr. Roman Martini, Dr. Jerzy Sawicki, and Karol Szwarc, was set up in the Ministry of Public Security to pave the ground for a trial to prove German culpability for the Katyn massacre.[824] The Communist government's plenipotentiary for the collaboration cases and the prosecutors soon joined forces in ensuring prompt and strict penalties for those who had blackened their names by collaborating with the Germans during the War and under German occupation in Poland.

As we might expect, their first joint initiative was the issue of arrest warrants for a number of journalists who had not only collaborated with the Germans but had also visited Katyn in 1943. On June 25, 1945 Dr. Roman Martini mounted a search for Jan Emil Skiwski and Ferdynand Goetel, and on July 7, 1945 for Marian Wodziński.[825] Rightly or wrongly, in the GG the first two were associated in the public mind with the reptiles, whereas Dr. Marian

---

[823] AIPN Kraków, sign. no. 1392, Spis Wydawnictw Książkowych Gadzinowych Autorów Polskich Okresu Okupacji [A list of books published by Polish authors who collaborated with the Germans under German occupation].

[824] Jankowski and Kotarba, *Literaci a sprawa katyńska 1945*, 85–86.

[825] AIPN Kraków, sign. no. 303/9, Listy gończe za Janem Emilem Skiwskim, Ferdynandem Goetlem i Marianem Wodzińskim [Warrants for the arrest of Jan Emil Skiwski, Ferdynand Goetel, and Marian Wodziński].

Wodziński had consistently avoided such collaboration, and as a matter of fact had shunned publicity of any kind. The only hint of his involvement was the result of a deception used by Władysław Kawecki, who faked an interview with Wodziński, who had served as head of the Technical Commission of the Polish Red Cross that worked in Katyn. As far as the opinion on Ferdynand Goetel's conduct during the War is concerned, Stefan Korboński emphasized that after some time Goetel quit collaborating with the Germans and "either to exonerate his name or to live up to his patriotic ideals joined the resistance movement and worked on the editorial board of *Polska Żyje*, the official journal of Komitet Obrony Polski (the Committee of the Defenders of Poland), an organization espousing radical nationalistic ideas."[826] Korboński also commented on Skiwski and counted him among the leading collaborators.[827]

The prosecutor's grounds for these three arrest warrants was the August 1944 decree issued by the PKWN Soviet-installed government, which described "activities detrimental to the Polish State." Skiwski's arrest warrant did not contain any information on his whereabouts, whereas Goetel's said that he had left Kraków on January 21, 1945 and might be staying in the vicinity of Warsaw. The prosecutor implied that Wodziński might be staying at one of the Polish health resorts. The interrogations conducted by the prosecutors in 1945-1946 provided two completely different opinions on Goetel and Skiwski. The former enjoyed a favorable reputation with his fellow writers, whereas the latter was branded an "ideological collaborator."[828] Prosecutor Sawicki urged the people he interrogated to contact Ferdynand Goetel and inform him that the authorities would rescind his arrest warrant if he made an official announcement that the Germans were responsible for the Katyn massacre.[829]

Mostly due to Soviet pressure, the Polish Communists treated the Katyn massacre as a priority, which accelerated the investigative work considerably and broadened its scope. This can be illustrated by the fact that the authorities were searching for the Polish journalists, writers, clergymen, doctors, and Polish Red Cross associates who had visited Katyn in 1943 as members of the

---

[826] Korboński, *Polskie Państwo Podziemne*, 147.

[827] *Ibid.*, 148.

[828] Jankowski and Kotarba, *Literaci a sprawa katyńska 1945*, 77.

[829] *Ibid.*

delegations organized by the Germans. There were 50 names on the search list.[830] In a few cases the journalists interrogated in 1945 were implicated both in the Katyn investigation and in the proceedings against reptile collaborators, some of whom, e.g. Marian Maak, had started collaborating even before the spring of 1943, that is before the departure of the Katyn delegations. What is exceptionally interesting, offering confirmation of the special significance the public prosecutors attached to the Katyn case, is the fact that the journalists interrogated on the Katyn massacre were not asked about their reptilian collaboration. After giving their statement they were free to go. It was not until somewhat later that their situation changed radically.

In my opinion, the change was due to three key events. The first was the mysterious death of prosecutor Martini on March 30, 1946.[831] The second was the fact that probably in connection with his death the Communist authorities decided to abandon their plan to stage a show trial, as they feared it could produce results contrary to what they had planned. The third was the widely publicized and commented fiasco of the Soviet attempt at the Nuremberg Trial to put the blame for Katyn on the Germans.[832] It seems that all these developments made the leaders of the PPR and its propagandists realize the futility of plugging their view of Katyn in Poland.[833] This, in turn, forced them to come up with something else. The news, however sketchy and incomplete, about the plan to prosecute those who had collaborated with the Germans had been in the air for some time. Thus it is likely that the trial of Stanisław Wasylewski,

---

[830] Wolsza, 'Wojenne i powojenne losy,' 8.

[831] For more on this see J. Bratko, *Dlaczego zginąłeś, prokuratorze?* An interesting view on the prosecutor's death is to be found the memoirs of Stanisław Salmonowicz, „*Życie jak osioł ucieka…" Wspomnienia* (Bydgoszcz and Gdańsk: Instytut Pamięci Narodowej. Komisja Ścigania Zbrodni Przeciwko Narodowi Polskiemu, 2014), 84–85. Another source quoted by Jankowski and Kotarba, (*Literaci a sprawa katyńska 1945*, 93) suggests that the prosecutor let Minister Henryk Świątkowski know that he would not take the case, as it was not a German crime.

[832] For more on this see Basak, *Historia pewnej mistyfikacji.*

[833] On this see S.M. Jankowski, 'Pod specjalnym nadzorem przy drzwiach zamkniętych,' 95–135; M. Golon, 'Zbrodnia katyńska w propagandzie PRL (1944–1989). 45 lat fałszowania historii,' in *Charków–Katyń–Twer*; Golon, 'Kary za prawdę o zbrodni Stalina,' 225–240; W. Wasilewski, 'Pamięć Katynia, Działania opozycji,' *Biuletyn IPN* 2009: 5–6, 60–69; Wolsza, 'Wojenne i powojenne losy,' 7–29; T. Wolsza, 'Konfabulacje Wacława Pycha w sprawie zbrodni katyńskiej (1952 r.),' in *Polska 1944/45–1989. Studia i materiały*, vol. 10 (Warszawa: Instytut Historii PAN, 2011), 7–21; Gasztold–Seń, 'Siła przeciw prawdzie,' 132–153; Motas, 'Materiały dotyczące zbrodni katyńskiej,' vol. 33, 232–252.

a reptilian editor, in December 1946, was meant to fill in the void left by the abortive Katyn trial. The more so as in June 1946, with much resolve and some confidence in the final verdict, the Polish press had announced a pending prestigious debate on Katyn in Nuremberg. When it did not work out the Communists kept their lips sealed and dropped the issue.

On the other hand, the date set for the trial of Helena Wielgomas and its context indicate that in this case, too, the Communists had a specific ad-hoc agenda. The trial opened in September 1948, that is after a detailed vetting process of the members of the PPR, when the Party leaders decided to purge it not only of fortuitous members and social climbers, but also of the so-called "inner enemy," who constituted a threat to the incontestably leading role of the Communist authorities. The final verdict was handed down in the fall of 1948, prior to the amalgamation of the PPS with the PPR. A harsh sentence imposed on a writer who had collaborated with the Germans was meant to show the public that the authorities were heavy-handed and uncompromising when dealing with traitors. The severe sentence was also intended to make Communists popular with postwar Polish society. There is another side to the story worthy of notice. Wielgomas was singled out as the only one out of dozens of Warsaw reptilians to be prosecuted at the time. This implies that the trial was prompt and tailor-made. In view of Wielgomas's CV – for a short time she had been a member of the PPR and the Society of Fighters for Freedom and Democracy, which I will discuss below – presumably the Party decided to cleanse its ranks of traitors. Wielgomas was notorious in Warsaw due to her publications in the reptiles, though she was never associated with the Katyn case. The propaganda impact of her trial was reinforced by the trial of the *Kurier Częstochowski* journalists, who received exceptionally harsh sentences.

The third trial was against the writer Jan Emil Skiwski and the journalist, writer and politician Dr. Feliks Burdecki, both well-known in the interwar period. Perhaps this trial, which was held in Kraków in June 1949, was in a way a much-desired response to the decisions taken at the Fourth Convention of the Professional Union of Polish Writers (ZZLP) in Szczecin in January 1949.[834] Additionally, I think it was an attempt to discredit Polish émi-

---

[834] On the Szczecin Convention see *Wokół zjazdu szczecińskiego 1949 r.*, ed. P. Knap (Szczecin: Instytut Pamięci Narodowej – Komisja Ścigania Zbrodni przeciwko Narodowi Polskiemu. Oddział w Szczecinie, 2011).

grés as such, because at the time Skiwski was already outside Poland. Finally, it should be noted that the Kraków trial was logically linked with a few other trials of journalists collaborating with the reptiles that were held successively in other Polish cities. Suffice it to mention the subsequent trial of the *Nowy Kurier Warszawski* journalists in Warsaw in January 1949, followed by another one in April of the same year. Also in April 1949 a dozen or so journalists and freelancers who had worked for *Kurier Kielecki* and *Dziennik Radomski* were put on trial in Kielce. On the other hand, the trial of the *Nowy Głos Lubelski* journalists that had been planned for 1949 was called off. The Lublin public prosecutor's office sent a list of authors and the headlines of their articles published in *Nowy Głos Lubelski* in 1940–1944 to other prosecutor's offices in neighboring cities (Kielce, Radom, and Kraków) in the hope of learning their whereabouts.[835] Despite the extensive search carried out by the Ministry of Public Security throughout Poland, not a single journalist from the list (Hipolit Szczotecki, Bernard Górecki, Tadeusz Marcinkowski, Bruno Widera, Kazimierz Bąkowski, Zofia Musielak, and Krystyna Szarska) was detained, whereas Jan Pelczarski, an editor whose name was also on the list, had already been incarcerated in a Kraków prison.[836] The documents kept at the Ministry of Public Security indicate that initially a separate trial of the journalists of *Dziennik Radomski* had been planned. Apparently security functionaries made several attempts to compile a list of collaborators with the reptiles and to learn what had happened to them during and after the War. They never completed the job. It seems that the list itself, which contained some very misspelled names, was useless. For instance, Eugeniusz Kolanko was recorded as Kolankowski. Sometimes agents were able to establish the pen-names only: "Stefan Kalicki" (the pen-name of Zygmunt Kawecki) and "Roman Moszczeński" (his real name is still unknown).[837] Zdzisław Koss, whom the Germans had shot during the War, also figured on the list.[838]

---

[835] AIPN Kielce, sign.no. 127/308, Pismo do obywatela Prokuratora Sądu Okręgowego [A letter to the Public Prosecutor of Radom Regional Court], sheet 205.

[836] AIPN Lublin, sign. no. 319/980, „Nowy Głos Lubelski".

[837] Piątkowski, *Okupacja i propaganda. Dystrykt radomski Generalnego Gubernatorstwa*, 58.

[838] There is no specific information on Z. Koss during the War. After the War he was on the Ministry of Public Security search list when the Communists were preparing the Katyń trial. I believe his name surfaced because of an interview on Katyn with Skiwski (headlined

There were eight trials of journalists charged with collaboration with the reptiles in 1946–1949 – three in Warsaw, two in Kraków, two in Częstochowa and one in Kielce. Only three journalists, Stanisław Wasylewski, Helena Wielgomas, and Krzysztof Caban, were tried individually. The other trials were collective – a total of 47 reptile journalists and writers (16 in Warsaw, 12 in Kraków, 10 in Kielce, and 9 in Częstochowa) were prosecuted. Some like Marian Maak faced more than one trial, as they had published in various papers and hence were involved in several proceedings. Theoretically, about ten more associates of *Nowy Głos Lubelski* could have been charged. However, the investigating officers decided not to file another suit. Instead, they started an investigation against Tomasz Rusek, an ex-priest accused of speaking in public in 1943–1944 on the circumstances of the Katyn massacre and publishing Katyn reports in *Nowy Głos Lubelski*.[839] We may say that the trial of Rusek, who had left the priesthood during the War, was different in character. Proceedings against him did not start until 1952, when a warrant was issued, followed by his arrest in Gdynia.[840]

Those who stood trial in Warsaw were Helena Wielgomas (in 1948 and in two other proceedings), Józef Antoni Dąbrowa-Sierzputowski, Alfred Szklarski, Ludwik Ziemkiewicz, Tomasz Pągowski, Kazimierz Mann, Tadeusz Trepanowski, Władysław Leśniewski, Czesław Pudłowski, Jan Wolski, Kazimierz Augustowski, and Mieczysław Kwiatkowski (January 1949); as well as Kazimierz Garszyński, Leonard Muszyński, Adam Królak, and Eugeniusz Riedl (April 1949). In Kraków proceedings started against Stanisław Wasylewski (1946); and Marian Maak, Piotr Paliwoda-Matiolański, Ewa Janina Smolka, Witold Rychlik, Witold Horain, Amelia Hanzlowa-Alterowa, Bronisław Król, Edward Kłoniecki, and Jan Borek (June 1949). On the other hand, security agents failed to find and arrest Feliks Burdecki and Jan Emil Skiwski, and that is why they were tried in absentia. In this particular prosecution charges were withdrawn against Witold Rychlik, Witold Horain, Amelia

---

'Czerwony bies atakuje kulturę' [The Red Fiend Is Attacking Culture]) published in *Goniec Krakowski* on Apr. 24, 1943. The interviewer signed his name as the mysterious KOSS, perhaps it was Zdzisław Koss.

[839] Golon, 'Kary za prawdę o zbrodni Stalina,' 229; Gasztold-Seń, 'Siła przeciw prawdzie,' 135.

[840] AIPN Lublin, sign. no. 326/132, Akta sprawy karnej Tomasza Ruska [Records of prosecution of Tomasz Rusek].

Hanzlowa-Alterowa, Bronisław Król, Edward Kłoniecki, and Jan Borek. Orest Marian Kałużniacki, Józef Kondek, Zbigniew Strzębalski, Marian Maak, Maria Hessel, Józef Głogowski, Wiktor Smenda, Jan Wierzbówka, Anna Kozłowska, and Zdzisław Tranda were prosecuted in Kielce (April 1949). Finally, the following journalists and writers were put on trial in Częstochowa in November 1948: Stanisław Homan, Zdzisław Józef Stanisz, Józef Stanisz, Ryszard Jeleński, Tadeusz Starostecki, Stanisław Jucha, Janina Tomza, and Stanisław Mróz; and Krzysztof Caban a couple of months later.[841] All the accused writers, journalists and technicians were charged with "spreading pro-German propaganda and undermining the spirit of resistance of the Polish people, which was an activity detrimental to the Polish Nation." In the media they were simply accused of collaborating with the Germans, which was the straightforward way of putting it to the general public. The issue of Katyn was hardly ever mentioned in court –it rarely came to the fore, and only in the investigation phase if at all. Some of the defendants tried to evoke the issue and present their own involvement in the best possible light.

Even before the trials were over Communist press reporters were vying with each other in denouncing the defendants, without paying much attention to how they defended themselves. For the reporters the journalists on trial were "collaborators," "traitors of the Polish Nation," "reptile accomplices", "renegades" and, of course, "fascists". When commenting on the trials of Jan Emil Skiwski and Feliks Burdecki, the headlines of the Kraków-based *Dziennik Polski* heralded 'The Heights of Polish Fascism' or 'They Cherished Fascism More than their Own Nation.' There were suggestions, as in the case of Helena Wielgomas, that "the indicted journalists would have done anything for money." In this case the press borrowed an opinion expressed in the documents of the Polish Underground State.[842]

Defendants defended themselves in a number of ways. The easiest line of defense was to plead guilty and claim that they had never realized their publishing activities would be regarded as collaboration with the enemy or betrayal of the Polish Nation. They claimed ignorance or that they were in

---

[841] Interesting details, especially on some of their publishing and writing activities, in Woźniakowski, *W kręgu jawnego piśmiennictwa, passim.*

[842] 'Współpracowniczka „gadzinówki" Helena Wielgomas przed sądem okręgowym w Warszawie,' *Życie Warszawy* 1948: 245 (Sept. 5), 3.

financial straits. Some defendants admitted they had realized the collaboration with reptiles was reprehensible and detrimental to Polish society, but saw an exonerating factor in the type of subject matter they addressed in their articles. They emphasized that the articles they had published were completely "innocuous" for Poles under the German occupation, as they were related to everyday matters (such as cooking, sewing, gardening, preserve-making, health concerns, searching for a job, etc.), leisure activities, excursions, and reading books.[843] Most of the defendants implied they had been "delegated" by the Polish underground authorities, either those of the Polish Underground State or those of the parties on the political left, to collaborate with the reptiles.

Interestingly enough, Communist prosecutors had a lot of respect for and trust in the opinions and judgments of the wartime underground courts, viz. the Special Military and Civil Courts, and they acknowledged documents produced by the Home Army Command, some of which they acquired after the War. In court they often resorted to arguments first expressed in *Biuletyn Informacyjny*, for instance, on the verdicts of infamy the Home Army courts passed on Skiwski, Burdecki, Wielgomas, Szklarski, and Dąbrowa-Sierzputowski.[844] One of the defendants who tried a line of defense based on the

---

[843] In his comments on this line of defense Szarota said, "one cannot forget that apparently innocuous, apolitical texts related to down-to-earth matters such as food, clothes or social security acquired a political character thanks to the fact that they were published in a German paper. What is more, they must have been published side by side with the articles glorifying the German army and the achievements of German pilots, including those who scored their first hits in September 1939." (Szarota, *Okupowanej Warszawy dzień powszedni*, 321–322).

[844] For instance, *Biuletyn Informacyjny* (Mar. 8, 1940) carried a notice entitled *Łajdactwo literata* [A writer's knavery] on Jan Emil Skiwski, who had published a novel with a German publishing house called Wydawnictwo Polskie. On June 28, 1940 *Biuletyn Informacyjny* called the collaborators of *Nowy Kurier Warszawski* scoundrels and pusillanimous fools. In an article headlined 'Infamia' [Infamy], published on September 18, 1941, *Biuletyn Informacyjny* wrote that the activities of three well-known Varsovians, Jan Emil Skiwski, Ferdynand Goetel, and Juliusz Nagórski, had been reported for review to a Special Civil Court. For more see Szarota, *Karuzela na Placu Krasińskich*, 83, footnote 52. Finally, on May 7, 1942 *Biuletyn Informacyjny* published an extensive list of reptile collaborators working for *Nowy Kurier Warszawski*, *Fala*, *7 Dni* and *Gazeta Lwowska* – Feliks Rufenach ("Editor R"), Józef Sierzputowski (pen-names "Zagłobicz" and "Rad"), Kazimierz Garczyński ("Cz"), Franciszek Wysocki, Halina Rapacka ("Mizantrop"), Władysław Mikulski, A. Poller, Hermina Bukowska, one Sandler (pen-name "Pękalski"), Janina Czarnocka, Łuczyński, Bilarzewski, Alfred Szklarski (pen-name "Murawski"), Jerzy Leżański (pen-name "Lubicz"), Aleksander von Schoedlin-Czarliński, Józef Ziemkowski, Stanisław Wasylewski, Edward Twardowski, Dr. Nalepowa, Nadalińska, Stefan Naider, Jerzy Bielański, and Zygmunt Szargut.

claim that the underground authorities had empowered him to collaborate with the reptiles was Zbigniew Strzębalski, who said at his trial that under German occupation he had belonged to the AL (the Communist-inspired People's Army). Marian Maak said he had been a member of the ZWZ Union of Armed Struggle (the predecessor organization of the AK Home Army), and that was why he signed his texts "AK". Moreover, he added that he had been actively involved in the production and issue of false ID cards. A similar line of defense was adopted by Orest Marian Kałużniacki, who said he had run a harmless chess column. Zdzisław Józef Stanisz invoked his underground activities in the Polish Freedom Union (Polski Związek Wolności). Józef Głogowski presented trustworthy documents to prove that he had worked as an editor in the underground *Biuletyn Informacyjny* and had served in a Home Army unit operating in the region of Kielce, Ostrowiec, Opatów and Radom. What is more, his service earned him the Krzyż Partyzancki (Resistance Fighter's Cross) and the Krzyż Walecznych (Cross of Valor). Wiktor Smenda allegedly took part in acts of sabotage and helped to harbor Jews. Józef Kondek had been a long-standing member of the PPS and worked in an underground printing house.

At the high-profile Warsaw trial of the collaborators of *Nowy Kurier Warszawski* and other reptiles, a number of defendants (for instance, Dąbrowa-Sierzputowski and Szklarski) attempted to persuade the court that their collaboration was part of a mission empowered by the authorities of the Polish Underground State.[845] They claimed they had acted as non-specified "operatives" and invoked their postwar membership of the Society of Fighters for Freedom and Democracy. But they were not able to give any details of their underground activities, apart from providing some irrelevant platitudes. They "forgot" to admit that *Biuletyn Informacyjny* had them down as disgraced. Alfred Szklarski had made it into *Biuletyn's* bad books no less than five times, including a verdict of infamy handed down on him. Appearing before a Warsaw court in 1949, Kazimierz Garszyński made an attempt to save his freedom by claiming that he had commenced his collaboration with a reptile having been instructed to do so by the clandestine editorial board of *Pobudka*, a paper issued by Obóz Narodowo-Radyklany (the Radical National Party), which was subject to the

---

[845] Schnepf, 'Losy pracowników niemieckiej gadzinówki,' 148.

authority of the Government Delegation for Poland. He had some documents to support his claim, but they were rejected by the court because at the time *Pobudka* was not regarded as an underground anti-German organization in the strict sense of the term. He was not rehabilitated until 1956.[846] Krzysztof Caban admitted that he had collaborated with the Germans, but emphasized that his collaboration had been short-lived and harmless to Polish people, because he had only published novels like *Córka kłusownika* (The Poacher's Daughter). He also told the court that the Germans had put him in a labor camp, which was confirmed by witnesses. Taking all this into consideration, the court passed the lowest possible sentence – three years in prison.[847]

The extant court records suggest that collaboration with the reptiles as a result of an order given by the Polish underground authorities was the hardest nut to crack for the judiciary, because it was difficult to verify the evidence provided by defendants or simply because there was no evidence at all. Defendants usually explained the want of evidence by the destruction of documents or the death of witnesses. Usually the court dismissed or simply ignored such arguments. There were also political reasons for this. The representatives of the Polish Underground State were usually staunch anti-Communists and as such could not count on prosecutors' and judges' forbearance. We may speculate that in some cases the sentences passed on defendants were not just a penalty for their work as editors of the reptiles but also for their service in the Home Army, Peasant Battalions (Bataliony Chłopskie) or National Armed Forces (Narodowe Siły Zbrojne). The Communists were happy to jump at the opportunity.

It is not surprising that only five defendants managed to convince the courts that they were innocent. Anna Kozłowska, the first of them, was a prewar employee of the check payment department of the company publishing *Ilustrowany Kurier Codzienny*. From 1940 on she published "casual" short stories and chatty columns in *Goniec Krakowski*, signing her articles with her real first and second name.[848] Her line of defense was a dramatic family situation

---

[846] *Ibid.*, 158.

[847] AIPN Katowice, sign. no. 562/317, Akta w sprawie karnej Krzysztofa Cabana [Records of the prosecution of Krzysztof Caban], sheet 43.

[848] AIPN Kraków, sign. no. 127/310, Akt oskarżenia przeciwko Orestowi M. Kałużniackiemu i innym [Indictment against Orest M. Kałużniacki and others], sheet 33.

and lack of money. Zdzisław Tranda, a professional journalist from Lwów and a regular correspondent of *Dziennik Radomski*, was another of those acquitted. The articles he usually published in the reptiles were on local matters, the work of the social security company or the Chamber of Commerce, and mutual assistance organizations.[849] What is more, after the War he contributed to a successful campaign to reactivate *Głos Ziemi Radomskiej*, a local daily. PPR activists commended him for this. Tranda also met Maj. Jerzy Borejsza over propaganda matters.[850] This, I believe, was the decisive factor for his getting off scot-free. Stanisław Wasylewski managed to prove in court that he had worked for *Gazeta Lwowska* at the behest of the Polish Underground State, which I shall come back to later. The Warsaw court acquitted Kazimierz Augustowski and Mieczysław Kwiatkowski on the grounds that "after a short period of time they quit their work in the reptile, which, anyway, was not creative, as they only delivered unrelated items of information that were not detrimental to the Polish state. They withdrew as soon as they realized the mistake they had made."[851]

Kazimierz Augustowski also proved that collaboration on his part was in fact "his military duty carried out for his country. He followed the order." Upon completion of his mission in *Nowy Kurier Warszawski* the Home Army assigned him another clandestine mission in the district of Błonie.[852]

The sentences passed on those who had collaborated with the reptiles were harsh. The Communist authorities of Poland ordered the press and radio stations to publicize the trials as much as possible. When Helena Wielgomas' Warsaw trial was over *Głos Ludu*, a PPR paper, ran the headline 'Wielgomas sentenced to six years in prison'. In January 1949 the news was splashed across the Warsaw papers that severe sentences were pending for "the reptilian traitors," with sample headlines like 'Crime and Punishment' or 'Guilt and Punishment'). The sentences were indeed harsh. Józef Antoni Sierzputowski was sentenced to 10 years in prison, and Alfred Szklarski to eight years. The most

---

[849] *Ibid.*, sheet 32.

[850] Ławrynowicz, 'A zaczęło się tak…,' *passim.*

[851] 'Surowe wyroki w procesie współpracowników warszawskich gadzinówek,' *Dziennik Polski* 1949 (Jan. 13), 3.

[852] 'Kiedy w Warszawie trwały egzekucje starali się złamać ducha ludności stolicy,' *Życie Warszawy* 1949: 4 (Jan. 5), 2.

drastic sentence was passed at the Częstochowa trial in November 1948 – it made the headlines as 'Death Penalty for Collaborating Journalist. Sentence Passed at the Trial of *Kurier Częstochowski* Collaborator'. It was the only death sentence imposed at any of the reptile trials. However, it is worth adding that during the War the court of the Polish Underground State had passed the same sentence on Stanisław Homan, the defendant in question, and the postwar prosecutors and judges knew it. The other defendants in the Częstochowa trial were given heavy sentences as well: Józef Stanisz received a life sentence, and his son Zdzisław Józef Stanisz 15 years in prison. The reptile trials and sentences were widely publicized to persuade the public that the authorities were effective and uncompromising in their treatment of traitors to the Polish Nation.

Those who were convicted were usually sent to labor camps in Upper and Lower Silesia, in the Opole and Kujawy regions as well as in Warsaw. Most were in prison until 1953, when they were amnestied. By working in mines and quarries, where many of them were treated like slaves, they were making amends for their errors under German occupation. At least this is how the Communist propaganda put it. Ironically, Polish soldiers fighting the Germans during the War, those fighting the Communists after the War, and veterans of the Polish Armed Forces in the West who had been brave enough to return to Poland, were kept in the same camps.

PROMINENT REPTILE TRIALS

Communist propaganda gave a lot of publicity to the trial of Stanisław Wasylewski, as it was the first public occasion to settle scores with a journalist who had collaborated with the Germans. It concerned *Gazeta Lwowska* and one of its editors. We know that other journalists collaborating with the paper were also in the crosshairs of the Ministry of Public Security. In my opinion reprisals against that paper's staff depended on the result of Wasylewski's trial.[853] A sentence imposed on him, the chief collaborator from Lwów, as he was called by the Communist propaganda, would remove the barriers to further proceedings. Arnold Gubiński, the public prosecutor who coordinated all the trials of collaborating journalists, shortlisted Dr. Witold Bełza,

---

[853] For more on Wasylewski's career in journalism see Hryciuk, „*Gazeta Lwowska*" *1941–1944*, 39–41.

Jerzy Bielański, Tadeusz Krzyżewski, Ada Nadalińska, Irena Nalepowa, Stefan Naider, Zygmunt Szargut, Edward Twardowski, and Józef Ziemkowski.

Although Stanisław Wasylewski had collaborated with the reptile press in Lwów, his trial took place in Kraków, where he lived after the War. The trial was triggered by a resolution adopted by the Polish Professional Writers' Union on September 2, 1944 to denounce Stanisław Wasylewski's behavior during the War and expel him, following a motion put forward by a delegate from Łódź. At the same convention a few writers, including Jan Kott, Adolf Rudnicki, and Julian Przyboś, who were all ex-editors and associates of the Communist daily *Czerwony Sztandar*, also attacked Ferdynand Goetel, and his collaboration with the Germans in the context of his Katyn visit in 1943. Adolf Rudnicki claimed that prior to the trip Goetel did not know how important the issue was. He only realized this once he had arrived on the site and that is why he recorded a brief statement. Others observed the harmful consequences, including the political ones, of the journey to Katyn. In a 1945 comment on the Katyn issue, Czesław Miłosz remarked that the general opinion on the atrocity changed from distrust to acceptance of the German version of the events. "The position of Polish society on the 'Katyn issue' changed with time from (1) general distrust of the German story and suspicion of a German provocation, through (2) a period of controversy and uncertainty, to (3) a general recognition that the German version was true."[854] Miłosz's opinion was borne out by Leon Kruczkowski, a writer with communist sympathies who spent the War in a POW camp in Gross Born. He stressed that "these observations led to a conclusion that unfortunately among about 2,000 officers [held as POWs in Gross Born] the 'Katyn provocation' to a large extent proved as effective as Goebbels thought it would be."[855] Ultimately the members of the Union did not press for an investigation of Ferdynand Goetel's case. There were unconfirmed reports that the writer himself would contact the public prosecutor's office.

However, the prosecution of Stanisław Wasylewski took a different turn. Jan Kott saw a need to denounce and punish Wasylewski, and wrote a column titled 'Spisek milczenia' (Conspiracy of Silence) in the weekly *Odrodzenie*: "The activities of writers, dead or alive, under wartime occupation have been passed

---

[854] Klecel, 'Pisarze ścigani za Katyń,' 69.

[855] *Ibid.*

over in silence; we are keeping silent about the activities of traitors. The name of Jan Emil Skiwski has been mentioned in our newspapers only once, when the public prosecutor issued the warrant for his arrest. Amazingly enough, the Polish Professional Writers' Union has never made a public statement on Skiwski and Wasylewski. Nobody should claim it is of no matter, because unlike France there were no more than four or five collaborators in this country. The silence was convenient. The Writers' Convention has broken that silence."[856]

The members of the Polish Professional Writers' Union did not make any further inquiries themselves but relied solely on Kott's opinion. What is more, the expulsion procedure was launched without any prior discussion. On the basis of the Union's decision the public prosecutor accused Wasylewski of collaboration with the Germans in 1941–1944, when he had worked for *Gazeta Lwowska*. His trial coincided with the widely publicized trial of Ludwig Fischer, a Nazi dignitary and an ex-governor, that was being held in Warsaw. Perhaps this was just a coincidence, but the reports on the trials were published in the daily press alongside each other, which was definitely not a coincidence.

Wasylewski chose a very effective line of defense. He invoked two key elements of his wartime biography to refute the prosecutor's allegations. A well-known and esteemed writer, Wasylewski claimed that he had joined the editorial board of *Gazeta Lwowska* at the behest of the Polish Underground State, and presented trustworthy witnesses to prove his claim. Furthermore, he argued that "the underground organizations wanted to have their men in *Gazeta Lwowska*, to obtain information on the activities of the German authorities."[857] This aspect of the case was also emphasized by the defense counsel and witnesses (for instance Zygmunt Szargut). One of them said, "Wasylewski acted neither on behalf of the occupying authorities, nor to the detriment of the Polish State. On the contrary, he took a personal risk to operate against the German propaganda and provide some spiritual consolation to the Poles living in the eastern borderlands of Poland, which was as uplifting as it could be. Even Polish schools, which did not have the schoolbooks they needed, used articles published in *Gazeta Lwowska*. Wasylewski was a guiding spirit."[858]

---

[856] J. Kott, 'Spisek milczenia,' *Odrodzenie* 1945: 41 (Sept. 9), 8.

[857] AIPN Kraków, sign.no. 1/1384, Proces Stanisława Wasylewskiego. Sąd zrehabilitował Wasylewskiego [Proceedings against Stanisław Wasylewski]. The court acquitted Wasylewski.

[858] *Ibid.*

Julian Przyboś, another witness and a well-known writer, who could not be counted among Wasylewski's champions, admitted in court that he had met Wasylewski when the latter was working on a stage performance on Adam Mickiewicz. Przyboś thought it was a successful cultural event. Juliusz Petry, one of the last witnesses and an ex-head of the Lwów branch of Polish Radio, characterized Wasylewski's activities in *Gazeta Lwowska* as beneficial, intended to "raise Polish spirits." Petry had heard of Wasylewski's engagement in the resistance movement, but did not know the details because they were responsible for different types of activities.[859] Wasylewski himself said he had written a number of articles for the underground press.

These were not the only arguments Wasylewski and his defense counsel raised. His attorney added two more facts which he considered of utmost importance. The first, which to my mind was particularly relevant to the propaganda objectives pursued by the Communists, was Wasylewski's refusal to take part in the German Katyn delegations in 1943.[860] Although *Gazeta Lwowska* published all the documents related to the Katyn massacre, it did not result from Wasylewski's personal engagement in the issue.[861] However, that does not mean he did not believe in the findings of the International Katyn Commission, which said the Soviets committed the massacre. Yet these were two different matters, and the court did not go into the Katyn issue. The second equally important argument also carried a propaganda aspect and strengthened the writer's line of defense. In 1944 Wasylewski had publicly distanced himself from Dr. Burdecki's activities. He turned down an offer of collaboration from the editors of *Przełom* and relocation to the GG. The fact that by the time of Wasylewski's trial a warrant for the arrest of the editors of *Przełom* had already been issued improved his position very considerably. His defense lawyer asked the court to acquit his client.

The press (for instance *Dziennik Polski*, a regional daily) was highly interested in the trial. Reports emphasized especially those aspects of the proceedings which "revealed the true face of Stanisław Wasylewski," who was of course guilty of all the crimes he had been charged with. Yet on the strength

---

[859] 'Stanisław Wasylewski przed sądem,' *Dziennik Polski* 1948: 348 (Dec. 19), 7.

[860] Hryciuk, „*Kumityt*", 68.

[861] Idem, „*Gazeta Lwowska*" 1941–1944, 59–61.

of the documents of the case and upon hearing all the witnesses, Eugeniusz Sawrycz, president of Kraków Regional Court, issued a verdict of not guilty. To support his decision he cited a few important facts. First of all, he was highly critical of the decision of the Polish Professional Writers' Union to expel Stanisław Wasylewski from its ranks. He asked – and it was not a rhetorical question – why none of the Union's members had made an effort to verify the information on the defendant for several months after the end of the War. He considered the expulsion too hasty and added that had the members not been driven by their emotions and taken the slander at face value, probably the trial would have never taken place. He also reiterated the defense counsel's claim that Wasylewski joined *Gazeta Lwowska* at the behest of a resistance organization.[862]

The court's decision made a big impact throughout the country, as the Communist authorities were sure Wasylewski would be convicted, or at least this was what the Communist press believed and published. That is why immediately after the writer was acquitted the press launched another, more sophisticated attack. The participants in the witch-hunt did not contest the court's verdict, instead they challenged Wasylewski's moral integrity. We could call it simply a wait-and-see strategy. Maksymilian Boruchowicz, a member of the PPS, published an article, which he signed as Michał M. Borowicz, in which he wrote: "I sort of felt relief when I learned of the court's decision, because under German occupation I was extremely sorry to hear that Wasylewski had started to collaborate with a reptile. Immediately upon learning this I let my underground organization (the PPS) know. At the time I also demanded decisive steps to be taken against 'apolitical' traitors. Wasylewski's 'work' published in the reptile was a blow to all of us, the more so as we used to believe in his humanitarian views. As for myself, whenever I thought of his collaboration, I could not overcome my bitterness."[863] Naturally enough, when asked by the judge for its position after the verdict, the Polish Professional Writers' Union expressed its opinion on the acquittal and the arguments advanced during the trial. The Union's authorities did not challenge the verdict itself but commented on Wasylewski's expulsion. They emphasized that they "could not pass

---

[862] AIPN Kraków, sign. no. 1/1384. [Proceedings against Stanisław Wasylewski]. The court acquitted Wasylewski.

[863] *Ibid.* (Papers from the aftermath of the Wasylewski trial.)

over in silence certain words which found their way into the grounds for the verdict and which were not only (…) unfair to the Union but inadmissible from the point of view of the separation of powers of the courts and the authorities of professional unions. We have to stress that just like an infringement of professional ethics is not a sufficient reason for prosecution, so the acquittal handed down by a court does not resolve the question whether a writer's obligations to his colleagues and his moral obligations have been duly met."[864] Briefly speaking, the Union's board stuck to its original allegations and still found Stanisław Wasylewski's activities reprehensible.

Wasylewski's case was appealed to the Supreme Court, which sat in Łódź, a city hostile to the writer. Just before the trial the dailies in Kraków and the whole of Poland were consistently reiterating the main allegation against Wasylewski, that is "collaborationism" or alternatively "collaboration with the Germans in the Goebbelsian *Gazeta Lwowska.*" This, I think, could be seen as an attempt to exert pressure on the court. Ultimately, on July 1, 1947 at a closed hearing that lasted several hours the Supreme Court decided to uphold the verdict passed by Kraków Regional Court and dismissed the public prosecutor's appeal.[865]

The trial of Helena Wielgomas was the first attempt in Warsaw to prosecute editors and writers who had collaborated with the reptiles. According to the court, under German occupation the defendant had published 230 short stories, opinion columns, and reviews.[866] Some of her articles, like those published in *Fala*, which were illustrated, had an erotic or pornographic undertone. Court experts counted 43 publications in *Nowy Kurier Warszawski*, 157 in *7 Dni*, and 30 in Fala.[867] She never raised the issue of the Katyn massacre, which in a way worked to her advantage. Tomasz Szarota, who tried to evaluate her services for the reptiles, called her a hack and the literary linchpin of the *7 Dni* weekly magazine.[868]

---

[864] 'Sprawa Wasylewskiego,' *Tygodnik Powszechny* 1947: 7 (Feb.16), 4.

[865] 'Sąd zatwierdził wyrok w sprawie S. Wasylewskiego,' *Dziennik Polski* 1947: 177 (Jul. 2), 3.

[866] According to Woźniakowski's estimate (*W kręgu jawnego piśmiennictwa literackiego*, p. 73) it was less: 138 poems, 56 short stories, and 6 theater plays.

[867] 'Wielgomasowa skazana na karę 6 lat więzienia,' *Głos Ludu* 1948: 248 (Sept. 8), 6.

[868] Szarota, *Okupowanej Warszawy dzień powszedni*, 324.

Wielgomas' first texts were published in 1940, and the last ones the "authoress" published in the Warsaw reptiles appeared in 1944, just before the outbreak of the Uprising. After the capitulation of the Uprising she published two opinion columns in Kraków in 1944. This turned out to be of utmost importance in the subsequent indictment, in which the public prosecutor wrote, "Under German occupation, in Warsaw between the spring of 1940 and the summer of 1944, she pandered to the German authorities and became a permanent collaborator of German papers published in Polish such as the daily *Nowy Kurier Warszawski*, the *7 Dni* weekly, and the *Fala* monthly. They were published by (…) the authorities of the German state, whose aim was to exterminate the Polish Nation; these papers were designed to weaken the moral standing of the people of Poland and their spirit of resistance against the occupying power. She chose to publish her literary texts in them, signed with her full, real name or with her initials, which was an activity against the Polish Nation and State."[869] During a brief hearing the court proved that the defendant had published her texts in these papers signed with her full name, with her initials H.W., or using the pen-name "Larysa," which was one of her given names: Helena Maria Magdalena Anna Larysa. The court dismissed her explanations that she had stopped publishing by 1943. This was one of her few lines of defense, completely useless as it turned out, apart from her deep conviction that collaboration with the reptiles was not an offense at all.

Almost all the witnesses testified against Wielgomas, including Stanisław Płoski, who was described in court as head of the Home Army History Bureau; and Władysław Sieroszewski, a prewar Supreme Court prosecutor and described in court as the chief magistrate of the underground Special Military Court. One of the witnesses said Wielgomas' claim that she had written "innocent" opinion columns, novelettes and short stories was not true. In 1944 he had read a text signed by her in *Nowy Kurier Warszawski*, in which she wrote of the greatest threat to Poland "coming from the East."[870] The opinions expressed by Stanisław Płoski and Władysław Sieroszewski, who were active in the administrative units of the Polish Underground State, turned out to be

---

[869] AIPN BU, sign. no. 0207/6864, Sentencja wyroku w imieniu Rzeczypospolitej Polskiej dnia 6–7 IX 1948 [Republic of Poland Sentence of Verdict of Sept. 6-7, 1948], sheet 107.

[870] *Ibid.*, sheet 109.

very significant for the outcome of the case. Płoski said that the reptiles had played an important propaganda role and created an image of an all-powerful Germany; but at the same time they created "a suggestion that the people living under German rule were free to pursue artistic activities in the field of culture."[871] Important evidence came from Sieroszewski, who said that in 1942 or at the beginning of 1943 he saw a court sentence imposed on Wielgomas, but was unable to specify what kind of sentence it was (infamy, flogging, or death).[872] The dubiety was clarified in the records held by the public prosecutors – it was infamy. It is almost certain that the special services of the Polish Underground State were interested in her activities. She was put under the Home Army's surveillance, as shown by what happened to her later. After the outbreak of the Warsaw Uprising, they arrested and detained her in a makeshift jail. A report on this appeared in the underground daily *Robotnik* on August 29, 1944.[873]

During the trial Helena Wielgomas finally conceded that her collaboration with the reptiles had been unquestionably detrimental to Poland and its people. She must have hoped the acknowledgment would make her sentence less harsh. She also said that during the Uprising she had volunteered to serve as an orderly in an uprising hospital. The court believed this (it was confirmed by one of the doctors), but did not accept the motives she had when she started this duty. She seems to have done it only on the basis of cold calculation, hoping to postpone the collaboration charge, even if for a short time, but she never showed any patriotic feelings or sympathy with the fate of the Home Army combatants. Neither could the court admit her claim that she had found a job with the reptiles at the behest of the resistance movement.

The court also knew other facts from her rich biography, especially those related to her exceptionally active life after the War. Helena Wielgomas realized she was finished in Warsaw, so she decide to find a safe haven in Kraków, where she went after the fall of the Warsaw Uprising and where she even received an apartment as a gift from the Germans. When the War was over

---

[871] *Ibid.*

[872] *Ibid.*, sheet 110. I did not find a reference in Leszek Gondek's book, *Polska karząca 1939–1945*, to say what type of sentence was passed on Helena Wielgomas by a Special Military or Civil Court.

[873] 'Współpracowniczka gadzinówki,' *passim.*

she changed her ways and according to the court became "brashy and art-ful."[874] For obvious reasons she used her maiden name, Larysa Domańska. She joined the PPR and relied on her stint as an orderly during the Warsaw Uprising to join the Society of Fighters for Freedom and Democracy. At the same time she made an attempt to obtain the Resistance Fighter's Cross and the Order of the Grunwald Cross, which was astounding in light of her CV. She found a job at the municipal office as a secretary to the mayor of Kraków. Finally, she became engaged in vetting journalists. As of the summer vacations of 1946 she organized artistic shows in the Recovered Territories of Poland. Her career advanced at an impressive pace. It was only briefly interrupted by her temporary arrest between March 19 and May 29, 1945.[875] Thereafter, until May 4, 1948, that is until her subsequent arrest, she remained at large. During that time only once was she up against the wall, when one of the journalists associated her new name Larysa Domańska with the wartime reptilian Helena Wielgomas. He sent a letter to the editors of the *Odrodzenie* weekly, in which he demanded severe punishment for her. She responded immediately by suing Jan Dąbrowski, the journalist in question, and, surprisingly enough, managed to convince the Kraków court that she was innocent. The defendant had to pay her damages and publish an apology in the papers.[876]

Warsaw Regional Court (presided over by Stanisław Zienkiewicz) was much more thorough and was in no doubt that Wielgomas was guilty. She was sentenced to 6 years in prison, forfeiture of public rights and confiscation of property.[877] Wielgomas appealed to the Supreme Court, which reviewed the case on April 20, 1949 and dismissed her appeal. She started her sentence in the Warsaw Central Prison II (the Gęsiówka). In 1950 she was moved to

---

[874] AIPN BU, sign.no. 0207/6864, Sentencja wyroku w imieniu Rzeczypospolitej Polskiej dnia 6–7 IX 1948 [Republic of Poland Sentence of Verdict of Sept. 6-7, 1948] sheet 116.

[875] *Ibid.*

[876] Z. Skup, 'Świadkowie przygważdżają wykręty Wielgomasowej. Pierwszy dzień procesu „literatki" wysługującej się okupantowi,' *Życie Warszawy* 1948: 247 (Sept. 9), 4.

[877] In Tomasz Szarota's opinion the sentence was too severe. This is what he writes about contemporary sentences in general: "At the time, public opinion was clearly displeased if a court acquitted a defendant, as happened with Stanisław Wasylewski, who was charged with collaborating with the *Gazeta Lwowska* daily published by the Germans. On the other hand, it approved of prison sentences of several years. From today's perspective and on the basis of the records of the proceedings, the historian sees them as far too high." (Szarota, *Karuzela na Placu Krasińskich*, 83).

Prokurator
Specjalnego Sądu Karnego
w Krakowie
dnia 19 lipca 1945.
Nr. II Ds Spec. 314/45.

W odpowiedzi na to pismo
należy powołać datę tego pisma
i numer akt.

List Gońc

Nazwisko: Skiwski

Imiona: Jan Emil

Wiek: około 45 - 50 lat

Ostatnie miejsce zamieszkania: Kraków ul.Król.Jadwigi

Wyznanie: rzym.kat. - zawód - literat,

Rysopis: wzrost średni, blondyn, twarz okrągła, czoło wysokie, oczy
           szare bystre, nos regularny - znaki szczególne: pochylony i
           zgarbiony, nerwowe mrużenie oczu,

Zarzucone przestępstwo: w okresie okupacji niemieckiej idąc na rękę
                         niemieckiej władzy okupacyjnej dopuścił się
                         działań na szkodę Państwa Polskiego tj.przest.
                         z art.1 § 2 dekr.P.K.W.N. z 31/8.1944. w brzmie-
                         niu dekr.P.K.W.N. z 16/2.1945.

Zarządzenie o aresztowaniu - wydane dnia 25 czerwca 1945.
Prokurator Specjalnego Sądu Karnego w Krakowie wzywa każdą osobę zna-
jącą miejsce pobytu oskar. Jana Emila Skiwskiego, do zawiadomienia o nim
najbliższej władzy sądowej lub najbliższego organu Bezpieczeństwa Publicznego wzgl. Milicji Obywatelskiej, a w miarę możności do zatrzymania go.
Wszystkie władze cywilne i wojskowe powinny zatrzymać i dostawić po-
szukiwanego do Prokuratury Specjalnego Sądu Karnego w Krakowie.

                                      Prokurator:
                     w.z.
                          p.o.WiceProkurator Rej.II.

                          Dr.Roman Martini

33. Arrest warrant for Jan Emil Skiwski, 1945

Grudziądz women's prison.[878] She was paroled on July 31, 1952 and later amnestied.

The Kraków trial of Jan Emil Skiwski, Dr. Feliks Burdecki, and other reptile collaborators was held in June 1949.

The arrests of the defendants began in December 1948. Those arrested were Witold Rychlik, Witold Horain, Marian Maak, Piotr Paliwoda-Matiolański, Amelia Hanzlowa-Alterowa, Bronisław Król, Edward Kłoniecki, and Jan Borek. Ewa Janina Smolka was arrested later. From the very beginning it was known that the main defendants, Skiwksi and Burdecki, would be tried in absentia, as both had left Poland illegally in 1945 and search warrants had been issued for them (on April 25, 1945 for Skiwski, and on September 17, 1946 for Burdecki). The main charge against them was for editing the political fortnightly *Przełom*, which had been published in Polish with the consent of the Germans.[879] These were not the only grounds for the charges against them. Skiwski had collaborated with *Goniec Krakowski* and *Nowy Kurier Warszwski*. In 1943 he was a member of a Katyn delegation. On his return he published articles in the reptiles, blaming the Soviet Union for the massacre.[880] The prosecutors acquired documents which showed that Jan Emil Skiwski "was the first man of letters to have departed from the common ground held by Polish writers against the Germans occupying Poland."[881] What is more, he published articles in *Ster* and *Zawód i Życie*, magazines for young people, and as such were considered particularly dangerous.

Feliks Burdecki's work was highly regarded by the Germans, who appointed him editor-in-chief of *Ster* and *Zawód i Życie*. He also published a propaganda pamphlet called *Nowy porządek w Europie* (A new order in Europe). On July 15, 1943 the Special Civil Court of the Polish Underground State sentenced him to infamy. The Communist judiciary had the indictment which had been issued by the court of the Polish Underground State against Skiwski

---

[878] AIPN GK, sign. no. 922/5, Centralne Więzienie Warszawa II Gęsiówka. Skorowidz więźniów, 1948 r. [Warsaw Central Prison II Gęsiówka. List of prisoners, 1948].

[879] For more on Skiwski's and Burdecki's collaboration see Głowiński, 'Kolaboracja do końca,' *passim*; and Urbanowski, *Człowiek z głębszego podziemia*.

[880] Wolsza, „*Katyń to już na zawsze katy i katowani*", 35–37; J.E. Skiwski, *Na przełaj*. For a discussion of Goetel's case, see Jankowski and Kotarba, *Literaci a sprawa katyńska 1945*.

[881] Gondek, *Polska karząca 1939–1945*, 140. This remark related to a note published in *Biuletyn Informacyjny* (Sept.18, 1941), which said Skiwski had been sentenced to infamy.

Prokurator
Specjalnego Sądu Karnego
w Krakowie
dnia 10 lipca 1945.
Nr. II Ds Spec. 314/45.

W odpowiedzi na to pismo
należy powołać datę tego pisma
i numer akt.

L i s t G o ń

Nazwisko: Goetel

Imię: Ferdynand

Rok urodzenia: 1890.

Miejsce urodzenia: Sucha pow. Wadowice

Miejsce zamieszkania w Warszawie przed powstaniem: Żoliborz ul. Targowa 44.

Ostatnie miejsce zamieszkania: Kraków, Rynek Kleparski 5.

Adres rodziny: Kraków, Rynek Kleparski 5.

Imię ojca: Walenty , Matki: Julia z domu Keller

Wyznanie: rzym.kat. - zawód: literat

Rysopis: wzrost średni, tęgi, szpakowaty i łysawy, twarz okrągła,

        oczoło normalne, oczy szare, rysy twarzy grube, zarost silny.

Według posiadanych informacji wyjechał dnia 21/1.1945. z Krakowa i

znajdować się może w najbliższych okolicach Warszawy.

Zarzucane przestępstwo: w okresie okupacji niemieckiej idąc na rękę

                niemieckiej władzy okupacyjnej dopuścił się

                działań na szkodę Państwa Polskiego tj. przest.

                z art.1 § 2 dekr.P.K.W.N. z 31/8.1944, w brzmie-

                niu dekr.P.K.W.N. z 16/2.1945.

Zarządzenie o aresztowaniu - wydano dnia 25 czerwca 1945.

Prokurator Specjalnego Sądu Karnego w Krakowie wzywa każdą osobę zna-

jącą miejsce pobytu oskar.Ferdynanda Goetla, do zawiadomienia o nim

najbliższej władzy sądowej lub najbliższego Organu Bezpieczeństwa Publicz-

nego wzgl. Milicji Obywatelskiej a w miarę możności do zatrzymania go.

34. Arrest warrant for Ferdynand Goetel, 1945

and Burdecki, enumerating their offenses against the Polish Armed Forces in Poland and against Poland's allies, as well as their work for the enemy (viz. for the Germans). This last charge concerned their work for *Przełom*."[882]

The other defendants had worked for the Polskie Wiadomości Prasowe and Telpress agencies, *Goniec Krakowski, Ilustrowany Kurier Polski, Siew*, and for radio. The included political journalists Witold Rychlik, Witold Horain, and Marian Maak; and columnists, short-story writers, and poets Amelia Hanzlo-wa-Alterowa, Bronisław Król, and Edward Kłoniecki. Piotr Paliwoda-Matio-lański had worked as a graphic designer and Jan Borek had served as a press photographer. The name of Ferdynand Goetel appeared almost every day in witnesses' statements and expert opinions, which in a way suggested that he should have been in the dock, too.[883]

As the main defendants were not present at the Kraków trial, the journal-ists covering it focused on those present. None of them pleaded guilty, that is none confessed that their work had been detrimental to Poland and the Polish Nation. Witold Rychlik emphasized that as a matter of fact he was a trans-lator (he knew German, Italian, and French) and had been sent to the reptile by a German employment agency. He added he had never translated propa-ganda texts. Like Rychlik, Witold Horain said he knew three foreign languages, German, English, and French. He said he had never intended to take up a job in a press agency but instead with a scientific publishing house. However, he was misled about the job and did not have enough courage to back out, as he was afraid of reprisals.

Marian Maak explained that first he had been employed as a driver with the Polskie Wiadomości Prasowe agency and later worked as a typist copying local reporters' texts. Also he admitted that in 1943 he had joined the Polish Red Cross delegation that visited Katyn. However, he was adamant he had neither published a single article on the massacre in any of the reptiles, nor delivered a report on the visit. He never mentioned the books he had published during the War under German occupation. He passed over in silence his short stories and romances, which were an embarrassment for his reputation and which literary critics later chose as examples of the Polish-language literature

---

[882] AIPN BU, sign.no. 1570/45, Akt oskarżenia przeciw Burdeckiemu Feliksowi i Skiwsk-iemu Janowi Emilowi [Indictment against Feliks Burdecki and Jan Emil Skiwski], sheet 3.

[883] Jankowski and Kotarba, *Literaci a sprawa katyńska 1945*, 59.

published by the Germans in occupied Poland. Krzysztof Woźniakowski went so far as to call Marian Maak "the pioneer of romance writing."[884] Witnesses testifying in court claimed that in his job as a typist he was more of an editor of the texts sent in by local journalists than a typist. As far as his Katyn visit was concerned, it turned out Maak had replaced Feliks Dangiel, a Vilnian Volksdeutscher, who was off sick. Maak had worked for Telpress as an editor of anti-Soviet articles. The court also held Maak's participation in the organization of the 1943 Harvest Festival at Wawel Castle against him.[885]

Piotr Paliwoda-Matiolański insisted that in his job with *Ilustrowany Kurier Polski* he was only responsible for the graphics and the cultural section. Amelia Hanzlowa-Alterowa, who had used the nom-de-plume Amelia Łuczyńska, admitted to having published her poems in *Ilustrowany Kurier Polski*, adding that at the time she thought they would be a comfort to readers. Bronisław Król confirmed that what the prosecutor had established was true – in 1941–1943 he had published in *Gazeta Lwowska* and *Ilustrowany Kurier Polski*. He was a fugitive from Łódź, and his family had no other source of income. When he learned that working for the reptiles was an offense he decided to withdraw his articles which had been endorsed for publication in these two reptiles. Those he had sent to *Gazeta Lwowska* were returned to him thanks to the services of Stanisław Wasylewski, but, he claimed, *Ilustrowany Kurier Polski* never responded at all to his request.

Edward Kłoniecki not only admitted to publishing poems and short stories in *Ilustrowany Kurier Polski*, but also added that he had published on Góral Mountain People in *Goniec Krakowski* and *Ster*. Jan Borek, a photographer for the prewar magazine *Światowid*, tried to exonerate himself by saying that he had been forced to work for *Ilustrowany Kurier Polski* by its German editors. He estimated that he had made about 200 thousand photographs. In addition, he said that before the War he had been suspected of being a communist sympathizer, and under German occupation he was afraid of reprisals should this have come to light. Hence his collaboration with the reptile was a security measure to cover up his leftist political sympathies.[886] The prosecution

---

[884] Woźniakowski, *W kręgu jawnego piśmiennictwa literackiego*, 325.

[885] Wolsza, 'Los dziennikarza,' 138.

[886] AIPN Kraków, sign. no. 1/1394, Akt oskarżenia przeciwko F. Burdeckiemu, J.E. Skiwskiemui innym [Indictment against Feliks Burdecki, Jan Emil Skiwski, and others], sheets 1–36.

Z notatnika obserwatora

Skiwski, albo człowiek bez pionu

„Dlaczego". To pytanie nasuwa się pierwsze każdemu, kto słucha przebiegu rozprawy. Wiemy wszyscy czym była okupacja, czym była w czasie okupacji linia podziału pomiędzy Polakami a Niemcami. Dlaczego ci ludzie stanęli po drugiej, nie polskiej stronie linii podziału? Dlaczego Maak jeździł do Katynia, dlaczego Smółka próbowała wmawiać, że Polakom wywiezionym na roboty do Niemiec dobrze się powodzi, dlaczego Matiołański opracowywał pismo, z którego szkodliwości musiał sobie dobrze zdawać sprawę, dlaczego Burdecki, dlaczego Skiwski?...

To pytanie nurtuje przede wszystkim opinię publiczną. Zainteresowanie sądu skupia się głównie na problemie jak było, na odsłonięciu przebiegu wydarzeń i ustaleniu faktów. Motywy postępowania są dla sądu okolicznością — bardzo ważną i istotną, ale tylko okolicznością. Dla szerokich kół społeczeństwa, dla czytelników pytanie „dlaczego"? — wysuwa się na plan pierwszy i my na to pytanie będziemy starali się odpowiadać. Będziemy odsłaniać motywy postępowania i okolicności na podłożu których zrodziły się uczynki sądzonych dziś ludzi.

A więc przede wszystkim Jan Emil Skiwski, bo tu sprawa jest pozornie najtrudniejsza do wyjaśnienia. Kim był człowiek, który na wiosnę 1944 r. po Oświęcimiach i Majdankach w momencie, gdy klęska Niemiec nie mogła nastręczać już żadnych wątpliwości wystąpił nagle jako rzecznik porozumienia z Niemcami, rzecznik stwarzania okupantom „pewnego i pomocnego zaplecza"? — i który robiąc to, nie szczędził swych niezaprzeczonych zdolności publicystycznych, aby

robić to jak najlepiej. Pomyślmy, na wiosnę 1944 roku!

Akt oskarżenia stwierdza, że działalność Skiwskiego była logiczną konsekwencją faszystowskiej postawy w latach międzywojennych i przypomina współpracę Skiwskiego w ozonowym „Pionie" i zachwyty nad książką Goebla „Pod znakiem faszyzmu". Niepozbawiony ironii będzie fakt, że na świadka oskarżenia wezwiemy dziś człowieka z obozu faszystowskiego — choć sprawiedliwość każe dodać, że Stanisław Piasecki redaktor „Prosto z mostu" nie poszedł śladami wielu innych i zginął z ręki niemieckiej w Lesie Palmirskim. Oto co pisał Piasecki o Skiwskim:

„Inteligencja rzeczywiście wysokiej klasy, a przy tym błyskotliwa... Skiwski uprawia intelektualne błąkanie się programowo. Nie chce mieć żadnej przystani. Poczytuje sobie za chlubę, że jej nie ma... Toteż w jego krytykach zaobserwować można całkowitą nieoblizalność. Gdyby był adwokatem, wiedziekbyśmy dlaczego podjął się w danej sprawie obrony, a w innej oskarżenia: kwestia zgłoszenia się tego właśnie, a nie innego klienta do kancelarii. U Skiwskiego-krytyka rzecz pozostawiona jest impulsom i urazom psychicznym. „Nieraz czytając jego krytyki odnosi się wrażenie, że równie świetnie, równie inteligentnie, równie błyskotliwie mógłby tę krytykę napisać z wprost przeciwnego punktu widzenia".

Ot i wszystko. Już wiemy o Skiwskim wszystko co nam potrzeba i już jesteśmy u źródeł jego zdrady. Źródłu temu na imię bezideowość — „indyferentyzm ideowy", jak mówi o nim

w innym miejscu Piasecki. Skiwskiemu było wszystko jedno: mógł pisać tak, mógł inaczej, stosownie do zamówienia. Aż na wiosnę 1944 r., kiedy Armia Radziecka stanęła u granic Polski, odezwał się uraz psychiczny — antyradziecki i antydemokratyczny. A pewnie coś więcej jeszcze: przyszło zrozumienie, że nadchodzą siły wobec których nie będzie można pozostać bezideowym indyferentem. I Skiwski wstąpił w obronie swego prawa do bezideowości, do sprzedawania swego pióra na drogę płatnej pospolitej zdrady.

„Przełom" wydawany przez Skiwskiego był pismem z propagandowego punktu widzenia dobrze i zręcznie robionym — lepiej niż jakiekolwiek inne preparowane nieudrabnymi często niemieckimi rękami. Pismem, które w kołach mniej uświadomionych mogło zrodzić i zrodziło wiele zła.

Skiwski uciekł z Polski i ukrywa się dziś gdzieś na Zachodzie. Jego rola w „Przełomie" jest od dawna zakończona i jeśli dziś tak wiele piszemy o nim, to dlatego, aby wszyscy mogli zdać sobie dobrze sprawę z tego, że Skiwski nie był jeden. Nie był zjawiskiem odrębanym. Tam na zachodzie takich jak Skiwski „emigrantów politycznych", obciążonych antydemokratycznym urazem, gotowych sprzedać się każdemu pod czyimi auspicjami mogą ocalić swą bezideowość, jest wielu. Proces, który toczy się obecnie w Krakowie, odsłania nie tylko pewne smutne fakty zdrady nielicznej grupy zdrajców-kolaboratów, ale demaskuje równocześnie bezideową postawę określonego typu ludzi z której rodzi się najhaniebniejsza zdrada.

ANDRZEJ KLOMINEK

35. Article published in the Kraków paper *Dziennik Polski* during Skiwski's trial with a headline reading 'Skiwski, The Man Who Was Not Straight'

accused Ewa Janina Smolka of having taken an active part in the publishing of the magazine *Siew,* by editing several sections in it (on what was being written from Germany, a "thousand curiosities" column, its games and puzzles section, and its letters to the editor column), and co-editing (with Zofia Łepkowska) a column on hygiene.[887] The prosecution argued that some of the letters published in the section on what was coming in from Germany were particularly harmful, because they commended deportation for slave labor in Germany. They also established that some of the letters were forged, written by the editors, quite possibly by the defendant herself.

---

[887] *Ibid.,* sign. no. 010/4450, Wyrok w imieniu Rzeczypospolitej Polskiej dnia 13 VI 1949 [Republic of Poland. Verdict of April 13, 1949], sheet 3.

The local press in Kraków gave the trial a lot of attention. Every day *Dziennik Polski* reported on its progress in court. The headlines served as a signpost to the lives of the defendants: "from nationalism to collaboration," they read.[888] In another article the journalist observed that he had seen a trial against the traitors of the Polish Nation.[889] Some articles focused on particular defendants. In one of them an anonymous author wrote that Piotr Paliwoda-Matiolański "felt offended by the people of Poland for not calling him a newspaper editor. (...) Now that reptilian 'editor' wishes he had never heard of that treacherous professional title."[890] Jan Emil Skiwski, and especially his life under German occupation attracted a great deal of attention from the press. "Who was that man who, in the spring of 1944, after all the Auschwitzes and Majdaneks, at the time when there could no longer be any doubt as to Germany's imminent defeat – precisely at that time he suddenly stepped forward as a spokesman for a deal with the Germans, speaking for the creation of a 'safe and helpful backing' for the occupying power? That man who did this without stinting his undeniable talent of journalistic rhetoric, to do it as best he could! Just think – in the spring of 1944!"[891]

In view of the fact that the two main defendants were beyond the reach of the Polish judiciary, in the speech for the prosecution the prosecutors spoke at length on the émigré aspect of the case. Both Skiwski and Burdecki had long since left Poland. Gustaw Auscaler, one of the prosecutors, did not know very much about the Polish émigré community and the various groups making it up, yet he ventured on the following remark, "This is the substance of the treason Skiwski and Burdecki committed. Those émigrés in London – all those Bieleckis, Cat-Mackiewiczes, and Goetels – followed the same political career, from fascism to outright treason. It's no coincidence that Skiwski and Burdecki made their way to those émigrés via Governor-General Frank's house in Bavaria, where they and their families stayed in 1945. Burdecki stayed in Geneva before moving on; Skiwski was in Austria and Italy, and now he is

---

[888] 'Od endecji do kolaboracji,' *Dziennik Polski* 1949: 157 (Jun. 10), 3.

[889] 'Proces zdrajców narodu polskiego,' *Dziennik Polski* 1949: 155 (Jun. 8), 3; 'Na pozycjach zdrady,' *Dziennik Polski* 1949: 154 (Jun. 9), 3.

[890] 'Ujawnia się rozmiar winy,' *Dziennik Polski* 1949: 157 (Jun. 10), 3; 'Wizytówki i fikcyjne listy,' *Dziennik Polski* 1949: 159 (Jun. 12), 5.

[891] A. Klominek, 'Skiwski, albo człowiek bez pionu,' *Dziennik Polski* 1949: 158 (Jun. 11), 3.

about to 'honor' Venezuela with his presence."[892] I shall only observe that this time the prosecutors did not say a word about General Anders, General Bór-Komorowski, or President Zaleski. The wartime and postwar exiles they referred to were not top-rank Polish émigrés. Prosecutor Auscaler also failed to mention another distinguished exiled writer, Józef Mackiewicz, who was in the Ministry of Public Security's crosshairs for a time, due to certain events in his life during the War, such as his visit to Katyn in 1943.

Having heard both parties to the case, on June 13, 1949 the court issued its verdict, which may be summed up in one word: "stiff." The two main defendants, who were tried in absentia, got life sentences, although "they deserved the death penalty," as the judge observed. But there was no certainty that notice of the date of the trial had been served upon them, so they could not attend. Marian Maak got a sentence of ten years. Surprisingly, Ewa Janina Smolka was sentenced to seven years – it was the highest sentence handed down on a woman who had collaborated with the reptile press, much higher than what Helena Wielgomas got, so we may say it was unreasonably high. Piotr Paliwo-da-Matiolański, the last defendant, got a four-year sentence.

There were several reasons why the sentences in this trial were so high. First, the absence of the two main defendants meant that those actually in the dock got higher sentences. In my opinion that was what the propaganda aspect called for. Second, the fact that Ewa Janina Smolka, Marian Maak, and Piotr Paliwoda-Matiolański were tried in the same proceedings with Skiwski and Burdecki did not augur well for them in the sense of expecting clemency. The fact that they were put together with Skiwski and Burdecki suggests the very opposite. Third, initially the prosecution had planned to bring charges against eleven persons. Once they had collected the evidence they dropped charges against six of them.

The trials held in 1949 in Warsaw and Kraków brought to a close several years of proceedings in the Polish judiciary to settle accounts with reptile journalists and associates. We may say that the Communist authorities of Poland succeeded in bringing to justice the most notorious reptilians, except for those who had left the country before hostilities were over or just after the War.

---

[892] 'Faszyzm był im bliższy niż własny naród,' *Dziennik Polski* 1949: 161 (Jun. 14), 3.

WACŁAW PYCH AND HIS TALL
STORIES ON KATYN (1952)

THE COMMUNIST KATYN CAMPAIGNS

In the early fifties, when the Madden Committee set about its work to clarify
the circumstances of the Katyn atrocity, in People's Poland the Ministry of
Public Security launched a large project to find and brief witnesses ready to
pledge and testify to the innocence of the Soviet Union.[893] The Ministry adopted a double agenda. First, it wanted to seek out a few of those who had been to
Katyn in the 1943 delegations the Germans had made a special effort to organize for their propaganda purposes. Those who had been on these expeditions
had already been invigilated and subjected to an in-depth investigation in
1945–1946, when prosecutors Dr. Jerzy Sawicki and Dr. Roman Martini were
collecting evidence for a Katyn trial in Warsaw which eventually failed to materialize. In that first wave of interest the prosecutors and the Ministry's agents
reached the physicians, Drs. Hieronim Bartoszewski, Edward Grodzki, and
Stanisław Plappert; the journalist Marian Maak; Father Stanisław Jasiński; the
top-rank RGO administrator Edmund Seyfried; Polish Red Cross associates
Kazimierz Skarżyński and Jerzy Wodzinowski; and Franciszek Prochownik,
a blue-collar worker from Kraków. For a short spell they were also on the
lookout for Dr. Adam Szebesta, who started a job with the Katowice branch
of the Polish Red Cross almost as soon as hostilities ended, and so was easy to
access. Other ex-delegates – Dr. Konrad Orzechowski, Dr. Jan Zygmunt Robel,

---

[893] See, for instance, W. Wasilewski, 'Komisja Katyńska Kongresu USA (1951–1952)', *Biuletyn Instytutu Pamięci Narodowej* (2005: 5–6), 71–84; Wolsza, „*Katyń to już na zawsze katy
i katowani*", 109–125.

326

and the prewar Olympic cyclist Stanisław Kłosowicz – fell into the hands of the NKVD. However, despite a tremendous effort the pursuers failed to establish the whereabouts of Ferdynand Goetel, Władysław Kawecki, Józef Mackiewicz, Jan Emil Skiwski, and especially Dr. Marian Wodziński, and apprehend them. The next round of arrests on charges of collaboration including involvement in the Katyn affair started in the late '40s. In 1948 the Cracovian writer and journalist Marian Maak was re-arrested and sentenced to ten years in jail for collaborating with the Germans. In the early '50s the Ministry turned its attention to Hieronim Majewski of Sieradz and Mikołaj Marczyk of Stalowa Wola, two of the blue-collar workers who had seen Katyn in 1943. Both got prison sentences, albeit the government did not disseminate news of their trials, quite understandably, since at the time (1950) the Communists did not want to make Katyn a public issue, and keeping quiet about it was in their best interest.

In outcome of the Ministry's activities, in the latter half of the '40s and early '50s a few individuals were blackmailed or pressurized with threats of jail into changing their standpoint on the circumstances and timing of the Katyn atrocity. The Ministry drew up a list of persons who claimed the Germans had perpetrated the Katyn massacre in the fall of 1941. The names on the list were Drs. Hieronim Bartoszewski, Edward Grodzki, Stanisław Plappert and Adam Szebesta, along with Franciszek Prochownik and Dr. Tadeusz Piechocki, a not very widely known persona.

1952 saw the start of stage two of the Katyn affair in People's Poland, this time with the Ministry of Public Security playing the leading role. Its decision-makers wanted to make use of all who had cracked up in the earlier episodes in its drive to bury the truth about Katyn under a mantle of lies. They were also out to find new witnesses ready to attest to Soviet innocence.

The matter was hyped up with a lot of propaganda. Radio broadcasts and the press kept the public informed about a new wave of "American Imperialist plots" designed to discredit the Soviet Union and undermine Polish–Soviet friendship. In the first days of March 1952 the government of People's Poland issued a declaration on the Katyn atrocity which straightaway appeared in the press under a striking headline: 'The American version of the Goebbelsian provocation will not resonate with the Polish Nation.' In this statement the Communist government said that for several months American propaganda had been attempting to promote "the work of a special

House of Representatives commission on Katyn." It went on to add that the people behind the campaign were "sponsors of Neo-Hitlerite revanchist policy, enemies of peace, democracy, and the Polish Nation – people like Mr. Bliss Lane, who, when he was the U.S. ambassador to Warsaw, had no qualms about making a personal contribution to a campaign against the Polish State and its independence, and since his return home has been specializing in shameful slander against Poland and the Soviet Union. (...)."[894] The Communist propaganda put the Katyn atrocity on an interminable list of Nazi German operations to exterminate the Polish nation. The declaration continued with "The Katyn atrocity was the work of Hitler's implementers of genocide whom today the Americans are releasing from jail and employing to prepare a new set of atrocities against the Polish nation and all peace-loving nations."[895] Next came the assertion that the German revelations on Katyn were shown up and disproved by the Burdenko Commission in 1943 in which – as the government unequivocally informed public opinion – Poles had participated. This last point deserves a comment. In 1952 it could neither be confirmed nor challenged. Today we know that Stalin had personally crossed Wanda Wasilewska and Bolesław Drobner off the list of the Soviet commission about to set off for Katyn.[896] The only Pole the Soviet authorities invited to join a special trip to Katyn and attend a press conference there was Jerzy Borejsza,[897] and, like Wasilewska, he contributed to the propaganda campaign by writing a press article entitled 'Śladami zbrodni' (Invesigating the crime) for *Wolna Polska*, and co-authored a discreditable brochure *Prawda o Katyniu* (The Truth about Katyn, 1945). However, perhaps what the compilers of the official statement had in mind was the military delegation headed by Gen. Zygmunt Berling and Col. Leon Bukojemski-Nałęcz which visited the site in January 1944 and paid a tribute to the victims.[898] A documentary film was made to mark the event, and was widely disseminated throughout Poland after the War.

---

[894] 'Amerykańska wersja goebbelsowskiej prowokacji nie znajdzie oddźwięku w narodzie polskim. Oświadczenie Rządu RP,' *Sztandar Ludu* 1952: 53 (Mar. 1–2), 1.

[895] *Ibid.*

[896] Materski, *Mord katyński*, 35.

[897] Jaczyński, *Zygmunt Berling*, 225.

[898] *Ibid.*, 221; Rutkowski, *Adam Bromberg*, 26.

The press followed up the government's declaration with more documents on Katyn. On March 4, 1952 readers of the Polish domestic press got the official Soviet position on the matter, in response to Ray Madden's letter of February 25, 1952 to the Soviet ambassador to the United States. Four days later the Soviet embassy reminded Americans that "the Katyn atrocity had been examined by an official Commission which had established that it was the doing of Hitler's Nazi criminals, and had published its findings in the press on January 26, 1944."[899] The TASS news agency made a special point in its communiqué of putting in the date when the Burdenko Commission closed its operations, because it went on to observe that in the eight years that had passed the American authorities had never questioned the results of the Soviet inquiry on Katyn. Polish readers at home got another straightforward message with the publication of a report on the work of the Burdenko Commission, which appeared on March 5, 1952, along with articles discrediting the members of the Madden Committee. The most spectacular publication appeared on March 3 in the Communist government paper *Trybuna Ludu*. Headlined 'Reżyserzy "komisji katyńskiej" ' (Stage-managers of "the Katyn Committee"), it was compiled by Henryk Podolski on the basis of documents supplied by the Ministry of Public Security and the journalist's own observations in the USA. Podolski, editor-in-chief of *Głos Ludu*, a Polish communist paper which came out in the USA, was a close associate of Bolesław Gebert, a reputed Soviet agent. In the mid-fifties Podolski repatriated to Poland, became involved in the activities of a pro-communist society sponsored by the People's Republic operating among Polish Americans. He was also a secret agent in the service of the Ministry of Public Security. [900]

The people of Poland were treated to two more helpings of nonsense on Katyn. On March 14 the domestic press published an interview with the Czechoslovak physician František Hájek and gave it an explicit headline – 'Prowokacje amerykańskie w związku z tzw. „sprawą katyńską" demaskuje

---

[899] 'Rząd radziecki w nocie do Rządu USA piętnuje nową prowokację amerykańską w sprawie katyńskiej jako nową próbę rehabilitacji zbrodniarzy hitlerowskich,' *Sztandar Ludu* 1952: 55 (Mar. 4), 1.

[900] S. Cenckiewicz, *Oczami bezpieki. Szkice i materiały z dziejów aparatu bezpieczeństwa PRL* (Kraków: Arcana, 2004), 45, 95; *idem*, Śladami bezpieki i partii. Studia. Źródła. Publicystyka (Łomianki: Wydawnictwo LTW, 2009), 20, 31, 68, 87.

uczony czechosłowacki' (American provocations on the "Katyń Affair" exposed by a Czechoslovak scholar), followed a week later by an interview with Dr. Adam Szebesta, 'Mogliśmy zobaczyć tylko to, co chciano nam pokazać' (We could only see what they wanted us to see).

NEW WITNESSES, NEW REVELATIONS...

Naturally enough, the press was not the only aspect of the propaganda employed over Katyn. The Ministry of Public Security was again invigilating those who had seen Katyn in 1943, just as it had done in 1945–1946. There was also a search going on for more witnesses to testify that Katyn was a German propaganda story now being revived by American Imperialists. One of these witnesses was the key figure in this chapter, Wacław Pych, a character who emerged completely out of the blue and was not connected in any way at all with the Katyn question. So who was this new guy entering upon a controversial issue, and what became of him?

Wacław Pych was born on July 15, 1906 in the village of Włoskowice in the Powiat of Puławy (now eastern Poland). His father was a carpenter, and his mother was the daughter of a blacksmith. In the 1920s he left school, having completed an evening course of secondary education, and got a job in Lublin, in a factory producing agricultural tools. In 1927 he attended a training course at the air force training center in Dęblin and started out on a military career with the Air Force Battalion stationed in Poznań, serving in the rank of sergeant right up to the outbreak of the War in September 1939. In 1936 he married Wanda Kute. These were all facts that made a significant impact on the later developments in his life.[901]

---

[901] I present Wacław Pych's biographical data on the basis of AIPN Lublin, sign. no. 00227/323, vol. 3. The data on him preserved in the card file of the Polish Institute and Sikorski Museum are sparse – sergeant, b. 1906; served in the Twenty-Third Infantry Battalion (Seventh Infantry Division. Base – Second Corps). Decorations: The Army Medal, 1946. Wacław Pych is not mentioned at all in the book by Zbigniew Wawer, *Znów w polskim mundurze. Armia polska w ZSRR sierpień 1941 – marzec 1942* (Warszawa: Zbigniew Wawer Prod. Film., Międzynarodowa Szkoła Menadżerów, 2001), though we can hardly hold this against this author, because Pych was neither an outstanding officer nor the commander of a unit, and his espionage operations were not very widely known at the time.

After the German invasion of Poland, he "found himself in an air force unit heading for the border with Rumania," as he would later write in his declaration for the Ministry of Public Security. "Near Zamość I left the unit, and with a party of about 50 men went on in the direction of Hrubieszów for the Soviet Union."[902] On September 16 the group reached Kowel (now Kovel, Ukraine), where they came up against the Soviet invasion. He decided to stay in the East (i.e. in Soviet–occupied Poland) and embarked on collaboration with the Soviets. He was disarmed and sent to a camp for Polish prisoners-of-war at Szepietowka, and subsequently to other POW camps at Zahorce near Dubno and at Radziwiłłów (now Zahirtsi near Dubno, and Radyvýliv, both places now in Ukraine). They operated as labor camps, and the Poles held in them were set to work building a 10-km stretch of the road that was to run from Kiev to Lwów. Pych started as an ordinary laborer, but by the late fall of 1939 he had been promoted to foreman, and by the end of the year to battalion chief. He was now an activist, and in January 1940 was given an order to "get things straightened out" in the Radyvýliv camp (as he later wrote).[903] He must have proved his mettle in propaganda work and invigilating other soldiers, because in May of 1940 the Soviets offered him a job as an NKVD informer. He assumed an alias, Semp (a misspelling of the Polish word for "vulture"). "My task was to eliminate fascist operations and propaganda, to keep up the soldiers' morale and look after their health and security," he would later write.[904] He turned out to be very active in other fields as well. If his declaration is to be believed, he took part in the setting up of new labor camps for Polish internees, at Sytno in the summer of 1940, Rodatycze (now Rodatychi) in the fall of 1940, Janów (now Ivaniv) in the winter of 1940/1941, and at Skniłów in the spring of 1941. All these were small places in the environs of Lwów, now in Ukraine.

When Germany invaded the Soviet Union Pych was appointed economic manager of the camps the Soviets had disbanded, and their inmates were marched out via Winnica (now Vinnytsia, Ukraine), finally reaching Zolotonosha, from where they were taken by rail to Starobielsk. Here they were set

---

[902] AIPN Warsaw, sign. no. 00231/124, vol. 2; W. Pych, 'Oświadczenie w sprawie mojej bytności poza granicami kraju oraz mojej w tym okresie działalności' [Declaration on my spell abroad and my activities in that period], sheet 251.

[903] *Ibid.*, sheet 252.

[904] *Ibid.*

to work on the construction of a military air base. Pych landed a management job, not surprisingly, since he was still helping the NKVD, and stayed in the post until the Sikorski–Mayski Agreement was signed in July 1941. When Gen. Kazimierz Wiśniowski, the special emissary of Gen. Władysław Sikorski, visited the camp, Pych knew that his mission had come to an end, at least for the time being. "I realized that my time was up," he remarked in his declaration for the Ministry of Public Security.[905] He was issued a letter of recommendation, and a special ID with a ticket valid for all the available forms of transport, and with the consent of his NKVD officer left for Moscow. From there he was sent to Totskoye in the Obvod of Orenburg (Western Russia), which he reached in October 1941. Poles released from Soviet gulags were rallying to Totskoye to join Gen. Michał Tokarzewski-Karaszewicz's infantry division. Pych observed and reported "a sharp anti-Soviet course organized and managed by Generals Tokarzewski and Okulicki, and all the officers of the Sixth Infantry Division," he wrote in his declaration.[906] He must have certainly kept his superiors in the NKVD informed about what was going on. In the winter of 1942, fearing his disclosure, the Soviets moved him on to a camp for sailors and airmen at Koltubanka. Here, too, he engaged in anti-Polish activities against the Sikorski government. He continued the same business at a camp in Kermine, Uzbekistan, which he reached in March of 1942. Eventually, as he wrote in his declaration, his name was put on the list of suspected communists and he was cashiered from Gen. Anders' army. As a result he was sent to the detention center established by the Polish military authorities at Guzar. His situation changed when Gen. Anders' forces were evacuated from the Soviet Union to Iran, when he re-established close relations with the NKVD and was given a guarantee of extensive assistance. However, in July 1942 he failed to obtain the consent of the Polish military command to leave for Iran. The Polish intelligence service classified him as a "Soviet sympathizer and a communist,"[907] so he was sent to the camp at Guzar again, where he once more sought assistance from the Soviets. "Next day I went to the NKVD, where I was recommended a rest to get used to the idea of working outside the USSR; I was given financial

---

[905] *Ibid.*, sheet 253.

[906] *Ibid.*, sheet 256.

[907] *Ibid.*, sheet 257.

assistance and advised to be cautious," he wrote in his declaration for the Ministry of Public Security.[908] Next he traveled from Guzar to Krasnovodsk and sailed for Pahlevi in Iran. He stayed at two Polish camps located in the Karasim and Quizil Ribat deserts. His prewar training course prompted him to try to join an air force unit, but he was rejected when he failed the vetting process, was qualified as a traitor and sent to the infantry. He was put into the Twenty-Third Infantry Battalion in the Seventh Infantry Division, which was a reserve unit and not part of the Second Corps. It seems that in spite of being suspected of Soviet sympathies he was allowed to serve in the Polish Army for a purely humanitarian reason. The commanding officers of the Second Corps tried to get all the Polish people who turned up at one of the rallying centers out of the Soviet Union. What's intriguing is why he was not dispatched to one of the detention camps the Polish Army set up in the East once it had evacuated its troops from the Soviet Union; for instance, to Latrun in Palestine, where a few other officers and NCOs found to have communist sympathies, such as Capt. Kazimierz Rosen-Zawadzki, Sgt.-Maj. Tadeusz Strzałkowski, and Cpl. Romuald Gadomski, were held.[909]

Pych claimed that he was under surveillance for the entire duration of his service in Anders' army – in Palestine, Egypt, and Italy. In Naples he established contact with "Soviet agencies" – if we are to believe him – and gave them a detailed account of the atmosphere in the Second Corps. In the San Basilio camp in 1945 he took part in an operation to get soldiers serving in the Second Corps to return home, yet stayed in Italy himself. We may conjecture that there were two matters which made him take this decision. First, he did not really have anyone to return to: his wife had been shot by the underground resistance in 1943 for maintaining intimate relations with the Germans (he did not say which resistance movement it was, or what its political orientation was). The same had happened to his brother-in-law, who was a Gestapo informer. And second, he was still working for the NKVD.

In the summer of 1946 he left for England. As soon as he arrived in London he got in touch with the embassy of the Polish People's Republic – as he took

---

[908] *Ibid.*, sheet 258.

[909] J. Pietrzak, '"Wyeliminowanie z szeregów elementu uciążliwego i niebezpiecznego". Sprawa Obozu Dyscyplinarnego Armii Polskiej na Wschodzie w Latrun w Palestynie (1944–1945),' *Dzieje Najnowsze* 2015: 2, 81.

care to point out in his declaration.[910] He engaged in the distribution of newspapers and magazines that came out in Poland among the Polish veterans who had fought in the Second Corps and on other fronts in the West. He wrote that he returned to Poland by sea, on December 6, 1947. According to Stefan Artymowski's research, there is no record of a ship carrying Poles repatriating from Britain arriving at a Polish port on that day.[911] Vessels bringing repatriates back to Poland berthed on December 2 and 4, so maybe Wacław Pych boarded the Eastern Prince and returned home on December 4, 1947. At any rate, his return was managed by 2nd Lt. Władysław Polkowski.

Pych headed for the place where his wife's family lived, not far from Dęblin. At first he and his mother-in-law engaged in black-marketeering. In 1948 he joined the PPR, and subsequently the PZPR. It is fair to assume that the Ministry of Public Security checked him out meticulously. He was appointed director of a state-owned business producing made-to-measure wear, and was later deputy manager of another state-owned enterprise called Centrolag. He established a close working relationship with the security service as Agent Cień (Shadow). [912] He had several tasks. First, he invigilated the community of ex-soldiers who had repatriated after having served in the Second Corps or other Polish units on fronts in the West. His reports for the Ministry of Public Security contain the names, ranks, and home addresses of scores of repatriated ex-servicemen, as well as their political views. In spite of his highly committed work for the Ministry, quite unexpectedly in 1951 he was removed from the Party. "Shadow did not do his work for the Security Office objectively, and did his best to discredit members of the Party," says the note in his personal file in the Ministry's records.[913] In addition some Party members had misgivings about his past. There were rumors that he had been a high-ranking officer in Anders' army, and some even thought he had been a commanding officer in no. 303 and 318 Polish Fighter and Reconnaissance Squadrons taking

---

[910] AIPN Warsaw, sign. no. 00231/124, vol. 2; W. Pych, 'Oświadczenie w sprawie mojej bytności poza granicami kraju oraz mojej w tym okresie działalności' [Declaration on My Sojourn Abroad and My Activities During That Time], sheet 261.

[911] S. Artymowski, *Repatriacja żołnierzy Polskich Sił Zbrojnych z Europy Zachodniej do Polski w latach 1945–1948* (Poznań: Wydawnictwo Poznańskie, 2012), 236.

[912] AIPN Lublin, sign. no. 00227/323, vol. 3, Charakterystyka „Cienia", 1954 r. [Description of Agent Shadow, 1954].

[913] *Ibid.*

part in the Battle of Britain and on the Italian front. Moreover, rumors went round in Lublin that he was a double agent, viz. that he was also working for the British and Americans. Although the Party had lost confidence in him, he continued to work for the Ministry, and it even gave him the chance to rehabilitate himself. Perhaps his expulsion from the Party was actually done to intensify his collaboration with the Ministry of Public Security? In 1952–1954 Agent Shadow was invigilating ex-members of the PSL, while still regularly informing on repatriated veterans. On January 23, 1953 he submitted an extensive report entitled 'Grupa Andersowców,' on dozens of ex-servicemen who had repatriated after serving in the Second Corps, giving the Ministry a detailed account of the officers – from Col. Pniewski, Col. Wicherkiewicz, down to Capt. Choiński. All this acted to his advantage, but he decided to improve his status as a secret agent, thereby speeding up the opportunity to rehabilitate himself with Party members. And his timing for this move – the spring of 1952 – was not a random choice, either.

On March 6, 1952 Wacław Pych sent a letter on Katyn to *Fala 49*, a program broadcast on Polish Radio and orchestrated by Col. Wiktor Grosz. "Dear *Fala 49*," the letter said, "as I listen to you, I feel I'm hearing the voice of my own conscience. Lately American and British capitalists and the posthumous offspring of Nazism have delved into the Hitlerite cold store and given a face-lift to one of Goebbels' rusty old weapons – the Katyn question. Dear *Fala*, we all know the British and American Imperialists have attributed this atrocity to the Soviet Union. They are lying disgracefully, just as they did in 1939, when they promised to help in the event of a Nazi German invasion. Those disgusting lies appall me all the more because I have the full knowledge on the Katyn affair, I know exactly what happened, and when it happened. I spoke to the people from those camps shortly before they were taken over by the Hitlerites. That's why I feel it is my duty to speak out and tell the whole truth. I want to tell the truth to all of my countrymen, because I know that among them there are other witnesses of what happened, and the time has come to clear out the hostile propaganda once and for all. I look forward to your reply, Sincerely yours."[914] Pych forwarded a copy of the same letter to the Lublin Municipal and Voivodeship Committees of the PZPR, and to *Sztandar Ludu*, the local

---

[914] *Ibid.*, *Fala 49*, 6 III 1952 r. [Mar. 6, 1952].

Party newspaper. In his closing sentence he wrote that he would be expecting a reaction, presumably meaning that he wanted to submit a fuller story to the paper. And that is in fact what he did – in March of 1952 he sent a "Report on Katyn" to the editor's office of *Sztandar Ludu*. In accordance with what he had hinted he would do in his letter to the radio program, he put into his article to the paper a few items of information to prove the Soviets were innocent:

"In August 1941 we reached the camp at Starobielsk and there I learned that the Polish officers had left shortly before for the camps near Smolensk, Kozelsk and others, and that Starobielsk was reserved for those who would be building an airfield for heavy bombers. (...) When I was working on this construction project I talked to rank-and-file men, NCOs, and officers who had come from all the camps, the camps around Katyn, and I learned from them that there were still more Polish officers, and more men would be joining us, and that the officers would leave for an officers' rallying point. In October 1941 we arrived at Totskoye to organize a Polish army, and I saw that a lot of officers had come there, too, more than enough for all the commissions. So here's where the hostile propaganda is foiled, you simply cannot believe that the Russians could have murdered the Polish officers in Katyn (...). Today, after over a decade, I have forgotten many of the facts, I've forgotten many of the names which would definitely have been very important for this matter today – but then again no-one could have imagined that the British and the Americans would be capable of such macabre villainy as to accuse the heroic Soviet Union of having committed the Katyn murders, nevertheless I think that if we make the right arrangements and get the right witnesses we will be able to give the ultimate blow to this evil propaganda and blot it out for good (...)."[915]

Straight after Pych's first intimation on Katyn the Ministry of Public Security received the full information both from the radio broadcasters and from the newspaper's editors. A special note drawn up by an officer in the Ministry for his superiors in the secret service said, "Wacław Pych, a white-collar worker from Lublin, has written a letter to the *Fala 49* radio program saying that he talked to Polish POWs from the camps around Smolensk shortly before they were rounded up by the Germans. During the conversation he told them he

---

[915] *Ibid.*, 'Doniesienie w sprawie Katynia, *Fala 49*, 25 III 1952 r.,' [Information concerning Katyn, *Fala 49*, Mar. 25, 1952].

was a provisions officer in one of the POW camps in the Soviet Union and that in August of 1941, during the retreat ahead of the Nazi invading force, he had been in the Smolensk area and had talked to Polish POWs working on the construction site of a new airfield. He did not know what happened next, because he left the area and traveled further east."[916]

However, the news supplied by Pych was not geared up for the propaganda campaign against the Madden Committee's findings. Instead the Communist propagandists turned to devices like the interviews given by František Hájek and Dr. Adam Szebesta. Didn't they believe Pych's revelations? We may indeed ask, but it seems they didn't. In his later disclosures Pych got so far-fetched that that even the decision-makers in the Party and security services thought it looked too much of a tall tale. It was Pych's way of trying to rehabilitate himself and have his Party membership restored. "Currently Pych is not a member of the Party, but he is constantly applying for a review of the decision to remove him from its ranks, because he thinks his exclusion was unfair," says a note in the Ministry's records.[917]

Pych was also hinting that he had information which was so significant that it would absolutely overturn the international discourse on Katyn. In his opinion his evidence was sound and unassailable. He sent a letter to the Central Committee of the PZPR introducing himself as a critic of Gen. Anders' Second Corps and an unswerving communist. He insisted he was also "a unique eyewitness for the matter of the murder of the Polish officers the Fascist Germans committed in Katyn,"[918] Quite obviously, such a declaration had to be followed up with action. So Pych made his earlier Katyn declaration even more unwavering, this time without taking the reaction of the "American imperialists" into consideration. Now he chose to follow the path already trodden by Stanisław Burgat, another crown witness to the Katyn affair. The only problem was that when Burgat made his deceitful

---

[916] AIPN Warsaw, sign. no. IPN 00231/124, vol. 1, 'Informacja nr 1 dotycząca dowodów prowokacji niemieckiej w sprawie Katynia z 3 IV 1952 r.,' [Information no. 1 concerning evidence for a German provocation in the Katyn affair, Apr. 3, 1952], sheet 10.

[917] *Ibid.*, vol. 2, 'Notatka o Pychu Wacławie z 10 II 1953 r.,' [Note on Wacław Pych, Feb. 10, 1953], sheet 248.

[918] *Ibid.*, 'List do Komitetu Centralnego Polskiej Zjednoczonej Partii Robotniczej z 5 II 1953 r.,' [Letter to the Central Committee of the Polish United Workers' Party, Feb. 5, 1953], sheet 249.

testimony he was already an inmate of Wronki penitentiary and no-one was likely to believe his story. Burgat claimed that he had managed to wriggle out of the execution the Germans had carried out at Katyn, saved by fluke thanks to "the cadaver of General Mieczysław Smorawiński." According to this witness the Katyn murders were like the mass executions the Germans conducted in occupied Poland using machine guns."[919]

Pych's declaration was indeed astonishing, and as such deserves to be presented in full. In the annex at the end of this chapter I present the most controversial of Pych's statements on the Katyn atrocity. It was submitted to the Lublin Voivodeship branch of the Security Office in April of 1953. The Katyn passage is part of a larger exposé entitled *Oświadczenie w sprawie mojej bytności poza granicami kraju oraz mojej w tym okresie działalności* (Declaration on My Sojourn Abroad and My Activities During That Time).[920] In the passage I present in the annex below it is very easy to test Pych's credibility. In practice he avoids giving names, except for a few cases, those of four colleagues from the army (perhaps former POWs from Kozelsk?) and a German commanding officer whose exact name he cannot recall (was it Arnes or Arne?).[921] Other details he gives are the number of the German army unit (537), and the information on the house in Katyn, its distance from the road and from the death pits. His frugality over facts of this kind was cautiously designed and intended to save him from embarrassment.

The names of the officers he gives are real. He even says that they may have been witnesses of the events he describes. The snag is that one of them, Roland Merski, was killed in Italy in 1945, just as he was about to pass on the

---

[919] *Ibid.*, vol. 1. 'Sprawa Stanisława Burgata z więzienia we Wronkach,' [The Stanisław Burgat case, sent in from Wronki prison], sheet 52. "I was held as a POW in Katyn concentration camp. When the mass shooting started I was in the first group due to be executed. When they started shooting I fell down, pretending to be dead. The corpse next to me, Gen. Smorawiński, fell on top of me and spattered me with blood. When evening set in I ran away. I joined an underground resistance unit at Kolpak, where I stayed, fighting the Germans until the Polish Army arrived. I joined the Kościuszko First Division as a volunteer and took part in its combat route as far as Warsaw" (*Ibid.*)

[920] *Ibid.*, vol. 2, 'Oświadczenie,' [Declaration], sheets 251–262; *Ibid.*, Katyń; for the full text (sheets 254–256) see the annex to this chapter.

[921] In fact the officer's real name was Friedrich Ahrens, and he served as a crown witness for the German defense against the Soviet charges at the Nuremberg Trial.

sensational news on Katyn (viz. that the Germans did it) to the British.[922] Pych actually says Merski died in 1945. Currently not much can be said about Capt. Miscjak and Maj. Dzieszyna, they can't be traced at all. But the fact that Pych mentions Lieut. Bolesław Doczyński proves that Pych's declaration is an outright hoax. The records on the Katyn atrocity list Doczyński as one of the victims executed by the NKVD in the spring of 1940.[923] So he could not possibly have met Wacław Pych in Kozelsk in the fall of 1941. There is no record in the documentary evidence relating to Katyn of either Pych or Merski ever being held as POWs in Kozelsk, Ostashkov, or Starobielsk. The source of Pych's data concerning the camp number of Kozelsk, the number of the German unit, the name of its commanding officer, and the description of the site of the atrocity is just as easy to explain. All he had to do was to use the Burdenko Commission's report, which was published in the press in People's Poland in 1952. There was no need for him to have been to Katyn in person.

I would add another point to the list of reasons why the security men of People's Poland decided not to use Pych's not very trustworthy revelations. He was not the first Polish soldier who had fought in September 1939 to claim after the War that he had gotten out of the graves of Katyn. In 1946 a note from Koronowo prison reached the hands of Leon Chajn, deputy minister of justice, notifying him that one of its inmates, Stanisław Burgat, had been telling fellow-prisoners that he had sent a letter to President Bolesław Bierut saying that he had been saved by sheer luck from the Katyn executions. In the investigation that followed it turned out that Burgat was suffering from spells of loss of memory and "fantastic delusions."[924] Later, when he was in the jail at Wronki in the early fifties, Burgat returned to the same story, so the decision-makers in the Ministry of Public Security treated the matter with a great deal of caution.

---

[922] AIPN Warsaw, sign. no. 00231/124, vol. 2; W. Pych, 'Oświadczenie w sprawie mojej bytności poza granicami kraju oraz mojej w tym okresie działalności' [Declaration on My Sojourn Abroad and My Activities During That Time], sheet 261.

[923] Tucholski, *Mord w Katyniu*, 94; *Katyń. Dokumenty zbrodni*, vol. 2: *Zagłada*, eds. W. Materski et al., (Warszawa: Trio, 1998), 119.

[924] Motas, 'Materiały dotyczące zbrodni katyńskiej w zasobie archiwum Głównej Komisji Badania Zbrodni przeciwko Narodowi Polskiemu Instytutu Pamięci Narodowej,' vol.33, 237.

ANNEX

KATYN

I got to Moscow, having taken a break in my journey at Ryazan, where the train had quite a long stopover. In Moscow I reported at the NKVD office, received instructions and a supply of food, and set out for the Polish camps near Smolensk. I was advised to make haste if I wanted to see them there, because the evacuation order had already been given.

I got to the Dnieper, where I had been told the bridge was damaged, but I managed to cross it. On my left I had Smolensk, I went round it from the north and on the road for Vitebsk I found the POW camps. The one I went up to was called no. 2ON. They didn't want to admit me, so I was taken to see the chief officer.

I noticed that everything was ready for the evacuation – the cars, the trucks loaded up with clothes and food supplies; the NKVD officers enthused about Soviet paratroopers being dropped at the rear of the German forces. When the chief officer had seen my credentials he gave instructions for them to take me back for the time being to no. 2ON and asked me to persuade the POWs in that camp to hurry up with their preparations, because time was running out and evacuation was imminent. He postponed the formalities of my registration to the next day.

When I got back to the camp I saw that the officers were not getting ready to leave, they were lounging on their beds and stopping those who wanted to leave from packing. The overwhelming majority wanted to leave, nonetheless they had been terrorized by the Polish commanding officer in the camp and especially by the Polish intelligence officers.

The POWs already knew of the Polish–Soviet agreement, which I think encouraged some to make inappropriate demands of the NKVD, such as saying they would only leave the camp in a convoy of vehicles, but not if they had to walk etc. Or that anyone who left the camp would be a traitor and would be court-martialed back at home. When I tried to tell them that Polish units were forming in the east and they were waiting for officers, I was told there would be no Polish army without them and that was why the Soviet Union had to treat them with respect and listen to their demands, in the end I was yelled at to shut up and not to prattle if I hadn't been asked to speak. The quarrels, disputes, and name-calling went on to far into night, especially among the senior officers.

In the morning I was woken up by the officers nervously yelling and I saw people rushing for the exit; when I got out after them I saw that the camp was surrounded by German guards.

Within a short time the Polish commanding officer had the POWs assembled in line and when the Germans arrived reported status. The Germans checked the attendance list, probably against a list taken on the NKVD, as people said that they took the NKVD officers along with the rest of the camp, and they had the camp regulations read out to them with the services of an interpreter. I learned that death would be the punishment for anyone who committed a second offense.

Next day, in line with instructions issued by the Germans, they started to organize groups to dig pits to serve as air raid shelters, the groups were formed on a voluntary basis, and they were promised that afterwards the best of them would be allowed to go home.

The officers got together in groups like they would to visit the officers' mess, using a lot of dirty tricks against me and other NCOs, they wouldn't admit us to their company, for, as I've said before, neither Capt. Miscjak, Maj. Dzieszyna, Lieut. Doczyński, nor me and my pal [Roland] Merski, none of us are officers.

While we were digging the air raid pits some of the officers were summoned to report to the so-called battalion HQ to check the list of those in the camp, most of them were senior officers, and one day when they came back they said they had been told to return without having done a report, as two Germans had arrived on motorcycles with some documents, and when the commanding officer had read these papers he dismissed them without conducting a report.

From that time on no-one was called to make a report. The POWs were allowed to write letters using "HQ of no. 537 Operational Battalion" as the return-to-sender address, which was what the commanding officer had said when the regulations were read out.

After a short time they started to take groups of officers out of the camp in vehicles. They took the groups which had been best on the job and drove off in the direction of Smolensk, to the train station, they said. Of course the time had come to say good-bye and forgive each other, promise to visit one another etc. Each group that left took with them letters to be sent home to Poland.

In the end I was the only one left in the barracks, and the German on duty had the interpreter ask me why I hadn't left. I told him that my name hadn't been read out, he checked the list, told me to get in the car and we drove off in the direction of Smolensk. After we had gone about 10 km the car turned off onto a country lane and went up to a house about 180–220 meters away from the main road. I was brought in to see Chief Officer Arne or Arnes, who listened to what the German who had taken me there had to say, then he took out a file and spent a fairly long time looking through it, asking for my ID card, I gave him my Polish one, as I had torn up all my other documents and thrown them down the toilet, the chief officer examined my ID card, checked the lists yet again and through the interpreter's services asked me how I had gotten there, I said I had run away from other camps and was trying to get home. On my way I had gotten to these camps.

I was told I was a communist sent there deliberately because I wasn't on the lists. Trying to save the situation, I started to explain that I really was a POW and had escaped from my old camp because I was its commander and when the amnesty was announced a hostile group tried to kill me, so I had to go on the run.

I was given a map and told to show them that camp, after I had done that I was asked how long I had been here, I lied, telling them it was about a month whereas in fact I'd been for just a few days, then they started talking in German, and all that I can remember is that they kept repeating, "*firer, gebels, befal,*" [viz. *Führer, Goebbels, Befehl* (orders) – translator's note].

After that conversation Arne patted me on the shoulders and said something out aloud in German, at which they all burst out laughing, while the interpreter told me that I would soon be joining my fellow countrymen.

At that I turned to the chief and said, "*Danke*," which was a German word I knew, and again they burst out laughing. No report was drawn up about me, and I didn't sign anything, one of the details I noticed was the sofa on which Arne was slouching and a glass cabinet full of liquor bottles at the back of the room.

A blond German of medium height came up to me, in the company of a taller, ginger one. The blond one took along another POW who had been standing by the wall, then he patted me on the back once more and told us to walk ahead in front of them. Both Germans reeked of liquor.

When we were outside we passed by two women who stared at us terrified, I smiled at them and waved to say good-bye…

We were escorted some 600–800 meters away from the house in the direction of the air raid shelters we had just dug, which were about 200–220 meters away from the main road, when I came up to the pit I felt a heavy thump in the back of the head and lost consciousness.

When I came round I felt a heavy weight on top of me, and a burning sensation in my mouth. It was dark and there was an indescribable stench. I wriggled out to the top and saw that I had been lying in a pit full of corpses covered with a thin layer of soil. Having brushed all the soil off myself, I managed to crawl up to the road despite the tremendous pain I was in, and there I hid in the bushes. I wiped the blood and soil off myself as best I could and started to run away into the fields, because there were yells in German coming from the house and you could hear dogs barking and howling. It turned out that the drunken German who had shot me hit me in the back of the head but hadn't killed me. I can show the scar now or any time, the scar his bullet left.

I fled over the fields, avoiding roads and people, but after a few days hunger forced me to go up to a man who was working on a cabbage patch next to his house, and ask for something to eat. He looked at me and straightaway took me into the house, where I was fed, washed, and given a change of clothes.

After a rest at night my host came with another, older man, who looked at my head wound and then asked me to give a full account of my story, with all the details. When he had heard my story he suddenly asked me for the password, and of course I played dumb, so the stranger burst out laughing and told me not to worry and get a good sleep.

That man, whom I still admire today, took me back to my own folks, leading me across the Dnieper. We scrambled past German tanks and then went along the byways, eventually reaching Soviet artillery set up in the bushes along the main road next to the river, from where they took us to their commander.

The commander listened to our story and made my companion stay behind. I was put into the care of an NKVD man who told me he was going on leave. He took me to Totskoye, traveling first by car and next on board a train. When we reached the place, I reported at the NKVD office at the station and then joined a group of Polish POWs who had just arrived to join the Polish army which had started to be established there. The camps from Starobielsk, Kozelsk, and other parts of the USSR were stationed at Totskoye, and there I met up with my friends [the original says "its friends" – author's note], the ones I have named above in this declaration.

Source: AIPN Warsaw, sign. no. 00231/124, vol. 2, Oświadczenie [Declaration], sheets 254–256.

THE KATYN ATROCITY IN LIGHT OF LETTERS TO THE *FALA 49* AND *FALA 56* RADIO PROGRAMS

ORIGINS AND FIRST YEARS OF *FALA 49* AND *FALA 56*

Research carried out by Paweł Szulc shows that 1949 marked an important caesura in the history of Polish radio broadcasting. It was the year when an institution known as Centralny Urząd Radiofonii was set up to supervise Polish Radio (Polskie Radio). There was a substantial rise in the number of listeners, to over a million. A new, state-of-the-art transmitting station was erected at Raszyn near Warsaw, and a high-class broadcasting center was opened in Warsaw. In October 1949 Program Two started broadcasting. Poland and the Soviet Union signed an agreement for the exchange of sound recordings.[925] The individual responsible for the political content of radio broadcasts was Jerzy Baumritter, an ex-officer of the First Army (viz. the Soviet-controlled force which in 1944 left the Soviet Union under General Berling and took part in the battle for Berlin). Baumritter had earned his spurs as a radio broadcaster working for Soviet radio as the editor of a Polish paper titled *Na Zachód*.[926]

---

[925] P. Szulc, '„Instrument wychowania człowieka socjalizmu". Polskie Radio Szczecin w latach 1949–1955,' in *Wokół zjazdu szczecińskiego 1949 r.*, ed. P. Knap (Szczecin: Instytut Pamięci Narodowej – Komisja Ścigania Zbrodni przeciwko Narodowi Polskiemu. Oddział w Szczecinie, 2011), 116.

[926] P. Szulc, *Zniewolony eter. Polskie Radio Szczecin w latach 1945–1989* (Szczecin: Instytut Pamięci Narodowej – Komisja Ścigania Zbrodni przeciwko Narodowi Polskiemu. Oddział w Szczecinie, 2012), 110.

And he was the Communist propagandist who said in July 1949 that radio had to be the mouthpiece of the Party, committed to the establishment of the new political order in Poland.[927]

In 1949 Polish Radio put a new regular program on the air based on an original idea put forward by Col. Wiktor Grosz, a well-versed broadcaster. The new program, *Fala 49* (Wavelength '49), was to serve a double purpose. First, to unload the political tension mounting up in postwar Polish society due to diverse socio-political issues and problems in everyday life; and second, to provide the Communist ruling class with information on public opinion and the patterns of behavior of ordinary people. Col. Grosz was not just a good broadcaster, but well-versed in various types of propaganda, especially radio propaganda. His CV was replete with the right kind of experience for the job – as an activist of the prewar KPP, as a Soviet agent, and as the pioneer behind the creation of a Polish section in the Ukrainian radio station based in Saratov (Russia). In addition, in 1944–45 he had served as a high-ranking officer in the Soviet-controlled Polish Army and head of its Central Political and Educational Board (viz. he was its chief *politruk*); after the War he was in the Ministry of Foreign Affairs, first in its Press Department and later serving as Poland's ambassador to Czechoslovakia. He was also the creator of a radio program called *Naszym zdaniem* (In our opinion) and head of a broadcasting station called Kraj (Home Affairs).[928]

The Communist authorities expected the people of Poland to respond to the opportunity to talk about their problems in a radio program and that this would encourage them to take a more sympathetic view of their rulers. The new program was to provide a platform for the refutation of at least some of the news and opinions disseminated by foreign radio stations broadcasting in Polish, such as Radio Madrid, the BBC, the Voice of America, and the Polish

---

[927] *Ibid.*

[928] Authors on the career of Wiktor Grosz include Cenckiewicz, *Długie ramię Moskwy*; M. Nurek, *Gorycz zwycięstwa. Los Polskich Sił Zbrojnych na Zachodzie po II wojnie światowej 1945–1949* (Gdańsk: Wydawnictwo Uniwersytetu Gdańskiego, 20090); A. Sobór-Świderska, *Jakub Berman. Biografia komunisty* (Warszawa: IPN. Komisja Ścigania Zbrodni przeciwko Narodowi Polskiemu, 2009); S. Ligarski, 'Twórcy a organy bezpieczeństwa państwa w latach 1945–1956,' in *Wokół zjazdu szczecińskiego*, 92.

Section of French Radio.[929] In the early fifties a new broadcasting station, Radio Free Europe, joined this group, and expanded at an amazing rate.[930]

Shortly after its launch in 1949 *Fala 49* added another explicit word to its name; henceforth it was *Fala 49 odpowiada* – "Wavelength '49 Replies." The program was to act as a sort of safety valve releasing the social tension that built up over a variety of issues which were problematic, awkward, or embarrassing for the authorities.[931] Listeners could voice their grievances, ask for advice, or even criticize the authorities. After the incidents that occurred in 1956 and the accompanying political thaw the program changed its name again, to *Fala 56*; and predictably to *Fala 80* following the eruption of mass strikes and the emergence of Solidarity in August 1980. All these developments in the program's history clearly show that its makers wanted to give their broadcasts at least the external trappings of credibility (and perhaps they did so on the initiative of top decision-makers in the PZPR). So they invoked the political turning-points of 1956 and 1980 to underpin the program's status and win the confidence of new listeners.

Fala 49 was managed by Leon Rawski, and its first speakers were Stefan Martyka, a second-(or even lower-) rate actor, and Wanda Odolska, a journalist of *Trybuna Ludu*, the paper reputed to be the mouthpiece of the Party and government. Odolska also published in other periodicals, such as *Po prostu* in 1951, the time of the show trial of the Warsaw *bikiniarze* (Bikini Boys – a youth subculture styling itself on contemporary groups in the USA and Western Europe).[932] Ministry of Public Security records contain information about an assassination attempt planned against her by an organization called Krajowy

---

[929] Recent publications on radio stations broadcasting from outside Poland include M. Bogdan, *Radio Madryt 1949–1955* (Łomianki: Wydawnictwo LTW; Warszawa: Uniwersytet Kardynała Stefana Wyszyńskiego. Instytut Nauk Historycznych, 2011); A.M. Jackowska, 'Działania Służby Bezpieczeństwa wobec Sekcji Polskiej Radia Francuskiego. Zarys problematyki,' in *Dziennikarze władzy, władza dziennikarzom. Aparat represji wobec środowiska dziennikarskiego 1945–1990*, T. Wolsza and S. Ligarski, (eds.), (Warszawa: Instytut Pamięci Narodowej. Komisja Ścigania Zbrodni przeciwko Narodowi Polskiemu 2010),, 358–380; K. Pszenicki, *Tu mówi Londyn. Historia Sekcji Polskiej BBC* (Warszawa: Rosner & Wspólnicy, 2009).

[930] Machcewicz, *„Monachijska menażeria"*.

[931] G. Majchrzak, 'Armia Krajowa na „Fali" w czasach „odwilży" (1954–1956),' *Biuletyn Instytutu Pamięci Narodowej* 2002: 8–9, 85.

[932] Z. Romek, 'Walka z „amerykańskim zagrożeniem" w okresie stalinowskim,' in *Polska 1944/45–1989. Studia i materiały*, vol. 5 (Warszawa: Instytut Historii PAN, 2001), 190.

Ośrodek Podziemia (the Domestic Resistance Center) and founded by Bruno Hlebowicz. The operation was never carried out, but in 1951 Stefan Martyka was assassinated by another resistance group called Kraj (The Home Country).[933] According to Marian Gołębiewski, who spent many years in jail under the People's Republic, after Martyka's death Odolska received a gruesome poison pen letter which said, "I'm in heaven now, Wanda dear, waiting to see you here." Following the political thaw of 1953 Odolska left Poland in disgrace and settled in France.[934]

Fala 49 was notoriously propagandistic and it was broadcast at various times of the day. Often it would interrupt other broadcasts, especially music programs popular with young people. The voice of its speaker would butt in on a piece of dance music, in a military style typical of the Cold War Period: "This is *Fala 49* speaking, *Fala 49* speaking. We're on the air now." This is what years later the expatriate writer Marek Hłasko had to say about the program and one of its speakers: "'This is *Fala 49* speaking, *Fala 49* speaking. We're on the air now.' And then the scoundrel would start to spit at the Imperialist countries, usually smacking the backside of the Americans, calling then cretins, beasts, idiots and the like, after which he would finish his tirade and sign off with 'We're going off the air now.'"[935] *Fala 49* put in a lot of effort to lambast the postwar anti-Communist resistance movement and denigrate its soldiers. It found itself a domestic enemy in the *kulaks* (well-to-do peasant farmers) and picked on them. And it never missed a chance to decry the Warsaw Uprising of 1944.[936] On the other hand the things on which the program lavished a lot of praise were the merits of the homegrown Communists, the campaign against

---

[933] Majchrzak, 'Armia Krajowa na „Fali" w czasach „odwilży" (1954–1956),' 88. Five members of Kraj were sentenced to death and executed. The women involved in Martyka's murder were given long sentences of imprisonment and held in isolation in Inowrocław prison.

[934] *„Bo mnie tylko wolność interesuje..." Wywiad – rzeka z Marianem Gołębiewskim (Nowy Jork, listopad 1988 – czerwiec 1989)*, interview with Marian Gołębiewski conducted by D. Balcerzyk, ed. J. Dudek (Lublin: Instytut Pamięci Narodowej. Komisja Ścigania Zbrodni przeciwko Narodowi Polskiemu, 2011), 357–358. The rhyming couplet addressed to the "obnoxious propagandist lady of *Trybuna Ludu*" is also quoted by Stanisław Salmonowicz in *„Życie jak osioł ucieka...",* 86. Listeners were still writing in about Wanda Odolska in 1956, following her aggressive comments on the air about the political changes in Poland. A. Leszczyński, *Sprawy do załatwienia. Listy do „Po prostu" 1955–1957* (Warszawa: Trio, 2000), 216–217.

[935] M. Hłasko, *Piękni dwudziestoletni* (Warszawa: Wydawnictwo Da Capo, 1994).

[936] Majchrzak, 'Armia Krajowa na „Fali" w czasach „odwilży" (1954–1956),' 86–88.

illiteracy, the growing housing industry, the country's electrification, and the growing number of radio sets its people had. And of course it promoted the Stakhanovite style of "socialist competition at work."

A large number of letters was sent to the program, so we may say that it enjoyed a considerable amount of popularity, and even that Col. Grosz had hit the bull's eye from the propaganda point of view. Listeners sent in scores of letters with a variety of questions, including ones which were extremely thorny for the Communist ruling class. Whether a letter received an answer was decided by the management of the radio station, on consultation with the top decision-makers in the PZPR. By the mid-fifties the correspondence office of Polish Radio was receiving an annual average of over 150 thousand letters, later rising to over 200 thousand, but falling to 50–70 thousand per annum in the seventies. A team of specialists was set up to analyze the incoming correspondence and compile *Biuletyn*, an in-house bulletin sent round to a very small number of addressees. At first it was issued in just 21 numbered copies, and 22 copies as of 1952, 14 of which went to the secretariat of the PZPR's Central Committee. The individuals who were on the shortlist of recipients were Bolesław Bierut, Józef Cyrankiewicz, Jakub Berman, Edward Ochab, Hilary Minc, Franciszek Mazur, Zenon Nowak, Roman Zambrowski, Władysław Dworakowski, Aleksander Zawadzki, Eugeniusz Szyr, Stefan Staszewski, Roman Kornecki, Artur Starewicz, Wilhelm Billig, Romuald Gadomski, Jerzy Baumritter, and Stanisław Radkiewicz. These people were the only ones with the exclusive right to receive a copy of the bulletin.

Later on the mandatory print-run expanded somewhat, and more top-brass PZPR activists – Roman Werfel, Leon Kasman, Władysław Matwin, Julia Brystigerowa, Jerzy Kowalewski, Ludwika Jankowska, Antoni Alster, Franciszek Blinowski, Eugenia Pelowska, the attorney-general Stefan Kalinowski, and Edward Uzdański, deputy chairman of the radio committee – got a copy. One copy was regularly deposited in the archives of the Central Committee. In October 1953 more Party activists and administrative officers were admitted to what was previously top-secret information. The new recipients were Zenon Wróblewski of the Central Committee's Press, Publishing, and Radio Department; Noe Wertzhajzer, Felicja Węgrowska, and Henryk Werner (all three from the Radio Committee); Kazimierz Mijal, head of the Office of the Council of Ministers; Wiktor Borowski, editor of *Trybuna Ludu*; Wilhelm Strasser representing the Voivodeship Committee for the Warsaw branch of the PZPR; Stanisław Pilawka, chairman of the board of the ZMP Communist youth organization; Franciszek Jóźwiak and Stefan Król of the Ministry for State Supervision; Hubert Miller; Wiktor Kłosiewicz, chairman of the Central Trade Union Council; Romana Granas, head of the Communist Party College; Piotr Jaroszewicz, vice-chairman of the Council of Ministers; Jan Dąb-Kocioł of the Ministry of Agriculture; Leon Chajn of the Ministry of Labor and Social Welfare; Antoni Bida of the Board for Religious Affairs; Edmund Pszczółkowski from the secretariat of the Central Committee of the PZPR; Jerzy Sztachelski for the Ministry of Health; and Feliks Baranowski from the Ministry of Public Management. In 1956 the exclusive list of individuals in receipt of the bulletin was yet again expanded, and the new recipients were Edward Gierek, Władysław Wicha of the Ministry of Internal Affairs, Włodzimierz Sokorski, the attorney general Marian Rybicki, Stefan Arski, Karol Małcużyński, and Stanisław Ludkiewicz. Initially the only representatives of the media who got the bulletin were the directors of Polish Radio, the magazine *Nowe Drogi*, and *Trybuna Ludu*. After 1955 it was circulated to the editors of more papers and magazines, *Gromada*, *Kraj*, *Życie Partii*, *Świat*, and eventually to the directors of Polish Television. Following the incidents of 1956 more media accrued to the list: the editorial boards of *Życie Warszawy*, *Polityka*, *Świat i Polska*, the radio program *Muzyka i Aktualności*, and the head of the PAP news agency. The new media men in receipt of the bulletin were Stefan Żółkiewski of *Polityka*, and Jan Pański of Polish TV.

The politicians who were now mandatory recipients were Władysław Gomułka, Edward Gierek, Józef Cyrankiewicz, Ignacy Loga-Sowiński, Zenon Kliszko, Edward Ochab, Adam Rapacki, Marian Spychalski, Roman Zambrowski, Aleksander Zawadzki, Jerzy Albrecht, and the heads of the various departments in the Central Committee of the PZPR. By the late fifties the bulletin was sent out to 106 recipients, including new ones such as the Board of the Women's League, the Headquarters of the Citizens' Police Force, the Board of the Union of Polish Writers, the Supreme Audit Office, the Documentary Film Studios, the Educational Film Studios, the Labor Agency, the Peasants' Mutual Assistance Union, the Polish Scouting and Guiding Association, the Union of Young Socialists (ZMS), the Rural Youth Association (ZMW), and the editorial boards of more periodicals (*Ekspres Wieczorny*, *Zielony Sztandar*, *Szpilki*, and somewhat later *Żołnierz Polski, Chłopska Droga, Sztandar Młodych*, and *Przegląd Kulturalny*). Individuals now added to the list included Andrzej Werblan, Jerzy Morawski, Irena Grosz, Mieczysław Rakowski, Henryk Korotyński, Leon Finkelsztejn, the theater director Adam Hanuszkiewicz, the writer and parliamentary deputy Leon Kruczkowski, the composer Witold Lutosławski, and the journalist Edmund Osmańczyk, albeit the last four were only sent issues on selected subjects, e.g. employment and professional matters.

There were two reasons behind this substantial expansion of the list of *Biuletyn* recipients. First, the letters listeners sent in covered a wide range of subjects, from political issues to ordinary, everyday problems. Hence the need for representatives of the ministries which handled matters that cropped up most often in the letters. Second, the character of the broadcasts changed – from a program which merely recorded problems to one which provided answers to them. That meant a need for specialists from a number of fields. In addition there was a gradual liberalization in the country's political affairs, and the Party's top decision makers became more open to accepting the blame for the "errors and aberrations" of the previous (Stalinist) era.

LETTERS TO *FALA 49* AND *FALA 56* AS A SOURCE FOR RESEARCH ON POLES IN THE SOVIET UNION DURING THE WAR

Letters to *Fala 49* have been used in research on several occasions. They have served as reference materials in the work of Dariusz Jarosz on social issues under the People's Republic,[937] and in the work of Anna Adamus[938] and Michał Jarmuż.[939] Scholars from the Institute of National Remembrance have examined an impressive number of these letters in studies on the Poznań incidents

---

[937] D. Jarosz and M. Pasztor, *Afera mięsna. Fakty i konteksty* (Toruń: Centrum Edukacji Europejskiej), 2004.

[938] A. Adamus, 'Doświadczenie gospodarki niedoboru w PRL – na przykładzie listów do władz centralnych w sprawie masła i margaryny z lat 1956–1978,' in *Polska 1944/45–1989*, vol. 10 (Warszawa: Instytut Historii PAN, 2011), 299–314.

[939] M. Jarmuż, 'Warunki mieszkaniowe w Polsce lat siedemdziesiątych XX wieku w świetle dokumentów osobistych,' in *Polska 1944/45–1989*, vol. 10 (Warszawa: Instytut Historii PAN, 2011), 315–330.

of 1956.[940] I have addressed the Church question as presented in them in an article on the arrest of Archbishop Stefan Wyszyński, Primate of Poland.[941] I have also referred this set of correspondence in work on the Katyn atrocity.[942] But neither the letters to *Fala 49* nor to *Fala 56* have been examined in studies on Poles in the Soviet Union in 1939–1956, while this problem does not occur at all in the *Fala 80* collection.

As I embarked on an examination of the *Biuletyn*, starting with its 1951 issues, I made an assumption that the Katyn atrocity might well have been a subject frequently addressed by some of the letter writers even if it was not the predominant theme. It could indeed have occurred in view of its gravity and the embargo the Communists put on its public mention in the media, yet there was no trace of any such phenomenon in the published bulletin. Perhaps the specialists who looked through the letters and selected those for publication in the bulletin decided to pass them over, on consultation with the Party's decision makers. I think that would be a sound conjecture to make, in view of the fact that until the end of November 1952 the correspondence office of Polish Radio had received dozens of letters on Katyn, out of which 15 were critical, 5 were hostile, and 26 were hostile and anti-Soviet.[943] We may assume that the letters classified as "hostile" were against the Polish authorities. Unfortunately none of them was qualified for publication in the *Biuletyn*.

But I am also quite certain that some of the letters on Katyn put the blame on the Germans. The staff working on the bulletin selected a few of them, not for publication but to be forwarded to the Ministry of Public Security. This was done deliberately in connection with the Communist propaganda campaign being conducted in Poland, the Soviet Union, Czechoslovakia, and

---

[940] *„My głodujemy – my chcemy chleba". Poznański Czerwiec 1956 r. w listach opublikow-anych w Biuletynach Biura Listów Komitetu do Spraw Radiofonii „Polskie Radio"*, ed. K. Bittner (Poznań: Instytut Pamięci Narodowej. Komisja Ścigania Zbrodni przeciwko Narodowi Pol-skiemu, 2011).

[941] T. Wolsza, 'Aresztowanie Prymasa Polski Kardynała Wyszyńskiego w świetle kore-spondencji do audycji „Fala 49",' in *Prymas Polski Stefan Kardynał Wyszyński na Ziemi Pomor-skiej i Kujawach*, M. Białkowski and W. Polak, (eds.), (Toruń ; [Bydgoszcz]: Dom Wydawniczy Margrafsen, 2014), 97–107.

[942] T. Wolsza, 'Konfabulacje Wacława Pycha w sprawie zbrodni katyńskiej (1952 r.),' in *Pol-ska 1944/45–1989*, vol. 10 (Warszawa: Instytut Historii PAN, 2011), 7–21.

[943] Archiwum Dokumentacji Aktowej TVP [Polish Television Archive of Written Records, hereafter ADA TVP], *Biuletyn* 1952: 52 (Dec. 12).

Bulgaria to discredit the Madden Committee, which after an inquiry lasting a couple of months established that the atrocity had been committed by the Soviets. The Ministry's secret agents checked every occurrence of letters of this kind very thoroughly. First of all they would visit the writer of the letter and question him on the circumstances of the matter. Hence only some of those who wrote to *Fala 49* on this subject went on the air or had their letter and their name published in the press. The majority of such letters made it into *Biuletyn*, as materials fit only for the eyes of the top-brass activists of the People's Republic.

From these letters the specialists extracted only those passages which could be utilized straightaway in the propaganda campaign, and sent them to the Ministry of Public Security. The Ministry's agents immediately set about questioning the senders of these letters. Below I give a few examples of such letters sent in to Polish Radio. In my first example "an anonymous fan of *Fala 49* from Hajnówka" wrote that he was in Battalion 202, which the Germans employed in the spring of 1943 to exhume the graves of the Katyn victims, and he saw "the Germans getting rid of the evidence and making it all look like it was done by the Soviet Union, to blacken its name." In another letter an anonymous woman wrote that when the Germans occupied Smolensk they arrested her sister Jadwiga and put her in a camp nearby. Her sister was made to work for the German commanders as an interpreter and she saw the Germans murdering Polish officers. In 1942 she returned home to the GG and told the writer of the letter what she had seen. Soon afterwards she died owing to her ordeal in the camp.[944] In a third letter Antoni Duchiński of Warsaw wrote that he knew what happened to Zygmunt Woźniak of Warsaw, whose name appeared in the list of Katyn victims published by the reptile press in April 1943. Duchiński wrote that he knew from Woźniak's wife that her husband had been arrested by the Germans on September 19, 1940, and so he could not possibly have been a Katyn victim. The Ministry took action immediately to clarify the matter. They interviewed the wife, who confirmed that her husband had been arrested by the Germans in 1940, and that a Zygmunt Woźniak appeared on the list published in the reptile, but

---

[944] AIPN Warsaw, sign. no. 00231/124, vol. 1, Informacja nr 1 dotycząca dowodów prowokacji niemieckiej w sprawie Katynia z 3 IV 1952 r., [Information no. 1 concerning evidence for a German provocation in the Katyn affair, Apr. 3, 1952], sheet 14.

with no further details, so she was not sure it was meant of her husband, who had not been heard of since his arrest.[945]

A couple of letters implied the Germans were guilty of the Katyn murders. I shall discuss three of them, later forwarded to the Ministry of Public Security. Bolesław Sitkowski wrote that under wartime occupation he heard from a man who worked on the railroad that in the winter of 1941 the Germans were transporting railcars full of dead Polish soldiers, taking them east via Chełm station. A woman wrote that in 1943 she heard from an engine driver named Ćwiklak that he had seen railcars full of corpses in Polish Army uniforms, which the Germans were transporting east via Tarnopol (now Ternopil, Ukraine). In yet another letter sent to *Fala 49* which eventually reached the hands of the Communist security service Anna Jackowska of Warsaw wrote that in April 1943 when she was on a train heading for Siedlce she saw a railcar with dozens of bodies inside.[946] The writers of all of these letters seem to be suggesting that Katyn was just a German hoax. To round off this list of examples I'd add one more which I have already discussed – the largescale Katyn mission conducted by Wacław Pych, an NKVD agent serving in the Polish Forces on the Italian front.

The first batch of letters on Katyn was put into the October 1951 issue of the bulletin, and the next one appeared in July 1952. In the second publication the question of Katyn appeared in the context of Gen. Sikorski, so I shall merely mention it in passing. The writers of this particular letter were blue-collar workers from Stalowa Wola, and they made the following request. "Please explain the Katyn affair and the question of Gen. Sikorski. Who murdered him? Not a single word has come on this matter from abroad. So who was he? According to our knowledge he was a friend of the Soviet Union. Was he an enemy of the nobility? Was he an enemy of the working class? We want an answer."[947] There are two points in the letter which deserve comment. The date when it was edited for publication, July 1952, marked the ninth anniversary of the Gibraltar airplane crash in which Sikorski was killed. We may speculate that the employees of the Stalowa Wola steelworks had discussed the subject, or

---

[945] *Ibid.* "Woźniak" is one of the most common Polish surnames (currently, 2018, the tenth most common), and "Zygmunt" is a typical first name for a man [translator's note].

[946] *Ibid.*

[947] ADA TVP, *Biuletyn* 1952: 63 (Jul. 30).

perhaps they had indulged in "whispered propaganda" (political jokes, which made those who cracked them liable to imprisonment).[948] The second point concerns Katyn. Why did the issue crop up in the Stalowa Wola steelworks, and why in 1952? If I may venture on a hypothesis, I think it could have had a background going back to the War. 1943. One of the members of the blue-collar delegation the Germans sent to Katyn in May 1943, Mikołaj Marczyk, was a steelworker from Stalowa Wola.[949] From his trip he brought home many souvenirs, such as officers' epaulettes, an army belt, fragments of uniforms, pieces of Soviet newspapers found on the bodies, and an incomplete list of victims' names. In addition the Germans instructed him to give talks on the atrocity, saying that the Soviets had done it, and to display the exhibits in a glass cabinet at work. Marczyk conscientiously carried out all that the Germans had told him to do, and his workmates must certainly have remembered his talks. In February 1950 the prosecution office of Rzeszów District Military Court found that Marczyk was living in Lower Silesia and initiated an investigation concerning him. Nearly twenty witnesses were questioned, including ten current and former employees of the steelworks who had known him since the War. They were asked what they knew about his visit to Katyn and the talks he subsequently gave.[950] In 1951 the court sentenced him to two years in prison. Another thing which I think must have prompted a rise in the interest in Katyn in Stalowa Wola was the campaign launched in Poland in March 1952 to counter the findings published in the Madden Committee's report.[951] These must have been the reasons which made a group of Stalowa Wola steelworkers interested in Katyn and encouraged them to write this letter to *Fala 49*.

---

[948] Several examples of what postwar relations between Poland and the Soviet Union were like are to be found in a selection of documents (including ones concerning Katyn) relating to a body called Komisja Specjalna do Walki z Nadużyciami i Szkodnictwem Gospodarczym (Committee for the Prevention of Economic Abuse and Harmfulness). See M. Chłopek, *Szeptane procesy. Z działalności Komisji Specjalnej 1945–1954* (Warszawa: Baobab, 2005). For more information on repressive measures against individuals who spoke out on Katyn, see Gasztold-Seń, 'Siła przeciw prawdzie,' 132–153.

[949] Madajczyk, *Dramat katyński*, 61; T. Wolsza, 'Wojenne i powojenne losy Polaków wizytujących miejsce zbrodni katyńskiej w 1943 r.,' 7–29; Jankowski, 'Pod specjalnym nadzorem przy drzwiach zamkniętych,' 95–135.

[950] AIPN Rzeszów, sign. no. 108/6521, Akta dotyczące Mikołaja Marczyka, [Records concerning Mikołaj Marczyk], sheet 74.

[951] Wolsza, 'Konfabulacje Wacława Pycha w sprawie zbrodni katyńskiej (1952 r.),' 9–11.

Another letter which I have already mentioned was sent from Szczecin on October 1, 1951. It was signed by Janusz Wardecki, who observed that Katyn was not being treated on a par with Auschwitz, Majdanek, and "other foreign human extermination camps."[952] He added that "the people exterminated in Katyn belonged to the privileged class, but they were humans, Polish people who had fought for a Poland that was our country after all, a Poland which issued people to whom today tributes are being paid and who are being commemorated with monuments. Surely those people must have stood up in opposition to something if they were dealt with so cruelly, and today we never mention them."[953] Wardecki went even further. He wrote that ZBoWiD (The Society of Fighters for Freedom and Democracy, the officially approved veterans' association) had neglected the Katyn issue: "They're commemorating the people who died in the concentration camps, but of course not all concentration camp victims held left-wing views. I would even venture to say that only a minority of the victims were left-wingers, nonetheless their memory is cherished, but Katyn is never mentioned."[954] In his letter to *Fala 49* Wardecki made an appeal to ZBoWiD, starting with a highly pertinent question: "Freedom Fighters, why have you forgotten the Katyn atrocity?"[955] And he continued by stressing that every atrocity should be condemned as a matter of course, "to stop any would-be perverted tyrants from thinking of perpetrating a new Katyn." He finished his letter with a few suggestions of initiatives which he thought could help to clarify the circumstances of the

---

[952] ADA TVP, *Biuletyn* 1951: 38 (Oct. 13).

[953] *Ibid.*

[954] *Ibid.*

[955] I did not find confirmation in Joanna Wawrzyniak's book, *ZBOWiD i pamięć drugiej wojny światowej 1949–1969* (Warszawa: Wydawnictwo Trio and Fundacja "Historia i Kultura", 2009) that Janusz Wardecki's letter reached the management of ZBoWiD and was discussed. In view of the political situation at the time, his appeal had no chance of being seriously considered in 1951. However, Wawrzyniak writes about another anonymous letter sent to ZBoWiD in the mid-sixties: "Mr. Rusinek, As a regular reader of *Życie Warszawy* I have again been lucky to see your name there. As Secretary of ZBoWiD, you will no doubt be speaking on the Nazi German crimes. You have said that one of the subjects you will be bringing up at the Congress will be the question of reparations. According to you those murdered at Katyn were victims of the Nazi Germans. So why have you never mentioned them in this context? One of the delegations attending will be a group representing the fraternal organization from the Soviet Union. Perhaps their presence will remind you about the Polish officers murdered in Katyn?" (Wawrzyniak, 282).

atrocity. "Besides, you Fighters should set up a Committee to identify those guilty of the Katyn atrocity. The Nuremberg Trial did not discover the names of these criminals, even though it named the criminals guilty of other atrocities. Ask the Polish–Soviet Friendship Society, which has close relations with the Soviet Union, to help you on this matter. The Soviet Union, a permanent member of the United Nations, could bring the matter up on an international forum. The atrocity cannot go unpunished, otherwise we will go down in history suspected of deliberately hushing it up and bereft of the sense of national dignity which should be a cherished symbol of great nations."[956]

What is striking about this letter are its forthright questions and hypotheses. Reading between the lines we see that Janusz Wardecki suggested, albeit clearly enough, that the Soviets were guilty of the Katyn atrocity. What made him do it? Surely not just to get an explanation of the backdrop to the crime. There must have been other reasons which made him brave enough to do this. Often a major motive behind such behavior is a family relationship. There is a 2nd Lt. Tadeusz Wardecki, an officer of the reserve forces (b. 1912) on the list of victims of the Soviet atrocity committed at Starobielsk in 1940;[957] and a Stanisław Wardecki (b. 1906) in the Register of the Polish Military Cemetery at Katyn.[958] Maybe this was just a pure coincidence, but on the other hand it is more likely there was a close family relationship (father and son, or perhaps brothers) at work here. This is what happened later, in a letter addressed to *Fala 56*.

In 1957 the Warsaw studio of Polish Radio broadcast a program in its series on the Warsaw Uprising, giving an opportunity for a discussion on the victims of World War 2. One of the letters to the editor concerned Katyn. "We commemorate the Soviet soldiers who fell on our territory, and we look after their graves," it said. "In many lands there are memorial on the graves of our soldiers, and the local people put up monuments and pay tribute to their memory. Well over ten thousand of Poland's best sons died at Katyn. Couldn't we make an effort to have them commemorated and put up at least a modest monument

---

[956] ADA TVP, *Biuletyn* 1951: 38 (Oct.13)

[957] Tucholski, *Mord w Katyniu*, 507.

[958] *Katyń. Księga Cmentarna Polskiego Cmentarza Wojennego*, ed. M. Tarczyński (Warszawa: Rada Ochrony Pamięci Walk i Męczeństwa, 2000), 669. "Wardecki" is not a very common Polish surname [translator's note].

on the site? If the Soviet Union has not done this yet, then let's pay a tribute to them in some other way."[959] The writer of this letter, Zofia Felicka of Jabłonna near Warsaw, signed it with her name and surname, writing that she was the widow of one of the Katyn victims. There is a Lieut. Stanisław Felicki (b. 1892) on the Katyn list, in the Kozielsk section. Lieut. Felicki was an infantry officer who served in the Eighth Region of the Toruń Corps.[960] Another publication provides the key information relevant to the case: Stanisław Felicki was the husband of Zofia née Zielnik, and the father of three children.[961] There is another individual with the same surname, a Lieut. Włodzimierz Felicki (b. 1891 as the son of Stanisław, a doctor from Greater Poland) on the list of Polish citizens held in Soviet captivity. In November 1940, once the NKVD had identified his real personal data, they transferred him from their camp at Równe (now Rivne, Ukraine) to Kozielsk.[962] But since this Felicki survived the spring of 1940, it is obvious that the Felicki in Zofia Felicka's letter was Stanisław Felicki. Another Katyn widow, Paulina Cieszkowska from Tarnów, wrote to *Fala 56* on the same matter, referring to Nikita Khrushchev's visit to Poland in 1959 to mark the fifteenth anniversary of the foundation of the People's Republic of Poland. "In his speech Mr. Khrushchev said, 'I don't want to be disrespectful to your religious feelings, but your beggar priests in black cassocks promise you heaven, while I'm promising you paradise on earth,' etc. I ask *Fala 56* – did he mean the same sort of paradise as Katyn, which is where my husband was killed?"[963] We have not as yet managed to find the name of Paulina Cieszkowska's husband on any of the lists of Soviet crimes committed in the spring of 1940, but since she signed her letter with her name and surname it is reasonable to assume she must have been certain her husband was killed in one of the NKVD atrocities.

In Poland the incidents of 1956 that occurred at home and the political thaw in the Soviet Union following the Twentieth Congress of the

---

[959] ADA TVP, *Biuletyn* 1957: 55 (Aug. 9).

[960] Tucholski, *Mord w Katyniu*, 100.

[961] *Katyń. Księga Cmentarna Polskiego Cmentarza Wojennego*, 135.

[962] *Katyń. Dokumenty zbrodni*, vol. 3: *Losy ocalałych lipiec 1940 – marzec 1943*, W. Materski et al., eds., (Warszawa: Naczelna Dyrekcja Archiwów Państwowych and Trio, 2001), 219.

[963] ADA TVP, *Biuletyn* 1959: 42 (Aug.).

Communist Party generally invigorated the public debate on Soviet issues, albeit only for a short spell. Its main theme was settling the account with Stalinism and matters involving the Soviet ruling class. But it also addressed things which happened during the War to Poles in the Soviet Union and their postwar fate. In 1957 an anonymous listener of *Fala 56* from the Jasło area of Sub-Carpathia sent in a letter asking which way the changes were going in the Communist Party of the Soviet Union, and who was culpable for the "Katyn murders."[964] Some members of KIK (the Catholic Intelligentsia Club) from Ziębice in Lower Silesia commented on a statement Khrushchev made in Prague, that currently Soviet–Polish relations were "excellent; all the incidents that had happened in the past were like a pimple on your face which had disappeared and was gone for good."[965] They went on to remark that Khrushchev's statement meant that Poland was "still in the Russian sack."[966] Only a few passages from this letter were published in the bulletin, so we shall have to speculate that the members of KIK who wrote it could perhaps have wanted to know more about the particulars of matters like Poles held in the Soviet gulags and Katyn.

In the late fall of 1961 the Katyn problem again surfaced in the bulletin published by the letters office of the Polish Radio Committee. We may conjecture that the subject again became current in connection with the Twenty-Second Congress of the Communist Party of the Soviet Union. "A Polish man from Warsaw" wrote in an anonymous letter to *Fala 56*, "Dear *Fala*, please get the name of the street changed from ulica Stalingradzka (Stalingrad Street) to ulica Ofiar Katynia (Katyn Victims' Street). Let it be the Polish reflection of the resolutions of the Twenty-Second Congress – oh, and get rid of Stalin from the name of the Palace [of Culture]. What we're seeing here is a return of 'Stalinism.' For instance, Gen. 'Gas-Pipe' Witaszewski [nicknamed 'Gas-Pipe' for saying revisionists should be 'thrashed with side-batons,' popularly known in Poland as 'gas-pipes'] has come back from Czechoslovakia and he's doing business in the Central Committee."[967] Another letter writer from Przemyśl

---

[964] ADA TVP, *Biuletyn* 1957: 54 (Jul. 30).

[965] *Ibid.*

[966] *Ibid.*

[967] ADA TVP, *Biuletyn* 1961: 27 (Nov. 21).

who called himself a 'Regular Listener' suggested a monument should be built for the victims of Katyn. "If the time has come for you to be saying the truth about Stalin," he wrote, "perhaps we could finally hear some specifics about Katyn. We are putting up monuments for Hitler's victims. Why have we not yet had a memorial erected to commemorate the victims of Katyn? There'll be no trouble with getting the money for it. Polish society will not be tight-fisted."[968] A month later (December 1961) the editors of *Fala 56* received more letters (unfortunately we don't know exactly how many) asking whether Nikita Khrushchev had put Katyn on the list of Stalin's crimes. The radio station did not answer this question.

The last sizeable batch of letters to the editor of *Fala 56* referring to the Katyn atrocity arrived in 1964. Its origins were connected with the activities of Radio Free Europe. In February and March of 1964 Radio Free Europe broadcast a series of programs on the thousands of Poles who has been imprisoned in Soviet gulags, and quite naturally the listeners of *Fala 56* took up the Katyn issue. One wrote, "I agree that war criminals should be prosecuted, and that's why I want you to explain to me this business with Katyn."[969] Another, "Anonymous from Warsaw," made an appeal in the same spirit: "Dear *Fala 56*, have you ever heard of Katyn? How many Polish people were murdered there? *Fala 56*, let my opinion be added to the campaign to bring in and prosecute war criminals."[970] In view of the content of these and other similar letters to the editors of *Fala 56*, we may assume that they were a response to an appeal made by Radio Free Europe, especially as the incidence of calls for the prosecution of war criminals in letters sent to *Fala 56* was rising. Yet another letter said, "In my opinion, and of hundreds of thousands of Polish people, all the war criminals should be wanted men, pursued and rounded up for as long as it takes the generation of murderers to die out of old age. For the Nazi German criminal hiding away to get no peace nor feel safe [for the rest of his life]. (...) That's one side of the medal. And now, Dear *Fala 56*, I'll come on to the other side. Why hasn't a single one of those Nazi war criminals who took part in the Katyn atrocity been

---

[968] *Ibid.*

[969] ADA TVP, *Biuletyn Wewnętrzny* 1965: 173 (Aug.)

[970] *Ibid.*

apprehended? Why is the Polish Memorial Committee doing nothing to look after the graves of those victims, why don't our radio and papers ever seem to want to speak to the nation about it? What's behind it all? We simple country folk know something about it, too. When the anniversary of the Battle of Monte Casino comes up, our ambassadors in Italy and Britain are there to lay a wreath. Same with Majdanek and Auschwitz. So, *Fala 56*, we're putting the question yet again, and we want an answer from you as soon as possible, for instance next Sunday."[971] Another letter arrived from an anonymous listener in Włodawa, saying that the blame for the Katyn murders should not be pinned on Stalin alone. "Dear *Fala 56*, let's be fair – the Stalinists were also enemies of the people of Poland. I remember how in Kozelsk they segregated the officers from the rank-and-file, whom they concentrated in another camp. And as they were saying good-bye the officers told the men that they would never see each other again. You can't just put all the blame on the Stalin cult. The commandants of the camps should be found and punished just like the Nazis are being punished, under the auspices of UN troops. The files of all the Poles who went missing in the Soviet Union can be found in Moscow archives. There are still Polish people in the gulags today; they want to come home, but our ambassador is too scared to do anything about it."[972]

We may sum up by saying that the aim of the propaganda the Communists conducted in Poland from 1945 on regarding the Katyn atrocity was to definitively erase Soviet culpability for the death of thousands of soldiers from the collective memory of Polish society. This was the purpose numerous books, articles in the press, and the activities of the censorship office were to serve, and it was coupled with a prohibition on the import of publications which presented the issue in any light other than the Communist version. In a way the operations of *Fala 49* and *Fala 56* were a sort of test to see how far these measures had succeeded, if at all. That is how I would explain Katyn cropping up now and again in these popular radio broadcasts. The Communist authorities were interested in collecting information to show that the people of Poland were confused about Katyn – in two minds whether the blame should be put on the Germans, or on the Russians. From the point of view of the propagandists

---

[971] *Ibid.*

[972] *Ibid.*

serving the People's Republic this sort of uncertainty seemed the best option. Every doubt, every ambiguity promised a better situation in the future. This aspect of the problem received frequent attention in the numerous publications (books, scholarly papers, articles, and reviews) Józef Mackiewicz wrote on Katyn.

Perhaps this is why the editors of the bulletin published a few of the letters whose authors were absolutely certain the Germans were culpable for the Katyn atrocity. Jan Ejgierd of Jelenia Góra made the following appeal: "Why isn't the Nazi German crime of Katyn – that mass grave of murdered Polish officers and men – being mentioned in the campaign against the Fascist perpetrators of genocide? A few days ago I read Bolesław Wójcicki's book *Prawda o Katyniu* (published in 1952). The book gives quite a full and convincing account of many details of how the German Fascists committed the Katyn murders and the evidence which they later fabricated, which only proves they were the real culprits. So why are neither the Polish government nor the public organizations doing anything about that mass grave, to save others the embarrassment, in the eyes of other nations and in their own eyes, for the negligence and sluggishness over the respect due to war victims?"[973]

An anonymous listener from Teresin wrote in with the following remark: "The German parliament in Bonn has decided under pressure from public opinion that it will continue to prosecute [those who committed] Nazi war crimes. And that's fair. My colleagues tell me that at Katyn the criminals were the Bolsheviks. I don't know about that – I wasn't there. Often you hear that such and such criminals from Auschwitz, Majdanek, Treblinka etc. have been caught and brought to justice. But there's silence over the mass graves of Katyn. Yet silence speaks volumes."[974]

Following the opinion of specialists working on the social history of the People's Republic of Poland, I would qualify the bulletins published by the letter office of the Polish Radio Committee as an important source also for Poland's political history after 1949, as regards questions such as public opinion and the general mood in the country. Yet there is something about the occurrence of the Katyn problem in the bulletin itself and on the air in the *Fala 49* and

---

[973] *Ibid.*

[974] *Ibid.*

56 broadcasts that leaves me with a sense of incompleteness. Although the correspondence on Katyn has been published, there are still two points to be made. Those letters on which the writer put his real name and surname and which attributed the blame for Katyn to the Soviets were usually the work of individuals who had grown desperate after years of waiting for their dear ones and the lack of an answer as to what had happened to them during the War. On the other hand those of the signed letters which made the Germans culpable tended to be an outcome of the endeavor to cover up the truth about the atrocity. Their writers, many of whom gave their address as well as their real name, most certainly expected a response and a reward from the Communist authorities.

While the bulletins, which were intended for a selected few in the topmost echelons of the Communist establishment, from time to time published letters on Katyn in an original version patently inadmissible from the point of view of the Polish and Soviet authorities, there was no discussion on the details of such matters in the radio broadcasts and the accompanying press articles and media commentary on current affairs. We could even say that the position taken up by the media became even more ossified. The most characteristic example of this is provided by an article by Stanisław Brodzki entitled 'Mordercy tańczą na grobach ofiar' (The murderers are dancing on the victims' graves). Brodzki was commenting in a series of Voice of America broadcasts, but he failed to mention that they triggered a fairly broad exchange of opinions on Katyn on Polish Radio, for instance in the popular program *Fala 49*. He took up a stance on the results published by the Madden Committee, but failed to mention its chairman's name. Brodzki's report was full of congressmen sympathetic to Hitler, Goebbelsian propaganda, and hooded witnesses testifying before the Committee, which only raised general laughter. His opinion of the Frankfurt round of witnesses' testimonies was that those who were invited to give evidence were "the very perpetrators of the Katyn murders and their buddies who had committed crimes elsewhere. The latter issued testimonials for the former, calling them gentle as lambs."[975] He threw in a remark that the bullets lodged

---

[975] S. Brodzki, 'Mordercy tańczą na grobach ofiar (Z komentarzy Polskiego Radia),' *Radio i Świat* 1952: 20 (May 18), 1. Brodzki had a prolific CV as a card-carrying Communist: he had been an activist of the Communist youth organization ZMP in prewar Kraków. During the War he had lived in Switzerland, Mozambique, and Palestine. In 1946–1947 he was the

in the bodies of the victims were German, but he never bothered to investigate this point. Listeners and readers wanted concrete, reliable information and arguments which would make the Communist version of the Katyn atrocity incontrovertible, but they got no satisfactory answer.

Polish press attaché in Jerusalem. He returned home in 1948, and ran the ideological depart-ment in *Głos Ludu* and *Trybuna Ludu*. J. Pietrzak, 'Działalność komunistów wśród polskiego wychodźstwa na Bliskim Wschodzie w świetle materiałów kontrwywiadu Polskich Sił Zbro-jnych (1944),' *Dzieje Najnowsze* 2006: 3, 126.

POSTSCRIPT.
WITNESSES AND WITNESS

For the Katyn atrocity we have no fewer than dozens of witnesses, and dozens of testimonies of diverse import and value. The most important in terms of significance are the accounts and recollections of those who actually participated in the events. I have in mind those who were lucky enough to be spared just before the execution. For various reasons the Soviets selected them and saved their lives. This group amounts to about 400 persons from the three camps, Kozelsk, Ostashkov, and Starobielsk. They were undoubtedly first-hand witnesses – eyewitnesses providing the key evidence for Soviet culpability. Next in order of importance I would put the comments and objective conclusions drawn by the observers who happened to see the site of the Soviet atrocity in April and May 1943, as members of the delegations taken there by the Germans. There were hundreds of them, important witnesses with detailed knowledge on the site, and medical experts, such as those from the International Medical Commission, who provided forensic evidence. Perhaps the key figures in this group were the journalists for the papers and radio, and the writers. On their return home they did what the Germans expected of them – spreading news of the atrocity throughout occupied Europe, naming the perpetrators, and presenting hard evidence of Soviet culpability on the basis of documents found on the bodies and the forensic results (especially the pioneering work done by the Hungarian pathologist Professor Ferenc Orsós, which dated the crime to the spring of 1940). Quite obviously, in the reptile press published in the GG Katyn was front-page news – a planned job for German propaganda, addressed in the first place to the families of identified Katyn victims and to all the Polish people. Katyn was also front-page news in the German press published in the Third Reich, with extensive details of the time and scale of the atrocity. Katyn was given extensive coverage in the press of other countries, especially in Paris, which was certainly no coincidence. Paris was the German-occupied city nearest London, and the British did not trust the German story. To put it briefly, in 1943 newspaper reports on the Katyn atrocity appeared in virtually the whole of Europe, from Wilno and Lwów to Madrid and Lisbon. There was yet another important group of witnesses and testimonials – the members of the Technical Commission who observed the site on behalf of the Polish Red Cross under the leadership of Dr. Marian Wodziński, who later compiled his invaluable Katyn report, the key document for the determination of the circumstances in which the victims of Katyn died.

The Polish government in London collected all the documents on Katyn successively sent in. It accumulated the reports arriving from units of the Polish Underground State, such as the testimonials of witnesses who had been to the site in 1943, and the articles which appeared in the reptile press. In this case we have to treat the reptile publications as detailed and trustworthy. This applies to the items published by Władysław Kawecki and the interview and commentary given by Jan Emil Skiwski and Józef Mackiewicz.

I would also attach considerable significance to those witnesses, many of them members of the Polish armed forces, who on their release from Soviet gulags started a search for their comrades-in-arms of 1939. The mission carried out by one such searcher, Capt. Józef Czapski, brought important findings. Pretty soon recollections, accounts, and documents relating to Kozelsk, Ostashkov, and Starobielsk, began to reach the Polish exiled authorities in London, though in 1941 and 1942 the authors of these testimonials were still not quite sure of what had happened to those officers who failed to report for duty in the Polish forces following the Sikorski–Mayski agreement. Several hypotheses were put forward. Yet few dared to speculate on the most tragic outcome – that the Soviets had executed these officers. The events of the spring of 1943 changed the situation. The first work based on evidence recording the fate of Polish army personnel in Soviet captivity started with the backing of the Polish authorities. The principal publication was undoubtedly *Fakty i dokumenty dotyczące polskich jeńców pojmanych w ZSRS podczas kampanii 1939 roku*, a document recording the facts and written records on Polish POWs held in the Soviet Union in the aftermath of the September '39 campaign. It was compiled by a team of researchers led by Dr. Wiktor Sukiennicki, a prewar lecturer at the Stephen Báthory University at Wilno. Another item, *Masowe morderstwo polskich jeńców wojennych w Katyniu*, published in London in 1946, was on the victims of Kozelsk, the method of execution, the scale of the atrocity, and – most importantly – it dated the time of their death to the spring of 1940. Both items were published in an English version as well.

There were also articles in the press published alongside the books and brochures. Personal recollections of life in Kozelsk were published by Władysław Jan Furtek, Tadeusz Felsztyn, Stanisław Lubodziecki, Jerzy Grobicki, Witold Ogniewicz, and Jerzy Lebiedziewski, the last-mentioned being the pseudonym of Stanisław Swianiewicz, whose family was in Poland. Two Second Corps officers, Stanisław Starzewski and Kazimierz Zamorski, showed a great deal of commitment to this kind of activity. They were co-authors of a book entitled *Sprawiedliwość sowiecka* (Soviet Justice), using the pen-names Piotr Zwierniak and Sylwester Mora. After the War, having joined the Second Corps, Ferdynand Goetel, a wanted man in Communist Poland, made a record of the account given by Ivan Krivozertsov, an eyewitness who was on the site of crime in the spring of 1940 and who went into hiding using the alias Michał Łoboda. The peak achievement in the publications was the issue of the book *Zbrodnia katyńska w świetle dokumentów* (first edition London: Gryf, 1948; English edition, *The Crime of Katyn*, London: Polish Cultural Foundation, 1965), with a foreword by Gen. Anders. The authorship of the book's first edition was claimed by two contenders for the honor: the writer Józef Mackiewicz, and Dr. Zdzisław Stahl, a Second Corps officer. The second and later editions no longer gave Mackiewicz as its joint author. Not much later Mackiewicz published his own book on Katyn in a German version.

In this brief summary I am skipping the group of licensed witnesses, brought to the site in January 1944 by the Soviets to cover up their crime. Nonetheless, the incident itself cannot be passed over in silence, because a few of them – locals of Katyn and Smolensk who had not managed to flee before the Red Army and NKVD entered the area – had earlier given testimony which cleared the Germans of culpability. In 1944, under duress from the NKVD and fearing for their lives, they changed their statements and now accused the Germans of the atrocity, saying that it was committed in the fall of 1941. A few British and American journalists published the Soviet lore on Katyn in their respective countries. They were joined by communist journalists. One Polish card-carrying Communist, the journalist Jerzy Borejsza, was a member of the Soviet delegation in 1944, and started his active involvement in broadcasting the lies about Katyn when he was still in the Soviet Union. Subsequently his story and the version cooked up for the Kremlin by the NKVD were disseminated by Communists in occupied Poland. The propaganda machine spread lies on Katyn to soldiers in the Polish army set up in the Soviet Union by Stalin and Polish Communists. Those Poles who were late and did not make it to Gen. Anders' army, or who never tried to make it, got the Soviet version. Anyone who challenged it risked being sent to the gulags or death. Soviet-appointed General Zygmunt Berling and his close associates always blamed the Germans whenever they got the chance to mention Katyn.

When the War was over in 1945 witnesses in Poland were again facing problems over their statements on Katyn. The reason was obvious. The Communists now started making preparations for a Katyn trial, following guidelines from the Kremlin. The Soviets gave them detailed instructions how to make use of witnesses and the findings of the Burdenko Commission. Naturally the final verdict was predetermined, and everyone knew it. The trial would be a pure formality. All the decisions had been made much earlier, definitely not in 1944 when the Red Army entered the Smolensk area. The Soviet point of view had been well-known since the spring of 1943, and endorsed by developments in Polish–Soviet relations, in particular by Stalin's breaking off of diplomatic relations with the Polish government when its prime minister, Gen. Sikorski, officially demanded a prompt International Red Cross investigation into the circumstances of the Katyn atrocity. The prosecution service of a now Sovietized Poland, in particular a team headed by Dr. Roman Martini, collected the available documents and decided to find the witnesses who had seen Katyn in 1943. The tactics were simple enough – to coerce all those whom the Communist services managed to detain to revoke the statements they had made earlier on the crime, in other words to disavow the German story of what had happened. Their plan was successful to a certain extent. Only a dozen or so of the witnesses who had made public statements in 1943 on Soviet culpability changed their minds in 1945. Professors František Hájek and Marko Markov, two of the physicians who had examined the bodies in 1943, did likewise and changed their earlier declarations under duress from the security services of their respective countries, Czechoslovakia and Bulgaria, which the Soviets had taken over.

The special services of Poland managed to intimidate some of the medical witnesses still in the country, Drs. Hieronim Bartoszewski, Edward Grodzki, and Adam Szebesta, and got them to make new statements. They also got Gen. Stefan Mossor to write public declarations; one of his articles obtained under duress was 'Palmiry – Katyń,' which appeared in the army magazine *Polska Zbrojna* in 1946. All of these witnesses now said that the atrocity had been committed by the Germans in the fall of 1941. A warrant for the arrest of Dr. Marian Wodziński proved ineffective. For the Ministry of Public Security, Prosecutor Martini, and the Communist propagandists Dr. Wodziński must have been one of the chief witnesses. Getting him to take part in the 1945 propaganda campaign and appear in court in the prospective Katyn trial would have been a considerable success for the Soviets. But the fact that he managed to flee the country and get to England saved him from their reprisals and most probably also from enforced participation in the lies about Katyn. Another witness lucky enough to escape from under the eye of the Communists was Kazimierz Skarżyński. Fearing imprisonment, after his preliminary interrogation he managed to leave Poland illegally and once in exile compiled a detailed report on what he had seen in Katyn in 1943. Three of the 1943 Katyn observers, Dr. Konrad Orzechowski, Stanisław Kłosowicz a competitor in the Amsterdam Olympics of 1928, and Bolesław Smektała, were imprisoned for a time by the Soviets, who put them in NKVD detention centers, such as the Rembertów camp, and subsequently deported all three to the Soviet Union, where they were held for over a year. Mikołaj Marczyk and Hieronim Majewski, blue-collar workers from the GG and Wartheland who saw Katyn in 1943, later paid for the experience in Communist Polish jails. Franciszek Prochownik, a blue-collar witness from Kraków, was terrorized and kept under surveillance for several years.

Katyn witnesses had an important part to play yet again in 1946 before the Nuremberg Tribunal, in the part of the trial which, on the initiative of Moscow's prosecution officers, was to clear the Soviet Union of culpability for Katyn. Prosecutor Col. Yuri Pokrovski put the following point on the list of charges: "The murder of 11 thousand Polish officers held as POWs, committed in September 1941 in Katyn Forest near Smolensk." It was obvious what he wanted. The wording was brief, but the allegation was quite clear: by putting a date to the atrocity the Soviets were accusing the Germans. They had endorsed a figure of 11 thousand for the number of victims, and had notified all the countries within their sphere of influence that this was the "right" figure. Not anticipating a debacle, the Soviet prosecutor called the crime an act of genocide. Not surprisingly, the defense lawyers representing Germany attached a considerable amount of importance to the Katyn charge, collected as much evidence as possible, and interviewed as many witnesses as they could. Aware of the complexity of the issue and absolutely sure of the course developments had taken in the spring of 1940, they appointed Col. Friedrich Ahrens of the Wehrmacht's 537th Communications Regiment as their chief witness. Earlier the Soviets had accused Ahrens of having been the commanding officer of the squad which carried out the Katyn executions. It was an evident sham, since Ahrens was not the commander of his unit, and he was elsewhere at the alleged time of the atrocity. The witnesses the Soviets put up turned out to be completely unreliable and their statements were muddled. For the British and American prosecutors the matter was absolutely clear. Moreover, they had information supplied by the Polish government-in-exile. Henry Szymanski, an American officer with Polish roots who had investigated the Katyn question during the War when he was in the Soviet Union, serving as a diplomat in Moscow, liaised between the Polish exiles and the American prosecutors. Szymanski was very well informed on the matter. The Polish émigré authorities considered the proceedings a very important event and followed the developments very closely. This is why, I believe, they passed on their materials unofficially, not only to the British and American committees at Nuremberg, but also to the German defense. So it was not hard to guess what the final outcome at Nuremberg on Katyn would be. The Soviets failed to prove their case against the Germans over Katyn, even though they tried very hard. In the final verdict issued by the International Military Tribunal on September 30, 1946, Katyn was not mentioned at all. Nonetheless, the silence spoke volumes, for if it wasn't the Germans, then who was it? The answer was perfectly clear. It was the Soviets.

In the 1950s, during the Korean war, Katyn was again a matter for public discussion in connection with the Madden Committee. The congressmen who joined this Committee decided to conduct a public inquiry into the atrocity and show their countrymen that the origins of the Communist crimes of 1950–1951 went back to the Soviet Union in the war years. The Polish émigré community treated the establishment of the Committee as the response they had wanted to the appeal they had made just after the end of the War. Gen. Anders said, "A committee set up by the US Congress to investigate the Katyn atrocity would answer the appeal for justice I had the honor to make on behalf of and in accordance with the wishes of the whole of Polish society, especially Polish soldiers, who stand on the side of the free world." The Madden Committee accomplished a gigantic task. In its sessions held in the USA, Britain, and West Germany it heard over 280 witnesses, including scores of Polish witnesses (e.g. Gen. Jerzy Wołkowicki, Lt. Władysław Furtek, Władysław Cichy, Col. Stanisław Lubodziecki, Stanisław Swianiewicz, Józef Romanowski, Maj. Adam Moszyński, Lt.-Col. Tadeusz Felsztyn, Capt. Eugeniusz Lubomirski, 2nd Lt. Zbigniew Rowiński, Ferdynand Goetel, Kazimierz Skarżyński, Stanisław Zamoyski, Józef Garliński, Józef Mackiewicz, Józef Czapski, Dr. Zdzisław Stahl, Gen. Władysław Anders, Gen. Tadeusz Bór–Komorowski, and Stanisław Mikołajczyk). Władysław Kawecki, chief editor of the reptile paper *Gazeta Krakowska*, delivered his testimony at the Committee's Frankfurt session. Other important witnesses who appeared before the Committee included members of the International Medical Commission, Ferenc Orsós, Helge Tramsen, and François Naville, who stood by their original statement that the atrocity had been committed by the Soviets. Lt.-Col. John H. Van Vliet Jr., an American officer held as a POW by the Germans during the War who wrote a report on what he had seen at Katyn, also testified before the Committee.

While the Madden Committee was conducting its inquiry the Communist propaganda machine in Poland, Bulgaria, Czechoslovakia, and the Soviet Union tried to discredit its work by presenting the witnesses who had been coerced by the Polish Ministry of Public Security or Soviet agents to change their statements and propagate their new opinion on Katyn. In return for a withdrawal of the threat of imprisonment hanging over them, these people now upheld the Soviet story of Katyn. To amplify the effect, the new statements these converted witnesses made were published in tandem, for instance interviews and articles by František Hájek and Adam Szebesta appeared side by side of each other. In addition, the Soviets asked why it had taken the Americans so long to raise the subject of Katyn, why they had not done so before 1951–1952, pointing out quite rightly that 1944, following the publication of the Burdenko Report, was the right time to have protested and challenged its findings. They regarded an inquiry carried out in the early '50s irrelevant and dismissed it as untrustworthy. For it was not until the early 1950s that it became evident that British and American procrastination and timidity to stand up to the Soviets over Katyn, and the fact that they had left the Polish government-in-exile to its fate, had been a grave political mistake.

LIST OF ABBREVIATIONS
AND GLOSSARY OF TERMS

AK   *Armia Krajowa* – the Home Army, the main Polish military and civilian resistance organization during World War 2

AL   *Armia Ludowa* – the People's Army, the official name of the army of People's Poland

CIC   the United States Counter Intelligence Corps

GG   the *Generalgouvernement*, the territorial unit established by Nazi Germany on Polish lands following the German invasion in September 1939. It was governed and administered by Germans, headed by Hans Frank as Governor-General.

The Government Delegation for Poland (*Delegatura Rządu na Kraj*) – the secret administrative authority on the territory of occupied Poland during World War 2 representing the Polish government-in-exile, and empowered to implement the government's policies, acting through the Delegate for Poland, his subordinates, and the Regional Delegations.

KIK   *Klub Inteligencji Katolickiej* – the Catholic Inteligenstia Club

KPP   *Komunistyczna Partia Polski* – the Communist Party of Poland, established in 1918 and disbanded by the Comintern in 1938; illegal in the Second Republic of Poland as of 1919 because it refused to recognize Polish independence.

MO   *Milicja Obywatelska* – **the Citizens' Police Force** – the police force of the People's Republic of Poland

NKVD   *Narodnyy Komissariat Vnutrennikh Del* – **the People's Commissariat (later Ministry) for Internal Affairs**, the internal ministry (or secret police) of the Soviet Union

OPW   *Obóz Polski Walczącej* – **the Fighting Poland Movement**, a Polish resistance group during World War 2

The People's Republic of Poland (also the Polish People's Republic) – Polish acronym **PRL** – the Communist state of Poland under Soviet tutelage, 1944–1989

PAP   *Polska Agencja Prasowa* – **the Polish Press Agency** (of People's Poland)

PAT   *Polska Agencja Telegraficzna* – **the** (prewar) **Polish Telegraphic Agency**

PKWN   *Polski Komitet Wyzwolenia Narodowego* – **the Polish Committee of National Liberation**, the Communist organization which established the Soviet-installed government of People's Poland in the summer of 1944

The Polish Council to Aid Jews (*Rada Pomocy Żydom*, aka Żegota) – a secret organization in occupied Poland during World War 2 subject to the authority of the Polish government-in-exile, set up to provide various forms of aid and life-saving assistance for Jews, such as arranging safe havens for Jewish children by placing them in non-Jewish families, foster homes, and Catholic convents, issuing false IDs to Jewish people etc.

POW   prisoner-of-war

PPR   **PPR – Polska Partia Robotnicza – the Polish Workers' Party**, a Communist Party founded in occupied Warsaw by Polish Communists who arrived from the Soviet Union; predecessor of the PZPR

PPS   *Polska Partia Socjalistyczna* – **the Polish Socialist Party** – the largest non-communist socialist party in Poland, founded in 1892; in 1948 the Communist authorities forcibly amalgamated the PPS with the PPR, creating the PZPR

PPS-WRN   *Polska Partia Socjalistyczna „Wolność Równość Niepodległość"* **– The "Freedom – Equality – Independence" Polish Socialist Party** – a socialist political organization derived from the prewar PPS operating clandestinely in occupied Poland during World War 2. After the War some of its members continued (anti-communist) undercover operations, risking repressive measures

PRW NiD *Polski Ruch Wolnościowy „Niepodległość i Demokracja"* – **the Polish Freedom Movement Independence and Democracy**, a Polish socialist organization founded in February 1945 in exile in London

PSL *Polskie Stronnictwo Ludowe* – **The Polish Peasants' Party**, aka **The Polish People's Party**, a political party traditionally associated with Poland's rural inhabitants, founded in 1895 and operating in a number of factions or offshoots. The PSL was the only party permitted to put up candidates in opposition to the Communists in the 1947 general election which was one of the official conditions made at the Yalta Conference for the postwar Polish State de facto put under Soviet tutelage to ensue "democracy". The Communists rigged the election, and the PSL was granted a disproportionately low number of seats in parliament in comparison with the number of votes actually cast for it. In 1949 the Communists delegalized the PSL; its leader, Stanisław Mikołajczyk, was forced to flee, and many of its members and activists were murdered or imprisoned.

The Polish Underground State – *Polskie Państwo Podziemne* (**PPP**) – the secret network of Polish state institutions operating clandestinely in occupied Poland during World War 2 subject to the authority of the Polish government-in-exile abroad (first in France, and later in Great Britain)

PZPR *Polska Zjednoczona Partia Robotnicza* – **The Polish United Workers' Party**, the ruling Communist Party in the People's Republic of Poland, created in 1948 by the enforced amalgamation of the PSL with the PPR

Reichsgau Wartheland – see *Wartheland*

RGO *Rada Główna Opiekuńcza* – **the Central Welfare Council**, the only Polish charity organization officially recognized by the Nazi German authorities in the Generalgouvernement (viz. German-occupied Poland during World War 2)

SD *Stronnictwo Demokratyczne* – **the Democratic Party**, a Polish prewar political (centrist) organization

SKSS *Stołeczny Komitet Samopomocy Społecznej* – **the Warsaw Social Self-Care Committee**, a welfare organization operating in German-occupied Warsaw during World War 2 (1939–1941)

375

SN   *Stronnictwo Narodowe* – **the National Party**, a nationalist political party operating in Poland from 1928, and clandestinely in Poland from the outbreak of the War until 1947, continuing its activities later in exile

SP   *Stronnictwo Pracy* – **the Labor Party**, a political (Christian democratic) party operating in prewar Poland and clandestinely after the outbreak of World War 2

SWAP   **Stowarzyszenie Weteranów Armii Polskiej** – the Polish Army Veterans of America

TPPR   *Towarzystwo Przyjaźni Polsko-Radzieckiej* – **The Polish-Soviet Friendship Society**, a political association in People's Poland, most of its activities were propaganda events promoting and celebrating the Soviet Union

TRJN   **Tymczasowy Rząd Jedności Narodowej – the Provisional Government of National Unity**, the coalition government installed in Poland in 1945, following the Soviet severance of diplomatic relations with the Polish government-in-exile and on the grounds of an agreement reached at Yalta between the Western Allies and the Soviet Union on the future of Poland. The coalition consisted of Communists and Mikołajczyk's splinter group of the PSL, but in reality the Communists were the dominant force

Wartheland   the name the Germans applied to the western territories of prewar Poland (viz. the region of Greater Poland) which they incorporated directly into the German Third Reich after they invaded Poland in September 1939

USSR   **Union of Soviet Socialist Republics**, Soviet Russia

WSS   *Wojskowy Sąd Specjalny* – **The Special Military Court**, the clandestine judiciary system operated by the authorities of the Polish Underground State during World War 2 in occupied Poland to try and punish individuals guilty of offenses against the Polish Nation (viz. various types of collaboration with the occupying powers). There were three kinds of sentence: a declaration of infamy, flogging, and death

WSW   *Wojskowe Służby Wewnętrzne* – **the Internal Military Service**, the military police force of Communist Poland

ZBOWiD   **Związek Bojowników o Wolność i Demokrację – The Society of Fighters for Freedom and Democracy**, the officially approved war veterans' association in People's Poland

ZMP   *Związek Młodzieży Polskiej* – **Union of Polish Youth** – the official Communist youth organization in People's Poland

ZPP   *Związek Patriotów Polskich* – **Union of Polish Patriots**, a group of Polish Communists living in the Soviet Union during World War Two

ZWZ   *Związek Walki Zbrojnej* – **Union of Armed Struggle**, a resistance organization in occupied Poland during World War 2, the predecessor of the Home Army

ZZLP   *Związek Zawodowy Literatów Polskich* – **The Professional Union of Polish Writers**

LIST OF ILLUSTRATIONS

1. A 1943 poster from France (courtesy of Musée de l'histoire vivante, Montreuil). I am grateful to Dr. E. Lafon for making a copy of this poster available to me.
2. Page One of *La Semaine*, May 13, 1943 (courtesy of Musée de l'histoire vivante, Montreuil).
3. Jan Rostafiński (Collection of Dr. Piotr Kardela).
4. Letter from the authorities of the Polish Red Cross inviting Professor Jan Rostafiński to attend the meeting on Katyn, May 1943 (Collection of Dr. Piotr Kardela).
5. Ferdynand Goetel, detail from a 1936 photograph published in the Kraków daily *Ilustrowany Kurier Codzienny*.
6. Letter issued by the prewar Polish court appointing Tadeusz Pragłowski to serve as a forensic expert, August 5, 1939 (Collection of Zofia Pragłowska-Gorczyńska).
7. Tadeusz Pragłowski (Collection of Zofia Pragłowska-Gorczyńska).
8. Letter issued by the postwar Polish court appointing Tadeusz Pragłowski to serve as a forensic expert, June 2, 1945 (Collection of Zofia Pragłowska-Gorczyńska).
9. Warrant for the arrest of Marian Wodziński, July 10, 1945 (AIPN Kraków, sign. no. 303/9).
10. Father Stanisław Jasiński conducting the funeral rites (obsequies) over the graves of Katyn. Photograph published by the Germans in *Nowy Kurier Warszawski*, *Goniec Krakowski*, and other reptile papers issued in the GG.
11. 'The Wedge,' This cartoon by David Low originally appeared in the British satirical magazine *Punch* in 1943, and was reprinted on page 209 of Low's album *Years of Wrath: A Cartoon History 1931–1945* (London: Simon and Schuster, 1946) Digital Library of India Item 2015.89514 https://archive.

378

org/details/in.ernet.dli.2015.89514 I am grateful to Professor T. Szarota for making a copy of this cartoon available to me.

12. Transcript of a letter from Father Kwiatkowski, dated Feb. 23, 1952; marked "Strictly Confidential". Document from the records of the Ministry of Public Security.

13. List of members of Arthur Bliss Lane's committee, the first American committee set up to investigate the Katyn atrocity (AIPN Warsaw, sign. no. 01419/78).

14. A witness (probably Kazimierz Skarżyński) testifying before the Madden Committee; American press photograph, 1952 (AIPN Warsaw, sign. no. 01419/78).

15. An article on Katyn, 'Sedno sprawy' (Heart of the matter), which appeared in 1952 in the Polish periodical *Nowy Świat* published in the USA (AIPN Warsaw, sign. no. 01419/78).

16. Page one of the article on Katyn published in 1952 in the American edition of *Reader's Digest*.

17. An April 1952 article on the annual Katyn memorial events, in *Orzeł Biały*, a Polish émigré paper published in London and registered as *White Eagle*.

18. Title page of the brochure published in 1943 by the Polish Underground State (AIPN Warsaw, sign. no. 0397/496, vol. 3).

19. Józef Sigalin and Jerzy Borejsza (Collection of Andrzej Skalimowski).

20. Józef Sigalin (Collection of Andrzej Skalimowski).

21. Władysław Kawecki (AIPN BU Warsaw, sign. no. 2386/709).

22. 1948 Polish translation of Lieut. Slowenczyk's letter to his wife on Katyn, 1943. A copy of the letter was passed on to a Polish People's Republic agent by someone in the editorial office of *Welt am Abend*. (AIPN Warsaw, sign. no. 01419/78).

23. Władysław Kawecki and his wife. (AIPN Warsaw, sign. no. 2386/709).

24. Władysław Kawecki at the time when the Communist intelligence kept him under surveillance (AIPN Warsaw, sign. no. 2386/709).

25. The second delegation from the GG at Katyn, April 1943. Photograph published by the Germans in *Nowy Kurier Warszawski*, *Goniec Krakowski*, and other reptile papers issued in the GG.

26. Edward Grodzki (Collection of Dr. Mirosław Grodzki)

27. Certificate issued by Col. Antoni Sanojca, for the posthumous conferral of the Home Army Cross on Dr. Grodzki for his work as a Polish Underground State physician in 1939–1945 (Collection of Dr. Mirosław Grodzki).
28. One of the photographs taken by Edward Grodzki at Katyn in April 1943 (Collection of Dr. Mirosław Grodzki).
29. Col. Stefan Mossor in Oflag II E Neubrandenburg. Detail from a photograph in the Mossor family collection.
30. Stefan Mossors's article, 'Palmiry – Katyń' in Polska Zbrojna 1946: 176.
31. Father Tomasz Rusek (AIPN Lublin, sign. no. 15/432).
32. An article in *Nowy Głos Lubelski* on the memorial mass, June 1943 (AIPN Lublin, sign. no. 15/432).
33. Arrest warrant for Jan Emil Skiwski, 1945 (AIPN Kraków, sign. no. 303/9).
34. Arrest warrant for Ferdynand Goetel, 1945 (AIPN Kraków, sign. no. 303/9).
35. Article published in the Kraków paper *Dziennik Polski* (1949: 158) during Skiwski's trial with a headline reading 'Skiwski, The Man Who Was Not Straight'.

BIBLIOGRAPHY

SOURCE MATERIALS

Archiwum Dokumentacji Aktowej TVP [ADA TVP], *Biuletyn* 1951: 38 (Oct. 13); 1952: 63 (Jul. 30); 1952: 52 (Dec. 12); 1957: 54 (Jul. 30); 1957: 55 (Aug. 9); 1959: 42 (Aug.); 1961: 27 (Nov. 21); 1965: 173 (Aug.)

Archiwum Instytutu Pamięci Narodowej [Archive of the Institute of National Remembrance, AIPN]. Archive collections in the Warsaw, Kraków, Rzeszów, Katowice, Kielce, Łódź, and Lublin branches of the Polish Institute of National Remembrance.

Armia Krajowa w dokumentach 1939–1945. Studium Polski Podziemnej, vol. 2: *Czerwiec 1941 – kwiecień 1943,* (London: Studium Polski Podziemnej, 1973); vol. 3: *Kwiecień 1943 – lipiec 1944*, (London: Gryf, 1976).

British cipher telegram (transcript), 5 Feb. 1942, from 30 Military Mission Moscow to The War Office. MIL 2706 cipher 2/2. Public Record Office Kew, FO 371/31078, C1370/19/55.

Byrdy, M. 'Prof. dr hab. Tadeusz Pragłowski w moich wspomnieniach' [Unpublished personal recollections of Prof. Pragłowski].

Drozdowski, H. *Stołeczny Komitet Samopomocy Społecznej. Fragmenty dotyczące Sekcji Zdrowia* [typescript, 1939–1941].

Dziennik czynności Prezydenta RP Władysława Raczkiewicza 1939–1947, vol. 2, ed. J. Piotrowski, (Wrocław: Wydawnictwo Uniwersytetu Wrocławskiego, 2004), 54–55.

Generał broni Władysław Anders. Wybór pism i rozkazów, ed. B. Polak, (Warszawa: Wydawnictwa Uniwersytetu Warszawskiego, 2009), 111, 187.

Instytut Polski i Muzeum Sikorskiego [The Polish Institute and Sikorski Museum], sign. no. Kol. 401/12.

Jagodziński, Z. *The Katyn Bibliography (Books and Pamphlets)*, (London: The Polish Library, 1976).

Jaworowski, G. 'Nieznana relacja o grobach katyńskich,' *Zeszyty Historyczne* 45 (1978), 4.

Kamiński M.K., and J. Tebinka, (eds.) *Na najwyższym szczeblu. Spotkania premierów Rzeczypospolitej Polskiej i Wielkiej Brytanii podczas II wojny światowej,* Polish translation of English documents by Iwona Sakowicz, (Warszawa: Wydawnictwo LTW, 1999), 84.

Katyń. Zamordowani. Mordercy. Oskarżyciele [no place of publication], 1943.

Kroll, B., 'Pierwsze sprawozdanie z Katynia. Raport Edmunda Seyfrieda,' *Życie Warszawy, Życie i Historia* 1989: 4 (Feb. 24), 1–3.

Księga bezprawia. Akta normatywne kierownictwa resortu bezpieczeństwa publicznego (1944–1956), selected and edited by B. Kopka (Warszawa: Instytut Pamięci Narodowej, 2011).

Materski, W., et al. (eds.), *Katyń*, vol. 1: *Jeńcy wojenni nie wypowiedzianej wojny. Dokumenty zbrodni,* (Warszawa: Trio, 1995); vol. 2: *Zagłada,* (Warszawa: Trio,1998); vol. 3: *Losy ocalałych,* (Warszawa: Trio, 2001); vol. 4: *Echa Katynia,* (Warszawa: Trio, 2006).

Motas, M. 'Materiały dotyczące zbrodni katyńskiej w zasobie archiwum Głównej Komisji Badania Zbrodni przeciwko Narodowi Polskiemu. Instytutu Pamięci Narodowej,' *Biuletyn Głównej Komisji Badania Zbrodni przeciwko Narodowi Polskiemu. Instytutu Pamięci Narodowej* 33 (1991).

Nasiłowski, W. *Życiorys Pragłowski Tadeusz (1903–1983)* [unpublished biography of Tadeusz Pragłowski].

O'Malley, O. Katyn: Dispatches of Sir Owen O'Malley to the British Government, (Chicago: Katyn Memorial Fund Commission 1973).

Polski Ruch Ludowy na emigracji (1944–1954). Dokumenty i materiały, Part 1; editor's note and introduction by R. Turkowski (Pińczów: Wyższa Szkoła Umiejętności Zawodowych, 2005).

Protokoły posiedzeń Rady Ministrów Rzeczypospolitej Polskiej, vol. 5: *Wrzesień 1942–lipiec 1943,* M. Zgórniak, W. Rojek, and A. Suchcitz, (eds.), (Kraków: Secesja, 2001).

'Raport Rządu Rzeczypospolitej Polskiej na Uchodźstwie. Masowe morderstwo polskich jeńców wojennych w Katyniu. Londyn 1946 r.' English version 'The Mass Murder of Polish Prisoners of War in Katyn.'

Skarżyński, K. *Katyń. Raport Polskiego Czerwonego Krzyża,* (Warszawa: Oficyna Wydawnicza Pokolenie, 1989) [samizdat publication].

Slowenczyk, G. Polish translation made in 1948 of a 1943 letter his wife on the events at Katyn, now in the Warsaw AIPN collection, sign. no. 001168/243.

Справка о результатах предварительного расследования так называемого "Катынского дела" [The Burdenko Report, 1944].

Świątkowski, H. *Notatka ministra sprawiedliwości Henryka Świątkowskiego o gromadzeniu materiałów zwalczających „hitlerowską prowokację" w sprawie Katynia, 7 XI 1951 r.* Archiwum Akt Nowych, Ministerstwo Sprawiedliwości, sign. no. 182, sheets 1–4.

Tarczyński, M. (ed.) *Katyń. Księga Cmentarna Polskiego Cmentarza Wojennego*, (Warszawa: Rada Ochrony Pamięci Walk i Męczeństwa, 2000).

Toczewski, A. 'Raport ppłk. dypl. Stefana Mossora o wizycie polskich oficerów z niemieckich oflagów w Katyniu,' *Niepodległość* 45 [25 in new series] (1992).

Tucholski, J. *Mord w Katyniu. Kozielsk, Ostaszków, Starobielsk. Lista ofiar*, (Warszawa: Instytut Wydawniczy PAX, 1991).

Wspomnienia Józefa Sigalina. [Document in the private collection of Andrzej Skalimowski].

Z listów do Mieczysława Grydzewskiego 1946–1966, R. Habielski (ed.), (London: Polonia, 1990).

Zbrodnia katyńska. Bibliografia 1940–2010, I. Kowalska and E. Pawińska (eds.), (Warszawa: Niezależny Komitet Historyczny Badania Zbrodni Katyńskiej, 2010).

Zbrodnia katyńska w świetle dokumentów, with a foreword by W. Anders, (London: Figaro Press, 1948 and later editions).

DOCUMENTARY FILM MATERIALS

Im Wald von Katyn. 1943 German newsreel documentary, directed by Fritz Hippler (8 min. 23 sec.).

Tragediia. Soviet documentary made by the Burdenko Commission, 1944.

The Graves of Katyn. Polish émigré documentary, directed by Stanisław Lipiński, script by Zdzisław Stahl and Władysław Cichy; several language versions, 1955 (5 min. 49 sec.).

Kraniet fra Katyn (The Skull from Katyn) Danish documentary film by Lisbeth Jessen, 2006 (30 min. 45 sec.).

NEWSPAPER AND MAGAZINE ARTICLES

'Amerykańska wersja goebbelsowskiej prowokacji nie znajdzie oddźwięku w narodzie polskim. Oświadczenie Rządu RP,' *Sztandar Ludu* 1952: 53 (Mar. 1–2), 1.

B.W. 'Lubliniacy wśród ofiar bolszewickich,' *Nowy Głos Lubelski* 1943: 91 (Apr. 18/19), 3.

Biuletyn Instytutu Pamięci Narodowej 2005: 5/6; 2007: 1–2; and 2010: 4.

„*Bo mnie tylko wolność interesuje…" Wywiad – rzeka z Marianem Gołębiewskim (Nowy Jork, listopad 1988 – czerwiec 1989)* [interview with Marian Gołębiewski conducted by D. Balcerzyk, ed. J. Dudek], (Lublin: Instytut Pamięci Narodowej. Komisja Ścigania Zbrodni przeciwko Narodowi Polskiemu, 2011), 357–358.

Bojarski, P. 'Gdy prawda jest zdradą,' *Gazeta Wyborcza* 2007 (Nov. 14).

'Bolszewicy zamordowali tysiące polskich oficerów. Delegacja Polaków z Ferdynandem Goetlem na czele oglądała wstrząsające cmentarzysko,' *Nowy Kurier Warszawski* 1943: 89 (Apr. 14), 1.

Borejsza, J. 'Śladami zbrodni,' Wolna Polska 1944: 4.

Bregman, A. 'Kto ma wyświetlić zbrodnię katyńską. Wolne narody powinny powołać nieoficjalny trybunał,' *Dziennik Polski i Dziennik Żołnierza* 1949: 28 (Feb. 2), 2.

Brodzki, S. 'Mordercy tańczą na grobach ofiar (Z komentarzy Polskiego Radia),' *Radio i Świat* 1952: 20 (May 18), 1.

Bukojemski-Nałęcz, L. 'Katyń,' *Nowe Widnokręgi* 1944: 4.

Burdecki, F. *Nowy porządek w Europie* [wartime reptile pamphlet].

'Byłem w Katyniu. Rozmowa z dr Hieronimem Bartoszewskim, lekarzem, członkiem Komisji Technicznej PCK w 1943 r.,' *Przegląd Tygodniowy* 1989: 18, 15.

'Cień katyńskiej zbrodni,' *Życie* 1956: 38 (Sept. 16), 4.

'Delegacja polskiego świata pracy w Katyniu,' *Nowy Kurier Warszawski* 1943: 126 (May 28), 1.

'Dożynki,' *7 Dni* 1943: 44, 11.

'Faszyzm był im bliższy niż własny naród,' *Dziennik Polski* 1949: 161 (Jun. 14), 3.

'Film o Katyniu,' *Dziennik Polski i Dziennik Żołnierza* 1956: 103 (May 1), 4.

G. 'Największa zbrodnia dziejów ludzkości,' *Nowy Kurier Warszawski* 1943: 90 (Apr. 15), 1–2.

'Gadzinowa farsa,' *Biuletyn Informacyjny* 1941 (Jan.9) [Polish underground news bulletin].

Glezer, A. 'Gehenna oficerów pod „opieką" NKWD w Kozielsku. Opowiadanie byłego jeńca, który wydostał się z obozu,' *Nowy Kurier Warszawski* 1943: 132 (Jun. 4), 1.

Goetel, F. 'Katyń. Rok 1943 i pierwsze wieści,' *Wiadomości* 1949: 43 (Oct. 23), 1.

Goetel, F. 'Katyń. *Po powrocie,*' *Wiadomości* 1949: 47 (Nov. 20), 2.

Goetel, F. 'Katyń. Rok 1943 i pierwsze wieści,' *Wiadomości* 1949: 43 (Oct. 23), 1.

Goetel, F. 'Katyń. *Wizja lokalna,*' *Wiadomości* 1949: 45 (Nov. 6), 2.

Goetel, F. 'Lot do Katynia,' sent to the press by P. Żaroń, *Przegląd Tygodniowy* 1989: 21 (Apr. 22), 10.

Goetel, F. 'Raport z Katynia do Polskiego Czerwonego Krzyża,' sent to the press by M. Kledzik, *Przekrój* 1989: 2297 (Jun. 18), 9.

Gostkowski, S. 'Week-end,' *Kultura* (Paris) 1965: 3, 83.

'Grausiger sowjetischer Massenmord an Kriegsgefangenen polnischen Offizieren. Aufdeckung von Massengraben bei Smolensk. Die Ermordeten in mehreren Schichten übereinander. 50 Leichen bisher identifiziert darunter bekannte Generale. Eine polnische Kommission am Tatort.' *Krakauer Zeitung* 1943 (Apr. 15).

Grobicki, J. 'Fakty katyńskie,' *Lwów i Wilno* 1947: 47 (Nov. 3), 2.

'Grudki polskiej ziemi padły na groby oficerów. Reportaż z pobytu delegacji PCK na miejscu kaźni pod Smoleńskiem,' *Nowy Kurier Warszawski* 1943: 94 (Apr. 20), 1.

Hudson, G. F. 'Who Is Guilty of the Katyn Massacre? Examination of the Evidence Leaves Little Room for Doubt,' *Reader's Digest* 1952: 7 (Mar.), 127–130.

Jeleński, K. 'List do Redakcji,' *Kultura* (Paris) 1957: 10, 151.

(jk), '*Świadkowie o roli prasy gadzinowej,*' *Dziennik Polski* 1949 (Jun. 11), 3.

'Katyń wobec opinii świata,' *Orzeł Biały* 1950: 18 (May 6), 1.

Kawecki, W. 'Wrażenia krakowskiego robotnika w lesie katyńskim. Specjalny wywiad Telpressa z członkiem polskiej delegacji Franciszkiem Prochownikiem, *Goniec Krakowski* 1943: 90 (Apr. 17).

Klominek, A. 'Skiwski, albo człowiek bez pionu,' *Dziennik Polski* 1949: 158 (Jun. 11), 3.

Kmiecik, S. 'Niewygodny świadek mordu na polskich oficerach,' *Głos Wielkopolski* 2010 (Apr. 17).

Kombatant, (Warszawa: Urząd do Spraw Kombatantów i Osób Represjonowanych, 2002 –).

Kontakt. Pismo Zjednoczenia Polskiego w Helsingforsie, dodatek [Supplement] 2008: 2.

Korczyński, A. 'Sprawa Katynia przed genewskim „Grand Conseil". List ze Szwajcarii,' *Dziennik Polski i Dziennik Żołnierza* 1947: 20 (Jan. 23), 2.

KOSS [Koss, Z.?], 'Czerwony bies atakuje kulturę' *Goniec Krakowski* 1943: 96 (Apr.24), 2.

Koss, Z. (?) 'Katyń – Fakty, które stały się symbolem w umysłach sercach i na ustach Radomia,' *Dziennik Radomski* 1943.

Kott, J. 'Spisek milczenia,' *Odrodzenie* 1945: 41 (Sept. 9), 8.

'Kozia Góra pod Smoleńskiem odsłania swą krwawą tajemnicę,' *Nowy Kurier Warszawski* 1943: 90 (Apr. 15).

Kozłowski, L. 'B. premier prof. dr. Kozłowski w Katyniu,' *Gazeta Lwowska* 1943: 126 (May 30/31).

Kozłowski, L. *Masowe morderstwo w lesie katyńskim. Sprawozdanie na podstawie urzędowych danych i dokumentów*, [no place or date of publication] 1943, unpaginated.

Kroll, B. 'Pierwsze sprawozdanie z Katynia. Raport Edmunda Seyfrieda,' *Życie Warszawy* 1989: 4 (Feb. 24, supplement entitled *Życie i Historia*).

'Łajdactwo literata,' *Biuletyn Informacyjny* 1940 (Mar. 8).

Mackiewicz, J. 'Do Zeszytu nr 45,' *Zeszyty Historyczne* 1978: 46, 226.

Mackiewicz, J. 'Katyń w *The Daily Telegraph*,' *Lwów i Wilno* 1949: 101 (Jan. 16), 1.

Mackiewicz, J. 'Tajemnica szwedzkiego dossier,' *Wiadomości* 1949; 41 (Oct. 9), 3.

Mackiewicz, J. 'Tajemnicza śmierć Iwana Kriwozercowa, głównego świadka zbrodni katyńskiej,' *Wiadomości* 1952: 15/16 (Apr. 20), 1.

Miński, K. [Edward Grodzki], 'Katyń w 1943 r.,' *Gazeta Kujawska* (Feb. 9, 1946), 1.

Mówią Wieki 2010: 4 and 2013: 4.

'Na pozycjach zdrady,' *Dziennik Polski* 1949 (Jun. 9), 3.

'Nabożeństwo żałobne za dusze polskich żołnierzy pomordowanych w Katyniu,' *Nowy Głos Lubelski* 1943: 136 (Jun. 13–14), 3.

'Nad grobami polskich żołnierzy,' *Nowy Kurier Warszawski* 1943: 93 (Apr. 19), 1.

Nieczuja, T. 'Zbrodnia katyńska,' *Przegląd Polski* 1948: 7.

Nowakowski, Z. 'Castrum Doloris,' *Wiadomości Polskie* 1943: 18 (May 2), 1.

Nowakowski, Z. 'Towary norymberskie,' *Wiadomości* 1946: 29 (Oct. 20), 1.

'Od endecji do kolaboracji. Trzeci dzień procesu Burdeckiego, Skiwskiego i towarzyszy,' *Dziennik Polski* 1949 (Jun.10), 3.

'Ofiarna praca ekipy PCK,' *Nowy Kurier Warszawski* 1943: 131 (Jun. 3), 2.

Palmieri, V. M. 'Rezultaty dochodzenia w Lesie Katyńskim,' *Tygodnik Demokratyczny* 1989: 22 (May 28), 18–19, 29.

Patricelli, M. 'Osaczony świadek Katynia,' *Do Rzeczy* 2013: IV, 48.

'PCK uczestniczy w ekshumacji,' *Nowy Kurier Warszawski* 1943: 93 (Apr. 19), 1.

'Pierwsze dni procesu współpracowników „gadzinówek" okupacyjnych' *Kielecka Trybuna Robotnicza* 1949 (Mar. 29).

Pióro, T. 'W lesie katyńskim,' *Polityka* 1989: 7, 12.

Podolski, H. 'Reżyserzy „komisji katyńskiej,"' *Trybuna Ludu* 1952 (Mar. 3).

'Potworne szczegóły masowej egzekucji na Koziej Górze. Sensacyjne wyniki badań zwłok w lasku katyńskim,' *Nowy Kurier Warszawski* 1943: 128 (May 31), 1.

'Proces zdrajców narodu polskiego,' *Dziennik Polski* 1949: 155 (Jun. 8), 3.

Pruszyński, K. 'Katyń i Gibraltar,' *Odrodzenie* 1945: 53 (Dec. 2), 4.

'Przegląd prasy,' *Dziennik Polski i Dziennik Żołnierza* 1944: 24 (Jan. 29), 2.

'Raport komisji sowieckiej o Polakach zamordowanych w Katyniu,' *Dziennik Polski i Dziennik Żołnierza* 1944: 22 (Jan. 27), 1, 4.

'Ręce złożyć w pięść. Robotnik polski na miejscu krwawej zbrodni. Żydzi z GPU mordowali polskich oficerów,' *Dziennik Radomski* 1943: 91 (Apr. 18), 1.

Rusek, M. 'Lot do Smoleńska, 1943,' *Gazeta Wyborcza* 2011 (Apr. 6), 11.

'Rząd radziecki w nocie do Rządu USA piętnuje nową prowokację amerykańską w sprawie katyńskiej jako nową próbę rehabilitacji zbrodniarzy hitlerowskich,' *Sztandar Ludu* 1952: 55 (Mar. 4), 1.

Saxen, A. [Interview], *Turun Sanomat* 1943 (Apr. 28).

'Sąd zatwierdził wyrok w sprawie S. Wasylewskiego,' *Dziennik Polski* 1947: 177 (Jul. 2), 3.

Skarżyński, K. 'Katyń i Polski Czerwony Krzyż,' *Kultura* (Paris) 1955: 5, 128–129.

Skiwski, J.E. 'Czerwony bies atakuje kulturę. Wywiad z literatem Skiwskim na temat Katynia,' *Goniec Krakowski* 1943: 96 (Apr.24), 2.

Skup, S. 'Świadkowie przygważdżają wykręty Wielgomasowej. Pierwszy dzień procesu „literatki" wysługującej się okupantowi,' *Życie Warszawy* 1948: 247 (Sept. 9), 4.

'Sosnowe krzyże na bratnich mogiłach w Katyniu. Wywiad z uczestnikiem delegacji polskiego świata pracy,' *Nowy Kurier Warszawski* 1943: 127 (May 29–30), 2.

'Sprawa Wasylewskiego,' *Tygodnik Powszechny* 1947: 7 (Feb.16), 4.

St. Sz., 'Nad grobami polskich żołnierzy,' *Dziennik Polski* (London) 1943: 854 (Apr. 22), 3.

[Stahl, Z.] Z.S., 'Kreml przerwał milczenie w sprawie Komisji Kongresu USA. Bierut zaniepokojony rozgłosem śledztwa w sprawie Katynia,' *Dziennik Polski i Dziennik Żołnierza* 1952: 53 (Mar. 3), 1.

[Stahl, Z.] Z.S., 'Moskwa zmuszona do zabrania głosu w sprawie Katynia,' *Orzeł Biały* 1952: 10 (Mar. 8), 4.

[Stahl, Z.] Z.S., 'Raport amerykański o Katyniu, *Orzeł Biały* 1952: 40 (Oct. 7), 4.

'Stanisław Wasylewski przed sądem,' *Dziennik Polski* (Kraków) 1948: 348 (Dec. 19), 7.

Sztejn, W. 'Proces redaktorów gadzinówek,' *Kielecka Trybuna Robotnicza* 1949 (Mar. 24).

'To co widziałem przekracza swą grozą najśmielsze fantazje,' *Nowy Kurier Warszawski* 1943: 92 (Apr. 18, 1943).

Tomiczek, H. 'O Katyniu – z oflagu.' *Tygodnik Demokratyczny* 1989: 34 (Aug. 20), 20.

Tomiczek, H. 'Woldenberski oddźwięk Katynia,' *Tygodnik Demokratyczny* 1989: 14 (Apr. 2), 21.

Tramsen, H. 'Wrażenia z podróży do Katynia w 1943 roku,' *Zeszyty Historyczne* 1989: 87, 155–157.

'Ujawnia się rozmiar winy,' *Dziennik Polski* (Kraków) 1949: 157 (Jun. 10), 3.

Vigil, 'Gdy milczą rządy niech się wypowie opinia. Trybunał dla sprawy Katynia,' *Dziennik Polski i Dziennik Żołnierza* 1949: 25 (Jan. 29), 4.

'W lasku pod Smoleńskiem wstaje groza. Cień 12000 oficerów woła z Katynia,' *Kurier Częstochowski* 1943 (Apr. 16).

Wasilewska, W. 'Mord w Katyniu,' *Wolna Polska* 1944: 4.

'Widziałem na własne oczy. (Józef Mackiewicz o swoim pobycie na miejscu zbrodni w Katyniu),' *Goniec Codzienny* 1943: 577 (Jun. 3).

'Wielgomasowa skazana na karę 6 lat więzienia,' *Głos Ludu* 1948: 248 (Sept. 8), 6.

'Winni są zdrady narodu. Motywy wyroku na kolaborantów prasy gadzinowej,' *Dziennik Polski* (Kraków) 1949 (Jun. 15), 3.

'Wizytówki i fikcyjne listy,' *Dziennik Polski* (Kraków) 1949: 159 (Jun. 12), 5.

'Wobec 10-ej Żałobnej Rocznicy Zbrodni Katyńskiej,' *Biuletyn Informacyjny Stowarzyszenia Byłych Sowieckich Więźniów Politycznych w Wielkiej Brytanii* 1950: 3,1.

'Wrażenia krakowskiego robotnika w lesie katyńskim. Specjalny wywiad „Telpressu" z członkiem polskiej delegacji Franciszkiem Prochownikiem,' *Goniec Krakowski* 1943: 90 (Apr. 17), 1.

'Współpracowniczka „gadzinówki" Helena Wielgomas przed sądem okręgowym w Warszawie,' *Życie Warszawy* 1948: 245 (Sept. 5), 3.

'Wstrząsający i potworny widok. Tajemnica cmentarzyska w lesie na Koziej Górze. Specjalny wywiad Agencji prasowej „Telpress" z redaktorem Wł. Kaweckim,' *Goniec Krakowski* 1943: 90 (Apr. 17).

'Wyrok w procesie redaktorów „gadzinówek",' *Kielecka Trybuna Robotnicza* 1949 (Apr. 1).

Z.S., 'Raport amerykański o Katyniu,' *Orzeł Biały* 1950: 40 (Oct.7), 4.

Zamorski, K. 'Katyń,' *Kultura* (Paris) 1951: 10, 144–148.

Zbyszewski, W. 'Nagroda Nobla,' *Kultura* (Paris) 1955: 10, 148–158.

REFERENCES (BOOKS AND ARTICLES IN SCHOLARLY JOURNALS)

Adamus, A. 'Doświadczenie gospodarki niedoboru w PRL – na przykładzie listów do władz centralnych w sprawie masła i margaryny z lat 1956–1978,' in *Polska 1944/45–1989*, vol. 10, (Warszawa: Instytut Historii PAN, 2011), 299–314.

Arczyński, M., and W. Balcerak, *Kryptonim „Żegota." Z dziejów pomocy Żydom w Polsce 1939–1945*, (Warszawa: Czytelnik, 1983).

Artymowski, S. *Repatriacja żołnierzy Polskich Sił Zbrojnych z Europy Zachodniej do Polski w latach 1945–1948*, (Poznań: Wydawnictwo Poznańskie, 2012).

Basak, A. *Historia pewnej mistyfikacji. Zbrodnia katyńska przed Trybunałem Norymberskim*, (Wrocław: Wydawnictwo Uniwersytetu Wrocławskiego, 1993), 68–69.

Bittner, K. (ed.) „My głodujemy – my chcemy chleba". *Poznański Czerwiec 1956 r. w listach opublikowanych w Biuletynach Biura Listów Komitetu do Spraw Radiofonii „Polskie Radio",* (Poznań: Instytut Pamięci Narodowej. Komisja Ścigania Zbrodni przeciwko Narodowi Polskiemu, 2011).

Bobkowski, A. *Szkice piórkiem,* (Warszawa: Wydawnictwo CiS, 2010).

Bogdan, M. *Radio Madryt 1949–1955, (Łomianki: Wydawnictwo LTW; Warszawa: Uniwersytet Kardynała Stefana Wyszyńskiego. Instytut Nauk Historycznych, 2011).*

Borák, M. *Ofiary zbrodni katyńskiej z obszaru byłej Czechosłowacji,* (Opava: Slezské zemské museum, 2011).

Bratko, J. *Dlaczego zginąłeś prokuratorze?* (Kraków: Stowarzyszenie Twórcze Krakowski Klub Artystyczno-Literacki, 1998).

Cenckiewicz, S. *Długie ramię Moskwy. Wywiad wojskowy Polski Ludowej 1943–1991,* (Poznań: Zysk i Spółka Wydawnictwo, 2011).

Cenckiewicz, S. *Oczami bezpieki. Szkice i materiały z dziejów aparatu bezpieczeństwa PRL,* (Kraków: Arcana, 2004).

Cenckiewicz, S. *Śladami bezpieki i partii. Studia. Źródła. Publicystyka,* (Łomianki: Wydawnictwo LTW, 2009).

Chłopek, M. *Szeptane procesy z działalności Komisji Specjalnej 1945–1954,* (Warszawa: Baobab, 2005).

Chojnacki, W. 'Jawna prasa polskojęzyczna na terenach włączonych do Rzeszy i w Niemczech w latach 1939–1935,' *Dzieje Najnowsze* 1985: 1, 101–147.

Chwalba, A. *Dzieje Krakowa,* vol. 5: *Kraków w latach 1939–1945* (Kraków: Wydawnictwo Literackie, 2002).

Cienciala, A.M., N.S. Lebedeva, and W. Materski (eds.) *Katyn: A Crime Without Punishment,* (New Haven and London: Yale University Press, 2007).

Ciesielski, A. *Katyń. Zamordowani. Mordercy. Oskarżyciele,* (Warszawa: Gebethner i Wolff [Kraków: Regierung d. G.G. Hauptabt. Propaganda, Abt. Aktivpropaganda], 1943).

Cytowska, E. 'W rocznicę ujawnienia zbrodni katyńskiej. Na marginesie publikacji amerykańskich dokumentów dotyczących sprawy Katynia,' *Dzieje Najnowsze* 2013: 3.

Cytowska-Siegrist, E. *Stany Zjednoczone i Polska 1939–1945,* (Warszawa: Neriton, 2013).

Cytowska-Siegrist, E. *Szkice z dziejów prasy pod okupacją niemiecką (1939–1945)*, (Warszawa and Łódź: PIW, 1986).

Czapski, J. *Wspomnienia starobielskie*, (Roma: Oddział Kultury i Prasy 2. Korpusu, 1944).

Czocher, A. *W okupowanym Krakowie. Codzienność polskich mieszkańców miasta 1939–1945*, (Gdańsk: Wydawnictwo Oskar: Muzeum II Wojny Światowej, 2011).

Dobroszycki, L. *Reptile Journalism: The Official Polish-Language Press under the Nazis, 1939–1945,* (Yale University Press: New Haven and London 1994).

Dymarski, M. *Stosunki wewnętrzne wśród polskiego wychodźstwa politycznego i wojskowego we Francji i w Wielkiej Brytanii 1939–1945*, (Wrocław: Wydawnictwo Uniwersytetu Wrocławskiego, 1999).

'Dzieje sprawy katyńskiej na przestrzeni siedemdziesięciu lat historii,' in *Jeńcy wojenni z Łódzkiego: ofiary zbrodni katyńskiej*, J. Żelazko and P. Zawilski (eds.), (Łódź: Instytut Pamięci Narodowej – Komisja Ścigania Zbrodni przeciwko Narodowi Polskiemu; Archiwum Państwowe w Łodzi, 2011), 35–62.

Eisler, J. *Siedmiu wspaniałych. Poczet pierwszych sekretarzy KC PZPR*, (Warszawa: Wydawnictwo Czerwone i Czarne 2014), 465.

FitzGibbon, L. *Katyn: A Crime Without Parallel*, (London: Tom Stacey; and New York: Charles Scribner's Sons, 1971).

Gasztold-Seń, P. 'Siła przeciw prawdzie. Represje aparatu bezpieczeństwa PRL wobec osób kwestionujących oficjalną wersję Zbrodni Katyńskiej,' in *Zbrodnia katyńska. W kręgu prawdy i kłamstwa*, ed. S. Kalbarczyk, 132–153.

Głowiński, T. 'Kolaboracja do końca. Wystąpienia radiowe dr Feliksa Burdeckiego w Krakowie jesienią 1944 r.,' *Śląski Kwartalnik Historyczny Sobótka* 2003: 3, 298.

Głowiński, T. 'Sprawa katyńska w oficjalnej polskojęzycznej prasie codziennej w Generalnym Gubernatorstwie: lipiec–sierpień 1943,' *Niepodległość* 28 (1996).

Głowiński, T. *O nowy porządek europejski. Ewolucja hitlerowskiej propagandy politycznej wobec Polaków w Generalnym Gubernatorstwie 1939–1945* (Wrocław: Wydawnictwo Uniwersytetu Wrocławskiego, 2000).

Goetel, F. *Czasy wojny*, Introduction by W. Bartoszewski, footnotes and postscript by M. Gałęzowski, (Kraków: Arcana, 2005).

Gogol, B. *Czerwony Sztandar. Rzecz o sowietyzacji ziem Małopolski Wschodniej, wrzesień 1939 – czerwiec 1941*, (Gdańsk: Wydawnictwo Uniwersytetu Gdańskiego, 2000).

Golon, M. 'Kary za prawdę o zbrodni Stalina. Represje polskich organów bezpieczeństwa w okresie stalinowskim (1944–1956) wobec osób ujawniających władze ZSRR jako sprawców zbrodni katyńskiej w świetle inwentarza dokumentacji przechowywanej w zasobie archiwalnym Instytutu Pamięci Narodowej,' in *Charków–Katyń–Twer–Bykownia. Zbiór studiów w 70. Rocznicę Zbrodni Katyńskiej*, A. Kola and J. Sziling (eds.), (Toruń: Wydawnictwo UMK, 2011), 225–240.

Golon, M. 'Zbrodnia katyńska w propagandzie PRL (1944–1989). 45 lat fałszowania historii,' in *Charków–Katyń–Twer–Bykownia. Zbiór studiów w 70. Rocznicę Zbrodni Katyńskiej,* A. Kola and J. Sziling (eds.), (Toruń: Wydawnictwo UMK, 2011).

Gomułka, W. *Pamiętniki*, vol. 2 (Warszawa: Polska Oficyna Wydawnicza BGW, 1994).

Gondek, L. *Polska karząca 1939–1945. Polski podziemny wymiar sprawiedliwości w okresie okupacji niemieckiej* (Warszawa: Instytut Wydawniczy Pax, 1988).

Gontarczyk, P. *Polska Partia Robotnicza. Droga do władzy 1941–1944*, (Warszawa: Fronda, no date of publication).

Gontarczyk, P. 'Katyń. PPR-owska szkoła kłamstwa,' *Pamięć.pl* 2013: 4, 24–27.

Górski, G. *Administracja Polski Podziemnej w latach 1939–1945*, (Toruń: Fundacja Inicjatyw Lokalnych Pomerania, 1995).

Grabowski, W. *Polska Tajna Administracja Cywilna*, (Warszawa: Instytut Pamięci Narodowej, 2003).

Habielski, R. 'Radiostacja „Wanda." Relacja Władysława Kaweckiego,' *Dzieje Najnowsze* 1989: 1, 167.

Habielski, R. *Niezłomni, nieprzejednani. Emigracyjne „Wiadomości" i ich krąg 1940–1981*, (Warszawa: Państwowy Instytut Wydawniczy), 1991.

Herling-Grudziński, G. *Dziennik pisany nocą*, *Kultura* (Paris), 1978.

Hłasko, M. *Piękni dwudziestoletni*, (Warszawa: Wydawnictwo Da Capo, 1994).

Hryciuk, G. *„Gazeta Lwowska" 1941–1944*, (Wrocław: Wydawnictwo Uniwersytetu Wrocławskiego, 1992).

Hryciuk, G. *„Kumityt". Polski Komitet Opiekuńczy Lwów Miasta w latach 1941–1944*, (Toruń: Wydawnictwo Adam Marszałek, 2000).

Hryciuk, G. *Polacy we Lwowie 1939–1944. Życie codzienne* (Warszawa: Książka i Wiedza, 2000).

Hugues, P. d' *Brasillach. Ofiara „kłamstwa katyńskiego"*, (Warszawa: ARTE, 2013).

Hułas, M. 'Rząd Władysława Sikorskiego czerwiec 1940 – lipiec 1943,' in *Władze RP na obczyźnie podczas II wojny światowej*, ed. Z. Błażyński, (London: Polskie Towarzystwo Naukowe na Obczyźnie, 1994).

Jackowska, A. M. 'Kłopotliwy temat. Francuzi wobec Katynia,' *Mówią Wieki* 2013: 4.

Jackowska, A. M. 'Polska emigracja polityczna wobec procesów sądowych Wiktora Krawczenki i Davida Rousseta (1949–1951). Przyczynek do historii zimnej wojny,' *Polska 1944/45–1989. Studia i Materiały* 10 (Warszawa, 2011), 61–122.

Jackowska, A.M. 'Działania Służby Bezpieczeństwa wobec Sekcji Polskiej Radia Francuskiego. Zarys problematyki,' in *Dziennikarze władzy, władza dziennikarzom. Aparat represji wobec środowiska dziennikarskiego 1945–1990*, Wolsza, T., and S. Ligarski (eds.), (Warszawa: Instytut Pamięci Narodowej. Komisja Ścigania Zbrodni przeciwko Narodowi Polskiemu 2010), 358–380.

Jaczyński, S. *Ocaleni z zagłady. Losy oficerów polskich ocalonych z masakry katyńskiej*, (Warszawa: Bellona, 2012).

Jaczyński, S. 'Stan badań i postulaty badawcze w zakresie problematyki katyńskiej,' *Łambinowicki Rocznik Muzealny* 30 (2007), 9–32.

Jaczyński, S. *Zygmunt Berling. Między sławą a potępieniem*, (Warszawa: Książka i Wiedza, 1993).

Jankowski, S.M. 'Pod specjalnym nadzorem przy drzwiach zamkniętych. Wyroki sądowe w PRL za ujawnienie prawdy o zbrodni katyńskiej,' *Zeszyty Katyńskie* 20 (2005), 95–135.

Jankowski, S. M. 'Sprawa Hieronima Majewskiego. Wyroki sądowe w PRL za ujawnienie prawdy o zbrodni katyńskiej,' *Zeszyty Katyńskie* 21 (2006), 83–107.

Jankowski, S.M., and Kotarba, R. *Literaci a sprawa katyńska 1945*, (Kraków: Wydawnictwo Towarzystwa Naukowego „Societas Vistulana", 2003).

Jarmuż, M. 'Warunki mieszkaniowe w Polsce lat siedemdziesiątych XX wieku w świetle dokumentów osobistych,' in *Polska 1944/45–1989*, vol. 10 (Warszawa: Instytut Historii PAN, 2011), 315–330.

Jarosz, D., and M. Pasztor, *Afera mięsna. Fakty i konteksty*, (Toruń: Centrum Edukacji Europejskiej), 2004.

Jasiewicz, K. 'Mechanizm podejmowania decyzji katyńskiej,' *Dzieje Najnowsze* 2013: 2.

Jasiewicz, K. 'Rola teorii, hipotez i spekulacji w wyjaśnieniu zbrodni katyńskiej. Rzecz o metodologii i metodyce badań,' *Przegląd Historyczno-Wojskowy*, (Warszawa: MON Wojskowe Centrum Edukacji Obywatelskiej) 2012: 4.

Jaworski, P. *Marzyciele i oportuniści. Stosunki polsko-szwedzkie w latach 1939–1945*, (Warszawa: Instytut Pamięci Narodowej, 2009), 167–177 [the chapter entitled 'Szwedzka dyskusja o Katyniu'].

Jerzewski, L. (Jerzy Łojek), *Dzieje sprawy Katynia*, (Białystok: Versus, 1989).

Jessen, A.E. *Kraniet fra Katyn. Beretning om massakren i 1940*, (København: Høst & Søn, 2008).

Jockheck, L. *Propaganda im Generalgouvernement. Die NS-Besatzungspresse für Deutsche und Polen 1939–1945*, (Osnabrück: fibre Verlag, 2006).

Kadell, F. *Die Katyn Lüge. Geschichte einer Manipulation. Fakten, Dokumente und Zeugen*, (München: F. A. Herbig Verlagsbuchhandlung, 1991).

Kadell, F. *Katyn – Das zweifache Trauma der Polen*, (München: Herbig Verlag, 2011).

Kadell, F. *Katyń w oczach zachodu*, (Warszawa: PWN 2012).

Kadell, F. *Kłamstwo katyńskie. Historia pewnej manipulacji*, (Wrocław: Wydawnictwo Dolnośląskie, 2008).

Kardela, P. *Stanisław Gierat 1903–1977. Działalność społeczno-polityczna*, (Szczecin: Wydawnictwo Promocyjne „Albatros", 2000).

Kardela, P. *Wojciech Rostafiński (1921–2002). Powstaniec Warszawy, naukowiec z NASA*, (Lublin: Norbertinum, 2008).

Katyń. Wybór publicystyki 1943–1988, (London: Polonia, 1988).

Kiersnowski, T. *Moje spostrzeżenia o Rosji Sowieckiej (1940–1942)*, Introduction by P. Łossowski, (Warszawa: Wydawnictwo DiG, 1997).

Klecel, M. 'Pisarze ścigani za Katyń,' *Biuletyn Instytutu Pamięci Narodowej* 2010: 4, 65–75.

Klementowski, R. *Służba Bezpieczeństwa w powiecie Lwówek Śląski (1945–1956)*, (Wrocław: Oddział Instytutu Pamięci Narodowej – Komisji Ścigania Zbrodni przeciwko Narodowi Polskiemu, 2009).

Knap, P. (ed.) *Wokół zjazdu szczecińskiego 1949 r.*, (Szczecin: Instytut Pamięci Narodowej – Komisja Ścigania Zbrodni przeciwko Narodowi Polskiemu. Oddział w Szczecinie, 2011).

Komaniecka, M, 'Orędownik sprawy katyńskiej. Profesor François Naville,' *Biuletyn Instytutu Pamięci Narodowej* 2010: 4, 82–85.

Korboński, S. *Polskie Państwo Podziemne. Przewodnik po Podziemiu z lat 1939–1945*, (Paris: Instytut Literacki, 1975).

Korboński, S. *W imieniu Polski walczącej*, (London: B. Świderski, 1963).

Korboński, S. *W imieniu Rzeczypospolitej...*, (Warszawa: Instytut Pamięci Narodowej, 2009).

Kossowska, S. *Mieszkam w Londynie*, (London: Polska Fundacja Kulturalna, 1994).

Kotarba, R. *Niemiecki obóz w Płaszowie 1942–1945*, (Warszawa and Kraków: Instytut Pamięci Narodowej, 2009).

Kozłowski, L. *Moje przeżycia w więzieniu sowieckim i na wolności w czasie wojny w Rosji sowieckiej*, B. Gogol and J. Tebinka, (eds.), (Warszawa: LTW, 2001).

Krasucki, E. *Międzynarodowy komunista. Jerzy Borejsza – biografia polityczna*, (Warszawa: Wydawnictwo Naukowe PWN, 2009).

Krawczyk, K. 'Działalność i rozbicie organizacji Katyń w Sieradzu (1947–1950),' in D. Rogut, ed., *"Precz z komuną!" Niepodległościowe organizacje młodzieżowe na Ziemi Łódzkiej w latach 1945–1956*, (Zelów: Atena, 2011), 220–222.

Król, E.C. 'Niemieckie czasopisma w języku polskim w Generalnej Guberni („Ster", „Mały Ster", „Zawód i Życie")',' *Kwartalnik Historii Prasy Polskiej* 1978: 1.

Kuberski, H. '*Świadkowie ludobójstwa*,' *Mówią Wieki* 2013: 4, 44.

Kunert, A.K. 'Kiedy ujawniono prawdę o Katyniu?' *Niepodległość* 28 (1996), 168.

Kuśnierz, B. *Stalin and the Poles: An Indictment of the Soviet Leaders*, (London: Hollis & Carter, 1949).

Kuśnierz, B. *Sprawa traktowania jeńców polskich i ich mordu. Masowe morderstwo w Lesie Katyńskim* M. Polak (Introduction); B. Polak and M. Polak (eds.); A. Golusińska (trans.), (Koszalin: Wydawnictwo Uczelniane Politechniki Koszalińskiej, 2012).

Kutta, J. 'Chmurowicz, Jan Władysław (1887–1965),' *Bydgoski Słownik Biograficzny*, vol. 6, ed. J. Kutta (Bydgoszcz: Kujawsko-Pomorskie Towarzystwo Kulturalne, 2000), 26–28.

Kwiatkowski, J.K. *Komuniści w Polsce. Rodowód – Taktyka – Ludzie*, (Brussels: Polski Instytut Wydawniczy, 1946).

Lacko, M. *Dwuramienny krzyż w cieniu swastyki. Republika Słowacka 1939–1945*, (Lublin: Oficyna Wydawnicza El-Press S.C., 2012).

Lenarczyk, L. 'Marian Borawski prezydent Głogowa (1982–1988) z wizją i charyzmą,' in *Głogów w latach 1945–1990. Studia z dziejów miasta*, R. Klementowski and K. Szwagrzyk, (eds.), (Wrocław: Oddział Instytutu Pamięci Narodowej – Komisja Ścigania Zbrodni przeciwko Narodowi Polskiemu, 2014).

Lerski, J. *Emisariusz „Jur"*, (London: Polska Fundacja Kulturalna, 1988).

Leszczyński, A. *Sprawy do załatwienia. Listy do „Po prostu" 1955–1957*, (Warszawa: Trio, 2000).

Lewandowska, S. *Prasa okupowanej Warszawy 1939–1945*, (Warszawa: Instytut Historii PAN, 1992).

Lewandowska, S. *Prasa polskiej emigracji wojennej 1939–1945*, (Warszawa: Instytut Historii Polskiej Akademii Nauk, 1993).

Libera, P. 'Za kulisami prawdy o Katyniu,' *Mówią Wieki* 2013: 4.

Ligarski, S. 'Twórcy a organy bezpieczeństwa państwa w latach 1945–1956,' in *Wokół zjazdu szczecińskiego 1949 r.*, ed. P. Knap, (Szczecin: Instytut Pamięci Narodowej – Komisja *Ścigania Zbrodni przeciwko Narodowi Polskiemu. Oddział w Szczecinie*, 2011).

'List Zygmunta Jundziłła do prezydenta Raczkiewicza,' *Zeszyty Historyczne* 19 (1971), 76–79.

Łambinowicki Rocznik Muzealny (Centralne Muzeum Jeńców Wojennych w Łambinowicach-Opolu 30 (2007).

Łogojda, K. '*Pamięć o ojcu. Refleksje z rozmów z rodzinami katyńskimi. Rekonesans badawczy,*' *Wrocławski Rocznik Historii Mówionej* 2014, 89–127.

Łysakowski, P. 'Prasa niemiecka o Katyniu. Jak niemiecka propaganda przedstawiała w 1943 r. sprawę mordu popełnionego na polskich oficerach,' in *Katyń. Problemy i zagadki*, ed. J. Jackl, (Warszawa: PoMOST, 1990), 88–114.

Łysakowski, P. 'W kraju o tragedii w Kozich Górach,' *Dzieje Najnowsze* 1990: 4, 81–95.

Machcewicz, P. *„Monachijska menażeria." Walka z Radiem Wolna Europa 1950–1989*, (Warszawa: Instytut Pamięci Narodowej, 2007).

Mackiewicz, J. *Fakty, przyroda i ludzie*, foreword by B. Topolska, (London: Kontra, 1993).

Mackiewicz, J. *Katyn – ungesühntes Verbrechen* (Zürich: Thomas-Verlag, 1949).

Mackiewicz, J. *The Katyn Wood Murders*, (first edition London: World Affairs Book Club, 1951).

Mackiewicz, J. *The Katyn Wood Murders*, (London: Hollis & Carter, 1951).

Mackiewicz, J. *Sprawa mordu katyńskiego*, (London: Wydawnictwo Kontra, 2009).

Madajczyk, C. *Dramat katyński*, (Warszawa: Książka i Wiedza, 1989).

Majchrzak, G. 'Armia Krajowa na „Fali" w czasach „odwilży" (1954–1956),' *Biuletyn Instytutu Pamięci Narodowej* 2002: 8–9.

Majewski, P. 'Kolaboracja, której nie było… Problem postaw społeczeństwa polskiego w warunkach okupacji niemieckiej 1939–1945,' *Dzieje Najnowsze* 2004: 4.

Malewski, J. (W. Bolecki), *Wyrok na Józefa Mackiewicza*, (London: Puls, 1991).

Maresch, E. *Katyń 1940*, (Warszawa: Świat Książki, 2014).

Maresch. E. *Katyn 1940: The Documentary Evidence of the West's Betrayal*, (Stroud: The History Press, 2010).

Massalski, A., and S. Meducki, *Kielce w latach okupacji hitlerowskiej 1939–1945*, (Kielce: Kieleckie Towarzystwo Naukowe; and Wrocław: Zakład Narodowy im. Ossolińskich – Wydawnictwo).

Materski, W. *Mord katyński. Siedemdziesiąt lat drogi do prawdy*, (Warszawa: Naczelna Dyrekcja Archiwów Państwowych, 2010).

Materski, W. *Od kłamstwa ku prawdzie*, (Warszawa: Oficyna Wydawnicza Rytm, 2012).

Materski, W. 'Zerwanie stosunków polsko-sowieckich,' in *Historia dyplomacji polskiej*, vol. 5: *1939–1945*, ed. W. Michowicz, (Warszawa: Instytut Historii PAN, 1999), 374.

Materski, W. 'Z początków wojny propagandowej wokół zbrodni katyńskiej. Sowiecka Komisja Specjalna (tzw. Komisja Burdenki),' in *Represje sowieckie wobec narodów Europy 1944–1956*, A. Adamczyk and D. Rogut (eds.), (Zelów, 2005), 19–28.

Młynarczyk, J. A. 'Pomiędzy współpracą a zdradą. Problem kolaboracji w Generalnym Gubernatorstwie – próba syntezy,' *Pamięć i Sprawiedliwość* 2009: 1.

Młynarski, B. *W niewoli sowieckiej*, (London: Gryf, 1974).

Moćkun, S. 'Niechciana prawda. Kanada wobec ujawnienia zbrodni katyńskiej (1943–1945),' *Dzieje Najnowsze* 2014: 1.

Mossor, S. 'Palmiry – Katyń,' *Polska Zbrojna* 1946: 176 (Jul. 26), 3.

Nicman, Z. 'Seyfried, Edmund,' *Polski Słownik Biograficzny*, vol. 36, fascicle 3/150, ed. H. Markiewicz, (Warszawa: Instytut Historii PAN, 1995–1996), 377–378.

Nicman, Z. 'Seyfried, Kamil J. (1872–1960),' *Polski Słownik Biograficzny*, vol. 36, fascicle 3/150, ed. H. Markiewicz, (Warszawa: Instytut Historii PAN, 1995–1996), 378.

Nurek, M. *Gorycz zwycięstwa. Los Polskich Sił Zbrojnych na Zachodzie po II wojnie światowej 1945-1949*, (Gdańsk: Wydawnictwo Uniwersytetu Gdańskiego, 2009).

Okułowicz, M. '„Kurier Białostocki" jako przykład hitlerowskiej prasy gadzinowej, wydawanej w okręgu białostockim w 1944 r.,' *Studia Podlaskie* 16 (2006), 209-260.

Orlicki, J. *Poprzez Starobielsk do Piątej Dywizji Kresowej. Pamiętnik wojenny lekarza - rezerwisty,* (London and Warszawa: Hanna Orlicka Kielim, 1992).

Orsós, S. 'Mój stryj Ferenc tam był,' *Biuletyn Katyński* 33, (1991: 1), 41.

Pałka, J. *Generał Stefan Mossor (1896-1957). Biografia wojskowa*, (Warszawa: Światowy Związek Żołnierzy Armii Krajowej: Oficyna Wydawnicza Rytm: Fundacja „Historia i Kultura," 2008),.

Paul, A. *Katyń. Stalinowska masakra i tryumf prawdy, (*Warszawa: Świat Książki, 2007).

Paul, A. *Katyń: Stalin's Massacre and the Triumph of Truth*, (DeKalb, IL: Northern Illinois University Press, 2010).

Peszkowski, Z. *Wspomnienia jeńca z Kozielska,* (Wrocław: Fundacja Centrum Ignacego J. Paderewskiego, 1992).

Piątkowski, S. *Okupacja i propaganda. Dystrykt Radomski Generalnego Gubernatorstwa w publicystyce polskojęzycznej prasy niemieckiej (1939-1945)*, (Lublin and Radom: Instytut Pamięci Narodowej. Komisja Ścigania Zbrodni przeciwko Narodowi Polskiemu, Oddział Lublin, 2013).

Pietrzak, J. 'Działalność komunistów wśród polskiego wychodźstwa na Bliskim Wschodzie w świetle materiałów kontrwywiadu Polskich Sił Zbrojnych (1944),' *Dzieje Najnowsze* 2006: 3.

Pietrzak, J. '„Wyeliminowanie z szeregów elementu uciążliwego i niebezpiecznego". Sprawa Obozu Dyscyplinarnego Armii Polskiej na Wschodzie w Latrun w Palestynie (1944–1945),' *Dzieje Najnowsze* 2015: 2.

Pietrzak, T. *Dokumenty mówią...* (Warszawa, 1944).

Piórkowska, K. *Anglojęzyczni świadkowie Katynia. Najnowsze badania*, (Warszawa: Muzeum Wojska Polskiego, 2012).

Podgórska-Klawer, Z. 'Orzechowski Konrad (1887-1964),' *Polski Słownik Biograficzny*, vol. 24, ed. E. Rostworowski, (Wrocław, Warszawa, Kraków, and Gdańsk: Polska Akademia Nauk, 1979), 282-283.

Pogorzelski, K. 'Sprawa katyńska w oczach mieszkańców Białostocczyzny,' *Biuletyn Instytutu Pamięci Narodowej* 2007: 10–11, 127–128.

Polak, B., and M. Polak (eds.), *Zbrodnia katyńska 1940. Dr Bronisław Kuśnierz o Katyniu*, (Koszalin: Wydawnictwo Uczelniane Politechniki Koszalińskiej, 2012).

Polak, B., and M. Polak (eds.), *Zbrodnia katyńska 1940. Polacy w Wielkiej Brytanii wobec ludobójstwa katyńskiego 1943–1989*, (Koszalin: Wydawnictwo Uczelniane Politechniki Koszalińskiej, 2013).

Polak, B., and M. Polak (eds.), *Zbrodnia katyńska 1940. Poszukiwanie prawdy 1941–1946*, (Koszalin: Wydawnictwo Uczelniane Politechniki Koszalińskiej, 2010).

Polak, M. 'Wanda Wasilewska o Katyniu. Przyczynek do pocztu renegatów polskich II wojny światowej,' *Mars* 2002: 12.

Polechoński, K. 'Ferdynand Goetel w Katyniu,' *Arcana* 2009: 1.

Polechoński, K. *Pisarz w czasach wojny i emigracji. Ferdynand Goetel i jego twórczość w latach 1939–1960*, (Wrocław: Wydawnictwo Uniwersytetu Wrocławskiego: Wydział Filologiczny Uniwersytetu Wrocławskiego, 2012).

Popielski, B., and W. Nasiłowski, 'Cienie Katynia w dokumentach i historii medycyny sądowej,' *Archiwum Medycyny Sądowej i Kryminologii* 47 (1997).

Prawda o Katyniu, (collected volume, W. Wasilewska, J. Borejsza et al., Moscow, 1944).

Przewoźnik, A., and J. Adamska, *Katyń. Zbrodnia. Prawda. Pamięć*, (Warszawa: Świat Książki, 2010).

Pszenicki, K. *Tu mówi Londyn. Historia Sekcji Polskiej BBC*, (Warszawa: Rosner & Wspólnicy, 2009).

Ptasińska, M. 'Korespondencja Jerzego Giedroycia z Józefem Mackiewiczem 1951–1982. Zarys problematyki,' in *Zmagania z historią. Życie i twórczość Józefa Mackiewicza i Barbary Toporskiej*, N. Kozłowska and M. Ptasińska (eds.), (Warszawa: Instytut Pamięci Narodowej. Komisja Ścigania Zbrodni przeciwko Narodowi Polskiemu, 2011).

Raczyński, E. and T. Żenczykowski, *Od Genewy do Jałty. Rozmowy radiowe*, (London: Puls, 1988).

Rogut, D. 'Polacy w obozach dla jeńców wojennych i internowanych NKWD–MWD–ZSRR po 1944 r.,' *Łambinowicki Rocznik Muzealny* (2007: 30).

Romek, Z. 'Walka z „amerykańskim zagrożeniem" w okresie stalinowskim,' in *Polska 1944/45–1989. Studia i materiały*, vol. 5 (Warszawa: Instytut Historii PAN, 2001).

Romer, T. 'Moja misja jako ambasadora RP w Związku Sowieckim,' *Zeszyty Historyczne* 30 (Paris, 1974).

Ronikier, A. *Pamiętniki 1939–1945*, (Kraków: Wydawnictwo Literackie, 2001).

Rutkowski, T.P. *Adam Bromberg i „encyklopedyści. Kartka z dziejów inteligencji PRL*, (Warszawa: Wydawnictwa Uniwersytetu Warszawskiego, 2010).

Sacewicz, K. *Centralna prasa Polski Podziemnej wobec komunistów polskich 1939–1945*, (Warszawa: Instytut Pamięci Narodowej – Komisja Ścigania Zbrodni przeciwko Narodowi Polskiemu, 2009).

Sacewicz, K. 'Katyń w prasie Polskiego Państwa Podziemnego,' *Biuletyn Informacyjny Światowego Związku Żołnierzy AK* 2015: 4, 31–39.

Salmonowicz, S. *„Życie jak osioł ucieka..." Wspomnienia*, (Bydgoszcz and Gdańsk: Instytut Pamięci Narodowej. Komisja Ścigania Zbrodni Przeciwko Narodowi Polskiemu, 2014).

Schnepf, Z. 'Losy pracowników niemieckiej gadzinówki „Nowy Kurier Warszawski" w świetle powojennych procesów z dekretu sierpniowego," in *Zagłada Żydów. Studia i Materiały* 2006: 2, 132–159.

Siemaszko, K. *„W trudnym okresie odbudowy państwa". Tak zwany mały kodeks karny w świetle orzecznictwa Sądu Okręgowego w Krakowie w latach 1946–1950* (Warszawa: Instytut Pamięci Narodowej. Komisja Ścigania -Zbrodni Przeciwko Narodowi Polskiemu, 2015).

Siwik, A. *Polskie wychodźstwo polityczne. Socjaliści na emigracji w latach 1956–1990* (Kraków: Abrys, 2002).

Siwik, A. *PPS na emigracji w latach 1945–1956* (Kraków: Księgarnia Akademicka, 1998).

Skiwski, J. E. *Na przełaj oraz inne szkice o literaturze i kulturze*, ed. M. Urbanowski, (Kraków: Wydawnictwo Literackie, 1999).

Sobór-Świderska, A. *Jakub Berman. Biografia komunisty*, (Warszawa: Instytut Pamięci Narodowej – Komisja Ścigania Zbrodni przeciwko Narodowi Polskiemu, 2009).

Sprzączki i guziki z orzełkiem ze rdzy... Obraz ofiar Zbrodni Katyńskiej w pracach plastycznych młodego pokolenia, ed. R. Cegieła et al., vol. 1, (Warszawa: Instytut Pamięci Narodowej, 2012); vol. 2, (Warszawa: Instytut Pamięci Narodowej, 2015).

Stanek, P. *Stefan Korboński (1901–1989). Działalność polityczna i społeczna*, (Warszawa: Instytut Pamięci Narodowej – Komisja Ścigania Zbrodni przeciwko Narodowi Polskiemu, 2014).

Stankowski, W. '*Życie codzienne ludności niemieckiej*,' in *Historia Bydgoszczy*, vol. 2, Part 1: *1939–1945*, ed. M. Biskup, (Bydgoszcz: BTN, 2004).

Swianiewicz, S. *W cieniu Katynia*, (Warszawa: Czytelnik, 1990).

Szarota, T. 'Jawne wydawnictwa i prasa w okupowanej Warszawie,' *Studia Warszawskie. Warszawa lat wojny i okupacji* 1972 (Series no. 2): 139–165.

Szarota, T. *Okupowanej Warszawy dzień powszedni. Studium historyczne*, (Warszawa: Czytelnik, 2010).

Szarota, T. 'Trudny temat – kolaboracja' in *Karuzela na Placu Krasińskich. Studia i szkice z lat wojny i okupacji* (Warszawa: Oficyna Wydawnicza Rytm: Fundacja Historia i Kultura, 2007), 71–147.

Szopa, P. *Zbrodnia katyńska 1940. Pamięci mieszkańców powiatu strzyżowskiego zamordowanych przez Sowietów w Katyniu, Charkowie i Twerze (Kalininie)*, (Rzeszów: Instytut Pamięci Narodowej, 2010).

Szubert, W., 'Wspomnienia o Departamencie Pracy i Opieki Społecznej Delegatury Rządu 1941–1944,' *Przegląd Historyczny* 1989: 1, 133–153.

Szulc, P. '„Instrument wychowania człowieka socjalizmu". Polskie Radio Szczecin w latach 1949–1955,' in *Wokół zjazdu szczecińskiego 1949 r.*, ed. P. Knap (Szczecin: Instytut Pamięci Narodowej – Komisja Ścigania Zbrodni przeciwko Narodowi Polskiemu. Oddział w Szczecinie, 2011).

Szulc, P. *Zniewolony eter. Polskie Radio Szczecin w latach 1945–1989*, (Szczecin: Instytut Pamięci Narodowej – Komisja Ścigania Zbrodni przeciwko Narodowi Polskiemu. Oddział w Szczecinie, 2012).

Szyszko-Bohusz, Z. *Czerwony sfinks*, (Roma: Polski Dom Wydawniczy, 1945).

Tarczyński, M. (ed.), *Zbrodnia katyńska. Kryzys prawdy 1940–2010*, (Warszawa: Niezależny Komitet Historyczny Badania Zbrodni Katyńskiej: Polska Fundacja Katyńska, 2010), 45–54.

Tebinka, J. 'Dyplomacja brytyjska wobec sprawy katyńskiej w latach 1943–1945,' in *Z dziejów Polski i emigracji (1939–1989). Księga dedykowana byłemu Prezydentowi Rzeczypospolitej Polskiej Ryszardowi Kaczorowskiemu*, M. Szczerbiński and T. Wolsza (eds.), (Gorzów Wielkopolski: IKF, 2003).

Tebinka, J. *„Wielka Brytania dotrzyma lojalnie swojego słowa". Winston Churchill a Polska*, (Warszawa: Wydawnictwo Neriton, 2013), chapter entitled 'Katyń,' 134–148.

Tucholski, J. *Mord w Katyniu. Kozielsk, Ostaszków, Starobielsk. Lista ofiar*, (Warszawa: Instytut Wydawniczy PAX, 1991).

Urbanowski, M. 'Szklarski, Alfred (1912–1992),' *Polski Słownik Biograficzny*, vol. 48, ed. A. Romanowski, (Warszawa and Kraków: Wydawnictwo Towarzystwa Naukowego Societas Vistulana, 2012–2013), 319.

Wasilewski, W. 'Decyzja Politbiura WKP(b) z 29 II 1952 r. ZSSR wobec komisji katyńskiej Izby Reprezentantów USA,' *Dzieje Najnowsze* 2013: 1.

Wasilewski, W. 'Komisja Katyńska Kongresu USA (1951–1952),' *Biuletyn Instytutu Pamięci Narodowej* 2005: 5–6, 71–84.

Wasilewski, W. *Ludobójstwo. Kłamstwo i walka o prawdę. Sprawa Katynia 1940–2014*, (Łomianki: Wydawnictwo LTW, 2014), 143–176.

Wasilewski, W. 'Pamięć Katynia, Działania opozycji,' *Biuletyn IPN* 2009: 5–6, 60–69.

Wasilewski, W. 'Z komisji do łagru,' *Pamięć.pl* 2015: 4, 28–31.

Wawer, Z. *Znów w polskim mundurze. Armia polska w ZSRR sierpień 1941 – marzec 1942* (Warszawa: Zbigniew Wawer Prod. Film., Międzynarodowa Szkoła Menadżerów, 2001).

Wawrzyniak, J. *ZBOWiD i pamięć drugiej wojny światowej 1949–1969* (Warszawa: Wydawnictwo Trio and Fundacja „Historia i Kultura", 2009).

Wieliczko, M. 'Na śladach dokumentacji prawdy o Katyniu,' in J. Faryś and M. Szczerbińsk, (eds.) *Historia i bibliologia. Księga dedykowana pamięci doktora Zdzisława Konstantego Jagodzińskiego (1927–2001)*, (Gorzów Wielkopolski: Zamiejscowy Wydział Kultury Fizycznej poznańskiej AWF, 2005), 301–306.

Witos, A. *Wszystko, co niosło życie. Wspomnienia*, ed. C. Brzoza (Wojnicz: Towarzystwo Przyjaciół Ziemi Wojnickiej, 1998).

Wolsza, T. 'Aparat bezpieczeństwa wobec polskich dziennikarzy wizytujących w 1943 r. miejsce sowieckiej zbrodni w Katyniu. Przypadek Władysława Kaweckiego,' in *Dziennikarze władzy, władza dziennikarzom. Aparat represji wobec środowiska dziennikarskiego 1945–1990*, T. Wolsza and S. Ligarski (eds.), (Warszawa: Instytut Pamięci Narodowej. Komisja Ścigania Zbrodni przeciwko Narodowi Polskiemu, 2010), 381–393.

Wolsza, T. 'Aresztowanie Prymasa Polski Kardynała Wyszyńskiego w świetle korespondencji do audycji „Fala 49",' in *Prymas Polski Stefan Kardynał Wyszyński na Ziemi Pomorskiej i Kujawach*, M. Białkowski and W. Polak, (eds.), (Toruń ; [Bydgoszcz]: Dom Wydawniczy Margrafsen, 2014), 97–107.

Wolsza, T. 'Gadzinówki przed sądem Polski Ludowej (1946–1949),' in *Polska 1944/45–1989. Studia i Materiały* 14 (Warszawa: Instytut Historii PAN, 2014), 359–360.

Wolsza, T. 'GUŁag z polskiej perspektywy emigracyjnej 1939–1956,' in *Sowiecki system obozów i więzień. Przykłady wybranych państw*, ed. J. Bednarek, (Łódź: Instytut Pamięci Narodowej – Komisja Ścigania Zbrodni przeciwko Narodowi Polskiemu. 2013), 111–131.

Wolsza, T. *„Katyń to już na zawsze katy i katowani". W „polskim Londynie" o sowieckiej zbrodni w Katyniu (1940–1956)*, (Warszawa: Instytut Historii PAN, 2008).

Wolsza, T. 'Kolaborant? Burzliwa biografia ks. Antoniego Wincentego Kwiatkowskiego (1890–1970),' in *Niepiękny wiek XX*, B. Brzostek et al. (eds.), (Warszawa: Instytut Pamięci Narodowej. Komisja Ścigania Zbrodni przeciwko Narodowi Polskiemu, 2010).

Wolsza, T. 'Konfabulacje Wacława Pycha w sprawie zbrodni katyńskiej (1952 r.),' in *Polska 1944/45–1989. Studia i materiały*, vol. 10 (Warszawa: Instytut Historii PAN, 2011), 7–21.

Wolsza, T. 'Los dziennikarza z tzw. gadzinówki w powojennej Polsce (Przypadek Mariana Maaka),' in *Nie tylko niezłomni i kolaboranci… Losy dziennikarzy w kraju i na emigracji w latach 1945–1990*, T. Wolsza and P. Wójtowicz (eds.), (Warszawa: Instytut Pamięci Narodowej. Komisja Ścigania Zbrodni przeciwko Narodowi Polskiemu, 2014), 134–142.

Wolsza, T. 'Polska emigracja o zbrodni katyńskiej,' *Dzieje Najnowsze* 2014: 2.

Wolsza, T. *Rząd RP na obczyźnie wobec wydarzeń w kraju 1945–1950* (Warszawa: Wydawnictwo DiG, 1998).

Wolsza, T. 'Wojenne i powojenne losy Polaków wizytujących miejsce zbrodni katyńskiej w 1943 r.,' in *Polska 1944/45–1989. Studia i Materiały*, vol. 9 (Warszawa, 2009), 7–29.

Woźniakowski, K. '*„7 Dni"* (1940–1944). Quasi-kulturalny gadzinowy tygodnik warszawski,' *Zeszyty Prasoznawcze* 1994: 1/2.

Woźniakowski, K. *W kręgu jawnego piśmiennictwa literackiego Generalnego Gubernatorstwa (1939–1945)*, (Kraków: Wydawnictwo Naukowe WSP, 1997).

Wójcicki, B. *Prawda o Katyniu*, (Warszawa: Czytelnik, 1952).

Wójcik, W. *Prasa gadzinowa Generalnego Gubernatorstwa 1939–1945* (Kraków: Wydawnictwo Naukowe WSP, 1988).

Zamorski, K. *Dwa tajne biura 2. Korpusu*, (London: Poets and Painters Press, 1990).

Zawodny, J. *Death in the Forest: The Story of the Katyn Forest Massacre*, (Indiana: University of Notre Dame Press, 1962).

Zawodny, J. *Katyń*, (Lublin and Paris: Editions Spotkania, 1989).

Zawodny, J.K. *Pamiętniki znalezione w Katyniu*, (Paris: Editions Spotkania,1989).

Zbrodnia katyńska: w kręgu prawdy i kłamstwa, ed. S. Kalbarczyk, (Warszawa: Instytut Pamięci Narodowej, 2010).

Zemła, M. 'Świadek ekshumacji w Katyniu,' *Sowiniec* (Dec. 2006), 135–137.

Zeszyty Katyńskie, (Warszawa: Niezależny Komitet Historyczny Badania Zbrodni Katyńskiej, 1990 –).

Żelazko, J. 'Dzieje sprawy katyńskiej na przestrzeni siedemdziesięciu lat historii,' in *Jeńcy wojenni z Łódzkiego – ofiary zbrodni katyńskiej*, J. Żelazko and P. Zawilski, (eds.), (Łódź: Instytut Pamięci Narodowej – Komisja Ścigania Zbrodni przeciwko Narodowi Polskiemu; Archiwum Państwowe w Łodzi, 2011), 35–62.

Żelazko, J. 'O Katyniu w Internecie,' in *Wokół spraw trudnych, bolesnych i zapomnianych*, E. Kowalczyk et al. (eds.), (Łódź: Instytut Pamięci Narodowej and Wydawnictwo Uniwersytetu Łódzkiego, 2014), 265–288.

Żelazko, J. 'Pamięć i propaganda. Sprawa Katynia po 1945 r.,' in *Represje sowieckie wobec narodów Europy 1944–1946*, D. Rogut and A. Adamczyk (eds.), (Zelów: Atena, 2005).

Żelazko, J. and P. Zawilski (eds.) *Jeńcy wojenni z Łódzkiego – ofiary Zbrodni Katyńskiej*, (Łódź: Biblioteka Instytutu Pamięci Narodowej w Łodzi, 2011).

INDEX OF, PERSONS